1972714

DESTINATION UNKNOWN

FIFTY YEARS OF LABOR RELATIONS

By

WALTER GORDON MERRITT

RIDER

New York

PRENTICE-HALL, INC.

1951

COPYRIGHT, 1951, BY

PRENTICE-HALL, INC.

PRINTED IN THE UNITED STATES OF AMERICA

To

I. H. M.

Preface

T HE SCENE IS an afternoon club meeting in a New York suburb. Someone has just been singing about fanciful things, and the hostess is speaking:

"We cannot always live in the land of flowers and seashells and mermaids—we have to come down to the prosaic things of life, and I take great pleasure in introducing Mr. Merritt!"

That is a tough introduction, but since, despite it, I have been persuaded again to toss some faggots into the bonfire of public opinion, I feel I should explain why I do so.

Since the beginning of the century, labor problems, and the relation of government to them, have changed so rapidly, and viewpoints have been so conflicting, that the public is in a state of utter confusion. Propaganda, often unanswered, has generated emotions and motivations based on many misconceptions of vital facts. In an effort quickly to gain desired ends, principles of priceless value—for which the world has fought and suffered —have been lightly tossed overboard without adequate realization as to what was happening.

To promote informed opinion in respect to these matters, it is certainly not amiss to review some of the forgotten but pertinent highlights of the last 50 years, so that those now living, and those who come hereafter, will be helped in their perspective.

I am undertaking this task because I am probably the only living person who participated in some of the most outstanding developments and the only living person who, through memory or memoranda, has access to important information that sheds light on what has taken place.

Obviously I cannot undertake to cover all phases of the different problems that lie within the limits of my title, but such omissions as are noted should not lead one to the conclusion that I exaggerate the importance of what I have written or undervalue what is omitted.

Also obvious is the fact that my generalizations, designed to portray outstanding trends and contours, are subject to many exceptions and, if applied to nonpattern groups, might work injustice, but no writer can sustain the reader's interest if he pauses to fish too many side streams.

I am also mindful of the fact that a book could be written on the arbitrary and oppressive conduct of certain segments of the employer class, which has been an important factor in provoking the excesses of unionism. That fact my book concedes as it proceeds to other matters. In a book of this length, equal emphasis could not be given to all phases of the problem, but I venture the belief that much that this book contains has not yet received its fair share of attention in the voluminous literature of the day.

My emphasis may be due in part to my early experiences. As a child I watched the growth of a labor power that did not always respect the rights of others, and at the outset of my career I enlisted in the cause of correcting what I conceived to be some of its abuses. In the small New England town of Danbury I could not see the right of a nationwide union to destroy my father's small business, but I did see the need to strengthen the dignity and power of the working man. I think I can truthfully say that I detested antiunionism and believed that the normal growth of unions in the sunlight of liberty was overwhelmingly important to the progress of democracy. Unions, it seemed to me, should repel the revolutionary spirit and plan to live within the framework of our laws—or, as I later announced in an address before M.I.T., where I shared the platform with Calvin Coolidge, "Government by strike should perish from the earth." I wanted this country to shun the European pattern.

At least that was the way I saw it in my early adult years and acted accordingly, rejecting all retainers that were inconsistent with my beliefs and publicly denouncing antiunionism, to the discomfiture of many employers.

Searching for a title to this book I have thought of many: *The Breaking Waves Dash High, We See Through a Glass Darkly, Labor Relations in the Making, As One Man Saw It, Then and Now, The End Is Not Yet, The System Is Still Working, The Battle for Control, Will a Common Fear Restrain Them?, Co-operation or Conflict?*, and finally *Labor Pains*, the last of which would have been adopted as suggesting something new and growing had it not been for my fear that it would seem flippant.   So I ended with a title that came to be the central theme of this book as my pen progressed.

W. G. M.

NEW FAIRFIELD, CONNECTICUT

Table of Contents

PREFACE . . . . PAGE V

PART I

CHAPTER

I. INTRODUCTORY 3
II. THE DANBURY HATTERS 7
III. GOMPERS TOYS WITH PRISON GATES 27
IV. THE APPEAL TO THE POLLS 33
V. THE CARPENTERS' BAN ON OPEN-SHOP WOODWORK . . 45
VI. THE CARPENTERS STRIKE BACK 50
VII. THE DOWNFALL OF LABOR'S MAGNA CARTA 55
VIII. THE PROSECUTION OF MIKE BOYLE AND OTHERS . . . 61
IX. THE SUPREME COURT AND THE STONE CUTTERS 65
X. WATER-FRONT WORKERS AND THE TEAMSTERS IN 1920 . 69
XI. A RETURN ENGAGEMENT IN 1934 76
XII. A HALF-WAY HOUSE 79
XIII. THE ROAD TO CONFUSION 84
XIV. WHEN THE SINFULNESS OF THE EMPLOYER IS VISITED ON
THE UNION 102
XV. SOMERSAULTS IN HIGH PLACES 111
XVI. UNION SECURITY AND INDIVIDUAL SECURITY 121
XVII. LIBERTIES BARTERED FOR BASIC NEEDS 138
XVIII. WAVES OF VIOLENCE 146
XIX. THE ANTHRACITE LESSON 185
XX. UNIONISM IN BUILDING SERVICE IN NEW YORK CITY . . . 209

PART II

XXI. INJUNCTION PHOBIA 239
XXII. INDUSTRY-WIDE BARGAINING AND STOPPAGES 250
XXIII. LEGISLATIVE EXPERIMENTS WITH UNION REGULATION . . 302

CHAPTER		PAGE
XXIV.	Onward March of Collective Bargaining	332
XXV.	Call to Battle	353
XXVI.	Collective Bargaining or Class Conflict	367
	Appendix A. State Legislation, 1937–1946	411
	Appendix B. Summary of Provisions of Delaware Act of 1947	416
	Appendix C. State Labor Legislation, 1947–1949	421
	Bibliographical References*	
	Footnotes	427
	Index	442

---

* Superior numbers in the text refer to notes in the bibliographical references.

PART I

I

Introductory

MUCH THAT IS SET FORTH in this volume presents the historic roots of important issues in the Taft-Hartley controversy—issues that are still unsettled. Thoughtful persons observing the transitional era in which we live are anxiously asking what will happen next and whether the turn will be to the right or to the left. Where two important segments of society, more dependent on each other than any other segments, are engaged in a conflict that seems unabating, it is clear that present-day institutions are not to remain unmodified. After serving many years with great distinction as a mediator between labor and management, Mr. Arthur S. Meyer says, "I am startled at the disclosures of mutual dislike."

Throughout the globe, except possibly in Canada, there is nothing comparable to the American pattern of labor relations, because in no other country is there the same legal protection of the right to organize, coupled with insistence upon the right of society to keep organized labor under some social control. In October, 1926, England passed the Trade Union Act to meet such problems as the general strike of that year. In the early 1930's the United States proceeded in the opposite direction by removing restraints from unionism. In October, 1946, England abandoned all controls by repealing the act of 1926. Eight months later the United States again moved in the opposite direction by tightening its controls.

What was done by us in the 1930's was undone in 1947, and what was done in 1947 was immediately put under political attack the following year. The country has been groping and stumbling. With contradictions between the policies of this coun-

3

try and the policies of Great Britain and contradiction between the
policies of one Congress and another within a few years, we are
confronted with uncertainty and instability in this field of labor
relations. Nothing seems to be settled. Perhaps many of the
unfortunate events that this book describes came about because
of the fact that those involved in labor relations are forced to stand
upon the shifting sands of shifting policies. Vacillation invites
challenge and resistance.

Thinking of the time of the enactment of the Sherman Anti-
Trust Law in 1890, or the beginning of this century, it is difficult
to recapture the total lack of public interest or public law in respect to the labor movement. As we view this subject today,
there was no recognition of the importance of the labor problem.
There was no Secretary of Labor. Newspapers did not normally
carry labor news because there was seldom any such news of interest to readers. Most workmen were not union-minded. The
giant-to-be was still slumbering. Employers had developed no
social philosophy for dealing with labor and were neither apprehensive nor defensive because they had had little or no experience
with collective bargaining. Most of them thought in narrow
grooves. Personnel departments as we now know them were comparatively unknown. There were no labor lawyers, and except
for a cluster of decisions arising out of the Pullman disturbances
in 1893, there was no considerable body of labor law. There
were no labor services like the Daily Labor Reports, Labor Relations Reporter, the Arbitration Reports of the Bureau of National
Affairs, or the various labor sources of Prentice-Hall, Inc., Commerce Clearing House, Inc., and others, such as we now daily con-
sult. There was no group of industrial arbitrators such as those
who now make a living from labor disputes. There was no multi-
tude of books and magazine articles discussing the labor situation.
In the absence of big unions and industry-wide bargaining, union
activities seldom affected the public interest and the conflicts in
which unions engaged were not conflicts with the public. The
spirit of class war was not abroad in the land.

But more important, the legal rights of the parties were undeveloped and indefinite, with the result that neither employers nor
employees were in a position to know the rules under which they
were supposed to live in a changing industrial society. It is no
wonder that unions and employers winced as the courts began to

lay down their social and economic philosophy in litigation of far-reaching importance.

In the years that followed this period of comparative vacuum, America changed more in a few years than Egypt changed in a thousand. In the first quarter of the twentieth century, the logical development of property rights and adherence to the traditional principles of individualism, to which our Constitution was dedicated, presented serious obstacles to the growth of collectivism. When this condition changed and changed quickly, the pendulum swung in the opposite direction. Rights of management were enormously curtailed and the individual rights of workers were swallowed by collectivism. Neither worker nor employer is now a free lance in an organized industry. Generally speaking, in the coal industry no harmonious productive organization of an individual employer and his employees can jointly work out its own labor relations. All are held in the vise of an industry pattern. An assertion of independence will be squelched by violence. As for the worker, it is only in the union hall that he may even hope to give voice to his wishes in respect to his terms of employment. It is now a part of our faith that the right of the individual worker to express himself in a collectivist group of his own kind is an expansion and improvement over his right as an individual to deal with a powerful employer.

All the sacrifices involved in turning to collectivism as contrasted with individualism and forcing the nonconformist to conform are thought to be justified by the over-all purpose of preventing the creative or creditor class from securing too much power. What is going on in this country is one manifestation of a world-wide effort to curtail property rights—sometimes by legislation, sometimes by united economic power, sometimes by the Gandhi policy of nonco-operation, and sometimes by revolution or organized lawlessness. It is a conflict between men and money —or persons and property—for the division of the fruits of industry; in Russia it has ended by a ban on money earning money. America, still clinging to the remnants of a free enterprise system, is guided by the hope that collective bargaining with powerful unions will work out a satisfactory accommodation between capital and labor; but the development and expansion of this process, instead of assuring the future of free enterprise, is creating new problems that now in turn imperil free enterprise. The days of private bargaining when each party pitted its economic strength against the other have led to strategic situations where the economic impact upon the parties is overshadowed by the impact on the public. The fate of millions of neutrals may lie in the hands of a few combatants. Never have we faced a situation where so many people are dependent on so few. Thus the curtain rises on government bargaining (or political bargaining) and its far horizons.

II

The Danbury Hatters

My FATHER LIVED on Main Street in Danbury, Connecticut, where I was born, and at the north end of that street was his hat factory. Next door lived Edmund Tweedy, who also operated a hat factory back of our house, just across a stream poisoned and discolored by hat dyes. Danbury had always been a hat manufacturing town from the latter part of the eighteenth century, when beaver hats were made in the upper stories of homes, and very early old-time craft unions had developed, both of hat makers, who made the hat bodies, and finishers, who put them through later processes. In 1880 there was organized the "United and True Assistant Society of Hatters in Danbury," from which the later hatters' unions evolved.

Thus Danbury had education in unionism—never since interrupted—long before the rest of the country became union-conscious.

In the late 1880's Edmund Tweedy conceived the idea of tying up with these unions upon condition that they protect the signatory manufacturers from the competition of the nonsignatory. His plan contemplated a far-flung scheme, between the hatters' unions and manufacturers, that would ensure no marketing of hats at prices that did not yield a fair profit. On paper the plan seemed perfect, and its conception preceded the antitrust laws by several years. Tweedy hopefully dreamed about it for some time. But the plan never was translated into action, and ultimately Edmund Tweedy became insolvent. Of course the manufacturers blamed local union pressure and outside nonunion competition for the financial plight of the industry, and that frame of mind laid the

7

foundation for the local hat strike that followed the great national depression of 1893.

When President Cleveland was quelling the Pullman riots of 1894, Danbury was having its less notorious troubles with a strike for unionism. My father, as president of a group of small local manufacturers, was singled out for unkind words. As usual, the manufacturers were not of one mind, some wavering in their resistance to union demands and others determined to go through to an open-shop victory. To this latter group my father belonged.

These were trying days for the womenfolk of our family, and all the children, including myself, were instructed not to let father answer the front doorbell. As a youngster I sat up all night with a brother 12 years my senior, while from a commanding window he guarded our home with a revolver. A watchman about the place was dubbed "Merritt's bodyguard," and another watchman guarded the factory. One night the factory watchman saw a head stuck out around the corner of the plant, but when he raised his gun a strident voice from the retreating head called out, "For Gawd's sake don't shoot—it's only Michael J. Keating, Chaif of the Polaice!"

Nature took its coure in settling this hat strike. A few, like the manufacturers of the famous Mallory hats, settled with the union and adopted the union label. Others like my father held steadfastly to their course and commenced operations on a truly open-shop basis, employing both union and nonunion men.

This partial unionization of Danbury led to developments in the last four years of the century that made that New England town the pilot station for America's union activities. There were such momentous developments as industry-wide unionism supported by activities of the American Federation of Labor to prevent the distribution of merchandise not bearing the union label. A national boycott was the weapon adopted to compel industry-wide unionism. In turn, this led directly to the formation of a defensive association of hat manufacturers, and finally to an employer association for legal defense covering many industries. The union activities placed my father's business in such a precarious state that I abbreviated my college and law school education and came upon the scene just as the battle lines were being drawn for the famous Danbury Hatters Case. The stage was set and the legal and political contest that arose out of these small beginnings has been carried on over since, with the lines forming and reforming.   How far may unions go in excluding goods and services from the market place and thus depriving the public of its right to choose?   What are the rights of the public?   What are the rights of those whose goods are excluded?   These are knotty problems.

Different conceptions concerning the rights of those engaged in industry there will always be, but the 15-year legal contest in the Hatters Case, based on happenings at the turn of the century, changed the course of industrial history in this country.   The American Federation of Labor, organized in 1886, had developed an astounding machine to destroy the goodwill and the business of manufacturers whom it was attempting to unionize.   In fact, that was its primary functional activity.   *Million Against One* was the title of one of my writings on this subject.   The machine was one of commercial persecution—persecution in a good cause, some may claim—but nevertheless persecution on a nationwide scale, with all organized labor of all trades in the Federation pitted against individual manufacturers.   So effective were its operations that in some cases the creation and savings of a lifetime were wiped out overnight.

At the time of the Hatters Case the A. F. of L. had over two million members organized into more than 25,000 local unions. These local unions reassembled around some 500 City Trades Councils in the country's main population centers.   Then in turn these local unions and City Trades Councils were affiliated with State Federations, of which there were 28 covering the principal industrial states.   Employed by the A. F. of L. were over 1100 organizers, who reported monthly to *The Federationist*, the official magazine, on the boycotts they were prosecuting.   Available also to distribute the tidings and propaganda relative to these boycotts were about 500 labor magazines or newspapers.

When any affiliated union wished to invoke a boycott against a recalcitrant employer, it made application to the Executive Committee of the Federation, which was authorized under the provisions of the A. F. of L. constitution to approve boycotts.   At annual conventions of the Federation a "committee on boycotts" reported to the convention as to boycotts approved or to be approved, and action was taken.   When approval was granted, Mr. Gompers, as president, issued a letter to all affiliated unions listing the victims who were regarded as unfair, requesting all union secretaries to

read this notice at union meetings, and likewise requesting the
labor and reform press to "please copy." Thereafter the unfair
list was published monthly in *The Federationist*. Unco-operative
unions were open to discipline for failing to push a boycott.

By January, 1897, 83 companies were listed as unfair. The
Federation saw the danger of diffusing its efforts and urged "that
in order to attain the highest degree of success we should concentrate our efforts upon a few of the concerns which have proven
themselves unfair." At its 1905 convention the same idea was
expressed more vividly:

We must recognize the fact that a boycott means war, and to successfully carry out a war we must adopt the tactics that history has shown
are the most successful in war. The greatest master of war said that war
was the trade of a barbarian and that the secret of success was to concentrate all your forces upon one point of the enemy, the weakest if
possible.[1]

To combat the boycott, the American Anti-Boycott Association
was organized early in the twentieth century. Its sole purpose was
to secure a clearer definition of the rights of employers and employees and to enforce the law. "A servant of greed," said
Gompers, "doing a nasty despicable job" and "casting about for
a stone to fit its sling has selected the law."[2]

To understand the incandescent leadership of the A. F. of L.
and its passionate devotion to the boycott, one must have at least
a passing acquaintance with the fiery little man who, with the exception of a slight interlude, was its president from the time of its
organization until his death in 1924.

My first glimpse of Samuel Gompers is unforgettable. At a
meeting of the National Civic Federation he was seated on the
platform with Mark Hanna, outstanding industrialist, the big political boss of the Republican party, and humorously known as the
king-maker. Of the two men it was Samuel Gompers who at-
tracted me. He was of a quality to inspire a small-town boy with
fear and admiration. Wholly un-American in appearance; short;
with large eyes, dark complexion, heavy-lined face, and hair
slightly curly but looking moth-eaten—he was impressive. As
I sat in the audience beside a writer for the *World's Work* I wrote
the name "Marat" on a slip of paper and handed it to my com-
panion. He nodded.

Gompers—not quite so overpowering in personality as John L.

Lewis—possessed a winsomeness that this other gentleman, when putting on his most courtly manners, never possessed. The suffering of the toilers seemed to have scarred Gompers' spirit. Given the right opportunity, he might well have gone to the stake. Mr. Lewis never forgot himself in his cause.

In September, 1902, while a mere boy, I drew Mr. Gompers' fire. In the short interval between my university and law school education, I prepared an article on the boycott entitled "The Neglected Side of Trade Unionism"; I referred to a phase that had been neglected by the public but not by the union. I can remember even now sitting on the front veranda of the home on Main Street and reading mediocre passages to my father, who was ever a patient listener. The article was offered to the *Outlook* for publication, and when that magazine rejected it my father, with parental instinct, wrote a letter of reproof! Then we—or rather my father—arranged to have it privately printed on cheap paper by a local printer. What, then, was our astonishment when this humble and poorly-clad messenger suddenly commanded widespread attention. Editorials appeared in prominent New York dailies and in other papers throughout the nation. Various specialized magazines reproduced it in full, and the *Literary Digest*, then an important weekly, gave it more than a full page with my college picture in the center. Of course I was flattered. But what was the explanation of this repercussion? The nationwide scheme of boycotting, which barred from the market place merchandise that people wanted to purchase, had startled and frightened the public. Here was something new that carried a national portent, and so this humble tract became a part of the history of the times.

But my greatest distinction came when Samuel Gompers himself honored the neophyte with attention. He described my pamphlet as "a truly wonderful and Pickwickian discovery" and defended the boycott with his usual forthrightness, declaring, "Why this may spell ruin and bankruptcy to the boycotted. Certainly it may." Then he tossed his gauntlet into the ring. "We beg to say plainly and distinctly to Mr. Merritt and his fellow-sympathizers that the American Federation of Labor will never abandon the boycott and that the threats against the Federation are idle, impudent and impotent." [3]

Only a few months later the Anthracite Coal Strike Commission, appointed by President Theodore Roosevelt in 1902 to settle the

famous anthracite strike, described the boycott as "a form of coercion" which when "carried to the extent sometimes practiced
. . . is a cruel weapon of aggression [,] and its use immoral
and antisocial."

It remained for the United Hatters of North America, an organization of some 9000 members that joined the American Federation of Labor in 1896, to make the most effective use of the
boycotting facilities of the Federation. In 1899 this organization
invoked the full force of a nationwide boycott against F. Berg &
Company of Orange, New Jersey, one of the largest hat factories in
the United States. A strike was first called to stop production and
the boycott followed to destroy distribution. That was the hatters'
strategy.

John Moffitt, president of the United Hatters (later a United
States Conciliator), said he obtained information as to the shipments by Berg and directed the union agents to chase down its
customers wherever they did business.[4] Reporting on the Berg
boycott, one boycotting agent wrote:

From the evidence he [the agent] had received when he left Orange he
was convinced that they [the Union] were right and Berg & Company will
be forced to make their factory fair or go out of business. There are six
men on the road working on the Berg & Company hats . . . that the hats
were coming back like an army of ants.[5]

With these incidents multiplied, the concern capitulated early in
September, 1900. Mr. Moffitt reported the union victory:

Success in the Berg fight, a struggle that will be historic in the annals of
the labor movement, was won after a battle of eleven months' duration.[6]

Shortly after the conclusion of this battle Mr. James P. Maher,
then treasurer of the hatters' union and who later served as a Congressman from 1910 to 1921, called on Mr. Loewe of D. E. Loewe
& Company of Danbury, destined to be the plaintiff in the Danbury
Hatters Case. The conference was tentative. Maher requested
unionization but later reported to his general executive board that
the union officials had made up their minds to carry the matter to
a conclusion.

Months slipped by, owing to one delay or another, until March
6, 1901, when Mr. Moffitt, president, Mr. Maher, treasurer, and
Mr. Lawlor, secretary, met Mr. Loewe and informed him that if he
did not accede to their demands they would employ their "usual

methods to force" him to unionize. At another meeting in the same month Mr. Lawlor made it clear to Mr. Loewe that if the factory were unionized some of the employees would have to be fired, since the union would not accept them as members. At this Mr. Loewe withdrew, and on April 22, 1901, he wrote his final answer rejecting their proposal.

Meanwhile, a local labor dispute arose in the hat factory of Henry H. Roelofs & Co. of Philadelphia, and diverted attention to that company. Roelofs' name took the place of F. Berg & Company on the unfair list of the A. F. of L. The usual activities followed. The United Hatters alone spent some $23,000 spying upon Roelofs' shipments and invoking the facilities of the A. F. of L. against all dealers who handled the Roelofs product. John Moffitt boasted that they had inflicted $250,000 damage, and suit for that amount was instituted by Roelofs against the board of directors of the union. After three months of futile defense Roelofs succumbed; on July 19, 1902, his company executed its surrender agreement and withdrew its suit.

Loewe's time had come. Five days later Mr. Maher telephoned Mr. Loewe from the Groveland Hotel in Danbury, stating that he desired a conference. Mr. Loewe refused, and the following morning his men were called to a union meeting.

Mr. Maher, flushed with victories, addressed the meeting. He emphasized the union conquests of Berg and Roelofs, and predicted it would be only a few days before Loewe would yield, after which, he said, no one would be allowed to work except a union man. Those who failed to strike, he said, would be fined five hundred or a thousand dollars or permanently deprived of their union cards. Nonunion men were told that if they responded to the strike call the officers would help them to secure union cards. Other officers told the employees that it would be to no avail for Loewe to fill his factory to the roof with nonunion men, since boycotting agents were ready to go on the road to ruin his business. Apparently these agents were to have no vacation.

Through these pressures the factory was almost stripped of skilled help, both union and nonunion. None of this disruption was initiated by the men in Loewe's employ or because of internal dissatisfaction. Mr. Loewe had risen from the ranks and had grown up with a large number of his employees, half of whom were union members. He knew most of them by their first names

and he still had faith in their unwillingness to injure him.   Mr.
Loewe told John Moffitt, "If you can bring to me a payroll of any
union factory making a similar class of goods that is as good as
ours, then I won't have another word to say." [7]

John Moffitt made no endeavor to meet the challenge.

On another occasion after the trouble had started, Mr. Moffitt
said, "Mr. Loewe, you don't know your people.   I had a talk with
them this morning.   I told them that *I* could not trust them.   They
wanted to know certain things.   I told them that I was running
this matter."   Then he added, "You seem to think a great deal of
them but you are mistaken about them." [8]

To which Mr. Loewe retorted, "Mr. Moffitt, it takes a bigger
man than you are to tell me that my people were not true to me." [9]

When Mr. Moffitt said he had a dozen affidavits showing grievances, Mr. Loewe replied, "Yes, Mr. Moffitt, if you have affidavits
in your pocket let me see them.   I do not believe it." [10]

Mr. Moffitt refused to produce any affidavits, and the extraordinary fact is that out of two or three hundred Loewe employees
and hundreds of distributors of Loewe hats, not one was produced
later by the union at the court trial to bear testimony against this
man.

When these men were called out they went like guilty men upon
a fearful summons.   They had no grievance when Maher planned
to start the attack in 1900, nor again in 1901, when attention was
diverted to Roelofs, and they had no grievance when the jugger-
naut car started rolling on July 24, 1902.   Loewe and his men
were but pawns in a national game originating with the national
officers.

Mr. Loewe was advised by his counsel that the members of the
union were responsible for acts performed in their behalf by their
officers and agents and communicated to them through reports
published in the official union journal.   Hence he decided to issue
a warning in order to give the union men an opportunity to stop
the attack.   In the local newspapers of August 23, 1902, he placed
this advertisement:

WARNING

To the Members of All Labor Unions.

Notice is hereby given that the undersigned will hold each and all the
members of all Labor Unions, individually and collectively responsible

for all damages which we may sustain in our property or business by reason of the unlawful acts of such Labor Unions or any of the officers or agents thereof.

The foregoing notice is issued in order that all members of Unions may be informed as to their individual liability for the unlawful acts of the Unions or officers or agents of the Unions, whether said acts meet with the approval or disapproval of the individual members of the Unions.

D. E. LOEWE & CO.

For some reason this warning went unheeded and the boycott proceeded. Spies reporting to President Moffitt, who kept headquarters at the Groveland Hotel, boarded trucks and visited railroad yards to list all Loewe shipments and the names and addresses of consignees. This information then was relayed by wire to the various local unions, trades councils, and state federations at the points of consignment throughout the country. A union delegate calling on a customer in Omaha stated that there was not a shipment that went out of Danbury, Connecticut, that they did not know about.[11] In Boston a Loewe customer was told that he had just received a shipment from Danbury, and when the customer denied this the union agent said, "You will soon receive them because I know they were put on the express wagon the night before."[12] From the Atlantic to the Pacific, through this system of espionage, customers were advised of shipments before they had received invoices and were called upon to cancel orders or to reject the goods when received.

Another representative of the hatters' union wrote:

I immediately started to visit the houses which were handling the product of the unfair Danbury concern. . . . Owing to the nature of my work and just entering a new fight, it requires a great deal of cautiousness and time, prevents me from writing a lengthy letter.[13]

A month later the same agent writes: I can't understand how any dealer can stand up and take the punishment when it is being dealt out in chunks of this size. . . .[14]

The pith of the attack was to block the agencies of distribution so that the consumer would have no opportunity to choose a Loewe hat. The report of one union representative shows how this was done:

I feel that it is money well spent to convince a dealer that the labor organizations would not patronize the concern which is handling unfair goods or patronize any retailer who will patronize the wholesale concern which persistently handles such goods. . . . Since my last journal report

I have operated in Pottsville, where I have found several customers of the unfair Philadelphia and New York wholesale houses. They all agree that they do not want to learn any lesson with organized labor of their city as their instructor, so I think we will accomplish something in that city.[15]

These boycotting agents operated from Astoria in the state of Washington to the Mexican border, from Atlanta, Georgia, to Portland, Maine, and through almost every industrial center of the country between these four points where Loewe hats were sold. In the cities of Baltimore, Philadelphia, and New York alone Mr. Loewe lost $132,000 of business in one year. In my enthusiasm at the trial of the suit that followed, I called them "bloodhounds" and looked upon the union manufacturers, who filled the cancelled orders, as "boycott beneficiaries."

Triest & Company of San Francisco was a commission house, distributing Loewe hats from Canada to Mexico and back to Utah and Idaho. Triest sold to wholesalers, who sold to retailers, who in turn sold to the public. Because of its importance as a distributor of Loewe hats, Triest & Co. became the center of concentrated attack. Moffit telegraphed the secretary of the San Francisco Labor Council: "Triest placed order with Loewe 198 dozen hats. Wire how much to send to start the boycott." And again: "Triest placed order for 160 dozen hats." [16]

One of the traveling agents of the hatters' union threatened the salesmen of Triest & Company with the ruin of its business, saying:

We have $100,000 to do it and do not care whether it takes one or two or three years. We have already obtained the firms of F. Berg & Company and H. H. Roelofs & Company and we do not think we will have a hard time beating you or Triest & Co.[17]

The entire forces of the California State Federation of Labor, the San Francisco Labor Council, the Oregon State Federation of Labor, the Portland Trades Council, the Washington State Federation of Labor, the Seattle Central Labor Union, the Western Central Labor Union, and the Tacoma Trades Council—all a part of the boycotting machinery of the A. F. of L.—dug in to destroy the business of Triest. The Trades Councils of 25 cities in California alone enlisted. It sounded like *The House that Jack Built*. Retailers who bought of wholesalers who bought of Triest & Company, who bought of Loewe, all had their businesses marked for destruction. The retailers received arrogant orders from the labor councils to show cause why they should not be boycotted.

This was no *appeal* to the American public not to buy Loewe hats. It was a scheme to keep these hats out of the reach of the people—to deprive them of their sovereign right of choice or right of commercial suffrage to decide what they wished to purchase. It was not a democratic boycott. It went beyond a private fight and became an attack on public rights.

The financial consequences of these activities were immediate. The Loewe business had proceeded with increasing prosperity down through 1901, when it reached a net profit of $27,700. Then when the blow was struck, in 1902 the balance sheet showed a loss of $17,000—a setback of $44,700 for the year. In 1903, when the production force had been partly reorganized and had emerged from the state of a kindergarten, the setback was only a little less.

It was about Labor Day, 1903, that the famous Danbury Hatters Case was started, against 240 members of the hatters' union, in the federal court of Connecticut under the Sherman Anti-Trust Law for treble damages aggregating $240,000. Since this was a pioneer case, a companion suit was started simultaneously in the state court as an anchor to windward. There had been trouble in securing a printer to print the complaints, and Daniel Davenport, senior counsel, had leaned his 250 pounds against the printer's door to block entrance while the work proceeded.

This was the first attempt of its kind ever made in this country to hold union members responsible as members for the acts of their union officials. The venture was necessary since the union did not have adequate funds with which to respond in damages.

I had just graduated from law school and I remember very well my agitation when my father drove me in a buggy to the town clerk's office to examine the real estate titles of homes of members of the union. My father turned to me and said:

"Son, you seem to be trembling. Is it excitement?"

And it was.

Suit was started by the attachment of 240 homes in Danbury, Bethel, and Norwalk, Connecticut, and the savings-bank accounts of union members. It was my expectation that the unions for whose activities these members were being sued would in the end

meet their responsibilities by paying any judgment that was secured. Any other result was unthinkable. No union could afford to desert its members under such circumstances.

The journey of this lawsuit covering nearly 14 years was a
difficult one. The union retained four attorneys for the trial.
Mr. Loewe, who was in financial difficulties, received $20,000
from his fellow hat manufacturers in full satisfaction of their
general defense pact, and in 1903 the American Anti-Boycott Association (later renamed the League for Industrial Rights) took
over the entire cost of the suit. The legal problems presented by
the case went three times before the Supreme Court of the United
States, in addition to appeals to the intermediate court.

The first appeal to the Supreme Court, which was disposed of
in 1908, involved the fundamental question as to whether or not
the Sherman Anti-Trust Law was applicable to labor unions seeking to prevent the national distribution of products. The
A. F. of L. filed a formal petition with the Court declaring that a
decision in favor of Loewe "would seriously obstruct and hinder
it in carrying out the purposes for which it was organized." In
1908 the Court did render such a decision and reasoned that any
combination "which essentially obstructs the free flow of commerce
between the states or restricts in that regard the liberty of a trader
to engage in business" violated the antitrust laws. The Court
quoted with approval the utterance of a famous English jurist,
Chief Justice Erle, who said, "At common law every person has
individually, and the public also has collectively, the right to
require that the course of trade should be kept free from unreasonable destruction." [18]

So Mount Sinai had spoken. The "liberty of the trader" was
entitled to protection against union encroachment.

The Federation promptly retorted: "No more sweeping, far-
reaching and important and unjust decision has ever been issued by
a Court. The Dred Scott decision did not approach it in scope." [19]
Mass meetings in every city and town in the United States were
urged. A conference of important labor leaders was convened
and the tocsin sounded: "Our industrial rights have been shorn
from us and our liberties are threatened." In time a new slogan
was found: "The Sherman Law—Amend it or End it." [20]

Almost immediately the Federation pledged the hatters and
especially those "whose homes and bank accounts are attached,

moral and such financial support as may be necessary in the pending contention." [21]

Meanwhile, interest was sharpened when the American Federation of Labor and certain of its officers, including Samuel Gompers and John Mitchell, were enjoined from prosecuting a boycott against the Buck Stove and Range Company of St. Louis, and the arena of battle was broadened to cover the political field.

The Federation continued its call for action:

We now call upon the workers of our common country to stand faithfully by our friends, oppose and defeat our enemies, whether they be candidates for President, for Congress or other offices whether executive, legislative or judicial.[22]

The press came in for a bitter attack from the union because it apparently was not prepared to accept the idea that Congress should relicense the boycotting industry of the A. F. of L. "We believe," wrote Mr. Gompers, "that it is a well-defined policy of the daily press to attack, ridicule and misrepresent every constructive and progressive step taken by the workers." [23] He added, "The whole idea of the daily press is to lull the people into a false sense of security while labor is being robbed of its inalienable rights." [24]

At a later date Charles Evans Hughes, running for the presidency, evaded heckling on the Hatters Case by saying that the original decision of the Court fixed the law of the case before he became one of its justices.

The Supreme Court had merely held that the case was sound if we could prove it. When it became necessary to prepare for trial in 1909 it fell to my lot to retrace the routes of the boycotting agents throughout the country and to take depositions of such witnesses as I could locate. I operated from Boston, Chicago, Philadelphia, Richmond, Lincoln, (Nebraska), San Francisco, Los Angeles, Portland (Oregon), and Seattle. Samuel Gompers and his associates were examined in Washington. To these locations witnesses were drawn by subpoena from considerable distances, sometimes from other states. Over a hundred witnesses were examined on the Pacific Coast alone. All these despositions, were returned under seal to the District Court in Connecticut to be read in evidence upon the trial.

The first trial began in Hartford in October, 1909. The defendants' four attorneys made much of the fact that these individual union men had not directed the boycotting agents, but the de-

fendants found it difficult to claim that they did not know what
these agents were doing in their behalf. The official hatters'
journal and the local newspapers had publicized the boycott and
the defendants were forced to admit on cross-examination that they
did nothing to remedy the situation or admonish their representatives, even when Mr. Loewe published his newspaper warning
over a year before the suit was started, or when finally they were
actually sued and their property was attached. Thus the jury
had the picture of union men who showed no desire to restrain
the wrongdoing that was being carried on for their benefit.

In my summation to the jury I made much of the fact that the
defendants had not dared to permit John Moffitt, the boycott captain,
to cross the threshold of the courtroom, notwithstanding the fact—
which was disclosed accidentally on cross-examination—that
Moffitt was actually staying in Hartford, at least during part of the
trial, for the purpose of consultation. Mr. Davenport, with
whom I was associated, recited the travails of Job as reflecting
Mr. Loewe's predicament:

O that I were as in months past as in the days when God preserved me,
when his candle shined upon my head and when by his light I walked
through darkness. . . . Now they that hate me without a cause are more
than the hairs of my head.[25]

The jury wept.

It was February, 1910, when the case closed and the judge
charged the jury that the defendants were liable, but left it for
them to fix the amount of damages. The jury, after long deliberation, returned a verdict for nearly the full amount of the plaintiff's
claim, which when trebled with costs resulted in a judgment of
$232,240.12. Since I had become engaged to a Hartford girl,
the New York *World* headlined our victory: "Went to Hartford to
Win Lawsuit and Won Bride."

On defendants' appeal it was disclosed that all of the defendants'
trial lawyers except John K. Beach had been dropped, and through
the intervention of the A. F. of L., Alton B. Parker of New York
and Frank L. Mulholland of Toledo had replaced them. The
intermediate court of appeals overruled the trial judge because he
had taken from the jury the determination of all questions except
the amount of damages.[26]

The reversal of that judgment was a bad day in my life, unseasoned as I was. That night, after spending many wakeful

hours, I dreamed that the Angel Gabriel, driving his chariot with two white chargers, came tumbling through the walls of my small bedroom, shouting, "Whoa, this is Judgment Day!" Whereupon, as I was coming to, I mumbled, "To Hell with all judges!"

So the case came back to Hartford for a second trial on August 26, 1912, with Judge Martin of Vermont presiding. This time the new counsel, Frank L. Mulholland of Toledo, together with John K. Beach, handled the defense. The trial lasted about seven weeks.

The second jury was sterner than the first. After considerable deliberation the jurymen asked the court whether they could award larger damages than the plaintiff claimed, and when informed that they could not, they ended by agreeing upon a verdict for the full amount of the claim, and sang the Doxology. This yielded a total judgment of $252,130.90. It was now October, 1912, over a year and a half after the close of the first trial.

So the defendants started the case on another journey through the higher courts. This time the court of appeals upheld the judgment [27] and Alton B. Parker, then retained by the union, and Frank L. Mulholland took it to the Supreme Court. But Judge Parker was no more successful than he was in running for the Presidency on the Democratic ticket. Again there was a unanimous decision—and this time by Mr. Justice Oliver Wendell Holmes—in which the main question was the liability of the rank and file for the acts of the union representatives. On this point the trial judge had charged the jury in effect that the defendants were liable if they knew, or ought to have known, what was going on and if the officers and agents acting in their behalf were warranted in believing that they were acting with membership approval. Commenting on this instruction Justice Holmes said:

It seems to us that this instruction sufficiently guarded the defendants' rights, and that the defendants got all that they were entitled to ask in not being held chargeable with knowledge as a matter of law. It is a tax on credulity to ask anyone to believe that members of labor unions at that time did not know that the primary and secondary boycott and the use of the "We don't patronize" or "Unfair" list were means expected to be employed in the effort to unionize shops.[28]

After the Supreme Court decided that the antitrust law was applicable, the outcome of the Hatters Case was never in doubt. At all stages judges and juries, except for Judge Platt's ruling at the trial, were unanimous. Nor did the jury seek seriously to compromise the amount of the claim in order to reach an agreement. No one who really faced the actual facts of the Hatters Case judged the union acts to be fair and right. The somber tones that have been drawn around it in our time are merely the result of propaganda. The contemporary public and press, knowing the facts, agreed with the unanimous judgment of courts and juries in condemning the union.

But that did not prevent John Moffitt from receiving a political plum. When ousted from the union in 1913 he was appointed Commissioner of Conciliation of the Department of Labor, a post which he held until he died in 1942 at the age of 76.

The collection of $252,000 was the next problem. Some labor leaders felt that the plaintiff would not dare to realize on the savings-bank accounts and the homes of the individual defendants, many of whom were quite old. Honest, fiery Andrew Furuseth, head of the seamen's union, preferred to sacrifice these defendants on the altar of unionism thinking the unions would profit by the emotional resentment to be engendered. Perhaps he was right. It took courage on the part of Mr. Loewe to proceed, but throughout this period of anxiety he showed that courage, although his bankers preferred to compromise.

In February, 1915, Judge Alton B. Parker and Samuel Gompers petitioned Congress for an appropriation of $290,000 to be placed in the general deficiency bill for the payment of the judgment and incidentals, on the ground that the law had been erroneously applied to union activities, but Congress turned a deaf ear. At the hearings before the Congressional committee Mr. Gompers was asked why the A. F. of L. did not come to the rescue of these men. He replied that such action would invite too many suits in the future. A Congressman then asked if an appropriation by Congress might not bring the same result.

The legal procedure to secure payment was neither simple nor pleasant. Since the plaintiff had no way of knowing the amount of the respective savings-bank accounts that had been attached, it was necessary to allege a belief as to the total amount so attached in each bank and ask for a report as to the credit standing in the name of each attached account. A blind amount of $100,000 was therefore sought from leading banks. By inadvertence the banks defaulted in answering the complaints at the very time when the term of court had expired. Under the rules then controlling, it was as if the court had ceased to exist, and there was no judicial power to relieve the banks from the monstrous injustice of a default judgment far in excess of the amounts in the attached accounts. Loewe could have enforced judgment against the banks for the total of his judgment for $252,000. Needless to say, no such advantage was taken of the banks and they were relieved of their default. The banks then raised the question as to whether Loewe was entitled to the accumulated dividends or interest of ten years, which had not existed when the attachments were levied. This accumulated interest was equal to about 50 per cent of the original account as attached.

The controversy over these dividends or interest had finally to be settled by a decision of the Supreme Court of the United States,[29] which held that the attachments carried with them the incidental accumulations. The total amount of these savings accounts, which was ultimately applied to the payment of the judgment, was about $52,000.

This issue as to the dividends, which was so thoroughly litigated, had little significance, since, as we afterwards learned, all these accounts had been purchased by the union for their face value, subject of course to the attachment lien.

But to sell the homes—homes of old people, homes that were loved—was something. Out of the 240 that originally had been attached, the defendant-owners of some 60 had died; also, a few had been "dropped." Thus the total number of homes involved had been reduced to about 175.

When the judgment for $252,000 was entered, judgment liens equivalent to mortgages had been filed on each of these homes in the towns of Danbury, Bethel, and Norwalk. Suits had then been started to foreclose these liens by selling the properties at auction. The date, hour, and place of each auction and a description of the property to be sold were advertised in the local papers, as required by law. This covered several pages of the newspapers. Under the schedule laid out, auctions were to start in July, 1917, at one end of each town with about 45 minutes allowed for each sale. Two weeks was allowed to complete the schedule.

A ghastly spectacle was thus projected. A few remarks by the auctioneer and in a matter of minutes a family would lose its home, which reflected the accumulation of a lifetime, just as overnight Mr. Loewe seemed to have lost his business, likewise the accumulation of a lifetime. I steeled myself for the worst. It was threatened that no home sold would ever find another buyer but that each would stand deserted and unused, like Balzac's "Accursed House."

Here was the picture. Auction day was approaching. Loewe's bankers wanted dollars. Sensational papers in New York City published pictures of beds and bedding thrown into the gutters and prostrated parents with clinging children standing by.

At that juncture another attorney acting for the A. F. of L. stepped into the picture, money having been previously raised by that organization by assessing each member an hour of pay. He asked us to settle this judgment for something less than the full amount. The bankers' committee was at my elbow urging compromise, but I did not wish to end what seemed to me a noble battle with an anticlimax of haggling; and so, surrounded by glowering glances of disapproval from the banking fraternity, I announced to the union attorney that there would be no compromise. That ended the negotiation. It looked like an impasse.

All this happened at the end of the week; I betook myself to the telegraph office, knowing that Danbury had many union eyes, ears, and tongues, and wired Mrs. Merritt, then visiting in the mountains, that all hope of settlement was off and I would join her on Sunday. It had the desired effect, since the union believed it had secretly acquired information that I was adamant. It was not long thereafter that a check for the full amount of the balance due was received. The homes of the defendants thus were saved from auction. At the end, as I understood it, the A. F. of L. and the United Hatters each paid about one-half of the judgment from assessments levied on their members. The total cost of the case to organized labor, as reported, was a little over $420,000.

Contemporary opinion never defended the union in the Hatters Case. The attack was ruthless and unprovoked and could not be defended except on the theory that fair ends justify unfair means. Today, when the facts have been forgotten, the case has become a byword in union circles, and emotions concerning it have been perverted by a flood of misrepresentation to the effect that the workmen lost their homes and bank accounts. Those statements reflect on the labor movement. They imply—what I never imagined—that a union like the A. F. of L. or the United Hatters would not run to the rescue of its members when they were held vicariously liable for union activities. Workmen battling together for self-protection and self-improvement could hardly be found wanting to a handful of fellow-members in such a crisis.

This case is in strange contrast with other battles in the trades-union world. There was no violence worthy of the name from the time the strike was called and the boycott instituted to the date the judgment was paid. Nor was there much vituperation. The bitter language of John Lewis or Philip Murray was lacking. Whatever ill will was aroused was of short duration. In fact, the secretary-treasurer of the local hatters' union of Danbury, writing about me in the Danbury *News* in 1941, said:

> I also wish to pay a compliment to attorney Walter Gordon Merritt, a native of Danbury and counsel for the Hat Corporation, for the great American manner in which he gave counsel and advice to the firm. It was the great American spirit of fair play used by President Montgomery, Superintendent Stack and attorney Merritt which other unAmerican manufacturers might profit by.

An echo of the Hatters Case came to me in 1947. Mr. Max Zaritsky, president of the United Hatters, Cap and Millinery Workers going over the union files, found the cancelled check of the Hatters' settlement drawn to my order, and sent me a photostat of it with a friendly letter of transmittal. Even deep wounds can heal.

Although I have enjoyed the confidence and friendly feelings of some union officers, it has been inevitable that during stormy periods, when "moments were as big as hours," I should have been the target of abuse, some of it as a part of the deliberate "hate-the-employer" campaign and some of it impulsive. Of course I have received many letters and telephone calls threatening my life, and Mrs. Merritt has shared these.

Humorously enough, I chose the wrong occasion to be frightened. One day it was announced in my office that Daniel Kearns wished to see me. The name meant nothing to me but since I was young and needed business, I unhesitatingly directed that he come in. Dan loomed in the doorway, a tall, powerful, glowering Irishman. I noticed that his hands were locked behind his back, and because it was shortly after the first judgment in the Hatters Case, I began to plan what I should do. Dan came a few steps toward my desk.

"You know who I am?" he inquired in a loud voice with an Irish brogue.

I replied, "No."

He came a step nearer, while I was preparing to jump into the well of the desk.

"You don't know who I am?" he shouted. "Why," he said, "I was one of the difindents in the Hatters Case and you cross-examined me."

Then to my relief he dropped his hands and I saw that they were empty.

Dan continued, "I have had trouble with the hatters' union and have given up my day's work and paid my railroad fare to come here, and I want to know how good a lagal opinion you can give me for foive dollars." Whereupon he slapped his five dollars on the desk.

When the story was told it was pretty clear that Dan had allowed his Irish temperament to run away with him and that his predicament was beyond legal treatment. So I sent him back home with his five dollars, after trying to outline a wise course for the future.

Whether in the days of the Hatters Case class conflict was less acute, or whether the hatters are essentially more law-abiding than many other crafts, the fact is outstanding that violence and hate were on the whole strangely lacking. It is the people of today, misled by decades of misrepresentation, who speak of that case with bitterness.

III

Gompers Toys with Prison Gates

SEVERAL YEARS BEFORE THE FIRST TRIAL of the Hatters Case, other legal battles were under way involving the "liberty of the trader" and the rights of the consumer. But in this chapter of events it was the injunction rather than a damage suit that challenged nationwide combinations of labor to blockade the channels of trade against contraband goods. Here the conflict reached the top level; it was waged between the head of the National Association of Manufacturers and the heads of the American Federation of Labor. Here, as in the Hatters Case, was posed the question as to whether or not there was to be any limit to the combined use of economic power by organized labor so long as it did not resort to means that were illegal in other respects. Mr. James W. Van Cleave, president of the National Association of Manufacturers, had recommended to his association that a sum of $500,000 a year be raised to "free this country from industrial oppression," by which he meant certain activities of labor unions. Mr. Gompers retorted:

Van Cleave's reptile hirelings may spend the $1,500,000 [for a period of three years] war fund in the campaign of character assassination, but it will be in vain.[1]

During this same decade Mr. John Kirby, as president of the Manufacturers Association, called labor leaders "serpents." The two groups were hissing at each other over the back fence.

In August, 1906, a strike took place in the factory of the Buck Stove & Range Company of St. Louis, of which Mr. Van Cleave was president. The ceremony of presenting grievances was overlooked, and the strike was said to be in violation of a written union agreement in one of the few industries where unionism and union agreements were already functioning. The company was placed on the unfair list of the A. F. of L. in March, 1907, and the special boycott notice to that effect appeared in the May issue of *The American Federationist*.

When the boycott started, the Buck Stove & Range Company, through Mr. Van Cleave, applied to the American Anti-Boycott Association for legal protection. In 1907 suit was instituted in the United States District Court in Washington for an injunction against the American Federation of Labor, Samuel Gompers, president; Frank Morrison, secretary; John B. Lennon, treasurer; John Mitchell, vice president; and other officers of the Federation. On December 18, 1907, a preliminary injunction was granted by Justice Gould. It restrained these defendants from boycotting and from distributing any papers declaring that the company or its products were on the "we-don't-patronize" or "unfair" list, and from doing anything to restrict the sale of such products or coercing others not to deal in them. On March 23, 1908, the injunction was made permanent.

Meanwhile there developed a deliberate intention to flout the injunction. Before the required bond or undertaking on the preliminary injunction was filed by the plaintiff, the defendants rushed the printing and distribution of ten thousand copies of the January, 1908, issue of *The American Federationist* containing plaintiff's name on the "we-don't-patronize" list. An editorial included this statement:

> The men of labor by their lives of devotion to the great cause of labor have earned and possess the confidence of their fellows. Tell your wives and friends all about Van Cleave's $1,500,000 war fund and the use to which it is being put.[2]

From time to time thereafter numerous statements were made by Mr. Gompers in public speeches that were reprinted in *The American Federationist*. The following, from a speech made in New York City in April, 1908, is a fair sample:

> They tell us that we must not boycott. Well, if the boycott is illegal, we won't boycott. But I have no knowledge that any law has been passed or any order issued by any court compelling us to buy, for instance, a range or a stove from the Buck Stove and Range Company.[3]

And again Mr. Gompers declared:

I might say just parenthetically about the Hatters' case that you are not now permitted to boycott the Loewe hats, but I want to call your attention to the fact that there is no law compelling you to wear a Loewe hat, nor has any judge issued a memorandum compelling you to buy a Loewe hat. That applies equally to Mr. Van Cleave's stoves and ranges. And by the way, I don't know why you should buy any of that sort of stuff. I won't; but that is a matter to which we can refer more particularly in our organizations.[4]

In the October issue of *The American Federationist* the editorial included this:

Until a law is passed making it compulsory upon labor men to buy Van Cleave's stoves, we need not buy them. We won't buy them and we will persuade other fair-minded, sympathetic friends to cooperate with us and leave the blamed things alone. Go to———with your injunction.[5]

Another editorial said:

In view of the combined attacks of the worst element of the capitalistic class, reinforced by sycophantic judges and supported by subservient politicians, it behooves the wealth producers to organize more thoroughly than ever and the organized toilers to be more alert, earnest and determined to stand for the right and for justice, not only for themselves but for all.[6]

Reacting to these inspirations, various affiliated unions and labor journals published such articles as this:

All the Justice Gould's Buck Stove and Range Company injunctions and United States Supreme Court Judges . . . will some day be in heaven or h——— but unionism will still flourish, so don't worry.
　　　　Neither Van nor his ally Judge Gould
　　　　And the combined forces of hell
　　　　Can bridle free speech in this country
　　　　And the same old story will tell.[7]

At the convention of the United Mine Workers of America in January, 1908, when John Mitchell was presiding, a resolution was introduced and passed:

Resolved, that the U. M. W. of A. . . . place the Bucks stoves and ranges on the unfair list, and any member of the U. M. W. of A. purchasing a stove of the above make be fined $5.00, and failing to pay the same be expelled from the organization.[8]

For utterances and actions such as these, of which there were too many to enumerate, contempt proceedings were instituted in the Supreme Court of the District of Columbia in July, 1908.

They resulted in a judgment sentencing Messrs. Gompers, Mitchell, and Morrison to respective jail sentences of one year, nine months, and six months.

From the court's ruling granting the injunction and from the judgments for contempt, the American Federation of Labor and its officers appealed first to the Court of Appeals of the District of Columbia and then to the Supreme Court of the United States.

Then death intervened. Mr. Van Cleave died and the new president of the company made peace with the union. Mr. Post of Postum and Grape Nuts fame, a vigorous advocate of the open shop and a large stockholder in the Buck's concern, tried to stop this by an injunction and, failing, then instituted a suit for $750,-000 damages under the antitrust laws. But all this came to naught. The Supreme Court, at the opening of the arguments on the union's appeals, found the injunction case to be moot because of the settlement, and therefore dismissed that appeal. On the other hand, the question as to whether the defendants were criminally liable for flouting an order of the district court still survived. If the injunction was a nullity because it abridged constitutional safeguards and therefore was beyond the judicial power of the court, there could be no contempt. If, on the other hand, the order was within the judicial power of the court, then the defendants were obliged to observe it while it stood, even though the higher court later was to hold that it was erroneous.

The Supreme Court held the injunction to be valid, saying it did not enjoin any publication but only certain "verbal acts" that always have been enjoinable. The comments of the Court were philosophical:

Society itself is an organization and does not object to organizations for social, religious, business, and all legal purposes. The law, therefore, recognizes the right of workingmen to unite and to invite others to join their ranks, thereby making available the strength, influence, and power that come from such association. By virtue of this right powerful labor unions have been organized.

But the very fact that it is lawful to form these bodies, with multitudes of members, means that they have thereby acquired a vast power, in the presence of which the individual may be helpless. This power, when unlawfully used against one, can not be met, except by his purchasing peace at the cost of submitting to terms which involve the sacrifice of rights protected by the Constitution, or by standing on such rights and appealing to the preventive powers of a court of equity. When such appeal is made it is the duty of government to protect the one against the many as well as the many against the one.[9]

In this interesting utterance we note again the conflict between individualism and collectivism. Liberty has become a "two-headed Janus"—the liberty to combine and the liberty to act alone—making it difficult to chart a course of conduct for the future.

Nevertheless, the defendants escaped their jail sentences on technical and procedural grounds; the court ended by saying that it acted "without prejudice to the power and right" of the lower court "to punish, by a proper proceeding, contempt, if any, committed against it."

The day after this decision the lower court appointed a prosecuting committee to start a new contempt proceeding, which, after the appropriate steps, resulted in the reimposition of the same jail sentences.

By 1913 the case again had arrived before the Supreme Court. This time the Court held in effect that when it sent the case back to the lower court with a suggestion of further proceedings, the statute of limitations had already barred further action.[10]

Throughout the excitement Mr. Gompers appeared to be trying to pry open the gates of prison in order that he might go to the stake for a great cause. But the end was unromantic; the principles for which he fought were lost, and the statute of limitations was pleaded and allowed, the Court appraising it as the "only real defense." [11]

The case was celebrated in its day because it was an organized contest between the president of the National Association of Manufacturers and the leading officials of the American Federation of Labor. Together with the Hatters Case it created history. In March, 1908, the "unfair" list of the A. F. of L. ceased to exist, Mr. Gompers announcing that the publication of such a list "makes the organization and the individuals composing it liable to monetary damages and imprisonment. . . ." And he added, "Labor demands relief at the hands of Congress; demands it NOW." [12]

Of the legal principles involved in these two cases, the Federation lost all. It had to abandon the boycott. As to fatalities, the score was more evenly balanced. The labor leaders did not go to jail and the Buck Stove & Range Company lowered its colors. On the other hand, Loewe the hatter continued making hats for some time thereafter, and people bought the hats. When I thought of the quiet and determined Loewe, I learned a lesson that since has proved useful. In times of industrial strife the person who shouts the loudest is not always the person who lasts the longest.

IV

The Appeal to the Polls

THE PHILOSOPHY OF MR. GOMPERS and the American Federation of Labor early in this century is in marked contrast with the union philosophy of today. Mr. Gompers was opposed to government intervention in any form, whether it originated in statute or court decision. Compulsory old age insurance and minimum wage laws were taboo. Any suggestion of a labor relations act to protect the right of men to organize, or a fair labor standards act to fix minimum wages or maximum hours, would to him have been revolting. Labor, he felt, could take care of itself if the government would keep its hands off.

An incident that well illustrates this attitude occurred in August, 1915, when O. B. Forshey, a proprietor of a barber shop in Colorado, installed a new razor-sharpening machine and advertised that he would sharpen razors for the public at prices lower than those fixed by union bylaws. A dispute arose. Both parties appealed to the newly created Colorado Industrial Commission, which stated that it would not attempt to bind either side but suggested that the union withhold action for a few days. Against this moderate action Samuel Gompers hurled his epithets in an editorial entitled "Invasion by Commission." He described this action as "invasion of the lawful rights of the barbers' union" and argued that "such regulating power exercised by any political agency . . . would sap the militant spirit and the resourcefulness and independence that have made the trade unions organizations of America the most powerful and most effective organizations which are to be found anywhere." [1]

This incident explains the objectives for which the Federation of Labor entered the political campaign in 1906. Its goal was negative. It sought no affirmative support or protection. It wished to escape from the entanglements of the law so that it might at all times engage in full freedom of action.

In the latter half of the decade which saw the commencement of the Hatters and Buck Stove & Range suits, this contest over the issue of nonintervention by government was being waged on two fronts: in the courts and in the committee rooms of Congress. It became a part of the activity of the Anti-Boycott Association, which was participating in the Hatters Case, to resist political efforts to exempt labor from legal restraints and responsibilities. Messrs. Daniel Davenport and James M. Beck were called upon to appear before committees in Congress in opposition to measures of this character. Their first appearance received sensational recognition from the press. The New York *Sun*, referring to this employers association declared, "But this session there appeared on the scene a secret organization, the ramifications of its membership extending into all parts of the country with abundance of means to employ the best of talent and guided and directed by men of energy, purpose and force." [2]

The legislative measures pertinent to government intervention in labor disputes, which came before Congress for consideration in these years and the following decade, covered a variety of proposals. Bills were proposed to exempt labor from the antitrust laws; to legalize boycotting and certain other forms of conspiracy; to declare that business was not property, and, therefore, not entitled to protection in a court of equity; to abolish injunctions; to provide that injunctions should not issue without notice of hearing; and that contempt proceedings for violations of injunctions should be tried by a jury.

The clamor for legislative relief would not down. The decisions of the courts secured by the American Anti-Boycott Association merely strengthened the union demand for legislation that would close the doors of the courts to so-called labor litigation. The utterances of organized labor were of growing intensity. *The American Federationist* repeatedly charged that the existence of organized labor was in jeopardy and that the right of free association and voluntary coalition had been denied. Editorials were defiant:

We have steadily fought the injunction—this outrageous, impudent, revolutionary invention of lawless plutocracy—and if the national and state legislatures are reluctant or slow to come to the relief of labor and put an end by appropriate legislation to the usurpation practiced by Judges more and more audaciously at the dictation of plutocracy, other lawful ways and means of resisting the abuse will suggest themselves.[3]

Do the worst elements of capitalism want a class struggle in the United States? Is it their purpose to convince labor that they control the courts, and can manipulate the law at their will? [4]

Under the caption "The Injunction Mania," Mr. Gompers wrote:

It is quite evident that there is a well defined campaign being conducted by the worst element in the capitalist class, countenanced by a considerable part of the judiciary to rob the workers of the rights and of the liberty to which they are entitled by the guarantees of the Constitution of our country.[5]

Year after year committees of Congress listened to the representatives of labor unions presenting their grievances and proposing a change in the laws, while employers' representatives and constitutional lawyers of distinction opposed them. Volumes of committee reports and articles in periodicals now record this. The issue became one of such outstanding importance that it found its way into the platforms of the two great political parties. In March, 1906, the Federation and prominent national unions presented their "Bill of Grievances" to Congressmen, Senators, and the President, calling for exemption from the antitrust laws and the abolition of labor injunctions and declaring that their repeated efforts to obtain redress from Congress had been in vain. They hoped their appeal would not be fruitless, "but if, perchance, you may not heed us, we shall appeal to the conscience and the support of our fellow citizens." [6] A categorical answer to the Bill was demanded for the purpose of definitely pledging each Congressman to the support of such measures or marking him for political slaughter at the fall elections. Answers were published in *The Federationist* and those that were evasive or hostile or which did not harmonize with the Congressman's record were briefly commented upon by the editor. "This," wrote the editor, "had the effect of convincing many that Labor's campaign was no bluff, and after that there were fewer attempts to evade or confuse the issue." [7] Answers promising to give the subject "careful consideration" and to vote for the "best interests of Labor" were not satisfactory because "the gentleman seems to know better than Labor what is for their best interest." [8]   The pledge demanded of the national legislators was not only to vote for certain bills or policies, but also to accept such changes in detail as might be thereafter approved by the legislative committee of the American Federation of Labor and the National Grange. The representatives of the people were to be rubber stamps. Never before that time was there such a public, bold, and systematic attempt in this country to make government a tool for class purposes. The quiet, unseen methods of secret lobbies and boss control, with which we were familiar through common gossip, were less startling, if not less dangerous. Labor's watchword, as announced by the A. F. of L. was:

We will stand by our friends and administer a stinging rebuke to men or parties who are either indifferent, negligent, or hostile, and, wherever opportunity affords, to secure the election of intelligent, honest, earnest trade unionists, with clear, unblemished, paid-up union cards in their possession.[9]

To realize how excessively class-conscious was this political venture, it is illuminating to follow the contemporary suggestion of one newspaper, which quoted one of Mr. Gompers' editorials after substituting the word "capital" for the word "labor":

The first concern of all should be the positive defeat of those who have been hostile or indifferent to the just demands of CAPITAL. A stinging rebuke to them will benefit not only the CAPITALISTS, but the people of the entire country. Wherever both parties ignore CAPITAL'S legislative demands a straight CAPITAL candidate should be nominated. . . .[10]

Congressmen and Senators who were fearless and outspoken in their opposition to such legislation on behalf of labor were attacked. This policy led to a personal campaign in the state of Maine by Mr. Gompers and his associates against Congressman Charles E. Littlefield. William Howard Taft and others of national renown went to Maine and campaigned in Mr. Littlefield's behalf. "The Parry-Post-Gripe-Nuts Manufacturers' Association and so-called Citizens' Alliance," according to the Federation, "had their henchmen in the field." [11]   It was a battle of national significance and Mr. Littlefield won by a greatly reduced plurality. The labor leaders were hopeful, thinking, no doubt, "As Maine goes, so goes the nation." The muse was invoked to strengthen optimism:

Three cheers for Samuel Gompers,
    And long may his name wave;
Against great odds he made a fight—
    it was a darned close shave—
Against the greatest speakers.
    Administration gave
        One Littlefield
        Was nearly peeled
And barely missed the grave.[12]

Labor then turned its attention to the coming campaigns of Congressmen McCall, "Uncle" Joe Cannon, Gillett, Palmer, Weeks, Gardner, Sherman, and others who were also marked for defeat, but the results were insubstantial. The political blacklist did not work.

Naturally labor leaders tried to convince themselves and their followers that the campaign was a great success. Political independence and courage must not be encouraged by the thought that there is no political penalty for independent action. So the official announcement went forth: "Labor's political work is just begun. The future is ours." [13]

An effort was made to explain to Congressmen why labor's initial effort did not accomplish more:

That labor was unable to exert its entire force in the recent campaign, we frankly admit, but in spite of great difficulties it accomplished enough to give more than a hint of what it can and may do when thoroughly prepared to exercise its political strength. . . . Let no Congressman delude himself with the hope that the recent campaign was merely a spasmodic effort on the part of labor to right its wrongs. Let no Congressman flatter himself that his future record will be concealed from the public.[14]

No such elaborate campaign on the part of the Federation was repeated for nearly 40 years. Efforts were made in subsequent elections, however, to write labor's demands into the platforms of the political parties and to capture more Congressional seats for union men in certain promising localities. From time to time *The Federationist* reviewed the results thus attained:

The year 1906 marked a concerted movement of organized labor into the field of national politics. . . . The records of Congressmen were scrutinized. . . . The first contest revealed the efficacy of the effort. Six trade unionists, in full standing with their respective organizations, were elected to membership in the national House of Representatives.[15]

The "dominant party refused to change its policy" and organized labor, proceeding with its campaign in the election of 1908, added "four additional trade unionists to the House. . . Congress and the public generally became convinced that Labor proposed to exercise its political rights, to the end that Congressional relief should be secured." Labor made its third campaign in 1910, thereby "augmenting the labor group to a total of fifteen." [16]

The counter-campaign of the National Association of Manufacturers during this era gives another startling picture of the times. In October, 1909, its president declared, "I am opposed to labor unions such as are represented by the American Federation of Labor. . . . To treat with criminals or to compromise principles that are sacred is forever wrong. . . ." [17] And again: "No organization of men, not excepting the Ku Klux Klan, the Mafia or the Black Hand Society, has ever produced such a record of barbarism as has this so-called organized labor society." [18] The closed shop was "a sin against humanity" and the union label was the "insignia of industrial slavery." [19]

Then at last in 1911 the same president of this association declared that "a representative of the American Federation of Labor has no more business to be in any manner affiliated with men or associations who are honestly and conscientiously endeavoring to promote the welfare of this nation . . . than has a tarantula a rightful place on the bosom of an angel." [20] Again the president of the National Association of Manufacturers declared, "The American Federation of Labor is engaged in open warfare against Jesus Christ and his cause." [21]

It is extremely difficult to explain the attitude of both these groups towards the National Civic Federation, a public-spirited organization formed by men like Mark Hanna, August Belmont, and others to bridge the chasm between classes and promote industrial peace. The National Association of Manufacturers attacked it vigorously calling it "a disloyal and unpatriotic organization," [22] and John Mitchell was expelled from the United Mine Workers for associating with it.

Returning now to the contemporaneous efforts of the Federation to secure political recognition of its grievances, we find it making substantial progress in securing public sanction, notwithstanding the attacks of the National Association of Manufacturers.

At the Atlantic City Convention of the American Federation of Labor in 1911, the executive committee was authorized "to take such action as in its judgment the situation may warrant in the presidential and congressional election of 1912." [23] The exhortation was slightly changed:

Men of Labor, grit your teeth, organize, unite, federate. Elect bona fide trade unionists to Congress. Get busy! [24]

The labor planks as incorporated in the national platforms were published in *The Federationist* and the speeches of two presidential candidates were reviewed with special emphasis on their references to the injunction.

The Federationist was careful not to dictate to its followers for whom they should vote for president, but recommended that they study the attitude of each candidate on the subject of relief from the Sherman Anti-Trust Law and from the issuance of injunctions. The unionist was reminded that Mr. Taft, the Republican candidate for the presidency being also the originator of the abuse of the injunction in labor disputes, was against any plan to weaken the courts or any form of class legislation.

In 1912 *The American Federationist* summarized the situation:

That issue was presented in the presidential and congressional campaigns of 1908. It was an issue in the congressional campaign of 1910. It is a paramount issue in the pending presidential and congressional campaign, and regardless of all other questions affecting the working people of the United States, all should be subordinated to the achievement of this one living, forceful issue, which the toilers and their sympathizers and all liberty-loving American citizens must determine in the election of November 5, 1912. [25]

The demands of labor unions had now become standardized. Most of them found expression in a Model Anti-Injunction Bill, which, in effect, declared that the right of a man to work and the right of an employer to conduct business should not be regarded as a property right entitled to protection as property in the courts of our land. These property rights were to be abolished *pro tanto*.

The Democratic platforms of 1908 and 1912 had pledged the party to a modification of the laws relating to injunctions in labor disputes. In 1913 conditions were more favorable. Politicians showed their states of mind by considering federal appropriation bills for law enforcement with provisos that none of the appropriated funds should be used against labor unions. Early in

1913, "after 23 years of effort, the labor proviso," says *The Federationist,* "was incorporated in a bill reported from a committee." This bill was vetoed by President Taft, but on June 23, 1913, a similar bill was signed by his successor, President Wilson. "This was a decisive victory for the rights and protection of labor," [26] wrote Mr. Gompers. A decisive victory indeed; a victory for class legislation when appropriations for the enforcement of laws provide that they shall not be utilized to enforce laws against a particular group! After that President Wilson annually signed bills with similar provisos. This was the beginning of several reprehensible approaches to this problem.

The ground was well harrowed for the events of 1914. A nationwide campaign, directed from the headquarters of the Federation at Washington, urged enactment of the Model Anti-Injunction Bill before the legislatures of various states. The Clayton Bill in Congress restricting injunctions and purporting to exempt labor unions from the antitrust law was ready for enactment. Hearings were shut off. The stage was set. Labor leaders sat in the galleries during the critical sessions of Congress and their presence had its effect.

The scene in the Senate was portrayed, as the Federation saw it and felt it:

The scene in the Senate on September 2 was intensely interesting. The day was very hot but the air was vibrant with the tenseness of the concentrated interest and earnestness of those men engaged in legislative deliberations. The quiet acceptance of Labor's contentions was very suggestive.[27]

By The Clayton Act, "After 24 years," wrote *The Federationist,* "the organizations of labor have freed themselves from this strange entanglement." [28] The Federation contended that unions did not need to be restricted by any such law. Unlike the captains of industry, they were not governed "by the same freebooting standards of ethics as the pirates of old." [29] The words of the new law were "sledge hammer blows to the wrongs and injustice so long inflicted upon the workers." The long-heralded declaration that "the labor of a human being is not a commodity or article of commerce . . . is the Industrial Magna Carta upon which the working people will rear their structure of industrial freedom." [30] The New York *World* beheld the event as "the most impressive legislative reversal of judicial decisions that has taken place in this country since the Dred Scott Judgment was overturned by the Civil War." [31]   The Executive Council of the A.F. of L. was complacent. It declared:

This law precludes the possibility of any similar suit being brought in the federal courts for the exercise of normal activities as performed by the Hatters—and thus the American Federation of Labor has performed its full duties to the Hatters and to all labor in the premises: [32]

Mr. Tumulty, the President's secretary, wrote Mr. Gompers on October 15, 1914, "I take pleasure in sending you herewith one of the pens used by the President in signing" this bill.   This pen, it was stated in *The Federationist*, will be "added to the collection of famous pens at the A. F. of L. headquarters" and "will be given the place of greatest honor," because "it is symbolic of the most comprehensive and most fundamental legislation in behalf of human liberty that has been enacted anywhere in the world." [33]

Oddly enough, although no authoritative decisions had found this law inadequate from labor's viewpoint, the Democratic platform in 1916 still carried a plank against "the unwarranted issuance of writs."

During this same period, when politicians had grown more responsive to the demands of labor unions, a few other laws of similar nature were passed in some of the states.   Only two played any conspicuous part in the history of this subject: the Massachusetts anti-injunction law, enacted in July, 1914, and the Arizona law, enacted in 1913.   Each of these, as well as the Clayton Act, commands attention, not for itself alone, but for the mishaps that befell it.

To understand the fate of these measures we must bear in mind the simple and fundamental concept against which organized labor was directing its energies: that the right to work or conduct a business was not a property right.   In the latter part of the eighteenth century Turgot declared:

God made the right to labor the property of every man since he gave to him needs and referred him to labor as the necessary means for satisfying these needs, and this property is the first, the holiest, the most imprescriptible.[34]

A century or more later the Supreme Court of the United States and state supreme courts were repeatedly declaring what from sheer common sense they could not avoid holding: The right of a man to earn a livelihood, whether it be the right of the workman to pursue his trade or the right of an employer to operate his business, is as much a property right as the tangible dollars with which he thereby fills his purse. Jurists agreed on this fundamental and granted these rights the same measure of protection they vouchsafed to other property rights. They remarked that it would be far less serious to deny protection to the goodwill or tangible property of business than to the workman's right to work.

These inalienable rights were the fortress to which nonunionists fled for protection. The artillery of the unions had been directed to the demolition of this fortress, because it lay athwart their path to more complete conquest. The end sought was the right to enlarge the union army by conscription. Bills declaring that the right to enter into the relation of employer and employee or to carry on business, or to labor, shall not be construed as a property right were therefore systematically introduced and pushed in Congress and state legislatures. Thus we came to the popular declaration that "the labor of a human being is not a commodity or article of commerce."

Curiously enough, that conservative old champion of individual rights, the Commonwealth of Massachusetts, was one of the first states to respond to this campaign by enacting such a law. To pass the law on the Fourth of July would have been irony, but it did not pass until July 7, 1914.

Shortly thereafter a branch of the Industrial Workers of the World sought an injunction against the hod carriers' union of the American Federation of Labor because that union had conspired to drive the members of the I. W. W. from their jobs by calling strikes of various trades upon buildings where they were employed. Under such a regime the hod carriers' union, being affiliated with the unions of other trades, was in control unless the law intervened. If the right to work were no longer a property right, as declared by the newly enacted law of that state, the complainants were helpless, but if the right to work were to be regarded as it had been regarded in the past, an injunction should issue. In 1916 the case was decided by the highest court of Massachusetts. It held the anti-injunction law to be unconstitutional, saying:

The right to make contracts to earn money by labor is at least as essential to the laborer as is any property right to other members of society. If as much protection is not given by the laws to this property, which often may be the owner's only substantial asset, as is given other kinds of property, the laborer stands on a plane inferior to that of other property owners.[35]

This decision created an uproar in the ranks of labor. *The Federationist* for August, 1916, in an article entitled "Americans, Wake Up!,"[36] spoke of it as the baldest usurpation. Another whole article, under the caption "What Shall Be Done with Judges Who Violate the Constitutional Rights of Labor?,"[37] was devoted to the subject. Mr. Gompers in an editorial in his own inimitable style declared that the "Massachusetts Court filches workers rights."[38] "Filches them," the court might reply, "of their right to filch the rights of brother laborers."

Punishment was promised the courts:

The organized labor movement will see to it that the judges either learn their lesson or that they are removed from places so potential for injustice; that the people through their legislatures will restore to the workers—the masses of the people—the rights and the freedom of which the Massachusetts court has undertaken to rob them.[39]

It is significant indeed that the Massachusetts case, which struck at the heart of the model anti-injunction bill and evoked this cry of defiance, was not a case brought by capital, but a case brought by members of one union to protect their right to join a union of their own choosing.

When the delegates of the Federation of Labor met in convention in Baltimore in November of the same year, their minds and their emotions were aroused by exhortatory appeals. A solution to the property-right controversy presented itself. If mere legislation could not by some precious alchemy change that which was a property right into something which was not a property right, the Federation must try a stronger chemistry and alter the Constitution. The convention went on record in favor of a constitutional amendment declaring, "that the labor of a human being is not a commodity or article of commerce; and the legislature shall not pass a law nor the courts construe any law of the state contrary to this declaration." But the convention did not stop there. It officially adopted a pronunciamento containing this:

We therefore recommend that any injunctions dealing with the relationship of employer and employee and based upon the dictum "Labor is Property" be wholly and absolutely treated as usurpation and disregarded, let the consequences be what they may. . . . Kings could be and were disobeyed and sometimes deposed.   In cases of this kind judges must be disobeyed and should be impeached.[40]

The next annual convention held in Buffalo in 1917 reiterated this program of court defiance,[41] and President Wilson in addressing the convention expressed his confidence in the patriotism of the Federation.   Finally the Federation concluded it must "Capture the Courts." [42]

Meanwhile "Labor's Magna Carta," the Clayton Act,—which was to introduce "a new era"—was not yet put to the test.   The President of the United States had declared that this did not legalize the secondary boycott.   The committee in Congress had declared the same.   The Federation of Labor, however, declared otherwise, claiming it had reversed the Hatters and Buck Stove and Range Cases.   But before we show the outcome of this controversy it is necessary to turn back the calendar slightly to deal with certain preliminary events leading to the downfall of labor's Magna Carta.

V

The Carpenters' Ban on Open-Shop Woodwork

Down to the present time, when recounting secondary boycotts of nationwide proportions, we have referred only to those
carried on primarily through combining purchasing power or
patronage. Boycotts of this type—at least on any nationwide
scale—died in the early part of 1908 when, bowing to the decisions in the Hatters and Buck Stove and Range Cases, the American Federation of Labor discontinued such activities. They were
never revived. But there is another type of secondary boycott
prosecuted by labor's refusal to work upon boycotted products or
on buildings or for employers when the contraband products are
used. This labor boycott began to gain headway about the time
that the patronage boycott ceased and has continued to be a matter
of active interest to organized labor. In fact it was the only type
of secondary boycott that became the subject of intense interest in
the debates that preceded the Taft-Hartley Act in 1946 and 1947
and in the debate that followed President Truman's effort to secure
its repeal in 1949.

Just as the Hatters Case typified the patronage boycott, so did
the activities of the carpenters' union typify this secondary boycott
prosecuted through secondary strikes.

This is the picture as it existed about 1910. The United
Brotherhood of Carpenters and Joiners of America, an affiliate of
the American Federation of Labor, represented a membership of
nearly 200,000 journeymen, who in turn were members of affiliated local unions, of which there were about 1900. This union
was definitely pledged to the elimination of all nonunion men and

45

all open-shop products.   It was to be accomplished through refusing to handle nonunion products and refusing to work on projects or for employers where open-shop products or nonunion carpenters were involved.   The carpenters' union was becoming a pretty tight monopoly.   Anybody expelled or suspended from any one of the 1900 locals could not become a member of any other local, except with the consent of the local from which he was expelled and a two-thirds vote of approval by the union to which he made application.   Thus a blackball on the Atlantic Coast controlled admission to a local union on the Pacific Coast.   A nonunion carpenter was to become a commercial leper.

Of the 200,000 members, about 160,000 worked in building construction alongside other organized crafts of which there were often 20 or 30.   If open-shop products were brought to the building, the union carpenters were called out on strike, and if any attempt was made to employ nonunion carpenters to do the work that the union carpenters refused to do, the other trades were usually called out.

Here was another effective machine of nationwide scope which exercised vast power over the distribution of products needed for homes and other structures.

In the spring of 1910 the concern of Irving & Casson, which operated mills in East Cambridge, Massachusetts, for the manufacture of decorative woodwork, wood carvings and special types of furniture, came into conflict with these boycotting operations of the carpenters' union.   The work of Irving & Casson was totally unlike that of an ordinary wood-trim manufacturer or carpenter contractor.   Its furniture deserved to be ranked with Phyfe and Sheraton.   Its art extended to church pews, statues, and such elaborate panels as the Lord's Supper carved in oak.   Because of its reputation, Mr. Ralph Cram, an outstanding ecclesiastical architect, arranged to have this company do important altar work in the Cathedral of St. John the Divine.   Then came the trouble. In April, 1910, the carpenters were called out on strike, and French of the carpenters' union threatened to call out the other trades, saying, "If you put on nonunion men I will close up that job as tight as a drum."   It was at that juncture that I secured an injunction in the federal court which saved the day.[1]

There were other instances of like difficulties where this concern was carrying on important work at West Point and in houses of wealthy owners, and there were instances where architects and builders threatened by labor troubles dared not do business with it. These scattered incidents were taken care of through a broader injunction enjoining the union from ordering men to strike against this material and its purchasers, and from threatening contractors and architects with trouble if they attempted to make such purchases.[2]

This suit was a mere skirmish. A year later I instituted a more comprehensive suit for an injunction in behalf of six large manufacturers of wood trim located in Oshkosh and Wausau, Wisconsin, and also in the states of Missouri, Iowa, Pennsylvania, and Tennessee, to protect them in their right to sell wood products in free and open competition in the city of New York. The defendants were some 23 officers of the carpenters' union, about 100 building contractors who had written agreements with the Carpenters' Union not to handle nonunion goods, and six local manufacturers in New York City who had entered into contracts with the carpenters' union, in which they agreed to employ only union members and in which the union agreed "that none of their members will erect or install nonunion material." The plaintiffs, who engaged in mass production of standard products, were equipped to furnish woodwork for building construction in New York City at a price 40 per cent less than that charged by the local union manufacturers. In order to force the transfer of the business of these larger manufacturers to the small local manufacturers, it was necessary to stifle competition. If that could be done the production of these goods would be shifted from country districts to the metropolitan area, and the public would be forced to pay the difference. The local specialty manufacturers would then do all the staple business. To accomplish this the New York manufacturers employed spies to track shipments of the contraband goods and then required the union to strike the job. So tight was this monopoly that even interborough competition was prevented. Open-shop manufacturers across the river on Long Island could not make sales in New York City at prices 25 per cent lower than the prevailing prices of the union material.

The secretary of the national union reported at the 1906 convention:

Two years ago we were face to face with the open-shop proposition . . . but thanks to the firm stand taken by the delegates attending the Milwaukee convention, the open shop has been a failure and is now a dead issue, as far as this organization is concerned.[3]

The president's report to the same convention recommended "that the work be continued along these lines until all mills and factories in the woodworking industry are under our jurisdiction." [4] Traffic in all but closed-shop products either had ended or was about to end. The union was embarked on a program of national control of wages and prices.

So attuned to these restrictions was the local market in New York City that our lawsuit, with its appearance of comprehensiveness and formidability, burst like a bomb upon the trade, and the numerous defendants gathered a battery of attorneys. The press heralded this move as a suit to burst the labor trust, and similar suits in the state courts followed which, in their early stages, met with great success, although later they failed.

The motion for a preliminary injunction having been granted in May, 1911, it then became necessary to prepare for trial. For this purpose I took depositions in Wisconsin, Tennessee, and various other points, with a view to proving the facts. Ultimately the case came on for trial and the judge dismissed the complaint, on the ground that it was of a broad, sweeping character which did not disclose a combination that aimed specially to injure an individual or single company.[5] The Circuit Court of Appeals agreed with the trial court.[6] The court, apparently staggered by the scope of our objective, did not relish the idea of endeavoring to control the forces of commerce on such a broad basis through a suit brought by private parties.

We appealed to the Supreme Court of the United States, which, after hearing argument, held the case for over a year and then restored it for reargument. When the decision was finally rendered it was 5 to 4 against the plaintiffs, with indications that if Justice Hughes, who resigned to run for the Presidency after the first argument of the case, had not been succeeded by Justice Clark, the decision would have been 5 to 4 in our favor.[7] "Time and chance happeneth to all men."

The majority opinion was scant and seemed to approach the case as a good housewife approaches a bad egg. It did not dispute the illegality of the combination under the federal laws but held that under those laws only the government could sue for an injunction. What I had looked upon as a vehicle with which to secure a real charter of rights failed of its accomplishment. Great expectations came to naught.

During this same period I secured several injunctions against the carpenters in the New York state courts. One of the cases which led to a rather lengthy trial was enlivened by a dramatic incident. In my possession, but hidden in my brief case, was the union minute book which contained boycott entries written in long-hand by five successive union secretaries over a period of years. These secretaries were all in court on subpoenas, which I had caused to be issued. One by one I put these secretaries on the witness stand. Successively they denied everything. They denied that they kept any permanent minutes when they were secretary. Under my persistent questioning, they fabricated testimony about the way in which they kept minutes on loose sheets, giving details as to the size and color of the paper and the lines on it. These sheets, they testified, were destroyed. No minutes were preserved. After each witness had dug in so deep that he could not escape, I asked the court for the privilege of recalling them, and on the first recall I produced the book. The consternation of the witnesses and the silence in the court room were startling. One by one these men threw themselves on the mercy of the court, one pleading that his wife had been so ill that his mind was upset. On another occasion I found the union minutes had apparently been altered in a critical sentence, so I rushed one of my junior associates to the phone to bring an ink and handwriting expert to the court. He came and that same day took the witness stand and proved that the minute book in this crucial passage had been recently forged to make it read otherwise than in the original entry.

The state Carpenters Case, which involved the concerted perjury, was appealed by the union to the Appellate Division of the Supreme Court of New York, which sustained the injunction, but when the union persisted and carried it to the highest court of the state, it was rewarded by a unanimous opinion that its activities were lawful.

Down to this time I had made no permanent headway against this type of boycott, but the end was not yet.

VI

The Carpenters Strike Back

THE CARPENTERS' UNION, large and resourceful as it was, did
not plan to remain on the defensive. It was only by accident that
I received advance information, via the Canadian wilderness,
as to its contemplated offensive. In 1911 Mr. John Kirby, who
as president of the National Association of Manufacturers had
denounced all labor leaders, was vacationing at a camp in the
Canadian woods when he met Charles Maitland Beattie, attorney for the carpenters' union. Mr. Beattie, not knowing the
identity of Mr. Kirby, told him confidentially of a program to
jail me and my associates of the Anti-Boycott Association. He
pointed out that Section 280 of the Penal Law of New York State
had long forbidden corporations to practice law, and the union
had been instrumental in having it amended to extend to associations like the Anti-Boycott Association. The maximum penalty
was a $1000 fine and a year in prison. This law, he said, "will
be applied to Mr. Merritt." Mr. Kirby wired me.

Of course this law was only intended to prevent business organizations from hiring a lawyer on a salary and subcontracting
his services at a profit. It had no application to voluntary groups
like unions or employers' associations not operating for profit but
uniting in the employment of a single attorney for some common
purpose in a limited field. Mr. Beattie felt otherwise.

The first step in the union program was to secure evidence in a
civil suit for an injunction. With the facts thus developed, whether
or not the injunction were granted, it would then be practicable to
resort to criminal prosecutions.

Proceeding according to plan, in November, 1911, the District

Council of Carpenters commenced its suit in the New York Supreme Court to enjoin the American Anti-Boycott Association from continuing its court activities. We employed the Honorable Charles E. Littlefield, former Congressman, to defend.

The complaint alleged that the association had raised vast sums of money to carry on litigation against labor organizations and had conspired against the Joint District Council of Carpenters by authorizing me, as a salaried officer and attorney, to act for members of the association in suits against the carpenters. The object of the association in such litigation, it was alleged, "is to harass and destroy said Joint District Council, and to impoverish it."

The first application for a preliminary injunction was dismissed without prejudice. On the second, Judge Bijur of the Supreme Court of the State of New York held on March 23, 1912, "I do not think that the defendant Association is shown to violate either the letter or the spirit of Section 280 of the Penal Law." The case dragged on until the end of the year, when on final trial Justice Ford held, "that the defendant's activities transgressed the statute in question seems quite clear." He added, however, that the carpenters' union had no standing in court to secure an injunction because it was merely seeking by indirection to enforce a criminal law. The case was accordingly dismissed. Subsequent efforts by the plaintiff to alter this decision by appeal proved unavailing but the ground was well ploughed for a criminal prosecution as planned.

On January 15, 1916, a marshal appeared in my office and laying the heavy hand of the law upon my shoulder informed me I was under arrest. When I inquired, "What for?" the officer replied, "For practicing law and giving legal advice." I was not quick to understand what was happening, although I had been forewarned, and I asked for what reason he supposed I studied law. The officer, then my custodian, laughed and said the whole matter was a mystery to him and exhibited the warrant, which stated the charge as "unlawfully practicing law and giving legal advice." We then hied to the Magistrate's Court, where I waived examination and was held on $500 bail, to appear before Special Sessions for trial.

The newspapers proclaimed the event with headlines—"Labor Hits at its Old Foe." The labor unions felt confident that this would be an end of organized effort to enforce the law against their illegal practices, and their feelings found expression in another headline, "Labor Leaders See End of Opposition in Court Decision." The union's attorneys declared, "This is the beginning of the end of the Anti-Boycott Association. It has operated against labor unions for fifteen years, and we will show that it is nothing more than a corporation of lawyers." Mr. Beattie, the union's attorney, declared, "Labor unions having come to the conclusion that it was time for the worm to turn, and prevent what they call a blind pool to fight labor, decided on the present criminal proceeding." To this I retorted, "The American Anti-Boycott Association is a public-spirited organization, formed to establish industrial peace and justice, and is now attacked by the carpenters' union on the ground that it furnishes counsel to secure protection of its members against unlawful conspiracies of labor."

The affidavit in support of the warrant of arrest was sworn to by a young man in Mr. Beattie's office. If charged me with starting and maintaining a dozen different suits against the carpenters' union in the city of New York, as well as a suit against the photo-engravers, and prayed "that the defendants be apprehended and dealt with according to law."

The case came on for trial November 15, 1916, before three judges sitting in Special Sessions, Brooklyn. After the evidence was taken, the defendant giving a full, frank and clear statement of its purposes and activities, the court dismissed the case, one judge dissenting.

In the summer of 1912, while the proceedings just described were dragging through the courts, the carpenters pursued another ingenious course. They had been unsuccessful in securing any court decision stopping the activities of the American Anti-Boycott Association. In order to secure a favorable decision without opposition, they applied to the Appellate Division of the Supreme Court, without notice to anybody, for a ruling as to whether the union could employ an attorney to act for its members or whether such activities would violate the penal law. The court was wary. It refused to pass upon the question and decided that when the carpenters' union had completed its form of organization it would be time enough to present the question for final decision.

Excitement ran high in New York City in 1912 as a result of this litigation with the carpenters' union. On October 26th, according to the newspapers, "an army of 25,000 men belonging to the building trades unions, every second man carrying a small American flag, marched last night from Fifth Avenue and 58th Street to Cooper Union to protest against injunctions restraining union men from boycotting the use of nonunion materials." [1] They had 20 bands and there was some disorder. "The red flag," according to union circulars, "was well represented in the demonstration and the workers' 'Marseillaise' was played continuously." Inscriptions called upon the courts to do something to wipe out the Anti-Boycott Association.

When the procession arrived at Cooper Union, a meeting was held with Eldridge H. Neal, secretary of the Carpenters' District Council, as chairman and Mr. Gompers as the chief speaker. The American Anti-Boycott Association, as well as the decisions of the courts enjoining boycotting, was excoriated. As reported by the New York *Times*, Mr. Gompers declared in substance as follows:

If the judges continue to abuse the power of injunction there may be many repetitions of the Lawrence affair and elsewhere. We are not bound to obey an injunction in excess of the power of the Court to issue it. Men who propose to exercise the rights of American citizens must take the consequences, whatever they may be.[2]

It was resolved that no member of the organized mechanics of the building trades unions will hereafter work for any member of the American Anti-Boycott Association.

To add to the agitation, inflammatory circulars were distributed in New York attacking me and the courts:

It is quite clear . . . that if you wish to get an injunction against the workingman under similar conditions, you do not need to go to the Supreme Court, but apply to the American Anti-Boycott Association, which will prepare the papers for you and they will compel the judge to sign the paper for you. You take no risk, therefore, in employing them, for you get the injunction in any event, and the judge no longer has anything to say about it.

At the Biennial Convention of the United Brotherhood of Carpenters, held in 1912, judges were referred to as "little pee-wee judges . . . without a single drop of red blood" [3] in them. The Anti-Boycott Association had been "caught red-handed" and the people connected with it were "criminals under the law." [4] The Committee on Legislation recommended "that the officers of this Council devote their time and money to fight the courts of our state and nation to the end that the wage earner shall have just as much right in expecting just and equitable decisions as the big interests." [5]

The convention also declared "that the reckless and unwarranted use of court injunctions has resolved itself into mere judicial anarchy. The frightful usurpation of unwarranted power has caused hundreds of thousands of the workers and toilers of our land to be led like sheep to the shambles." [6]

One can never tell to what results such venom as this may lead, whether poured out by labor leaders or stars of less magnitude. It starts emotional forces that are beyond control. In these early days our Chicago correspondent was blackjacked and left for dead in an elevator and never again fully recovered his faculties. Francis J. Heney, a brilliant district attorney representing us in the Loewe case on the Pacific coast, was actually shot through the face when engaged in one of his prosecutions.

VII

The Downfall of Labor's Magna Carta

THE CARPENTERS' CASES settled nothing as to the scope of labor's
Magna Carta in the Clayton Act. In the meantime another situation had arisen in the spring of 1914. I did not then regard it
as important as a test case, but it finally turned out to be the
historic case—the stone which the builders rejected.

The Duplex Printing Press Company of Battle Creek, Michigan,
employed about 250 mechanics, most of them machinists, in the
manufacture of large printing presses for metropolitan newspapers. These presses weighed from 10,000 to 100,000 pounds,
and the delivery of a single order sometimes required four railroad cars and of course many trucks. Once the unassembled parts
of the press started on their journey the responsibility for unloading, trucking, erection, and operation lay with the purchaser, who,
however, was entitled to the supervision and technical guidance of
a field man from the Duplex Company. This made the draymen,
loaders, and erectors the employees of the customers.

Duplex operated an open shop. Its three competitors, who
controlled over 90 per cent of the printing press business, had
closed-shop agreements with the International Association of Machinists, which was even at that time a union of about 60,000
members. Naturally the machinists and the competitors wished
to bring Duplex into the fold. With the help of some other trades,
the union started a campaign to force the unionization of Duplex.
First they called a strike of 11 union machinists, who constituted
5 per cent of the total force employed in the company's factory,
and then they required the withdrawal of labor from customers
who attempted to haul, unload, erect, or operate the open-shop

55

presses.   All labor in all parts of the country was to suspend work wherever these presses appeared in connection with their jobs, and in this way the presses were to be treated as "unclean" and made unusable.

In one instance the threatened customer, in an effort to avoid strikes of other trades, stopped the work of installation until Saturday and Sunday, when no other men were employed on the building.   To this adroitness the union delegate replied:

You put one over on me this time but you will never do it again and I am going to make it more and more difficult for the Duplex Printing Press Company to make installations and will interfere with their work in every way possible.[1]

In another case where a press was sold to *The New York Law Journal*, the same delegate said that he was "going to do all possible to prevent the wheels of the *Law Journal* press revolving."[2]   He added that the unions had unlimited financial means with which they could fight the Duplex Printing Press Company and which they were to use for that purpose.   Workmen engaged in unloading the machinery were called off and half of the load was left on the sidewalk.   Repairmen in local shops were ordered not to repair Duplex machines and the union representative spoke insinuatingly of breakdowns.   Workmen were threatened with a general blacklist by the union if they handled the boycotted machines.   Pressmen threatened not to operate the presses.   The International Association of Machinists passed a resolution saying that all members "will prevent, if possible, the installation of presses by scab labor and will use our influence to prevent the placing of orders for presses manufactured under unfair conditions."[3]   Union appeals said that the members "will not be permitted to handle the product of the Duplex Company, no matter who wanted them."[4] They told of presses tied up throughout the country, including New York.   Twenty-one building trades were called on strike to prevent the employment of nonunion men to do the work which the union men refused to do.[5]

"This company has admitted," wrote the union, "that much harm has been done them on the outside, with many publishers having cancelled orders, and their machinery not being erected," and it urged "all to get in touch with the local printing tradesmen."[6]

The matter came to a head in April of 1914 when the National

Exposition Company was to hold an exhibition of printing press machinery in the Grand Central Palace in New York City. Since contemporaneously the American Newspaper Publishers' Association and the Associated Press were also holding conventions in the city, the opportunity to exhibit was considered of great value. The exhibition was scheduled to open on a Saturday night. That day representatives of the machinists' union served notice upon the exposition company that none of their men would be allowed to install the Duplex machines for the exhibit. If nonunion men were employed, they stated, all the union men employed by all the exhibitors would strike and the entire exhibition would be closed. The exposition company representatives called attention to their contract with the union, but the union replied that the existence of a contract would not make any difference. After many powwows in which the exposition company pointed out that a general strike would also injure the concerns with which the union was friendly, the union delegate replied, "I cannot help it. I have orders from Johnston at Washington and we will pull all the labor union men out if the Duplex is allowed to exhibit." [7]

I then applied to the Federal District Court for an injunction, which was served on the union delegate in Grand Central Palace on Saturday afternoon. The delegate grabbed the injunction, threw it on the floor, and stamped on it. He declared he would pay no attention to it, but calmer considerations prevailed. He went down to union headquarters for guidance and never called the strike.

The suit instituted on these facts involved some serious legal complications. The case was started and the preliminary injunction obtained in the spring of 1914, but the case was not actually brought to trial until 1917. Meanwhile, in October, 1914, the Clayton Act, declaring that "the labor of a human being is not a commodity" and forbidding injunctions against so-called peaceful acts in labor disputes, was enacted. The same statute, however, by giving a private party the right to an injunction had cured the defect that had led the Supreme Court to dismiss the Carpenters Case. Here was the problem: In the absence of the Clayton Act this combination was clearly a violation of the antitrust laws but not enjoinable on the application of a private citizen. What effect, then, did labor's Magna Carta have upon the case when it permitted injunctions but undertook to restrict their use in labor cases?

In the trial it was held that the Clayton Act barred any relief to the company because the act by its terms forbade injunctions against strikes or boycotts.[8]

On appeal to the Circuit Court of Appeals the company again lost by a decision of 2 to 1.[9]

We appealed to the Supreme Court, which, with three judges dissenting, decided in January, 1921, that the company was entitled to an injunction. The majority of six drew a distinction between a primary and secondary boycott. It held that the restrictions placed on injunctions by the Clayton Act extended only to situations arising between the immediate parties to a labor dispute where the relation of employer and employee existed or had just previously existed and did not free labor from injunctions where the weapons of the strike and boycott were employed against neutrals, such as the customers of Duplex. Attacks on noncombatants were held to be still subject to legal condemnation and restraint. Justice Pitney, speaking for the Court, said:

> To instigate a sympathetic strike in aid of a secondary boycott cannot be deemed "peaceful and lawful" persuasion. In essence it is a threat to inflict damage upon the immediate employer, between whom and his employees no dispute exists, in order to bring him against his will into a concerted plan to inflict damage upon another employer who is in dispute with his employees.[10]

The opinion described the combination as "imposing a general embargo upon the products of the establishment and a nationwide blockade of the channels of interstate commerce."

Justice Brandeis, supported by Justice Holmes and Justice Clark, dissented in a scholarly and vigorous opinion, which in later years has been cited with a great deal of effect. The Clayton Act, they believed, "was the fruit of unceasing agitation which extended over more than twenty years and was designed to equalize before the law the position of working man and employer as industrial combatants." They could not accept the conclusion that the act was intended merely to redeclare, and not to expand, the rights of labor unions.

Of course the decision of the Court brought great resentment and started a new drive for legislative relief. Broadly speaking, its effect was to declare that the Clayton Act, designed to define employment relations, had not changed the law, as labor had contended. The decisions of the Debs Case, Hatters Case and

Buck Stove & Range Case stood unshaken as bulwarks of individual liberty against the tide of collectivism. The broad contention that all labor could organize against all capital was rejected. Class war was not to be a lawful occupation. Class solidarity was not to be regarded as an economic relationship that justifies concerted action by all members of a particular class to assist one of their fellows in fighting a member of another class. The privileges of economic action must have a rational connection with the economic interest of the participants. A learned jurist has said:

A sympathetic strike or a boycott must be held unlawful as not within the immediate field of competition. Persons who have nothing to do with the trade dispute—noncombatants—cannot be compelled, by such means, to take part in the struggle. A "boycott," as that term is ordinarily used, and a sympathetic strike, are attacks upon society itself. They are only justified when revolution is justified.[11]

The Federation of Labor treated the decision in characteristic fashion. "Rights Judicially Purloined" was the title of its article. "A blow at the movement for human freedom"[12] was its substance. But again it was the human freedom of unionists to destroy the freedom of 95 per cent of the Duplex employees who desired to produce printing presses without joining the union. The *Federationist* editorial spoke of the normal and natural rights of labor unions. In exasperation at the fiasco of labor's campaign against courts and injunctions, it declared, "We cannot admit that the court has a right to define those rights."[13]

Mr. Andrew Furuseth asserted the opinion to be against the "commands of Jesus Christ" because it forbade workers from "bearing each other's burdens."

So it happened that labor's Magna Carta did not improve labor's position in respect to the antitrust laws, but strengthened the position of the employers by extending to them what had previously been denied, the right to apply for injunctions.

Again the Federation recorded its defiance of judicial decisions by declaring as follows:

The American Federation of Labor and its president have declared that manifestly unjust decisions of courts must be defied and there is no disposition to recant.[14]

To meet this emergency the executive council of the A. F. of L., under Mr. Gompers' direction, called a conference of national trade unions which adopted a declaration to remove from the courts the power to declare laws unconstitutional, to provide for the election of judges, to exempt labor from all anticombination and conspiracy laws, and to repeal all industrial court acts.[15]

VIII

The Prosecution of Mike Boyle and Others

IN THE SUMMER OF 1914, when Germany was invading Belgium, I was commissioned by some of the largest electrical equipment manufacturers to go to Chicago and undertake through legal proceedings to end a boycott of their products enforced by the local electricians' unions with the help of the powerful Chicago Building Trades Council. Prior to 1911 the electrical contractors in Chicago bought electrical switchboards, from manufacturers throughout the country, including General Electric Company, Westinghouse Electric & Mfg. Co., and many others, in a free and open market. Switchboards, incidentally, are sizable equipment normally ranging in value from $5000 to $20,000. Beginning around 1911, the Chicago Switchboard Manufacturers Association, composed of local manufacturers who assembled switchboards from parts which they purchased, entered into agreements with Local 376 of the electrical workers' union, which controlled the men employed in the factories, and Local 134, which controlled the electricians who installed equipment on the buildings. These agreements provided that the local manufacturers would unionize and that, in return for this unionization, Local 134 would give them complete protection from outside competition. The agreement with Local 376 contained this amazing paragraph:

This increase in wages is to go into effect only in the case the union has succeeded before October 1, 1911 in bringing about a condition which will permit of none but union label switchboard work to be installed in the City of Chicago.

The leading figure in this arrangement was Mike Boyle, business agent of Local 134, backed by all the power of the Building Trades Council.

Although Local 376 originally controlled the employees of the local manufacturing companies and accomplished its work of organization through Mike Boyle's control over installation, Boyle later decided to throw over the sister local and seize control of the factories. To that end he notified the local manufacturers that thereafter only switchboards manufactured under the jurisdiction of Local 134 would be installed. Since Boyle and his Local 134 were in the saddle, the manufacturers merely handed their employees over to Local 134.

Out of these arrangements and internal fights between gangs within the unions grew graft, corruption, terrorization, property damage, violence, and even murder, but Boyle seemed always on top. To the businessman he at least had the practical virtue of "delivering the goods" and keeping his word. If fixed, he stayed fixed.

Boyle's method of procedure was to serve notice on a contractor to meet him at Johnson's saloon at a given hour and there Boyle awaited him with a hooked-handle umbrella hung over the bar. As Boyle and the contractor faced each other Boyle would remark, "Chip in $250," and if the contractor argued Boyle said, "Make it $500." He never went backwards. The money was then tossed into the umbrella and the bartender notified Boyle that someone wanted him on the telephone. Whereupon Boyle would enter the telephone booth, empty his umbrella of its contents, and then resume his place at the bar awaiting the next victim. For this Boyle was described in the headlines of the Chicago papers as "Umbrella Mike." The extortions ran high, and in the case of the erection of a building by one Chicago Company, $20,000 was paid for immunity. Boyle also had a financial interest in the States Electric Company, one of the local manufacturing companies, and when strikes were instituted, or threatened, against electrical equipment brought in from outside the state, it often took no more than a nod to have the contract transferred to the States Electric Company.

Boyle accumulated a fortune, and when asked to explain how this could happen with his modest salary, he replied, "By exceeding thrift." Boyle was also a powerful political factor, and policemen doffed their hats to him.

When I arrived in Chicago in the summer of 1914, terror over these activities was running amuck. About that time there were some murders and the press was on the job. I stealthily interviewed various businessmen who had experienced difficulties. One who was of outstanding importance locked the office door, covered the keyhole, and took me to the farthest corner of the room to whisper his story. Samuel Insull, the utility king, was very shy. He felt he had to work with Boyle and not against him. No one would sign a statement, but most of the men I saw "spilled" their story.

With the facts thus gathered I presented a statement to the United States District Attorney, who I was informed, advised the grand jury that these matters were solely of local significance and did not constitute an offense under the federal antitrust laws. To surmount this barrier and get my material before the grand jury, it was finally necessary to arrange with one of the federal judges to present it over the head of the District Attorney. That was done, and the grand jury, "raring to go," was again discouraged by the local prosecutor. The usual authorities in the Department of Justice would not become active in the matter, and it was finally left in the hands of a young man, now a prominent Chicago attorney, with whom I collaborated to draft the indictment, ultimately returned by the grand jury.

The matter then dragged, because of apparent reluctance on the part of the Department of Justice to proceed in the normal way, but pressure finally made it no longer possible for the Department to sidestep a trial. This same young man was then placed in charge of the trial in 1917 and did an excellent job with such help as we were able to extend him outside the courtroom. The jury returned a verdict against both the local manufacturers and the union. The court gave Boyle the full sentence of $5000 fine and one year imprisonment. On appeal to the Circuit Court of Appeals [1] in July, 1919, the court referred to the evidence as picturing Boyle "in the role of a blackmailer, a highwayman, a betrayer of labor and a leech on commerce."

Despite the outrages thus exposed, the political forces working in behalf of Boyle and his associates did not abate, and President

Wilson released him after he had served a few months of his sentence.

Then the extraordinary happened, as recounted by the author of *Labor Czars:*

"It's going to cost somebody something," "Umbrella Mike" warned when he came out of prison. Not even the shiny new $4,500 automobile presented to him by his loyal union subjects assuaged his anger. To show the world that he was not a man to be trifled with, Boyle called a strike of the powerhouse employees which tied up all the surface cars in Chicago. The reason for the strike, the *Chicago Tribune* commented, can be presented in a few words: "Umbrella Mike Boyle is out of jail." [2]

IX

The Supreme Court and the Stone Cutters

In 1924 I started a new case against some 40 union officials and unions in the United States District Court in Indiana on behalf of some 25 producers of stone in the Bedford-Bloomington district. In principle, but based on less forceful and colorful facts, the case was the exact replica of that which had been brought nearly 15 years earlier against the carpenters' union, building contractors, and local union manufacturers in New York City. The Carpenters Case, it will be recalled, was lost in the Supreme Court by a decision of 5 to 4, on the ground that a private party was not entitled to an injunction. The Stone Cutters Case, on the other hand, had the advantage of the Clayton Act, which expressly gave a private party the right to protection by injunction, but the request for an injunction was based on much weaker evidence. Judge Anderson, known as the injunction judge, dismissed the case without an opinion, and his action was sustained by the United States Circuit Court of Appeals.[1]

We thereupon took a further appeal to the Supreme Court of the United States. The evidence showed that plaintiffs produced stone in Indiana amounting to about $1,500,000 a year and shipped it to contractors in various states to be used in connection with the construction of buildings. The local unions in Indiana, being unable to reach a collective-bargaining agreement with the producers, undertook, with the co-operation of other locals and other trades, to prevent the use of this product in various states and cities by requiring union employees not to handle it. No stone was to be installed in any state or any city which had been produced in whole or in part by a nonunion stonecutter. The purpose of interference with the use of the stone at the point of installation was to blockade the flow of these articles of commerce to the public market and thus to create a backwater with such an impact on the sources of production in Indiana that the employers would grant the union demands and employ only union men.

The Supreme Court, with two justices dissenting, upheld the plaintiffs' position on the authority of the decision in the Duplex Printing Company Case, and said:

The strikes ordered and carried out with the sole object of preventing the use and installation of petitioners' product in other states necessarily threatened to destroy or narrow petitioners' interstate trade by taking from them their customers.

Justice Brandeis felt otherwise and said:

Members of the Journeymen Stone Cutters' Association could not work anywhere on stone which had been cut at the quarries by men working in opposition to it without aiding and abetting the enemy. Observance by each member of the provision of their constitution which forbids such action was essential to his own self-protection. It was demanded of each by loyalty to the organization and to his fellows. If on the undisputed facts of this case refusal to work can be enjoined, Congress created by the Sherman Law and the Clayton Act an instrument for imposing restraints upon labor which reminds of involuntary servitude.[2]

More picturesque than this case was the suit brought by the Decorative Stone Company of New Haven against the Building Trades Council of Westchester County, the Stone Cutters' Union, and others, to enjoin a combination of these various unions that prevented the plaintiff from shipping his products for use in buildings in New York City. Here again it became obvious that the union was acting with the approval of local stone producers to protect them from outside competition. A "stone wall" was erected around the New York market to exclude outsiders. In addition to causing strikes on buildings where the contraband material was used, the union also initiated strikes in the factory of the plaintiff in New Haven, where otherwise the conditions of employment were satisfactory, to prevent the employees from producing stone that was destined for New York City. Stone for other markets was produced without interference.

The most glaring incident in the case was a strike called against the junior high school in New Rochelle in the summer of 1925 to prevent the Board of Education from carrying out its contract purchasing $18,000 of building stone for which the lowest bid from union manufacturers had been $52,000. Much of the stone had been delivered and was lying on the ground about the half-erected structure when this school building was struck. There it lay during an 18 months' strike as a dismal monument to industrial strife. The union was stubborn and refused to meet with either the mayor or the board of education, while the school children were denied adequate schooling facilities. A final injunction, issued in 1927, [3] was later affirmed in the United States Circuit Court of Appeals [4] and the work of completing the building was resumed.

Since the court held that it had no power to consider the question of damages as an incident to the suit for an injunction, the plaintiff later brought suit for damages. After a jury trial this action resulted in a judgment of over $43,000.

Perhaps the most ridiculous application of this specie of union boycott—even more ridiculous than the discrimination against the carved woodwork of Irving & Casson—was a requirement by the New York building trades concerning the installation of elaborate Aeolian organs. For all practical purposes, these organs could be sold only on the basis of complete installation by the manufacturer and his expert craftsmen, but the union insisted that they must be assembled and installed by ordinary building craftsmen on the job, rather than by Aeolian Company employees.

It took a long legal battle to escape from even this preposterous situation. A motion for a preliminary injunction was denied, [5] and on appeal that denial was sustained by the Appellate Court. [6] When the case was finally tried, the court dismissed the complaint and it was not until a further appeal to the Circuit Court of Appeals that the company was accorded the relief to which it seemed to me it was so obviously entitled. [7] If manufacturers of elaborate and delicate instruments, such as large organs, cannot carry their skilled help to the building to perform the work of assembling and installing without having the combined forces of the Building Trades Council turn against the owner of the building, it is a sad day for purchasers of such equipment.

In fact, various situations of this kind imposed by building trades unions, through their closed-shop power, account in part for the inflated costs of building. In large cities these unions in many instances control both the selection and installation of important materials and equipment. They sometimes require that work that is normally done in the factory as a part of the production process shall be performed on the building site under great disadvantages and at greatly increased costs. Agreements, between contractors and unions, that the workmen will not handle any materials or equipment that are not purchased by the contractor are not unwelcome to the contractor for they protect his opportunity to earn a buyer's commission or margin. These restrictions are all costly. If the contractor were free to select his equipment in a free market and the manufacturer were free to have his own expert employees perform technical services at the building, the public would be better served. All these facts were developed in an investigation by the Gwynne Committee of Congress.[8]

From the time of the initial difficulty on the Cathedral of St. John the Divine in 1910 as described in Chapter V until the decision against the stone cutters, which clearly answered the question of the right to enjoin discrimination against open-shop products, 15 years had slipped by. The courts had toyed with the problem, pushing it aside as long as possible, because they were reluctant to come to grips with it. One judge warned me that my activities were dangerous to the peace of society. Congress had once legislated satisfactorily to the labor movement, and the courts had whittled down the legislation by judicial interpretation in a way that offended many liberals and certainly the leaders of labor. This gave rise to added unrest. Obviously nothing was settled. The salmon beats its head against the rocks in trying to climb the waterfall, but in the end its resoluteness is rewarded. Labor was gathering more political power than in the days of its futile efforts to defeat Charles E. Littlefield for Congress and was ready to seize the opportunity offered it by the New Deal program of the 1930's.

X

Water-Front Workers and the Teamsters in 1920

FROM EARLY DAYS it has been recognized by common law, and later reinforced by statute, that there are certain commercial activities so strategic in importance and so essential to the lives of individuals and the conduct of commercial enterprises—and, in some cases, so inherently monopolistic—that they are "clothed with the public interest." Of this character are transportation companies like railroads; street railways; steamship companies; telephone and telegraph companies; and water, electric, and gas companies, as well as operators of taxis, trucks, and buses who hold themselves out to serve the public. Some of these have a monopoly and exercise the power of eminent domain. Most of them, by virtue of their importance, are by law compelled to serve the public without discrimination and are not even free to discontinue service so long as they hold their franchise. As a Supreme Court Justice said, "The common carrier has no right to refuse to haul a passenger even if he has been convicted of arson."

Following the depression of 1893, these rights were put severely to the test and were strongly vindicated by decisions of courts, including the Supreme Court of the United States. Efforts by labor unions to treat these quasi-public agencies as puppets to further the cause of unionism were decisively met by government.

In Chicago the American Railway Union, acting under the leadership of Eugene V. Debs, its president, refused to operate trains carrying Pullman cars because the Pullman Company had a strike, and the federal government through its Attorney General secured an injunction. Debs and others were held for contempt in violating this injunction, and the case went to the Supreme Court, which sustained the sentences.[1]

An engineer by the name of Lennon abandoned his train at a way station because it carried some of the boycotted cars, and the court found that he "did not quit in good faith but intended to continue in the company's service and that his conduct was a trick and device to avoid obeying the order of the court." He was found guilty of contempt and his sentence was sustained by the Supreme Court.[2]

In effect the court said, "You are not constrained to remain in the employ of common carriers, but if you choose so to do, your duty is to serve all members of the public alike."

At about the same time Judge William H. Taft, sitting with another judge in a federal district court, enjoined certain of the officers of the Brotherhood of Locomotive Engineers. The injunction prohibited the brotherhood from enforcing a union rule preventing employees of the Pennsylvania Company and others from combining to deny connecting facilities to the Ann Arbor and Northern Michigan Railroad, which was having a strike, and required the Pennsylvania Railroad to perform its usual duties as a connecting railroad.

The court said:

What the employees threaten to do is to deprive the defendant companies of the benefit thus accruing from their labor in order to . . . compel the companies and their managing officers to consent to do a criminal and unlawful injury to the complainant.[3]

Even earlier the Illinois Supreme Court had held that a Chicago railroad was not justified in refusing to accept nonunion men as passengers, on the ground that it might provoke attacks of hostile mobs, endangering other passengers.

"The nonunion workmen," said the court, "were committing no offense. They were earning their living in an honest way, by legitimate labor, in a lawful occupation. To hold that, because they were so doing, a common carrier was authorized to refuse to give them passage over its road, would be to maintain a monstrous doctrine indeed." [4]

The American Federationist described the Debs decision as "the worst ever made by such a court so far as the interests of labor are concerned," but held out hope "that labor will find redress in some form or another, and that ere long." The decision by Judge Taft was called "a humiliating precedent." [5]

The principle involved in these cases seems too fundamental to be debated. If a nonunion man—or even the writer—were to be denied electric current and telephone and transportation service, or if a businessman operating an open shop could not ride from his home in a suburb to his office in the city or could not ship his products by railroad or steamship company, groups carrying on such discriminatory activities would exercise an unfair control over the lives of others.

Those engaged in furnishing services essential to human existence and the conduct of business should not be free to discriminate against others whose way of life they do not approve. In our modern civilization the right to enjoy the services of subways, railways, and steamship companies, as well as the services of telephone, water, and lighting companies, is as important a part of civil liberty as the right of free speech, the right to own property, or the right to travel unhindered on the city streets. To permit owners or workers occupying such a strategic position to discriminate for selfish ends or class domination is to place the power of commercial life or death in that group. Discrimination by carriers led to the establishment of the Interstate Commerce Commission to end the abuse.

So far as I recall, after the reaffirmation of this principle in the latter part of the nineteenth century, it remained without serious challenge until, about 1920, a disturbance of no mean consequence in New York City again brought the issue to the front—or shall I say to the water front.

In the summer of 1920 commerce in New York City, the greatest port in the world, was seriously threatened by the Transportation Trades Council, a federation of many unions, comprising dock workers, longshoremen, teamsters, and others. This group covered most of the labor forces involved in the movement of goods in and about the metropolitan area. That council adopted this program: None of the members would handle any nonunion goods or any goods transported in any way by firms, corporations, or individuals, who refused to employ union labor or refused to enter into a contract to transport their goods under union terms.

What was the outcome? Union merchandise was separated from nonunion merchandise and the latter left on the docks to perish. The ocean-going steamship companies, threatened by strikes of their clerks, checkers, and others employed at their steamship piers, refused to receive goods delivered by nonunion teamsters. The Coast Line Steamship Companies, which were undergoing a strike and were employing nonunion men on their docks, were tied up because the unionized teamsters of New York City refused to permit the merchants to deliver goods to the docks or to take freight away from the docks. Undistributed freight accumulated in huge piles.

The alarmed merchants of the city convened on May 5 in a mass meeting which overtaxed the ballroom of the Hotel Astor. In my address to that gathering I remember referring to the fishermen of Edgartown, Provincetown, and Martha's Vineyard who fearlessly prosecuted their perilous trade after the fashion of their forefathers without thought of union affiliation. I then stated:

When large shipments of fish from distant fishing villages arrive at our wharves, union truckmen separate the union fish from the nonunion fish and cart away the union fish while the nonunion fish are left to rot until condemned as a menace by the Board of Health.

After reciting this and other similar situations I threw out this challenge:

Are you, as responsible leaders of our commercial interests, to stand quiescent while the commerce of the city stifles under the ever-contracting grip of a strangling combination; while industry slips quietly away to a more congenial clime, and the supremacy of the port is imperiled; while foodstuffs rot and people hunger? The time has arrived to emancipate trade from these shackles and place all transportation facilities in or about this community on a fair and just basis, where the interests of all the public shall be served without discrimination.

Referring to the fact that Mr. Frederick J. Koster, an outstanding figure facing similar problems in San Francisco, was with us, I continued:

When once the people of this nation have grasped this issue and their passion for human liberty is aroused, you can rest assured that such attempts at tyranny will be driven friendless from the market place. That is why San Francisco and New York, the Pacific and the Atlantic, meet today on this common platform in recognition of a common peril.

And this was my closing:

We have not courted and do not court a struggle, any more than this government sought war with the Imperial German Government, but the rights of neutrals are again assailed and we are not "too proud to fight." We have been patient; we have suffered much; but there is a limit to human endurance; there is a time to yield and a time to stand, and now is the time to stand.

The assembly then prepared for action by passing a resolution which, while long, so completely sets forth the facts and what was believed to be the crisis of the time, that I feel compelled to submit it in its entirety.

WHEREAS, the commercial life of the City and the welfare of our people largely depend on the free flow of merchandise through impartial and uninterrupted service of transportation and trucking facilities; and

WHEREAS, a large portion of the trucking business of the City has been unionized and there has been a growing tendency on the part of union truckmen to use the power of this strategic position to control the outcome of industrial disputes in other lines of activity by refusing to haul to and from places where such disputes exist; and

WHEREAS, the leading trucking contractors, for a consideration, have made a deal with the Truckmen's Union not to receive, haul or deliver merchandise to or from certain points where industrial disputes exist, and have thus bartered away an important part of the public rights; and

WHEREAS, the Merchants of New York have been made the innocent victims of such unfair discrimination and the citizens of this City have thus been made to suffer by a stoppage of distribution in perishable foodstuffs and other materials;

Now, THEREFORE, be it

RESOLVED, that the facilities and agencies for the hauling and transportation of merchandise are so essential to the commercial life of the City, that they must not in any way be misused to aid strikes or promote the cause of unionism or nonunionism in other lines of activity, but must at all times serve the commercial needs of the City without discrimination or unnecessary interruption; and be it further

RESOLVED, that all points for the receipt or delivery of goods, whether manned by union men or nonunion men, and regardless of whether they are suffering from strikes or lockouts, and all goods, whether of union or nonunion origin, must receive impartial service from those engaged in the movement or transportation of merchandise; and be it further

RESOLVED, in view of the public distress which has arisen out of the present emergency, that we, as representative merchants, feel compelled to agree that we will employ only such truckmen, teamsters and trucking contractors as will carry out the letter and spirit of these resolutions and render impartial service for the benefit of the public; and be it further

RESOLVED, that, acting in the interests of the public welfare, we appoint a Committee to carry out the terms of these resolutions in cooperation with a Committee representing THE MERCHANTS' ASSOCIATION OF NEW YORK, THE CHAMBER OF COMMERCE OF THE STATE OF NEW YORK, BROOKLYN

CHAMBER OF COMMERCE, BRONX BOARD OF TRADE, NEW YORK BOARD OF TRADE AND TRANSPORTATION, and CHAMBER OF COMMERCE OF THE BOROUGH OF QUEENS, and that, if occasion so requires, said Committee shall definitely make arrangements for such independent trucking facilities as may be needed in the premises, for adequate police protection and the enforcement of the law through appropriate legal proceedings; and be it further

RESOLVED, that we are compelled to take this action for the protection of the supreme rights of the public, without regard to the merits of unionism or nonunionism, the open shop or the closed shop, upon which questions we are not now expressing any opinion.[6]

Out of this resolution grew the Citizens' Committee, of which I was counsel, and it proceeded to take active charge of a program to provide the city with trucking facilities to and from the water front. A Citizens' Trucking Company, incorporated to do the work which the union teamsters refused to do, manned its trucks with uniformed soldiers of World War I and furnished prompt and efficient service with comparatively little disturbance. Overt acts were prosecuted in the courts.

Setting up this emergency service met only part of the problem because the steamship lines, under threats of strike, refused to accept or deliver freight handled or to be handled by nonunion teamsters. That problem had to be solved by litigation which invoked the principles of the Debs Case.

For Burgess Brothers Company, lumber dealers in Brooklyn, I sought an injunction in the Supreme Court of New York against the Trades Council, its affiliated unions, and the overseas steamship companies, claiming all were engaged in a conspiracy to deprive the lumber company of its right to fair and impartial service under the Federal Shipping Act. The judge described the situation in unequivocal terms:

This seems to me to be a combination to gain control over transportation and to blockade the channels of trade against all but union merchandise and against all concerns who do not make union contracts. Such a combination to exclude open shop merchandise from the channels of trade and commerce and from the markets of the nation is a conspiracy against public welfare and deprives the public of their sovereign right of choice to purchase such goods as they want, because by artificial methods it keeps such goods out of the market. . . .

While it is indisputable that a man may enter any vocation that he chooses, yet if he sees fit to select the field indissolubly linked with the rights of the public, such as that of a common carrier, he must subserve his own rights to that of the public welfare and must at all times stand ready and willing to assume all of the exacting duties which he knows are owed the public. When he enters the public service he impliedly acquiesces in assuming all of these obligations. He must either get out of the transportation business or serve all persons alike.

Employees of steamships, and those employed in and about the docks and all others associated in or connected with and necessary to, the conduct of business of common carriers should perform their usual services regardless of whether the merchandise is worked upon, or handled, received or delivered by union or nonunion men, and such service should be impartial and uninterrupted.[7]

Suit was also brought in the federal courts in behalf of Buyer & Co., a garter manufacturer, against the Old Dominion Transportation Co. and the unions of the water-front employees to enforce rights to transportation by water to Norfolk, Virginia. The water-front employees had refused to accept Buyer's merchandise when delivered by the Citizens' Trucking Company, and the steamship company acquiesced in such action and refused to render carrier service for fear of labor conflict. After an initial failure the suit was successful in the higher court and the principle was established.[8]

By that time the contest had been pretty well won in all its aspects and commerce resumed its normal flow. It was the pressure of two forces that won this battle: the resourcefulness and resolution of the merchants in uniting to supply their own trucking service and the action of the state and federal courts in supporting their efforts. If the state or society is interested in its own protection, it must at times be sufficiently stalwart to endure privations while it proves its capacity for self-defense. They only deserve rights who will play their part in safeguarding them. There is too much inclination to surrender principles for the sake of avoiding discomforts that in many cases are not serious. The spirit of the Citizens' Committee of 1920, and of like committees, if sufficiently determined, can impose moderation on those who plan to take unfair advantage of society.

XI

A Return Engagement in 1934

NOTHING IS EVER STATIC in the field of industrial relations. In 1934 New York City was again plagued with a recurrence of the same difficulties that arose in 1920, but this time with less public excitement.

The Transportation Trades Council, working with the teamsters and longshoremen, the locals of which were represented in the Council, agreed to prevent any business concern from utilizing any coastwise steamship line so long as it employed any chauffeurs or drivers not members of the teamsters' union or so long as it employed nonunion men in its factories. Piers and docks were picketed. Trucks calling to receive or deliver cargoes were turned back by pickets, who stated that it would be useless to enter the piers or docks as no nonunion freight would be received or delivered. Those employed on the piers were threatened with disciplinary action by the union if they performed services in connection with such contraband cargoes, and steamship companies were threatened with strikes of all their employees and a boycott of their docks by all teamsters if they violated the embargo. Some strikes were actually called against steamship lines for trying to perform their public duty, and in the end all carriers refused transportation of the boycotted articles in order to avoid stoppages. The plan was put into effect by union officials without a vote of the rank and file and its extension to railroad terminals was definitely threatened.

The New York Shipping Association, of which most of the carriers were members, protested to the heads of the unions and appealed to civic organizations. The latter used their powers of persuasion. The result of their interference was that the unions modified their program by limiting the boycott to incoming and outgoing cargoes where nonunion teamsters called at the piers, except for the requirement that no merchandise that came from a factory on strike would be handled, regardless of who delivered it or called for it. No shipments of manufactured articles or raw materials could thus be made without union sanction.

In October, 1934, I commenced suit in behalf of about 150 manufacturers and merchants against the Transportation Trades Council, the International Brotherhood of Teamsters and some ten of its locals, and the International Longshoremen's Association, its district council, and some 15 of its locals, together with some 50 steamship lines and terminal companies. The purpose was to enjoin all defendants from discriminating against the plaintiffs in respect to water transportation. Senator Burton K. Wheeler was called from Washington to present the union defense.

The case was tried before Judge Humphrey of the New York State Supreme Court, and all facts were elaborately proved. Judge Humphrey, relying on decisions growing out of the troubles of 1920, granted an injunction. His decision was followed by protest strikes in the area. On appeal of the unions and the carriers to the Appellate Division of New York, it was held that since the case involved admiralty law and the United States Shipping Act, the state courts were without jurisdiction.[1] When I appealed to the Court of Appeals of the State of New York, the court decided against me without an opinion. No one doubted the importance of the case. Thousands upon thousands of persons were parties or were represented by associations that were parties. The trial court and the Appellate Division had disagreed, but the only answer of the Court of Appeals was to sustain the action of the Appellate Division with the cryptic comment, "No opinion." Neither side was given the slightest indication as to what the highest court of the state would regard as a proper course of conduct in the future. I then prevailed upon the Court of Appeals to amend its order, so that it would at least appear that a federal question was involved and thus make it possible for me to apply for review to the United States Supreme Court.[2] But all this was of no avail, for the Supreme Court in 1936 refused to grant my petition. Important as this matter was to the people of New York, the courts gave them very little light.

In these water-front difficulties of the early 1930's, neither of the factors that made it possible to protect the freedom of the port in 1920 existed. Court decisions did not support the efforts of civic organizations to defend the commerce of the city, and the steamship companies preferred illegally to discriminate, as the union demanded, rather than to endure stoppages. The battle was lost, and the consequences, direct and indirect, have ever since been felt. A city having a water front is particularly vulnerable to coercive unionism unless it is willing to defend itself. What has happened on the Pacific coast gives remarkable support to this assertion.

With the passage of New Deal legislation, and the Norris-La-Guardia Anti-Injunction Act of 1932, secondary boycotts to compel common carriers to discriminate against "hot cargoes" or other goods that the unions hold to be contraband, had an open season until the enactment of the Taft-Hartley Act in 1947. During that interim period of 15 years it was the federal law that unions pursuing normal objectives could organize to ruin an employer's business unless he would consent to become a law-breaker. It was common practice on both the East and the West coasts for longshoremen and marine workers to force carriers illegally to deny transportation facilities to goods to which unions objected.

XII

A Half-Way House

In the decade of the 1920's, sandwiched as it was between World War I and the New Deal era, encouraging forces, which were not sufficiently spectacular to be noticed, were at work. Labor unions, having gained nothing by the Clayton Act, resented the treatment received at the hands of the Supreme Court, while some employers were beginning to philosophize over changing conditions in industrial relations. Vaguely industrial leaders recognized that labor must have a voice in fixing terms and conditions of employment. The voice, as they saw it, must be consultative and not authoritative. Management should listen to get understanding and guidance, but the responsibility of management must remain unimpaired. There should be an interchange of ideas to secure co-operation and to make doubly sure that justice was done, but militant dictation from labor was not contemplated. Out of this more liberal approach grew employee representation plans, of which I was a diligent advocate.

Men like John Leitch inspired many of us to believe that production sharing, rather than profit sharing, offered a way out of the labor conflict in some factories. He contended that labor should receive not only its regular wage but also a group bonus based on the productivity of a particular room or department, and he proved by experience that such group sharing turned labor against the drones and placed it on the side of efficiency in order to reap the fullest rewards. Of course such a program was impracticable in many operations, but it was the germ of an idea that had some value.

The broader aspects of employee representation began with the plan that Mackenzie King formulated for the Colorado Fuel & Iron Company, which was adopted and advocated by leaders like the International Harvester Company and the Pennsylvania Railroad. Such plans reflected the hope that a labor conflict was not inevitable and that, through organized means of communications in the factories, understanding and co-operation could be built on sound foundations. Part of this optimism was a postwar rebound to the high idealism of World War I. Even the coal and railroad strikes of 1922 were not sufficient to squelch it. There was a feeling that we were in a world that was shifting to a broader brotherhood and that the America we had known was to leave its chrysalis and turn into something more beautiful. The British Labor Party published its pronunciamento, and it was republished in this country. Mr. Gompers, sensing the spirit of the times, declared:

Under the burning heat of necessity civilization is now in a fluid state. . . . That group which has the most intelligent self-interest will control developments. . . . The world cataclysm swept away conventions and barriers to aspiration. . . . This is the time when the impossible is achieved. . . . It is idle to talk of returning to the status quo ante— America and the world of before the war have gone, never to return.[1]

President Hoover declared that "one looming shadow of this war is its drift towards socialism."

It was the contagion of this feeling that led the more advanced employers to look with sympathy towards plans that would afford a more attentive hearing of the needs and problems of the workers.

I was excited by all this, and not having learned to separate surface ripples from ocean currents, was naïve enough to place hope in the adequacy of works councils, democratically elected in each factory, as a durable step towards industrial co-operation. I dreamed of each factory as a self-contained unit of management and of men who thought only of outside production units of employers and employees as their rivals in interest. Naïve, you may agree. Yes, I reply, but it was a pleasant dream and led me to write such pamphlets as *Factory Solidarity or Class Solidarity* and *The Four C's—Contact, Conference, Confidence, Co-operation*.[2] I had great faith in the effect of following through from contact to co-operation and put my faith into action by establishing industrial relations plans along these lines in various factories, some of them large. In *The Four C's* I wrote:

Conflicts arise from barriers to understanding. The removal of these barriers tends to conformity of ideas. . . . The average employer is no philosopher or reconstructionist and has little comprehension of the psychology of the worker. The average employee knows little of the problems and embarrassments of business. Unless the gulf is bridged and the traffic of ideas resumed, our existing industrial instititutions and constitutional rights of liberty and property can scarcely survive.

That I had no illusions about the need of education on both sides is shown by the following:

One is tempted to create one purgatory to which certain employers should be sentenced for a period to ponder the literature of the workers and another where the workers should ponder the literature and balance sheets of employers. When these people returned from their unpleasant sojourn the solution of industrial questions would be visibly nearer.

To the employers who felt that such councils and committees would multiply grievances I replied:

Far better is it that the complaints of employees, many of which are minor difficulties the employer gladly meets, should come to the surface instead of breeding irritation and resentment. It is told that the inventor of the French helmet found it difficult to induce the authorities to try it, and when they did so they were discouraged at the first test because it brought an unusually large number of wounded to the hospitals. The inventor replied: "Those who are now numbered among the wounded were previously numbered among the dead." Better far that the employer should endure the burden of giving preventive treatment than operating with a lifeless morale.

Perhaps one more quotation from this pamphlet is necessary to suggest the opportunity which, as an idealist, I thought should appeal to the industrialist in the 1920's:

No opportunity for education was ever afforded any group of persons comparable to that afforded large employers who daily convene millions within their reach. Through employe representation factories can better become universities for the broader phases of economic education upon which sound conceptions of industrial relations must be based. The average worker will be inoculated against the false and misleading statements of unfair agitators and the employer fortified against narrow conservatisms and complacency.

Whether the loss of that opportunity was due to lack of intelligence on the part of the employer or to underlying forces too powerful to control is a question for anyone to answer, but the tragic result is that the employer has largely lost his audience.

My naïveté was shared by others. In the early 1920's about a million workers, or one tenth of the industrial employees, were working under such plans. The President's Second Industrial Conference in its final report of March 6, 1920, declared for established channels of expression in each factory and emphatically endorsed the movement. A convention of employers in Canada called by the Canadian Minister of Labor dealt primarily with this subject and employers' associations in this country dignified it as a major point of discussion.

Nor was interest limited to this country. In Germany, Austria, Italy, Great Britain, Czechoslovakia, and other European countries such councils were recognized by statute, and interest extended to South Africa and India.

My optimism grew as I watched the arrival of industrial missions from other nations that were visiting our country to analyze the causes of our happy state of industrial peace. The fact that these fortunate conditions accompanied an unprecedented increase in labor productivity was looked upon by me, whether rightly or wrongly, as a result rather than a cause of good feeling.[3]

Employee representation or works councils, as instituted during the period of development, were an excellent salve to heal minor irritations. And that is important. They correspond more nearly to what we now call grievance procedure but they were based on the mistaken idea that existing relationships had come to stay and that the only problem was to keep the machine well oiled. The proponents of these plans failed to visualize class militancy and class war marching ever forward, challenging the justice of things that are, and seeking more and more to apply the process of attrition to the rights of management and property.

The Wagner Act of 1935, in spite of pious language, emphasized the conflict of interests as it had not been emphasized in the era of works councils. It placed less emphasis on the community of interest between employers and employees. As stated at the outset by one of the first members of the National Labor Relations Board, the Wagner Act meant that the employer had no interest in what the employees did in respect to unionism, even though the employees were hoodwinked or swindled. The old-time fatherly employer was legislated out of his benevolence. It became risky for him to exchange confidences with his men. The "four c's" were outlawed, for the employer could not deal frankly with his employees—not even with a nonunion employee who distrusted the union leaders. Thus the era of class conflict, encouraged by some unwise provisions of the Norris-LaGuardia Act, was pushed forward, and as far as I can see, has received such momentum that no wise person would dare predict that its ultimate destination will fall short of revolutionary changes.

XIII

The Road to Confusion

LABOR WAS NOT SATISFIED with individualism or even with edging toward collectivism through works councils. It sought the unlimited right to marshal the economic strength of the entire labor movement to accomplish its ends. Under provisions of our Constitution, which were designed primarily to protect individualism and property rights, there developed logically and inevitably a system of law unadapted to modern industrialism and collectivism. In buttressing the rights of ownership the courts followed the Biblical suggestion: "Is it not lawful for me to do what I will with my own?" Sooner or later there had to be a modification of legal theories if the labor movement were to strengthen. It is not surprising, although regrettable, therefore, that in many instances needed changes were brought about by objectionable and irregular means. To escape from the rigidity of a written Constitution, intended to protect a certain sphere of industrial liberty from encroachment from any source, both courts and legislatures did strange things.

For nearly four decades following the Debs episode the fundamental principles of law involving the liberty of the trader to engage in commerce remained unimpaired, notwithstanding labor's Magna Carta in the Clayton Act of 1914. Just before the New Deal, labor saw victory ahead for its long-discouraged efforts to change these established principles. Congress was pliant, and while the court-packing bill was defeated by a frightened public, appointees to the Supreme Court were chosen from those who were known to be devoted to a new and different philosophy. Both legislative and judicial obstacles on the road to change were thus eliminated. The smart of past defeats, when the courts whittled down labor's rights under the Clayton Act, contributed no little to the lack of judgment and loss of balance embodied in what proved to be the controlling law in this field from the early 1930's to the passage of the Taft-Hartley Act in 1947. When we scan the major defects in this panicky legislation, the surprising fact is that the American voter endured it so long.

To begin with, the Norris-LaGuardia Act, passed in March, 1932, was primarily an anti-injunction law and did not purport to make lawful what was unlawful. It dealt with the injunction remedy. The cases that it sought to reverse were not the Hatters Case, where the action was for damages, but the Bucks Stove & Range, the Duplex Printing Press Company, and the Bedford Stone cases, where injunctions without damages had been sought and granted. The act itself begins by saying:

that no court of the United States, as herein defined, shall have jurisdiction to issue any restraining order or temporary or permanent injunction in a case involving or growing out of a labor dispute except in strict conformity with the provisions of this act.

The reports of the Senate and House committees that framed the act confirm this limited purpose. In a book entitled *The Labor Injunction*,[1] written by Frankfurter and Greene before Professor Frankfurter became Justice Frankfurter, it was said that the model bill that later became the anti-injunction law did not change the substantive law and that which was "hitherto unlawful conduct remains unlawful." Notwithstanding this history, a majority of the Supreme Court, speaking through Justice Frankfurter in a case involving a secondary boycott held that this act changed the substantive law. The decision exempted labor not only from the antitrust laws but also from any charge of illegality in connection with strikes, picketing, or boycotting, even though such activities were employed to accomplish a criminal end. "So long as the union acts in its self-interest," said the court, "and does not combine with nonlabor groups," the licit and illicit nature of the end is immaterial where strikes, picketing, and boycotting are involved.[2]

This is my first indictment of the Norris-LaGuardia Act: It permitted the use of industrial war with all its distressing concomitants to further criminal and antisocial ends.

The majority decision, which Justice Roberts tartly criticized, was revolutionary doctrine, and it seems to me it was antisocial doctrine. Heretofore it had been a fundamental rule of human conduct that anyone who aided or abetted a crime, even though he aided by an act that was otherwise lawful, was a participant in the crime and criminally liable. It seems to me that this Supreme Court decision announced as a proposition of federal law that coercion through strikes, picketing, and boycotting may be lawfully applied to strangle a business and the life of a community, solely for the purpose of compelling an employer to commit a crime. The employer had the dubious choice of inviting injury to his business or violating the laws of the land. Of course this statute controlled only federal courts and did not necessarily prevent a contrary result where state statutes provided otherwise.

Heretofore it had been the law of the land that no rights were absolute or unqualified. The right to acquire property, the right to work, the right of speech, and the right to travel the streets had all been subject to the qualification that they must not be employed to accomplish a purpose forbidden by law. But under the new rule the right to strike, to picket, and to boycott may be employed to attain unlawful ends. Thus an earlier unanimous decision of the Supreme Court of the United States rendered by Justice Holmes, who declared that "the most innocent and constitutionally protected of acts or means may be made a step in a criminal plot," [3] was reversed so far as these union activities were concerned. Here was egregious class distinction. Reversed also was another unanimous decision of the Supreme Court rendered by Justice Brandeis, in which it was declared that "a strike may be illegal because of its purpose, however orderly the manner in which it is conducted." [4] Now no strike could be unlawful under federal law. Mrs. Roosevelt as the first lady said she made it a matter of principle never to cross a picket line. Her theory seemed also to be that pickets are always right. With this point of view, one regards a picket line as a symbol or fetish, and it loses its character as an instrument of justice. It is not an instrument of free speech, because the minds of its observers are closed. It was nine years later that Judge Learned Hand, speaking for the Circuit Court of Appeals in dealing with the Taft-Hartley Act, rejected the argument that labor activities were absolutely privileged and said:

He who provokes or instigates a wrong makes himself a party to the wrong, and is equally liable with the perpetrator. . . . It appears to us highly unlikely that . . . Congress meant to abolish a doctrine so deeply imbedded in our civil and criminal law.[5]

Several grotesque results flowed from this disturbing doctrine. The court held that unions could employ their economic power without recognizing legal boundaries only so long as they did not act in collaboration with a nonlabor group. The test in the future was not what was done but who did it. For example, according to the above decision, if labor, the exempt group, collaborated with a nonexempt group like building contractors, then according to familiar principles of law they were all in the same boat and equally liable. The labor unions thereby lost their special dispensation because they had associated with the sinful ones who had no special dispensation.

Here is another absurdity. One of the declared purposes of this law was to promote the peaceful settlement of disputes, but curiously enough it erected barriers to settlement. Let us assume that a union demanded that a carrier refuse to accept or transport merchandise that has been produced or handled by nonunion men. The carrier, if he wished to keep out of legal difficulty, had to reject the union demand and continue to endeavor to perform his legal duty to serve the public without discrimination. The union, on the other hand, was legally free to fight for its illegal demand and to employ destructive forces to secure it. This dual standard confronted both parties with a dilemma. If the employer, prizing his business above his liberty, yielded and made an agreement with the union to ban the proscribed cargoes, then both unions and employers become legally liable, since the union had united with a nonlabor group and the taint of the employer thus contaminated the union. To avoid this pitfall the union could have continued to fight for its antisocial and illegal objects but could not seek them through the peaceful processes of negotiation, mediation, or arbitration. The area of legitimate objects that industrial war may seek was broader than the area of objects that may lawfully be attained by the more peaceful means of collective bargaining. The union could lawfully fight for terms that the employer could not legally grant. Thus a statute designed to promote peaceful settlement sanctioned labor disputes that the parties are forbidden to settle. Nor was this a dialectic dilemma. Every steamship company is faced with it when asked to handle "hot" cargoes.

The same statute undertook to exempt labor unions from the fundamental rule of Anglo-Saxon society which holds the principal liable for the acts of his agents or the master liable for the acts of his servants.[6] The profound importance of this special dispensation deserves more than passing comment. In order that people might live together on a fairly practical basis, it has been the law of Anglo-Saxon countries for over 500 years that when one employs another to carry on his affairs, that employer must be liable for the acts of his *alter ego*.

Except under the Norris-LaGuardia Act, everything that the servant does in furtherance of his master's business, whether commanded or forbidden by his master, whether known or unknown to his master, is the act of the master. By legal fiat the master, morally innocent though he may be, is civilly responsible. The doctrine derives its title of *respondeat superior* from the early statutes of Edward the First and is defined by the United States Supreme Court as follows:

The rule of "respondeat superior," or that the master shall be civilly liable for the tortious acts of his servants, is of universal application, whether the act be one of omission or commission, whether negligent, fraudulent or deceitful. If it be done in the course of his employment, the master is liable; and it makes no difference that the master did not authorize, or even know of the servant's act or neglect, or even if he disapproved or forbad it, he is equally liable, if the act be done in the course of his servant's employment.[7]

The necessity for the rule is supported by two arguments. First, if the master feels responsible for his servant's conduct, he will safeguard his own interests, and incidentally the public interests, by care in the selection of his servant and by a restraining influence upon his servant's conduct. Second, it is a nearer approximation to justice that the employer, who is usually a man of substance, should respond in damages for the wrongdoing of the servant who is acting in his behalf, and perhaps for his profit, than that the injured party should be virtually denied relief. By imposing this vicarious liability on the employer, the injured party is more likely to reach a full purse.

Originally in the fourteenth century it was necessary for the injured person first to sue the agent and collect what the agent was able to pay, before proceeding against the principal for the deficit. Now the practice is reversed. The principal is the underwriter. He usually pays first and if he is morally innocent he may, in turn, seek indemnity from his agent.

So familiar and fundamental is this doctrine that we do not even pause to analyze its significance. In effect it means that a principal employs an agent at his peril, and for that privilege must indemnify anyone who suffers injury while the agent is acting within the scope of his authority. Corporations and other large aggregations of business are thus constantly held responsible for acts performed by thousands of agents. Perhaps half of all remedial lawsuits in this country depend on this doctrine. If we were to undermine it our commercial standards would indeed be worsened.

In some respects conditions prevailing among labor unions and employers' associations involved in labor disputes call more eloquently for this rule of liability than do many other activities of life. A corporation may have ten thousand agents for which it is liable and an individual employer often several hundred. In the case of a labor union or an employers' association, the condition is reversed, for one may find a thousand principals for each agent. The agent who is jointly employed by a thousand union men exercises a power and influence to inflict damage far in excess of any ordinary individual and far in excess of one of the numerous agents of an ordinary corporation. His power is to be measured by the combined influence of his constituents and he can inflict damages out of all proportion to his ability to make indemnity.

This issue of union liability boils down to a question of forcing union members, who in this case are principals, to feel some responsibility and exercise some restraint in respect to their officers and organizers. No institution occupying such a position as that occupied by organized labor can endure and properly acquit itself of its large responsibility towards society if the duties of its vast membership terminate with the payment of dues. Who is to spend that money, what it is to be spent for, and how its officers are acquitting themselves of their trust are questions that every member of a labor union would have an incentive to know if the funds of the union were involved and concerning which he has every incentive to remain ignorant if knowledge is the danger signal of a liability not otherwise incurred. If lawlessness on the picket line is to be curbed, union responsibility should be extended to include positive efforts at control, rather than contracted to cover only acts that are expressly authorized. That would be a sound rule for employers' associations, as well as unions.

The Anthracite Commission in the famous Award of 1903, which dealt with lawlessness in the coal strike, apparently felt the same way:

Surely this tendency to disorder and violation of law imposes upon the organization, which begins and conducts a movement of such importance, a grave responsibility. It has, by its voluntary act, created dangers, and should, therefore, be vigilant in averting them. It has, by the concerted action of many aroused passions, which, uncontrolled, threaten the public peace; it, therefore, owes society the duty of exerting its power to check and confine these passions within the bounds of reason and of law. Such organizations should be the powerful coadjutors of government in maintaining the peace and upholding the law.

If liability or responsibility to society can be avoided through silence or secrecy on the part of the bosses, whether they represent unions or employers' associations, it is perfectly obvious that bossism, graft, secret crime, and irresponsibilty will become rife and the democratic administration of association affairs by conservative law-abiding men will be discouraged. It would seem to be too clear for argument that wholesome unionism was not promoted by the provision in the Norris-LaGuardia Act that protects unions and employers' associations from responsibility for the acts of their agents. Just why such a privileged exemption should have been given to associations engaged in a labor dispute, where society needs maximum protection and where restraint is urgent, is difficult to explain except on the basis of political expediency. Collective action must be accompanied by collective responsibility and the combatants of industrial disputes must learn that this applies to them.

This question of the responsibility of labor unions has a historical background. In 1901 in the famous Taff-Vale Case in Great Britain, it was held that labor unions were legally suable and responsible. In that connection Justice Farwell said:

For . . . the wrongful conduct of the agents of the society in the course of managing a strike, . . . the defendant society is, in my opinion, liable. . . . I have already held that the society are liable for the acts of their agents to the same extent that they would be if they were a corporation, and it is abundantly clear that a corporation, under the circumstances of the case, would be liable.[8]

In meeting the union argument that it could not be reached through the courts because it was not incorporated, Justice Farwell said:

If the contention of the defendant society were well founded, the Legislature has authorized the creation of numerous bodies of men capable of owning great wealth and of acting by agents with absolutely no responsibility for the wrongs that they may do to other persons by the use of that wealth and the employment of those agents.

The Trades Dispute Act passed by Parliament in 1906 changed this rule and placed unions beyond the reach of civil process— that is, beyond the reach of the courts—in connection with acts "in furtherance of a trade dispute." The shock which the judges of Great Britain felt over this result found expression in many of their decisions. Justice Darling, in dismissing a suit against a labor union in 1908 because of this new law, said:

From the humiliating position of being on a level with other lawful associations of his Majesty's subjects the statute of 1906 has relieved all registered trade unions, and they are now *super legem*, just as the medieval Emperor was *super grammaticam*.[9]

In another case in the same year, Lord Justice Farwell said:

It was possible for the courts in former years to defend individual liberty against the aggression of Kings and barons, because the defense rested on the law which they administered. It is not possible for the Courts to do so when the Legislature alters the law, for they can only administer the law. The Legislature cannot make evil good, but it can make it not actionable . . . it inflicts a cruel hardship on the plaintiff, and it is no consolation to him that far greater hardships will doubtless be inflicted in the future on persons even more innocent than himself. . . . To use as nearly as possible Lord Justice Romer's language—

The conduct of the defendant morally is unjustifiable molestation of the man, an improper and inexcusable interference with the man's ordinary rights of citizenship; but those rights have been cut away and the remedy for them destroyed by the Legislature.[10]

After the general strike in England in 1926, Parliament passed some regulatory legislation that made unions suable in limited cases, but after the Labor government came into power at the close of World War II, all this was repealed with great éclat.

In this country, it will be recalled that in the hatters decision in 1914 the Supreme Court, speaking through Justice Holmes, had held that the members of a union were liable for the acts of their officers "if they knew or ought to have known what was being done in their behalf." At least as stringent a rule would have been applied if the union, rather than its individual members, had been sued. In 1921 the Supreme Court in a unanimous decision reached somewhat the same conclusion as was reached in the Taff-Vale Case in Great Britain 20 years earlier, and held that, in view of the various statutes which had been enacted recognizing labor unions as entities, the union, even though unincorporated, might be sued. The Court said:

It would be unfortunate if an organization with as great power as this International Union has in the raising of funds and in directing the conduct of 400,000 members in carrying on in a wide territory industrial controversies and strikes, out of which so much unlawful injury to private rights is possible, could assemble its assets to be used therein free from liability for injuries by torts committed in the course of such strikes.[11]

In the Decorative Stone Case in the federal courts, as I have already pointed out, the unions were held liable for damages in a boycott, and in a considerable number of industrial states like suits could be maintained in the state courts. Such in general was the state of the law on this subject when in the early 1930's Congress undertook to undermine union responsibility. The Norris-LaGuardia Act provided that no organization involved in a labor dispute shall be responsible for any of the acts of its officers, agents, or members as such except upon clear proof of "actual authorization of such acts or of ratification of such acts after actual knowledge thereof." By this fundamental change of law an employers' association or a union engaged in a labor dispute was relieved from responsibility merely by giving its officers blanket authority and remaining ignorant of what they were doing.

There is still another outstanding fault in this Norris-LaGuardia legislation. It may be said to be a concept of civilized society that one should exhaust the resources of diplomacy or bargaining before declaring war. This is a desirable concept whether you deal with international or domestic clashes—military or economic ones. We do not like the Pearl Harbor idea. Ludicrous as it may seem, the Norris-LaGuardia Act followed the reverse of the civilized standard. It declared in effect that the union may attack at dawn without notice and if it resorts to fraud and violence the employer may not defend himself by an injunction, unless he proves that he first resorted to negotiation and mediation and even offered arbitration.[12] In other words, the right of the aggressor to attack without notice was upheld, but the right of the aggrieved to defend by seeking court relief was conditioned on his willingness to compromise with fraud and violence—all of which came pretty close to compounding a crime or rewarding a crime. Why any remedy against violence or fraud should have been so burdened is difficult to understand. If injunctions should not issue against fraud or violence in labor disputes, that is one thing; but there is no justification for tolerating and condoning such wrongdoing by giving the placator a remedy which is denied to those who insist on law enforcement.

It was further provided in this law that no injunction should be issued against fraud or violence unless it was shown that the employer would suffer more by having the violence continue than the union would suffer by stopping it. Let me state this in reverse. If the union had more to gain by continuing violence than the employer had by stopping it, then the violence was not to be enjoined. It seems to have been a doctrine of comparative need. When coal was stolen by 20,000 bootleggers in Pennsylvania it had to be decided whether the thief or the owner needed it more. Violence when practiced by unions seemed to gather some kind of moral sanction. On the picket line it had a tolerated or condoned status.

This law was a fair reflection of the tendency to condone union violence and was in marked contrast to the temper of the times when Grover Cleveland declared, "If it takes the entire army of the United States to deliver a postal card in Chicago that card will be delivered."

But times have changed and this statute reflected and strengthened the demoralized notion that violence on the picket line is not an unmixed evil.

A few years ago the Wheeling Steel Company had to protect the safety of its willing employees from strikers by keeping them in the mill and sending them food by parcel post. The Postal Department of the United States refused to order its employees to pass the picket line. On other occasions federal officials have sought and received permits from pickets to perform their official duties. With such dramatic illustrations, multiplied by many evidences of a disinclination to maintain order in labor disputes, it would be a rash man who would assure his children that the time will come in their lives when it will generally be safe for a workman to cross an organized picket line.

The federal antiracketeering law is another instance where the government was ready to look obliquely at the use of violence where it aimed to help unionism. That law forbade an attempt to obtain payment of money by violence, but there is special dispensation in respect to the use of violence to force the payment of money as wages. As a result, when union men lay in wait for trucks crossing from New Jersey to New York to beat up the drivers unless they would step down and let the assailants run the trucks for a charge of $9.42, or pay the $9.42 for protection without stepping down, the court held this did not constitute a violation of the law.[13] "Holdups" for jobs, or wages in lieu thereof, were given a preferred position as compared with other "holdups." Whether we look to anti-injunction laws, antitrust laws, or antiracketeering laws, or whether we observe the inaction of the law enforcement officers in times of strikes, it becomes apparent that our new public policy has been to deal indulgently with labor for acts of violence and that this public policy has received encouragement at the hands of the legislative, the judicial and the executive branch of government. And of course unionism must see some partial sanction of lawlessness in the indulgence.

On the general subject of labor injunctions, with which the Norris-LaGuardia Act primarily dealt, much remains to be said. There is no occasion to criticize the crusade against labor injunctions, which began 40 or 50 years ago, except to say that it got completely out of hand. We can assume that there was justification for the slogan of "Government by Injunction." On the other hand, the legitimate usefulness of an injunction to further a broad social policy should not be overlooked or discarded. But more of this in Chapter XXI.

The Norris-LaGuardia Act as a piece of pre-New Deal legislation was begotten in part of the leading boycott cases I have described. They were always in the foreground when the legislation was being debated, and their reversal was frankly acknowledged to be one of its major objectives. It legalized all boycotting, and it remained for the Taft-Hartley Act of 1947 to restore in part the rights of the buyer to the free flow of commerce.

Under the Taft-Hartley Act the secondary boycott, when carried out by secondary strikes, was again made illegal. For some unexplained irrationality, however, the secondary boycott, when carried out by the use of the power of patronage—though equally incompatible with the right of the public to enjoy a free competitive market—was not made illegal. Moreover the right of an injured party to secure relief from illegal boycotts was limited to suits for damages, with the remedy of injunction excluded. Congress was not yet prepared to be consistent.

The distinction between the primary boycott and the secondary boycott is the most important consideration. Of the primary boycott, which is a democratic appeal to a consumer's right of commercial suffrage, there can be no criticism. It is a part of the fundamental right of free speech. But the secondary boycott is the antithesis of this; it attacks neutrals like carriers, merchants, and contractors who control the gateways to the public markets in order to deprive the public of the right to express itself through its purchasing power. It is a denial to the consumer of the very right that labor asserts; the right to bestow or withhold patronage. The consumer, whether acting through sentiment or self-interest, is thus shorn of his liberty as a buyer, which is as important a part of the same package as the liberty of the trader. Moreover, the familiar practice of A. F. of L. unions in boycotting C.I.O. goods is in conflict with the right of the producers' employees to join a union of their choosing.

In dealing with the problem of secondary boycotts the question will long be debated whether the legislation of the 1930's, which permitted boycotts without limitation, or the more conservative legislation of 1947, which forbade them in part, represents the soundest public policy. When the principles are explored and understood, only those who favor class dictation can defend the secondary boycott. Simple indeed is the question to be answered. Should the highways of commerce and the facilities of transportation be open to all traders, subject only to governmental regulations, or should it be permissible for labor unions to utilize them as pawns to promote the enforcement of their private regulations?

The nation was built on the underlying concept that there must be a national economy, not a sectional or segmentary economy.

The barriers of trade that colonies like New York, New Jersey and Connecticut had erected prior to the adoption of the federal Constitution and the injury they were causing trade were predominant reasons for convening the Constitutional Convention of 1789 and for the final adoption of a Constitution giving Congress supreme power to regulate interstate and foreign commerce. Unless Congress has by statute indicated otherwise, the rule of law that the people should enjoy the benefits of a free interchange of goods in the course of interstate commerce must prevail. This rule may, of course, be qualified by Congress in the interests of the public. Thus Congress may forbid the transportation of dangerous or objectionable goods, stolen cars, and even drugs and food, except under appropriate regulations. It may forbid the distribution of misbranded goods or unfair methods of competition, as it has done by the Trade Commission Act, and it may forbid the transportation of goods made under substandard labor conditions, as it has done by the Fair Labor Standards Act.

But after the list of Congressional regulations and prohibitions has been exhausted, the underlying rule in respect to all other goods requires that commerce must continue free and open and that the rights of the public to choose and buy must be maintained. That certainly is national policy as implemented by the antitrust laws, but from these laws, as we have shown, labor unions were exempted. Is it desirable, when the interests of the people are so directly concerned, that labor, acting privately and with its major responsibility to one segment of our population, should have delegated to it the right to exclude from commerce goods that Congress has not excluded? Is such a delegation of power at all necessary when Congress has already recognized the social problem by forbidding the transportation of goods made under antisocial conditions? The producer or the trader, whichever you call him, should have the right unhindered, except so far as public statutes hinder him, to distribute his goods overland or over the high seas to any destination of his choosing, and the consumer is entitled to this free flow in order that he may exercise his sovereign right of choice or commercial suffrage. So long as Congress has taken over the problem of minimum labor standards by defining what is contraband and what is legitimate, private embargoes for this purpose should not be tolerated.

Society should beware of private combinations that obstruct the free flow of commerce or the free distribution of products, because such combinations are an attack upon the people. To restate it in other words: Society should beware of legislation that permits special interests to obstruct the free flow of commerce or the distribution of national products, or to deny the facilities of distribution or transportation to merchandise which the public wishes to buy.

The Norris-LaGuardia Act aimed primarily to prevent judicial interference with unionization. It outlawed yellow-dog contracts, gave legal sanction to the use of union coercion even for antisocial and criminal ends, and further relieved unions from the normal responsibility imposed upon others by exempting them from the familiar rules of principal and agent. Having thus necessarily increased resistance to union recognition, the next legislative step was to compel the employer to deal with these organizations of attenuated responsibility. To accomplish this end the National Labor Relations Act of 1935 came into being.

Again history repeated itself and the New Deal made several notable errors because of the unbalanced thinking of the time. The Act required the employer to deal with the union, regardless of its standards or conduct. It did not require the union to deal with the employer under any conditions. The union had an unrestricted option either to bargain with the employer or to strangle his business through its unlimited right to strike, picket, and boycott. On one occasion I was brought to the bargaining table by an employer and on my appearance the union president looked up, shouted profanely, and with his henchmen following walked out of the conference. Nor was that all. Within an hour thereafter pickets were marching up and down in front of the place with banners that stated, "This Company Refuses to Bargain." Again in Philadelphia, when I represented a carpet manufacturer, the union challenged my presence. I merely asked whether the company as well as the employees should be represented by someone of its own choosing or whether each side should be given the power to veto the name of one of the representatives of the other side. That quieted the storm and we proceeded without vetoes. But it was not only in the matter of choosing representatives that unions sometimes balked at collective bargaining when it suited their purposes. At times we couldn't even lead the horse to water, to say nothing of making him drink. With the union this was lawful; with the employer it was unlawful.   In summary, no obligations or restraints of any kind were imposed upon the unions in return for the compulsion imposed upon the employer to recognize and deal with them.

The second travesty arose from the fact that the union could invoke the aid of the Labor Relations Board to enjoin unfair labor practices or to enforce union recognition and could then resist the Board's decision by industrial warfare if the union deemed it unsatisfactory.   On the other hand, the employer could be sent to jail for failure to comply with the Board's order after it was confirmed by the court.

Thus it happened again and again that the union, as was its legal right, organized attacks to strangle the employer's business, because, in order to keep out of the clutches of the law, the employer endeavored to adhere to the decisions of the Labor Board. In fact, the statute by its very terms fairly invited the unions to strike against Board decisions which they found to be unsatisfactory, since it expressly provided that nothing in the Act should be construed to "diminish in any way the right to strike."   So far as this Act was concerned, the union could do no wrong.   So far as the Norris-LaGuardia Act was concerned, picketing, boycotting, and striking could never be unlawful.

The purpose of this Labor Relations Act was to avoid strife and interruptions to commerce through collective bargaining and through the friendly adjustment of industrial disputes by imposing a kind of compulsory wedlock between employers and unions.   It was really a command to co-operate imposed on the employer, without any corresponding command imposed on the union.   It was like regulating a sales contract or a service contract with responsibilities imposed on one side and responsibility entirely removed from the other side.   Congress was deaf to the very suggestion that its purpose of securing greater union recognition by reducing sales resistance would at least be promoted by reducing some of the union evils that caused such sales resistance.   The liberal frequently claims voluntariness and education as the best means of promoting improved conduct, but in this instance Congress relied solely upon legal coercion to attain its ends and ignored the very factors that would have led more employers voluntarily to respect the objectives of the legislation.

In this connection my remarks in opposition to the Labor Relations Act as a piece of lopsided legislation seem to me as sound today as when I presented them in Washington in 1935. I then argued:

By the passage of the Norris-LaGuardia Anti-Injunction Law, and other statutes, unions have been relieved, to a very large extent, from effective legal restraint, in respect to many unlawful activities. The Wagner Bill goes a step further, and, as we will show, in effect compels dealings with these labor organizations, if a majority of the employees desire it, regardless of the legality, reasonableness, or good faith of the practices of these unions. Thus, in a short period of time, we are taking momentous steps of first relieving labor unions from legal responsibility, and secondly, forcing industry and society to function through these unrestrained organizations. If our industrial society is thus forced to function through these organizations, and their recognition is to be induced by legal compulsion rather than by the value of their service, they should be required to maintain certain standards of social conduct, as a condition of such recognition. In this respect, the Wagner Bill is strangely silent, and imposes no restraint or condition upon labor organizations for the privileges that are bestowed.

This extraordinary bill puts governmental power and the injunctive process behind the recognition of all unions alike, whether good or bad, lawful or unlawful.

The right to select individuals and institutions for mutual intercourse is of the very essence of sound social policy and freedom of contract. It is only through such selections that individuals succeed or fail, and institutions rise or fall by reason of a kind of social suffrage and social sanction. To compel dealings by law, regardless of the deserts of a private organization, is to undermine the ordinary incentives for good conduct upon which private and social sanctions depend, and thus to suspend the ordinary laws of reward and punishment.

The time has come, therefore, when certain requirements in the nature of a code for labor unions should compel them to observe certain standards of law-abiding conduct, fair dealing, reasonableness, integrity of contract and proper democratic administration and internal government as a condition precedent to the enjoyment of the broader privileges which have been bestowed on labor unions, and which the new bill proposes to bestow on them. In dealing with industrial relations, there is no occasion for drifting from the usual anchorages of sound social policies, which in all other fields are accorded almost universal sanction.

The situation thus developed by this compulsory wedlock, which makes no distinction between good and bad organizations, might conceivably place the employer in a position whereby he is compelled to become a party to a crime. . . . If one institution is by statute ordained to do business with another institution, it is necessary for the protection of society that the institution which is thus buttressed by statutory enactment should be regulated and made responsible.

Thus I urged what to some extent was recognized over a decade later by the passage of the Taft-Hartley Act.

I argued that there should be written into the Wagner Bill, as an amendment, "a proper definition of a lawful labor union of the kind which society should encourage and sanction and thus limit the compulsory requirements of the bill to that type of labor union."

It seemed to me that if, for the first time in our history and the first time in the history of any free country, the government were to require compulsory wedlock between employers and unions, it should at least require that both spouses measure up to standards reasonably necessary to a satisfactory alliance.

But all arguments such as these accomplished nothing in the political atmosphere of 1935. A tidal wave was rolling.

Since unions were left free to use their economic powers destructively, without social responsibility and moral restraint because they were guaranteed standing and recognition, regardless of their deserts, they could hardly be expected to measure up to their responsibilities to the rest of society. If under such unmoral encouragements they slipped into practices which were antisocial, the blame should be directed, not at the unions, but at the public opinion and the statutes that lured them down the wrong trail. I hesitate to imagine what employers might have done with like encouragement.

Anyone who adds together the Norris-LaGuardia Act of 1932, which permitted labor to use its combined economic power for antisocial objectives, and the Labor Relations Act of 1935, which compelled employers to recognize and deal with these unrestrained organizations, comes up with an amazing paradox. Congress and the courts first vested the unions with the unqualified right to engage in concerted nonintercourse for the attainment of any end, however criminal, and then proceeded to follow this with another law that forbade the employer to exercise the right of nonintercourse, to promote a socially desirable end. Inevitably the result was confused and intolerable. So it was only six years after the Supreme Court gave its enlarged interpretation to the Norris-LaGuardia Act, and 12 years after the passage of the Labor Relations Act, that an aroused public opinion and an awakened Congress brought some of these absurdities to an end by the passage of the Taft-Hartley Act of 1947. Those who would not listen to the voice of reason were reached by the voice of experience.

I have made no attempt to ascertain the full extent to which the tidal wave in favor of special privileges for labor expressed itself in state laws, but one or two examples come to my mind. In Pennsylvania an arbitration law, providing for procedures and binding awards in voluntary arbitration, expressly exempted labor because labor did not wish to be compelled to abide by awards, even after it had agreed to arbitrate. In New York State, Sec. 600 of the Penal Law provides penalties for wilful resistance or disobedience of a lawful process or mandate of the courts "except in cases involving or growing out of labor disputes." Thus a man who refuses to testify or produce documents in any lawsuit can be punished by the court under this Section unless the case, whether it be a criminal prosecution or a civil suit, grows out of a labor dispute. Perhaps the point is not of practicable importance, as there may be other ways of enforcing compliance with the mandates of the court. Of overwhelming importance, however, was the readiness of legislators to accept class dictatorship by the enactment of laws that in express terms aimed to corrupt the administration of justice. Our fundamental concepts of liberty would rest on shaky foundations if illustrations like this, and others I have not named, were multiplied.

XIV

When the Sinfulness of the Employer
Is Visited on the Union

B Y THE MIDDLE 1930's, as the record now shows, Congress had
largely written the epitaph of labor litigation as exemplified by
the leading labor cases of the previous quarter of a century.

Thereafter the Department of Justice struggled again and again
by well-selected cases to protect the public from antisocial combinations that it believed came within the purview of the antitrust
laws.   Its leading prosecution involved activities of the carpenters'
union in St. Louis and grew out of a jurisdictional dispute between carpenters and machinists as to who would erect machinery
in the plant of the Anheuser-Busch Brewing Company.   Because
the company employed machinists, the carpenters and affiliated
trades declared a strike and a boycott against the employer, who
was powerless to adjust the trouble.   It was in this case that the
Norris-LaGuardia Anti-Injunction Law was found to legalize all
such activities when carried on by labor unions in furtherance of
self-interest.[1]

In another case a Labor Board election was held on the application of rival C.I.O. and A. F. of L. unions, and when the C.I.O.
won, the A. F. of L. unions boycotted the employer for living up
to the order of the Labor Board, as the law required him to do.
The A. F. of L. union did the same thing in New Orleans, again
attacking building employers who recognized the C.I.O. truckers
who won a Board election.[2]   In both of these cases the court refused to recognize the employer's plight and upheld the right of
unions to engage in an organized attack against an employer be-

102

cause he refused to defy the law. Prosecution of the unions that prevented the use of building stone that was fabricated at the quarry, or the use of modern machinery [3] or prefabricated houses, or the manufacture, sale, or use of records or electrical transcriptions [4] all came to naught. In one of these cases, where violence was used, the grand jury found that the existing conditions were such as "should never be countenanced in a free society." In all these suits the union won and the public lost. Officially reporting on this condition in 1946, the Department of Justice writes:

The net result of all the labor cases brought by the Antitrust Division in recent years is that none of the restrictive agreements involving restriction in production, price fixing, allocation of markets and boycotts are violations of the Sherman Act if practiced by the labor unions alone.[5]

That was the statutory law of the United States—although not understood even by lawyers—when in 1935 I had a case tossed in my lap by the leading electrical manufacturers. The problem was to find some legal relief from a tripartite combination to prevent the use on buildings in New York City of certain kinds of electrical equipment unless it were locally assembled or produced by members of the local electrical union. Since all building operations of substantial size in the city were thoroughly unionized and nonunion operations were practically impossible, the simple tactic for the combination was to threaten a tie-up of any construction job that used electrical equipment brought into the city from the outside. One of the three parties to this combination, Local 3 of the International Brotherhood of Electrical Workers, was interested in broadening the work opportunities of its members, who were employed by the local contractors and the local manufacturers. The local manufacturers were interested in monopolizing the metropolitan market for their products. They felt that this market was their private preserve, where, with the help of the union as a policeman, all outsiders should be treated as poachers. The local union contractors were interested in having more equipment built on the job instead of in the factory and also in the protection afforded them as dealers by the union agreement to handle only manufactured products that were purchased by the contractor. For these advantages they accepted the union requirement that only goods of local union manufacturers be supplied.

The net result was that concerns like the General Electric Company, Westinghouse Electric & Mfg. Co., Allis-Chalmers Company and other giants in the trade were excluded from the New York market, and the people of the city paid more for their equipment than they would have paid if open competition had prevailed. So complete was the barrier that some local union manufacturers issued two price lists, one for use in the protected area and another when they sought to compete with concerns like the General Electric Company in an unprotected area. In some instances the price charged by these local manufacturers for the closed market was more than double the price charged in the open market.

This picture of trade relations in a great metropolis reflects one of the most significant situations ever existing in the field of union activities. Originally composed of some 7000 electricians engaged in electrical construction, the union had grown rapidly by extending its organization into the manufacturing field until it reached a membership of over 15,000. Picketing, boycotting, violence, sabotage, and the united power of the Building Trades Council, with a membership of 200,000, prevented electrical construction work, whether public or private, from being conducted on a nonunion basis. Cafeterias, retail stores, and shopkeepers of all kinds were picketed if they employed a nonunion electrical contractor, and even banks that loaned money to nonunion contractors were picketed. There was considerable violence, and the local union always poured in union funds for bail and defense. Local 3 and the local contractors' association united in the adoption of a voluntary code to protect themselves "from unscrupulous competition among themselves and from outside nonunion sources." A "closed ring" was established under the administration of the union officials to prevent any additional journeymen, contractors, or manufacturers from entering the trade unless in the judgment of the union it was deemed expedient to admit them.

The union contractors were union vassals and accepted uneconomic restrictions in return for union protection. Pressure on them was twofold: punishment if they tried to break away and reward if they co-operated—"threats of hell and hopes of Paradise."

The director-general of the voluntary electrical code declared:

Alone the contractor can do practically nothing. The union, on the other hand, has a certain power and influence, even when making its effort by itself, but when it makes that effort it automatically helps the union contractors. With both working for the same end, much can be accomplished.

Of course, under these conditions the contractor is not in a position to quibble over small details when the union wants something that would be a help to its members.[6]

Vassals never quibble.

The members of the union were likewise subject to a political dictatorship. Voting rights were limited to the construction electricians, so that the majority of members in other classifications, whose dues constituted more than half the union's income, were denied the right of suffrage—taxation without representation. The books of the union were closed so that only those who were the sons and brothers of members were admitted into the union. This action entailed the right to work at the trade; as a result, a father excluded from the union and treated as a commercial leper for the purpose of working at this trade carried the taint to his children—a new kind of infant damnation.

Those who were lucky enough to be union members had to watch their step. They could not directly contact an employer for a job or continue indefinitely to work for the same employer, for fear that overly friendly relations would be established. One member was sentenced to suspension for three years because he broke this rule by seeking employment from an employer—three years' exile from his trade and a family to support! Those desiring employment first had to be placed on the union waiting list and were then assigned to jobs in accordance with the number of credits for picket duty that were punched in their cards. During the course of the trial of the lawsuit brought by my clients, picket credits were given to those who attended the trial.

When the union decided that the industry could carry a new employer and that he was to be organized, his nonunion employees were often barred from the job. In case the union was displeased with the way in which a particular employer was behaving and did not wish to take direct action against the employer in violation of contract, it assigned riffraff or incapable workers to him who would run up the labor costs. As one employer testified during the trial, concerning one of his employees: He had lumbago so he couldn't lean over and piles so he couldn't sit down.

Rebellion was easily squelched. When a few union members brought suit because of favoritism and the dissipation of union funds, they were fined $300 each and suspended for a year. It was only the action of the court that prevented the enforcement of these sentences. Unemployment insurance, which was important during the depression of the 1930's, was applied first to the payment of the union dues of the unemployed, rather than to the living needs of wives and children. Organizing political opposition to a union officer and engaging in free assembly for a discussion of union affairs were made penal offenses, and every member was a compulsory spy because he was liable to discipline for failure to report any violation of union rules. The rule was captioned "Failure to Prosecute." In all, the union bylaws contained about 40 penal offenses, which remind me of a quotation from Browning:

> There's a great text in Galatians,
> Once you trip on it, entails
> Twenty-nine distinct damnations,
> One sure, if another fails.[7]

No journeyman, contractor, or manufacturer within this ring was a freelance. Commercial extinction was the price of resistance. Perfect co-ordination was thus assured in boycotting all products that came from outside the state. This boycott was enforced even against products made by members of a brother local of the same international union—a fact that led Chief Justice Stone, on the argument of the case before the Supreme Court, to comment, "That's where the Brotherhood came in."

A few graphic illustrations of this boycott are desirable. The Ten Eyck Low-Cost Housing Project needed switchboards and secured a bid from a local union manufacturer of $133,000. The Westinghouse bid was $56,000, but that company was told that it could not have the contract at any price because it could not produce a union passport. Finally the contract was awarded to the local manufacturer for $110,934—low-cost housing!

At Rockefeller Center, where 2000 building craftsmen were employed in building construction, strikes took place because certain complicated control equipment produced in a factory— where it should be produced—had come to the job completely wired and assembled. The demand was that the control equipment be disassembled and unwired and reassembled and rewired on the job, notwithstanding the fact that the cost of wiring and assembling on the job would be double that of wiring and assembling in the factory. To settle this issue several contractors' associations and the unions assembled in the offices of the Building Trades Employers' Association, and after excluding the boycotted manufacturers from the meeting, proceeded to decide just what products could be made in the factory and what products should be built on the job site. That settled the Rockefeller Center strike.

In conformity with this arrangement, when the General Electric Company was supplying control equipment for the Ward's Island sewage plant, the contractor, at union dictation, had to unwire and disassemble and rewire and reassemble the equipment at an added cost of $17,550. The net result was that the money might just as well have been thrown into the East River. When the General Electric Company supplied lift machinery for the Triborough Bridge, there was a duplication of work for the same reason amounting to $5800 on control equipment that cost considerably less than $20,000. In some cases even equipment made in local union factories had to be unwired and disassembled on the job site in order to duplicate work. The make-work program was running wild.

There was another complication in the situation. Electrical equipment made in the factory usually received a certificate of approval from the Underwriters Laboratories, Incorporated, which entitled the user thereof to reduced insurance rates. If there were no such label, the equipment was characterized as substandard and insurance rates were automatically increased. The rebuilding of electrical equipment on the job, after it had been completely built in the factory and had received the certificate of the Underwriters Laboratories, of course jeopardized recovery of insurance in case of a fire loss. The laboratory certificate had no validity in respect to rebuilt equipment.

It is more than significant that this whole combination went beyond orthodox unionism and sought to deprive New York City of the benefits of our national economy by excluding all products, union as well as nonunion, if they came from outside the state. If this destruction of interstate competition were to continue, Chicago, St. Louis, and Philadelphia, whose manufacturers had already felt this exclusion from New York, would inevitably retaliate and shut their gates against the influx of outside products. Self-interest would multiply imitations of this program, and the economic integrity of the nation would be impaired, just as it was menaced by state governments before the Constitution delegated to Congress the power to regulate interstate commerce.

It was Daniel Webster who pointed out that no factor was more prominent in the minds of statesmen, when seeking a federal constitution in 1787, than the necessity for establishing the free flow of interstate commerce. Senator Sherman, urging the passage of the antitrust law bearing his name, made a like comment:

The want of this power was one of the leading defects of the Confederation and probably as much as any one cause induced to the establishment of a Constitution. It is a power vital to the prosperity of the Union and without it the government could hardly deserve the name of a national government and would soon sink into discredit and imbecility. It would stand as a mere shadow of sovereignty to mock our hopes and involve us in a common ruin.[8]

Such was the importance of the issue presented to me by my clients in 1935 when they sought relief from this intolerable situation. The legal problem was difficult. With the Norris-La-Guardia Anti-Injunction Law on the statute books, it seemed doubtful indeed that an injunction could be secured. In the minds of most lawyers at that time, however, it was not believed that this anti-injunction law had changed the boundaries of what was lawful and what was unlawful. Accordingly it was decided to seek a declaratory judgment in which the court without a jury would determine what was lawful and what was unlawful as applied to these facts, and at the same time to ask for an injunction as an incidental measure to enforce the declaratory judgment. If, as a result of that suit, the courts declared the acts to be illegal but denied an injunction, it would then be possible to recover treble damages under the antitrust law, with the question of illegality already determined and the jury serving only to compute the amount of damages.

Following this strategy, a declaratory judgment case was instituted December 9, 1935, and was followed a year later by a suit for $1,300,000 treble damages. In both of these suits only the union and its officers were made defendants, but it was set forth that they were combining with the employer groups. The defendants' attorneys abetted our strategy by entering into stipulations, which adjourned the damage suit and sent the declaratory judgment suit to a special master to determine all issues of law and fact. Hearings then proceeded, with various adjournments, for over two years and involved the examination of over 400 witnesses, with a stenographic record of about 25,000 pages, in addition to

1000 and more exhibits. During the course of the trial Mr. Frank P. Walsh, chief counsel for the defendants, died of a heart attack on the courthouse steps, but after that his able assistant, Mr. Harold Stern, carried on.

The special master found in favor of the plaintiffs,[9] and his opinion was sustained by the District Court.[10] The union appealed to the Circuit Court of Appeals, which by a vote of two to one reversed the District Court.[11] On behalf of the plaintiffs I appealed to the Supreme Court of the United States, which sustained the position of the plaintiffs, with Justice Murphy dissenting, and granted an injunction.

The Supreme Court relied entirely upon the fact that the union had lost its exemption from the antitrust laws by uniting with contractors and manufacturers, nothwithstanding the fact that it was only the union and its representatives who were made defendants. The Court squarely espoused the doctrine that labor unions were exempt from the antitrust laws except when they combined with those who were not exempt. Speaking of these dual standards the Court said:

The result of all this is that we have two declared congressional policies which it is our responsibility to try to reconcile. The one seeks to preserve a competitive business economy; the other to preserve the rights of labor to organize to better its conditions through the agency of collective bargaining.[12]

Again it said:

Our problem in this case is therefore a very narrow one—do labor unions violate the Sherman Act when, in order to further their own interests as wage earners, they aid and abet business men to do the precise things which that Act prohibits? [13]

Having reached the conclusion that labor unions as an exempt group forfeit their exemption when they unite with a nonexempt group, the Court said:

Our holding means that the same labor union activities may or may not be in violation of the Sherman Act, dependent upon whether the union acts alone or in combination with business groups.[14]

Thus the final test is not what was done, but who did it. The real embarrassment confronting the court, which it had brought upon itself by earlier decisions, was in dealing with situations where the exempt and the non-exempt groups unite in furtherance of a common purpose. Under such circumstances the Court could not quite accept the idea that half of the collaborators were criminals and the other half were innocent. For the purpose of this decision, therefore, the Court returned to the sound legal standard that both groups are equally liable when they play together, thus making it dangerous for them to play together where the union is lawfully pursuing an object that the employer is forbidden to countenance.

The remarks in Justice Roberts' concurring opinion are worth quoting:

This court, as a result of its past decisions, is in the predicament that whatever it decides must entail disastrous results. . . . If the present decision is, as I think, a retrogression from earlier holdings, I welcome it; if it is but a limitation of them I concur in the partial alleviation of an impossible situation.[15]

According to a report of the Department of Justice made in 1946 to a special Senate committee, this Electrical Case "was the first case since 1926 in which the Supreme Court has held labor union activity as violative of the Sherman Act where the activity was related directly to terms and conditions of employment."[16]

Repeated suits and prosecutions by the Department of Justice failed. Although the purpose of the antitrust laws was to protect the public from undue economic burdens imposed by artificial and monopolistic practices, the legal doctrine of this Electrical Case left the public defenseless from indefensible labor practices so long as labor acted alone. Mr. Thurman Arnold, when in charge of antitrust prosecutions for the federal government, pointed out its helplessness when labor sought (1) to prevent the use of cheaper materials, improved equipment, or more efficient methods; (2) to fix prices; (3) to compel the employment of useless or unnecessary labor; or (4) to employ graft and corruption. That intolerable state necessarily called for correction when the Taft-Hartley Act was passed.

The decision in the Electrical Case, although technically a victory for the public, exposed the vulnerability of the public interests when attacked by such combinations of labor. The evidence upon which the case was based was convincing proof to Congress of the need for action.

XV

Somersaults in High Places

Early in this century Samuel Gompers, joined by many liberals, again and again reproached the United States Supreme Court for what was called "judicial legislation" and for usurping the power of Congress to make or change the law. In 1907 he said, "Judicial usurpation has overreached itself. After all, America is not Russia." [1]

But in the 1930's this liberal group, abandoning its political ideals, apparently determined to reverse legal trends by using the very tools they had criticized. The country again witnessed the familiar phenomenon of a group appealing for a principle or ideal that serves its own ends and being guilty of apostasy when the principle works in the other direction. In matters of fundamental political philosophy few people are capable of faithfully following a principle and letting the chips fall where they may.

In the 1930's "judicial legislation" became a deliberate objective of the liberal group. Although the court-packing bill was defeated, the objective was brought within the reach of the New Deal movement through the appointments which Franklin D. Roosevelt was called upon to make to fill vacancies in the Supreme Court. Through this process there was created an opportunity for more radical and avowed "judicial legislation" than had hitherto been known. Significant changes in the interpretation of our laws and our Constitution were effected without an act of Congress or an amendment of the Constitution. In the field of labor relations alone this new judicial attitude, coupled with the Norris-LaGuardia Act and other New Deal legislation that I have discussed, brought about changes which in their totality may be characterized as truly revolutionary.

111

White was changed to black and black was changed to white by the changed personnel of the Court. What had been declared to be rights protected by the Constitution, so that the legislature could not destroy them, were taken away by statute and Court decisions. What were once wrongful acts, according to earlier decisions of the courts, became Constitutional rights which neither Congress nor state legislatures could take away. Here is something momentous, and yet it all took place without undue excitement and without any adequate realization of what was happening. Even though many may believe, as I do, that some sort of change was long overdue, they may nevertheless challenge the method of change and the authority of the Court to alter our fundamental principles of law without legislation or a change in the Constitution.

Illustrations will be illuminating. It was repeatedly held by the Supreme Court of the United States, and generally by the highest courts of the different states, that the employer had an inalienable Constitutional right to refuse to employ a union man or to demand, as a condition of employment, that the employee agree not to join a union.[2] That right was held to be embraced within the Constitutional guarantee of liberty of contract. Injunctions could even be obtained against unions seeking to persuade an employee to disregard his employment agreement not to join a union, because it was wrong wilfully to induce anyone to breach a contract.[3] State and federal acts making it unlawful for an employer to demand such antiunion contracts were declared to be invalid as an infringement of individual rights. The employer was thus given the power to suppress unions and to punish by discharge employees who gave aid or comfort to them.

This has now changed. Today under the National Labor Relations Act and similar state laws an employer may be sent to prison if he persists in discriminating against a union man. Moreover under fair employment acts the employer may not discriminate against races. Thus the domain of property rights is contracted. Without a Constitutional amendment it has now become unlawful to do that which a quarter of a century ago was held to be a Constitutional right.

While, by judicial process, the rights of employers shrank, by the same process the rights of unions enlarged. By judicial alchemy that which was once illegal for a union to do has been transmuted into a Constitutional right—without legislation or amendment to the Constitution. Twenty-five years ago, or there-abouts, some federal courts held there can "be no such thing as peaceful picketing, any more than there can be chaste vulgarity, or peaceful mobbing, or lawful lynching" and that "peaceful picketing was a contradiction in terms."[4] Statutes forbidding injunctions against picketing were of doubtful validity.[5] Now this has been overturned. In the last decade the Supreme Court has held that peaceful picketing is a part of the Constitutional right of free speech.[6] By these decisions no legislation, no municipal ordinance, and no court decision, except another reversal by the Supreme Court, could forbid that which a couple of decades ago was declared by some courts to be an unlawful act. In this respect states and cities are deprived of the right of self-government and Congress is not entirely free to respond to a popular demand, if there should be any, to forbid all picketing. But since 1945 the same Court has been veering away from this doctrine and is inclined to qualify the Constitutional right to picket.[7]

By these decisions Constitutional walls to protect property were razed and Constitutional walls to protect labor were built on the same site. Where formerly there was a Constitutional right to obstruct unions, there was substituted a Constitutional right to obstruct business. Formerly it was charged that under decisions of the Supreme Court "it is Constitutional for corporations to discriminate against union men but unconstitutional for union men to discriminate against corporations."[8] Now the reverse is more nearly true.

Judicial treatment of labor under the Sherman Antitrust Law presents a similar picture. In 1908 the Supreme Court, speaking unanimously through its Chief Justice in the Danbury Hatters Case, decided that this law was designed to protect "the liberty of the trader" and that it applied to everybody including labor unions.[9]

The Clayton Act of 1914, including labor's Bill of Rights, was passed in 1914 as an amendment to the Sherman Antitrust Law, and the Supreme Court held that this Bill of Rights did not substantially change the status of union activities.[10] This decision was tartly criticized as defeating the purpose of Congress. That was the Court in its pre-New Deal form protecting the rights of employers. What the new Court did in the other direction I have already recounted but must again mention.

In 1941 a divided Supreme Court found the Norris-LaGuardia Act of 1932 threw light on what Congress intended by the Clayton Act in 1914 and in that new light it appeared the Clayton Act legalized activities of unions that theretofore were thought to be illegal.   Thus the Court did what many Congresses had repeatedly refused to do for 18 years from 1914 to 1932—exempted labor. It legislated new privileges for unions.   It is just such legal adroitness, in labor issues, that the man on the street cannot understand and that used to be the butt of attack by those who called themselves liberals.   Mr. Gompers' "judicial legislation" was becoming useful and popular with those who had condemned it.   In a dissenting opinion in the same case Justice Roberts, supported by the Chief Justice, excoriated this procedure:

I venture to say that no court has ever undertaken so radically to legislate where Congress has refused so to do. . . . In the light of this history, to attribute to Congress an intent to repeal legislation which has had a definite and well-understood scope and effect for decades past . . . seems to me a usurpation by the courts of the function of the Congress not only novel but fraught, as well, with the most serious dangers to our constitutional system of division of powers.[11]

Judicial treatment of labor's rights thus shows a tendency to give effect to the social viewpoints of the judges rather than to the letter of the law, and the Court in recent years has made this tendency most pronounced.   If a union combines with a "nonlabor" group, which is a nonprivileged group, the union loses rights, which it would otherwise have, to restrain or monopolize trade.   If it operates alone it may travel far without feeling the restraint of law.   This flowed not from Congressional action but from judicial legislation.

Before 1930 it was the general conclusion of the courts that an antitrust law which exempted labor was unconstitutional as arbitrary class legislation.[12]

A more prophetic statement on this subject is found in the unanimous opinion of the Criminal Court of Appeals of Oklahoma in 1912, where the court rejected the idea that labor and capital must receive the same treatment, and said:

Labor is natural; capital is artificial.   Labor was made by God; capital is made by man.   Labor is not only blood and bone, but it also has a mind and a soul, and is animated by sympathy, hope, and love; capital is inanimate, soulless matter.   Labor is the creator; capital is the creature. . . .

Labor is always a matter of necessity. Capital is largely a matter of luxury. Labor has been dignified by the example of God. The Savior of mankind was called the "carpenter's son." We are told in the Bible that "the love of money is the root of all evil." This statement is confirmed by the entire history of the human race. The love of money is the cause of the organization of trusts and monopolies. With what show of reason and justice, therefore, can the advocates of monopoly be heard to say that capital is the equal of labor? [13]

The language of the Oklahoma court, which I used to read to employers' meetings, is a bit flowery and picturesque. But it was at least prophetic in recognizing what ultimately has come to be the prevailing judicial opinion: that the problems of labor and capital, and the relation of the public to them, are so different that it is entirely within the Constitutional power of the legislature to treat them separately by different types of laws.

The next judicial somersault is even more startling because it concerns a fundamental law of human relations. It is a rule of law, declared by Justice Holmes, that "no conduct has such an absolute privilege as to justify all possible schemes of which it may be a part. The most innocent and constitutionally protected of acts or omissions may be a step in a criminal plot. . . ." [14] That is a profound, practical, and fundamental rule of law but apparently the Court has reached the conclusion that it no longer applies to strikes, picketing, and boycotting by unions. "So long as a union acts in its self-interest and does not combine with non-labor groups . . . the rightness or wrongness" of the purpose is immaterial. [15] The Supreme Court thus imputed to Congress—erroneously, I believe—an intention to legalize certain militant activities carried on by unions for the purpose of compelling an employer to do things for which he might be fined or imprisoned. This places these union activities in a preferred status over other human rights. An ordinary citizen who abets a crime is an accomplice, but one who by strike compels a crime may be free of taint. The net result is a complete reversal of the law laid down in the unanimous decision of Justice Brandeis, declaring that "a strike may be illegal because of its purpose, however orderly the manner in which it is conducted." [16]

Not so many years ago the Supreme Court held that Congress had no power to regulate hours and wages in manufacturing and could not even forbid the transportation in interstate commerce of

merchandise manufactured under substandard labor conditions.[17]
The regulation of wages and hours in manufacturing was held to be
a matter exclusively within the jurisdiction of the state. In recent
years the Court has held that Congress has the power even to
regulate the wages of elevator operators, porters, and cleaning
women employed by a real estate owner because space in the building is leased to various tenant manufacturers who produce goods
for interstate commerce.[18] According to some recent court rulings
those employers who relied on former decisions are liable for a
penalty of double overtime pay of time and a half for five years
back, and apparently no union, attorney, or individual employee
has the power to waive any part of such pay by way of settlement.[19]
These penalties imposed on innocent employers who had acted in
entire agreement with the union on what was supposed to be the
law amount to hundreds of millions of dollars. The payments
thus exacted were in direct conflict with collective bargaining
agreements where, over a period of years, everybody assumed that
the employees had currently been paid in full. This unconscion-
able liability, including the penalities, is based upon a radical
reversal of the viewpoint of the Supreme Court and the application
of that reversal back to a period which antedates the reversal.
The results were so highly unsatisfactory that Congress later found
it necessary to correct some of them by enacting the Portal to Portal
Act.

Formerly, according to decisions which President Theodore
Roosevelt called "judicial nullification," it was held to be a part of
the Constitutional liberty of the worker in ordinary industry to
work for as long hours and at as low wages as he might accept.[20]
We now have a federal act fixing minimum wages and maximum
hours for employees.[21]

In 1928 the Supreme Court held that employment exchanges
had a Constitutional right to fix the fees that they charge, which
right could not be taken from them by legislative enactment.[22] In
1941 the Supreme Court held that the former decision "is no
longer the law" and even upheld a law that prescribed a fixed fee
in securing employment for professional workers—a ruling that,
in its practical effect, permits the destruction of freedom of contract for employment exchanges seeking to obtain positions even
for professional men.[23] I argued both of these cases before the
Supreme Court, and on the argument of the second case, in re-

ferring to the first case as a precedent, I paraphrased Omar Khayyám by saying that I realized that it was not an instance where the moving finger writes, and having writ, moves on, but that the Court's piety and wit could wipe out every line of its previous decision. And the Court did.

In 1842 the Supreme Court of the United States, speaking through Justice Story, held that the District Courts of the United States were free to exercise independent judgment as to matters of general law and were not in this respect bound to adopt the doctrines of the highest court of the state in the area in which the District Court was sitting.[24] This had been important doctrine in labor cases, for the federal courts were presumed to be, and usually were, more independent of local waves of influence. In fact the District Courts were established to avoid the local pressure of corporate influence. Accordingly it was the law for nearly a century that these courts should exercise independent judgment on matters of general law. In 1939 this rule was overruled by the Supreme Court, without the intervention of the legislature.[25] Regardless of whether the court was right in the nineteenth century or in the first half of the twentieth, the significant fact is that this fundamental rule of law was changed by the Court after nearly a century of legislative and public sanction. The dissenting opinion, commenting on the impropriety of such an unwarranted change in the law, said:

Evidently Congress has intended throughout the years that the rule of decision as construed should continue to govern. . . .[26]

More recently the Supreme Court seems to have streamlined its process of changing laws through the reversal of previous decisions. In the flag-saluting case the Court reversed its decision made only three years earlier.[27] The trend has come to such a pass that the Justices have been chiding each other. Perhaps Justice Douglas would now revise his remarks in which he said, referring to another case, it "dies a slow death." Justice Frankfurter was chided by Justice Black, who, in a concurring opinion, said:

And for judges to rest their interpretation of statutes on nothing but their own conceptions of "morals" and "ethics" is, to say the least, dangerous business.[28]

Justice Roberts, in another case, said:

The evil resulting from overruling earlier considered decisions must be evident. . . . The law becomes not a chart to govern conduct but a game of chance . . . the administration of justice will fall into disrepute. Respect for tribunals must fall when the bar and the public come to understand that nothing that has been said in prior adjudication has force in current controversy.[29]

A later opinion by this same Justice, protesting a reversal of a decision only nine years old, expressed the idea more popularly:

The reason for my concern is that the instant decision, overruling that announced about nine years ago, tends to bring adjudications of this tribunal into the same class as a restricted railroad ticket, good for this day and train only.

It is regrettable that in an era marked by doubt and confusion, an era whose greatest need is steadfastness of thought and purpose, this court, which has been looked to as exhibiting consistency in adjudication, and a steadiness which would hold the balance even in the face of temporary ebbs and flows of opinion, should now itself become the breeder of fresh doubt and confusion. . . .[30]

Now we come to the fire insurance decision of June 5, 1944. From 1869 to 1944, a period of 75 years, according to repeated decisions of the Supreme Court the business of fire insurance was not interstate commerce. During that period Congress enacted the Sherman Anti-Trust Law, without intending its application to fire insurance; states passed regulatory laws, many of them recognizing the right to fix insurance rates by agreement, subject to state approval.

Notwithstanding this established rule of law, the Department of Justice indicted insurance men as criminals for relying on these rulings of the Supreme Court and for condoning a program of rate fixing that had been the industry practice for the indefinite past. On June 5, 1944, when the indictment was before the Supreme Court, the law was changed by the decision of four Justices. Insurance became interstate commerce and that which men had done in reliance on Supreme Court decisions became criminal. Nothing but abhorrence can be felt for any act of government that jeopardizes the reputation and liberty of men by charging them with criminality for acts that were innocent and proper at the time they were done. In this case it was equivalent to passing an *ex post facto* law in 1944 to punish men for what they had done in 1943. As pointed out by Chief Justice Stone in his dissenting opinion, a state of utter chaos was created by this sudden demolition of the established foundations upon which this industry and the various state governments and Congress had relied for many decades. Again Congress had to step in to alleviate confusion created by judicial legislation.

It is no mere accident that this same tribunal, which thus reversed former decisions in order to extend the antitrust laws to insurance, three years before reversed former decisions to remove unions from the antitrust laws.

Nor have I attempted to state all of the recent instances of reversal of law by the Supreme Court. The frequency of these changes in the last ten years has made us callous to the significance of this trend. We hardly realize how far we have travelled. The stability of our Constitution and laws, as we used to measure it, is greatly lessened. Excepting war legislation, the Court has done as much to change our institutions in the last ten years as has Congress itself.

To what extent the decisions of the old Court or new Court were right or wrong, I express no opinion. That is not material to the discussion in this chapter. The question is, who shall make our laws or amend the Constitution? Shall it be the Justices of the Supreme Court, who are chosen for life in order to be beyond the tendencies of the weather vane; Congressmen and Senators, who are supposed to reflect the changing demands of the people; or the people themselves?

Many are familiar with the alarm sounded by Thomas Jefferson over possible judicial usurpation:

It has long been my opinion . . . that the germ of dissolution of our federal government is in the constitution of the federal judiciary, an irresponsible body, . . . working, like gravity, by day and by night, gaining a little today and a little tomorrow, and advancing its noiseless step like a thief over the field of jurisdiction until all shall be usurped from the states and the government of all consolidated into one.[31]

The overeager reformer will have little sympathy with this discussion. If the results are desirable, he will say, why quibble over the means? A little violence and a little usurpation of power, here and there, now and then, are of little consequence. I wonder. If law and order are desirable and if our governmental structure of three co-ordinate branches is worth while, the functioning of these branches should not be permanently impaired in the cause of accelerated progress. That is placing temporary expediency above fundamental principles. Benito Mussolini, by overthrowing democracy, temporarily brought great material benefits to the Italian nation—but at what price?

The irrevocable harm done our institutions through an impatient desire to arrive by short cuts can never be undone. The position of the Supreme Court as an independent interpreter of law and governmental powers, with democratic trends as they are, would have been difficult to maintain under favorable conditions, but once abandoned can never be regained. The indispensability of an independent judiciary to the permanent stability of democracy presents a question upon which our forefathers and present-day progressives may differ. Certain it is that those who established this government honestly believed that the danger of democracy was too much democracy, and equally certain is it that the present standing of the courts has opened the gates to a more direct democracy.

XVI

Union Security and Individual Security

To WHAT EXTENT shall collectivism devour individualism? To what extent may the union conscript new members? These questions embrace the subject of the closed shop and union security, and our treatment of them within the last half-century reminds one of the chamois of the Alps, which jumps from crag to crag.

In the middle of the nineteenth century the Supreme Court of the United States declared that the ordinary trades must be "free in this country to all alike upon the same conditions," and that this "is a distinguishing privilege of citizens of the United States, and an essential element of that freedom which they claim as their birthright." [1]

In 1888 the Supreme Court held that a combination of members of the Knights of Labor, in which they agreed not to work with a suspended member or for anyone who employed a suspended member, was a heinous offense requiring a jury trial. [2]

Our very Constitution, with its checks and balances, predicated on our founders' fear of totalitarian government, was dedicated to the idea that there was a certain sacred sphere of individual liberty with which every man was endowed, even against the will of overwhelming majorities. One Supreme Court decision expressed this sententiously by saying that the purpose of the Constitution "was to prevent experimentation with the fundamental rights of the individual." [3]

In 1776 Europe regarded our new venture in government, with its exaltation of individual rights, as radical and visionary, and then through some strange cycle, by adherence to this faith of our fathers this government became the most conservative of industrial nations. With us both courts and legislatures undertook to protect individual liberty. "The trader is not a free lance," says one court. "Fight he may, but as a soldier, not as a guerrilla." [4] The Sherman Anti-Trust Law was enacted in 1890 to protect the liberty of the trader, and various other regulatory agencies like the Interstate Commerce Commission and the Federal Trade Commission were established at the beginning of this century and earlier to protect the individual from oppressive use of economic power. As already pointed out, in 1908 the Supreme Court asserted "the duty of government to protect the one against the many, as well as the many against the one."

Opinion on the closed shop early in the century makes interesting reading. Such leaders as Theodore Roosevelt and William H. Taft were advocates of the open shop and believers in unions. Woodrow Wilson declared, "I am a fierce partisan of the open shop. . . ." Herbert Hoover stated, "The principle of human freedom requires the open shop." Herbert Croly, an editor of *New Republic,* wrote a book that recommended the abandonment of the nonunion men, while Charles W. Eliot, president of Harvard University, spoke of the scab as a type of American hero. Cardinal Gibbons wrote:

The right of a non-union laborer to make his own contract freely and perform it without hindrance is so essential to civil liberty that it must be defended by the whole power of the government.[5]

Most of the intellectual leaders of that time were opposed to union restrictions on the right of any man to work either in time of strike or peace.

Warren S. Stone, president of the Brotherhood of Locomotive Engineers, one of the foremost unions in the country, said:

I do not believe in forcing a man to join a union. If he wants to join, all right. But it is contrary to the principles of free government and the Constitution of the United States to try to make him join. We of the Engineers work willingly side by side with other engineers every day who do not belong to our union, though they enjoy without any objection on our part the advantages which we have obtained. Some of them we would not have in the union; others we can not get. What I say is, make the unions so good that they will want to join.[6]

The Anthracite Coal Strike Commission in its award of 1903 adjudged:

That no person shall be refused employment, or in any way discriminated against, on account of membership or nonmembership in any labor organization; that there shall be no discrimination against or interference with, any employee who is not a member of any labor organization by members of such organization.[7]

Mr. Louis Brandeis, in a letter of October 6, 1910 to Lawrence F. Abbott of the *Outlook*, said:

The objections, legal, economic and social, against the closed shop are so strong, and the ideas of the closed shop so antagonistic to the American spirit that the insistence upon it has been a serious obstacle to union progress.

Nearly two years later he wrote Lincoln Steffens on February 26, 1912:

But the American people should not and will not accept unionism if it involves the closed shop. They will not consent to the exchange of the tyranny of the employer for the tyranny of the employees.

John Mitchell wrote that the time would come when compulsory union membership would be no more of a grievance than compulsory attendance at school. "The inalienable right of a man to work," he said, "will then be on a par with the inalienable right of a child to play truant, and the compulsion exercised by the trade union will be likened to that of the state which, in the interest of society, forces an education upon the child. . . ." [8]   Mr. Mitchell did not state what would happen in the event the school expelled the child and thus abandoned it as a wandering waif in our society, but at least he recognized that the union was looking forward to the exercise of sovereign powers or their equivalent.

The typographical union required a pledge from the members that their fidelity to the union should be above "any allegiance that I may now or hereafter owe to any other organization, social, political or religious, secret or otherwise," [9] while Mr. Gompers' motto was, "May my union always be right, but whether right or wrong, my union." He recognized the seriousness of the problem, however, when he declared that expulsion from a union in an organized industry was equivalent to "capital punishment." [10]   He recognized no such middle ground as a genuine open shop, for he commented: "As the immortal Lincoln said, 'This country cannot long remain half free and half slave.' So say we that any establishment cannot long remain or be successfully operated part union and part non-union." [11]

The decisions of the courts, both state and federal, in the early part of the century were faithful to the cause of individualism. The employer, being the owner of his factory, was free to choose his own employees, and in the process of choosing might lawfully discriminate against union members. As already noted, any law, state or federal, that attempted to take that right from him was a nullity as an unconstitutional interference with his property right. He might even force his employees to sign agreements not to join a union and could then enjoin a union, as an intruder, from trying to persuade employees to violate that agreement. Thus the ordinary peaceful process of unionization and organization could be blocked because of the breadth of this conception of property rights. In public employment, on the other hand, since the funds were contributed by the taxpayer, there could be no discrimination between union or nonunion men, citizens or noncitizens.

The right of union men to band together not to work with non-union men was open to question. In many courts this right was positively denied, particularly where a closed-shop system existed throughout an entire industry, either nationwide or in a single community.

This body of law was the logical and consistent outgrowth of current conceptions of individual rights. The individual worker was legally free to choose his associates and to refuse to work with nonunion men. He could do what he wished with himself, but to combine with others to exclude the nonconformist from a factory was quite another matter. The employer, if he wished, could require his employees to sign yellow-dog contracts, but if he combined with other employers for the purpose of maintaining a blacklist, he fell under the same condemnation as did the union. Unrealistic as this may seem, this reasoning had some logic behind it as an intellectual feat.

As for myself, I could not look tolerantly on the use of yellow-dog contracts forbidding an employee to join a union and the use of an injunction to protect those contracts from outside intrusion. I believed too strongly in unionism.

In 1917 when the Hitchman Coal & Coke Company was maintaining its suit against John Mitchell and others to protect its anti-union employment contracts from interference even by persuasion from outsiders, its counsel approached me for a conference in respect to its appeal to the United States Supreme Court. I immediately expressed my positive disapproval of such a use of property rights to suppress unionism. Frankness naturally eliminated the possibility of my being retained. The Supreme Court, however, with three dissenters, sustained the position of the company in a decision that in most of its aspects is now outdated law.[12] That decision became a great comfort to employers, who thought that through yellow-dog contracts they could immunize their enterprises from unionization.

So strongly did I feel about this situation that in 1920 I editorialized the issue as follows:

Shall employees be thus driven to sell their birthright for a mess of pottage? Can the resourcefulness of radical leadership devise any means better calculated to influence the workers and the public against the employing class? In the name of justice—in the name of public policy—in the name of many other considerations—let us have an end of this.[13]

The same editorial, then referring to the position of the League for Industrial Rights, an employers' association, continued:

An organization like the League which stands for human liberty and against oppressive restrictions on individual action, believes in the open shop. It defends the right to organize which carries with it the right to remain unorganized and opposes unfair action on the part of employers or labor unions to restrict a worker's liberty in this regard. The closed shop, whether union or nonunion, is incompatible with this principle. The employer should not boycott union men and the union should not boycott nonunion men. If such principles were adhered to, unions would grow wholesomely in the sunlight of liberty, and the number of their members would depend on service and not on force. If that policy were observed we believe that anti-unionism, which is but the foster-child of closed-shop unionism, would never thrive in the United States.[14]

It may be something of a disappointment to those who have taken pleasure in branding me as a union-buster to know how far I went in advocating unionism in the days when so much of industry was antiunion. In March, 1918, a fairly formidable employers' movement was organized to reduce me to innocuous desuetude because I pamphleteered for union recognition in the interest of industrial co-operation in time of war.

In 1922 when delivering addresses in different parts of the country, I issued this prophetic warning:

It is the strong who seek battle; it is the weak who seek peace and security. If employers teach the spirit of battle now that they are strong, labor will teach the spirit of battle when it is strong.

The closed-shop monopoly goes far beyond the necessities of union recognition and raises some serious problems. Unaccompanied with any safeguards or regulations to protect a member from being driven from his trade, it can never be justified. It places the power of commercial life and death in the hands of a private society and creates a condition contrary to our fundamental concepts of liberty. If a union card is to become the symbol of the right to work, then the state must have some voice as to the issuance or withdrawal of such a card even though the voice is limited to a review of arbitrary action.

Concrete illustrations are sometimes most illuminating in determining the importance of a principle or a generalization. In 1922 *The United Mine Workers Journal* listed disciplinary actions, taken against union members in the closed-shop coal mining industry, which showed in the aggregate that within a period of 16 weeks 1236 members were expelled for a total of 66,784 years and fined a total of $171,852. The boilermakers, iron shipbuilders and helpers' union published a record of four or five hundred expulsions and fines for a period of about a year, which ranged from $5.00 up to $9,999.99 and expulsions which ranged from one year to 99 years. Men have been expelled for years for insisting upon an accounting of union funds. Cecil B. DeMille was expelled from the union and deprived of his opportunities "on the air" because he refused to pay an assessment of one dollar to support a political program to defeat a referendum vote on a law to forbid the closed shop. Other men have been expelled and deprived of their jobs for reasons that were wholly unjust and unmoral. Other men, with wives and children to support, have been refused a union card and driven from their jobs when their employer was unionized, and all because they were neither sons nor brothers of some member. Races have been discriminated against, and men have been driven from their trades because their wives acted contrary to union edicts in another trade.

If the conditions that give rise to these extreme examples of tyranny were rare, it is unlikely that Congress would have been disturbed by them in 1947, but the facts are to the contrary. Sumner H. Slichter, writing for the *Quarterly Journal of Economics* in February, 1949, says:

Trade union membership had increased about five-fold between 1933 and 1945 and about twofold between 1940 and 1945. About one-third of the members were concentrated in six large unions—the Teamsters, the Automobile Workers, the Steel Workers, the Carpenters, the Machinists, and the Miners. About seven million jobs were covered by closed-shop or union-shop contracts (about three times the entire A.F. of L. membership in 1933), and four million more were covered by maintenance-of-membership clauses. This meant that large areas of American industry were open only to union members or to persons whom the unions were willing to admit, and that in these areas loss of good standing in the union meant loss of one's job.[15]

It is the magnitude of the problem that has led people to urge that in this field, as well as in others, a monopoly must be regulated or abolished.

Of course the closed-shop issue is aggravated when the union closes its books or when it discriminates against Negroes or otherwise enforces restrictive practices such as excessive initiation fees that deny men a fair opportunity to enter the trade. I had supposed that the closed shop with a closed union had no considerable number of defenders, even among union men, and was therefore shocked when in the summer of 1949 a public official in New York City urged the Longshoremen's Union to close its books because there was a surplus of men competing for this work. In effect he was urging that an ironclad monopoly, enforced by the monopolists without public regulation, is a proper remedy for overproduction or overmanning.

Although I am inclined to think of this problem in terms of the rights and freedom of the employees, it is of course not to be forgotten that the evils of monopoly are many-faced. It is industries maintaining the closed shop that have presented the most outstanding examples of antisocial practices. The printers, the musicians, and the building trades are sufficient examples.

The evils of a closed-shop monopoly grow as the institution expands. If the closed-shop union controlled substantially an entire industry, as in the case of the coal industry, or an entire industry throughout a community, as in the case with the construction trades in many cities, it used to be condemned by the courts because it interfered with the liberty of men to engage in the monopolized trade. Now such monopolies are not uncommon.

A labor case involving the closed shop was sandwiched into my schedule while the celebrated hatters' litigation was in its most active stage. In the latter part of 1909 three journeymen hatters under cover of darkness knocked at the rear door of our home

on Main Street and sought a conference with "Lawyer Merritt."
As they unfolded their story, it developed that the predicament of
each was identical. As union members they had responded to
a strike call early that year and under the bylaws of that union
were entitled to strike benefits of $7.00 a week, which were not
forthcoming. After the strike was called off they refused to pay
union assessments, on the ground that a larger sum of money was
due them for strike benefits. For this their employer, who operated a union shop, was forced to discharge them under threat of
strike. Their situation was indeed distressing, since practically
all factories in Danbury were unionized and nearly all commercial
activities in the community were accustomed to bow to the union
will.

One of these men, whom we shall call Pat, was particularly
notable for his tautness. He had a worn-out wife and too many
children. Later Pat reached the conclusion that the officers of the
hatters' union had a machine that pressed on his head and permitted them to see everything that was going on in his home. Not
long after that he was arrested while going downtown in Danbury
to shoot the Catholic priest. When Pat finally ended up in the
Middletown State Hospital he used to write me letters and in one
of them said: "They leave the door open here so I will soon escape." He did, and again appeared in my office. He had then
decided that his wife had murdered his baby, and he wished a
divorce. I pacified him, but by some ill-fated chance he ended
up as an armed guard for a large company in New Jersey, and I
never again saw him.

For the second man I was able to effect a reasonable settlement.

The third man was Dominick Connors, whose case became a
cause célèbre. He was made of different stuff—short, stocky,
and determined. Dominick never turned back. He asked for no
help or comfort. Not being able to secure employment in Danbury he moved to Yonkers, where he went to digging ditches for
the gas company and thus supported himself through the years
of the legal battle that followed.

Dominick's case against the local union and some of its officers
was commenced in March, 1910, and after many legal skirmishes
caused by technical maneuvers of the union, it came to trial before
a jury in the Superior Court in Danbury.

Of course I should have known better than to have permitted

the case to be tried in Danbury. The town was surcharged with excitement.

The timing of the trial was also unfortunate. Hatting was slack in this unionized hatting town, so union hatters had nothing better to do than to attend the trial. The aisles and doorways of the courtroom were packed. Dominick was driven from his boardinghouse, and after court hours, when I accompanied him as a bodyguard, he was stoned. The atmosphere was compelling and the jury decided against Dominick, who went on digging ditches in Yonkers.

I appealed to the Supreme Court of Errors of the State of Connecticut, claiming that the whole labor monopoly in Danbury was illegal and that, if basically legal, the union still could not throw a man out of his job for nonpayment of dues, when it owed him a larger sum for strike benefits.

The Connecticut Supreme Court sitting in Hartford in the spring of 1913 listened an entire afternoon to the argument of my opponent, who always fished up side streams. He was quick to take encouragement from the action of a nearsighted judge who was squinting at his pad and jerkily making notes. When court adjourned, the judges filed out but the nearsighted jurist left his notes behind. That was too much for my opponent. He walked up behind the bench and scanned the lines with an inscrutable expression. Later I learned that this was what he read: "Why don't you stop? Why don't you stop? Go to hell. Go to hell."

The decision, which came down before summer, was unanimous and eloquent. The court did not deign to deal with our contention that the injury to this man was unjustifiable because the union was really his debtor, and turned to our fundamental contention that the entire union monopoly in Danbury was against public policy. It held as a matter of law that where unionization "takes in an entire industry of any considerable proportions in a community so that it operates generally in that community to prevent or to seriously deter craftsmen from working at their craft . . . without joining a union, it is contrary to public policy."

In support of this conclusion the court said:

Monopolies of things of common use and need, whether created by governmental grant or by the acts of private persons or corporations, are odious, and their existence is contrary to public policy. . . . They are especially intolerable where they concern the basic resource of individual existence, to wit, the capacity to labor.[16]

A new trial was accordingly ordered.

The defendants then filed various new answers and pleas. To these I objected by filing a formal statement to the effect that the defendant's papers contained allegations known by defendants and their counsel to be false and sham. My opponent objected to this, saying it was all very well to accuse his clients of making false statements but that it was unethical to accuse a fellow lawyer. When I stood my ground, he brought proceedings before the grievance committee of the bar association of Fairfield County to disbar me.

The grievance committee with a fair measure of shrewdness decided to await the decision of the court on the papers in question before proceeding with an inquiry. They did well to do so. The court finally ruled in my favor, with an opinion in which it said:

If the defendants' counsel really cannot understand what he may or may not do in the defense of this action he should give place to some counsel who can. Any further attempt to cumber the record and delay the trial by conduct contemptuously disregarding rules and principles which have been plainly stated may have serious results for him who makes the attempt.[17]

That ended the grievance proceeding.

Facing the prospect of a second trial, I moved to have the case transferred to Bridgeport, on the ground that a fair trial was not possible in the hostile climate of Danbury. That motion was granted, and since the case was beginning to assume greater importance, the union retained the law firm of Homer S. Cummings, who later became Attorney General of the United States and was one of Connecticut's most brilliant barristers.

The Bridgeport trial was short. The sturdy Dominick stood up well on cross-examination and never failed to remember that he was fighting for his rights as an American citizen to pursue his livelihood and not for contract rights with the union.

In the course of my summation I quoted Elihu Root as saying that the first client of every lawyer is his country, and I presume I tended to wrap the American flag around the little Irishman as a defender of liberty. At any rate the jury brought in a satisfactory verdict, and in congratulating me said that they did what they did for their country.

Six years after he was driven from his trade Dominick received his money without any deduction for fees, for I was filled with admiration for the way in which he faced his hardships. As I looked back over the years of struggle, wondering at this man's decision to fight, I was reminded of Josh Billings' comment on the cow who sought to derail a train—he admired her courage but not her common sense.

Of Dominick Connors, the humble but doughty warrior, an editorial in *The New York Times* said:

He was hooted and stoned in the streets, driven from boarding places and finally from town. Nevertheless he persevered and has won his case and deserves no less well of his fellow-citizens than Loewe, who vindicated the rights of capital. . . . That Connors deserves well of those who do not wish to be unionists is too plain to remark.[18]

Instances such as I have cited explain the reluctance of many disinterested people to support the closed shop and such compromises as the preferential shop and the maintenance of membership provisions.

The maintenance of membership clause adopted by the National War Labor Board early in World War II had good as well as bad features. At least it did not force a man into the union in order to hold his job. The employer agreed merely that once an employee elected voluntarily to join a union, he must continue to maintain his membership during the term of the contract. That would have been all very well if the agreement had been intended and interpreted as a mere requirement that the employee would at all times endeavor to remain a member, but unfortunately it was interpreted as a guaranty on the part of the employer that the man would maintain his union membership, even if the union insisted upon depriving him of it. The union could expel a man for any cause or without a trial, and then require his discharge. Thus men lost their jobs because they informed their employers of thefts or refused to strike in violation of the union agreement. Imagine the absurdity of compelling an employer to discharge an employee on the demand of the union because the employee insisted upon living up to the existing agreement with his employer! It seemed to me unjust for the War Labor Board to urge agreements of this character where *ex parte* judgment by the union could require the discharge of an employee without any review of the arbitrariness of the union action. It seemed particularly unjust because, at the same time, the Board was directing the adoption of another clause requiring the employer to arbitrate the justice of discharges initiated by him.   Although this injustice of maintenance of membership irked me considerably, I nevertheless refused an important retainer to contest it in the courts.   I felt it was no time to rock the boat and did not wish to see the War Labor Board embarrassed.

The same inconsistency exists today when unions, through their insistence on the closed shop, ask for the unreviewable right to expel an employee from the union and from his job, while, on the other hand, demanding contract provisions in union agreements requiring arbitration of the justice of any discharge initiated by the employer.

Whatever flows from the ever-recurring discussions of the closed shop, it becomes more and more apparent as the issue is clarified that if a closed-shop monopoly is allowed to continue in any form, it must be subject to reasonable regulation.   If union membership is to be equivalent to a license to work, its protection must be lifted above the precarious level of membership in a private society. The real problem, which even maintenance of membership does not grasp, is the right of a man in a free society to enter and remain in the "economic world" or, if you will, a free labor market.

The Congressional hearings on labor legislation in 1946 and 1947 produced such overwhelming evidence of the abuses which arise under a closed-shop regime that Congress was, in general, well united in its opinion as to the necessity of regulating or qualifying such a monopoly.   With the Taft-Hartley Act, Congress met the union man's resentment against fellow workers who bore no part of the cost of securing the benefits of the collective bargaining agreements by imposing the cost of union dues upon all employees within the bargaining unit where a majority so voted.   But Congress eliminated any form of union security whereby the union might demand the discharge of a worker for nonmembership in the union except where that nonmembership arose from a failure to pay reasonable initiation fees or regular dues.   Unfair situations—of which there were many—where the union unfairly denied membership to a worker or unfairly expelled him were thus prevented by the Taft-Hartley Act.

To many people this seemed like a reasonable compromise. Since the union insisted upon contract provisions requiring arbitration of all discharges, it did not seem consistent that the union could arbitrarily order discharges.

Personally, I would have been ready to go a step further and require that when a majority of all the employees voted by secret ballot in favor of the kind of union security that the Taft-Hartley Act sanctions, that issue should no longer be the subject of industrial conflict or collective bargaining, and that any step by either party to establish a different arrangement would constitute an unfair labor practice. That would entirely remove this controversial issue from the field of industrial conflict. To say that this is an unfair encroachment on the rights of the individual worker is scarcely realistic. As the law now stands, such taxation for union dues may be imposed on the individual by act of the majority of all of the employees, only if the employer consents. As I view it, carrying out this will of the majority of the employees should not depend on the consent of the employer. The question of limited liability for union dues is hardly a matter for his determination. Moreover it will soon appear clear, from what I am about to write, that this added encroachment by collectivism on the rights of individual employees is slight indeed compared with the accumulation of encroachments that they now must endure. Already the employee no longer has the right to name his own conditions of employment if a majority have voted to be represented by a union.[19]

It is not necessary to accept the Taft-Hartley Act as the last word on this problem. Certainly an arrangement whereby a man may insult, cheat, and defy his union in order to invite expulsion and escape the payment of dues may ultimately result in loss of union discipline aimed at achieving the orderly performance of contract obligations or employee duties. As the law now stands, a man expelled from the union because he steals either company funds or union funds may not be discharged because he is no longer a union member. In fact, the man wins by his own wrongdoing because he may thereafter hold his job without the payment of union dues. Under such eventualities discipline might be undermined, to the detriment of both management and the union. This question of discipline, particularly in some industries where union stabilization has been valuable, should not be overlooked.

If under the Taft-Hartley Act lack of disciplinary authority over union members proves embarrassing, it may be necessary to supplement the pertinent provisions of that Act with some additional paragraph providing that the nonpayment of reasonable fines imposed for just cause may carry the same consequence as the nonpayment of dues, subject to an appeal to an administrative board empowered to review all phases of the case including the severity of the punishment. This would restore to the union a degree of disciplinary authority over members who engage in wildcat strikes or otherwise disrupt the negotiation or administration of collective-bargaining agreements.

An interesting suggestion, which was designed to meet this question of discipline and which shows a reasonable and intelligent recognition of the fundamentals of the problem, was proposed by a committee appointed by the Governor in a report to the Senate and House of the Commonwealth of Massachusetts in 1947. That committee, of which Sumner H. Slichter was chairman, recommended against a law prohibiting the closed shop but found that safeguards were necessary to protect against its abuses. The committee proposed the enactment of a law that would define as an unfair labor practice any act calling for the discharge of an employee for loss of union status, pending a hearing of all the available appeals permitted by the union constitution and bylaws. The proposal further provided that any employee so disciplined for any cause, other than malfeasance in office or failure to pay dues or assessments, should have the right, after exhausting his remedies under the union constitution, to appeal to the Labor Relations Board. The enactment of such provisions, it was thought, would insure sufficient scope for discipline and would protect the status of an employee as a union member under a closed-shop contract. To that extent the proposal would partially answer one of the main criticisms of the closed shop.

But let us examine the practical applications of this proposal. When an employee is discharged by an employer for some real wrongdoing and the issue goes to arbitration under the collective-bargaining agreement, it is almost certain, except in extreme and unusual cases, that the arbitrator will rule that the penalty is too severe and will soften it. If that is the result when a man is discharged by a single employer, how much more pronounced would the tendency be if arbitrators were dealing with a closed-shop industry in which a man, once condemned to expulsion and dismissal, could nowhere pursue his trade? What would a poor arbitrator do if faced with the question of making a man an outcast throughout an entire industry? What are the circumstances under which any agency, whether a public official, a private union, or an arbitrator, might fairly rule that a man must become a commercial leper?

It is difficult for a union audience to be patient with such a discussion of principles or to believe that anyone who advances such principles is not an enemy of the labor movement. On a Sunday afternoon when I debated with Andrew Furuseth in what was then the Lexington Avenue Theatre in New York, I tried earnestly to couple my opposition to the closed shop with an outspoken advocacy of unionism. But it was no use. A voice from the gallery shouted "You don't believe what you say. Why don't you get off the fence?" I paused, walked to the end of the stage nearest him, and, shaking my finger in his direction, retorted, "I am trying to keep my balance and you would do well to do likewise."

A recent brief filed in behalf of unions in the Supreme Court of the United States contains this amazing statement:

There exists no constitutional right to work as a non-unionist on the one hand while the right to maintain employment free from discrimination because of union membership is constitutionally protected. . . . We say that just as a state may not make the right to be a slave a cornerstone of its legislative policy, so may it not make the right to work as a non-unionist, a cornerstone of legislative policy.[20]

Deep-seated is the idea that nonunion men have no economic rights and that they are legal, as well as moral, outcasts. The same union that would deny them legal rights wishes to reserve without regulation the power to decide whether they shall enter the union portals in order to obtain equal rights of citizenship.

The problem of union security and individual liberty, although the unions refuse to recognize it, is a delicate and difficult one, and it is not made easier by the over-all demand that unions remain free from legal responsibility. The power of the union to control its membership through reasonable discipline must be preserved, but the right of the individual to protection in the exercise of one of his most important rights as a citizen must not be withdrawn.

Philosophizing over the problem in the 1920's I indulged in this language:

The right to organize must not overthrow the right to remain unorganized. One may venture to believe in voluntary associations without giving approval to involuntary associations. The rights of the group, the mob or the class must not destroy the rights of the individual. "Our fundamental law recognizes no class, no group, no section," says Mr. Harding, "Ours is a government of individuals." We all believe in collectivism as an agency of co-operation, but collective self-help must not unduly infringe upon that ancient and more important right of individual self-help. Individual self-reliance is of far more importance to a nation than reliance upon the collective power of a class. It is the individual human being whom we cherish. God made him a unit of responsibility and no earthly power can change that immutable fact. He must primarily look to himself and his own talents to work out his career. The destiny of the individual is above the destiny of any group or class. His character, initiative and service are the pillars of our republic. So far as collectivism promotes the development of individuals, it is good, but so far as it obstructs such development, it is bad. The aim of modern life must be to work out an adjustment between individualism and collectivism, but the solution when reached must not be unmindful of the fact that the organization of groups as well as the organization of the state, is but a means of securing the best life for individuals.[21]

Reading over that statement after the lapse of over a quarter of a century, I am not satisfied with its generalizations, but I am more inclined to supplement it than modify it. If under union practices and labor relations acts, the right of every individual to pursue his trade and to determine the terms of his employment, as well as his right to decide when he will work and quit work, is to be sacrificed to the voracious appetite of collectivism, then it would seem that the organizations taking over these responsibilities become governmental in their functions and must accept some regulation from the over-all sovereign. Perhaps there is no room for the nonconformist or the rebel soul in the field of economics, but at least he should be protected in his right to become a part of the team when he conforms. In our thinking we seem to be back just where we were nearly 50 years ago, unless we accept some compromise like the Taft-Hartley provision or the Sumner Slichter proposal. Today we still pose the questions: Shall the right to organize wipe out the right to remain unorganized? Shall voluntary associations be displaced by involuntary associations?

The need for union security, which is often the antithesis of free unionism, or the need to conscript members has waned since the day when Congress forbade the federal courts to protect the individual and later, in 1935, buttressed the powers of unions by affirmatively protecting collectivism. Prior to the Taft-Hartley

Act, the union might strike to compel the discharge of members of a rival union, and the employer might then be penalized for yielding by being compelled to re-employ the men with back pay. Today the subject has largely been removed from private determination by the Taft-Hartley Act. Under the policy of the Act union-shop requirements become legitimate only after a majority of employees have voted for them. Were I spokesman for the employer group, I would gladly surrender the option to reject the Taft-Hartley brand of the union shop for a governmental policy that eliminated all stricter forms of union security.

If, by any chance, proponents of the closed shop are to win in any new legislation, it might be wise to search for some arrangement whereby closed-shop unions shall be automatically subject to a set of laws or regulations, not required of open-shop unions. As always, regulation must be the price where monopoly is the lesser of two evils, and in this case it would be a regulation to prevent arbitrary exclusion from a trade.

If we abandon the nonconformist in the field of economics, we shall tighten the grip on the rebel souls by demonstrating that there is little room in this world for him who dissents from his class. If we have to accept the goose step or the lock step, we must find some way to guarantee that all other values of individual expression and individual talents are not lost by a sense of individual hopelessness and despair. Because the worker in the early part of the century was subject to the caprice of the employer is no reason why he should now be subject to the caprice of union leaders. Nothing should blind us to both sides of the problem.

Mr. Harold Cox, editor of *The Edinborough Review,* published an article in the London *Times* on April 10, 1922, in which he quoted with approval my statement at that time concerning the problem of union security as follows:

We all believe in collectivism as an agency of cooperation, but collective self-help must not unduly infringe upon that ancient and more important right of individual self-help. Individual self-reliance is of far more importance to a nation than reliance upon the collective power of a class. . . . The aim of modern life must be to work out an adjustment between individualism and collectivism, but the solution when reached must not be unmindful of the fact that the organization of groups as well as the organization of the State is but a means of securing the best life for individuals.

XVII

Liberties Bartered for Basic Needs

CURIOUSLY ENOUGH, my title for this chapter is inspired by a sentence in President Truman's message to Congress in December, 1947. Referring to the consequences that might ensue if we did not help Europe, he declared that their peoples might be driven by despair to "the philosophy which contends that their basic wants can be met only by the surrender of their basic rights. . . ." That is the underlying principle of unionism. Workmen have surrendered individual rights to the union in return for the well-recognized benefits of collectivism and the right to speak and vote in the union hall. Thus the untrammelled flowering of this associational right becomes of paramount importance.

The loss of the liberties of the individual workman in the United States is not the product of philosophy, ideology, or preconceived planning. Dogmas as to individual rights, which played such an important part in this field in earlier years, came into collision with economic actualities. Changes were induced by stark realism, pragmatism, and economic necessities.

Following the Civil War, our national philosophy had been individualistic and not social, with emphasis on the liberty of everyone, high or low, to carve out his destiny by harnessing his own talents and with rich rewards awaiting the exercise of special talents. With the development of large corporate employers, the individual workers in mass industries drifted into a position of comparative helplessness. Frustration drove them to seek a change. That change was the creation of unions which would govern them.

This did not restore individual liberty to the worker but further restricted it because there were new masters, and the new masters were inescapable. Formerly the workers could, in most cases, choose between competing employers in a free economy, but today where national unionism prevails there is no escape from one of the masters. Laws that regulate conditions of employment or nationwide or community-wide unionism fix the workers' status. It is this fence around the rights and responsibilities of the individual worker that deserves discussion.

Sir Henry Maine, in his volume on ancient law,[1] first published in 1861, declared that "the movement of the progressive societies has hitherto been a movement from status to contract." "Status," in the sense in which Sir Henry used the word, means a fixed relationship not temporary in its nature nor terminable at the will of the person. Uppermost in his mind was the gradual transition of man from a serf, who is fixed like a cabbage to the spot, to a free worker who determines his position by making contracts. Sir Henry, unaware of the problems of modern industry, could easily formulate such a comment, but had he lived in our time he would have been cognizant of many intermediate forms between the extreme of serfdom and free contract. He would have visualized unions as free institutions of free men acting for individuals in making contracts.

Today the industrial workman has lost his liberties to the state, the employer, and his union. His recent surrender of rights to the state and his trade union is based on the conviction that such a sacrifice is essential to protect him from greater evils. He saw no future for himself as a competitive freeman scrambling for a job and bargaining individually with the centralized hiring power of employers. He saw greater opportunity for self-expression in the union meeting hall than he did with his employer, at least this was the case in mass industries.

Of course there is a vast difference between losing rights to a dictator as in Russia, to a political majority as in England, or to an employer who is all-powerful and entrusting those rights to a group of your own kind. But in any case it is authoritarianism, to the extent that it enters an area of individual liberty that our founding fathers thought should be inviolable. It was Lenin who said, "Liberty is precious—so precious that it must be rationed." He knew that liberty spelled economic inequality.

The underdog has a hard time in this world. If he doesn't

look out he is likely to be shoved around by someone. The only question seems to be who shall do the shoving. Mass production has done more than any other modern force to improve the underdog's economic lot, but it has been at the cost of other values.

Joe Doakes is growing accustomed to less freedom and responsibility. No longer is he responsible for himself. In return for his loss of self-control he expects to be taken care of. That is the philosophy of today. If Joe is to be shoved about, he naturally has some preference as to who shall do the shoving. The employer group? Reasonably enough, Joe says "no" to this, for he believes that there is too much conflict of interest between the "likes of him" and the employer. Shall it be the State? To this Joe may possibly reply that the State includes too many segments of population whose interests are not identical with his. Then it must be the union, Joe's own association, which is made up principally of people whose interests are the same as his own. Even though he knows of union racketeering and unfair union politics, and even though he may have felt the heavy hand of union tyranny, Joe Doakes would sooner entrust his rights as an employee to the union, including his sacred right to work, than leave them to the employer or the government. Joe will listen credulously to what union leaders say, while turning a deaf ear to others. If he is a coal miner, he would listen to John Lewis rather than Harry Truman. So when we talk about protecting the individual rights of the worker against the sweep of collectivism, we must not forget Joe's preference. After all, it is his rights we are shouting about. In the last analysis, his is but a Hobson's choice.

Viewed cumulatively, the encroachment on the rights of individual workers, as employees, is reaching a point where it will almost totally eclipse those rights. However necessary this may be for an individual workman of mediocre talent, it must often prove irksome to those of superior talent, and it is bound to take its toll in efficiency of production.

Let us paint the picture with a large brush. Whether he be union or nonunion, by authority of law if a majority so votes, Joe forfeits to the union or its officers his rights to bargain as an individual for the hours, wages, and terms of employment for which he will hire out, and, to some extent, his right to decide when and where he shall work. If a majority of the employees so decides, he may be required to bargain through a union that is not of his choosing.

The United States Supreme Court has pointed out:

that the Statute which grants the majority exclusive representation for collective bargaining purposes, strips minorities within the craft of all power of self protection for neither as groups nor as individuals can they enter into bargaining with the employers on their own behalf.[2]

There is little left to individual agreement except the act of hiring.[3]

The law of the land has vested the majority of the workers with the power to seize these rights without Joe's consent. Even if he is a particularly gifted workman to whom the employer would give preference, he is forced to toss his talents on the altar of collectivity by agreeing that in layoffs and rehiring, and sometimes in promotions, he shall give way to inferior workmen of greater seniority. Prior to the passage of the Taft-Hartley Act, according to the rulings of the Labor Relations Board he also lost his right to settle his own grievances with management.

Under a closed-shop regime, important political and moral rights were endangered and sometimes forfeited. If Joe is a coal miner, whether he is a Republican or a Democrat, he must join the United Mine Workers in order to carry on his trade. Prior to the Taft-Hartley Act the union could take his dues, and the dues of other members, and contribute $600,000 to the election of a Democratic candidate for President. His political rights were undermined, because his money could be conscripted to support candidates whom he opposed.

Since we in America have gone so far as to express faith in collectivism and loss of faith in individualism, I cannot be shocked over the idea that a majority of the workers should decide the minor question as to whether a minority of nonconformists, who have already lost their rights to bargain for themselves, should not pay a few dollars a month towards the collective-bargaining expenses of the union that determines their terms of employment. It is natural that unions, having imposed on them by law the responsibility of giving equal attention to the rights of all employees, union and nonunion, should insist that those whom they must serve should not play the role of free riders.

But Joe has lost his individual rights in other ways. By action of government, he cannot work more than 40 hours a week unless the employer will bear the financial burden of paying him an additional 50 per cent of the basic rate for overtime, and no person, however incapacitated, can work for less than a minimum wage. A quarter of a century ago the Supreme Court of the United States would have held that this constituted an encroachment on the liberty of the worker, which it was one of the major purposes of our Constitution to forbid.   Now a more socialized concept prevails.

Neither can the worker decide whether or not he wishes old age insurance, and if he does wish it, where he shall purchase it.   The state assumes he is incapable of deciding this question for himself. If he were regarded as competent to pass upon his own individual problems he would at least be given the opportunity to decide whether or not he will take out government insurance.   In other words he should be "sold" the idea.   Then he would be educated. But it is these same men, shorn of their liberties and responsibilities because they are not deemed competent to handle their own affairs, who as voters are regarded as competent to pass upon important national policies.

As we drift nearer and nearer to the dangers of direct democracy, with modern communications making our public officials more promptly responsive to the will of the voters, we go further and further away from policies that tend to develop individual responsibility and self-reliance among industrial workers.   With one exception, the worker lives less and less under a system of free contract.   The exception is his right to be heard in the union meeting hall.   That residue of his individual rights must be zealously guarded.   If that right is not encouraged and expanded, if the worker grows to look upon that right as futile or impeded by unpleasant and discouraging surroundings, then this resort of the individual in the collective world will be of little avail.   In a collectivist world, unless we conserve all spiritual and moral values in what is left of individual expression, man as a personality will surely shrivel.   It seems to me that it is almost as important to guard that right as it is to guard the right of workers to vote in primaries and public elections.   We must see to it that the worker has not sold important rights without receiving full compensation.

By that I do not mean to supervise union meetings or elections but to require union bylaws to conform to certain minimum standards and to provide legal remedies, readily available to the well-intentioned members who have the will to protect their democratic rights.

This problem of promoting or protecting the democratic process within the union is not a class question and should not be highly controversial. Its relation to industrial relations is only of secondary importance. Generally speaking, the employer should feel that as an employer he has no special interest in this problem, albeit, like the rest of us, he has an outstanding interest in it as a citizen. In my experience I have not discovered that a union democratically run invariably serves the immediate interests of the employer more satisfactorily than a union which is autocratically run. Nor have I found that radical leadership in a union is necessarily more disadvantageous to the routine administration of affairs in a factory than a union with conservative leadership. Sometimes the democratic union with conservative ideology is more dependable and sometimes it is not. It is on the basis of these considerations and this experience over many years that I repeat: The employing class as a whole has no direct immediate self-interest in promoting the democratization of a union. The problem should be placed on a much higher level than any possible controversy between employers and union leaders.

If unions were to accept a reasonable degree of regulation so that their conduct would more fully conform to democratic ideals, I would not be averse to the idea that such dynamic functional groups should exercise broad powers of self-government subject to overriding laws to protect the public. Within these specialized groups, people activated by self-interests and possessed of direct knowledge of the matters with which they are dealing are more likely to exercise a more active and intelligent participation in matters that come before them, than can be hoped for in a political democracy where problems are impossibly complex and direct interest seems so far removed. The major problem, which is already with us, would be to protect society as a whole from overreaching or to prevent attempts to substitute economic coercion for the democratic process.

In applying this principle to Joe Doakes, who is more ready to comply with union authority than outside authority, these associations, I feel, should exercise important powers of government among members but should always be subordinate to law and public interests. Commensurate with that power must be laws providing individuals or minorities with legal remedies to enforce fundamental principles of fair play. For the unions to oppose such laws, on the ground that they do not know where government intrusion will end, is understandable. Employers have been taught that such fears are well founded. On the other hand, it seems that flat resistance to all regulation is losing public favor and injuring the union movement. If all that remains of the rights of an individual as an employee largely resides in the union meeting hall, then that outlet, that bastion of individual expression, must be preserved at all hazards. His right to speak and vote at union meetings and his relation to the union may sometimes seem of more practical concern to him than his right to vote for the President of the United States, and his membership in the union may seem of more vital importance than a mere matter of citizenship.

Describing the union man's new status Stuart Chase writes:

He has more protection against arbitrary power exerted by his employer than by his union officials. He is often under very severe penalties for exercising ordinary civil 'rights' in his union, such as organizing minority parties, issuing leaflets, holding meetings, denouncing officials. He can damn the President of the United States until he is black in the face, but he had better keep his mouth shut about Mr. Big in his union front office. The effective power of top officials is greater, their grip tighter, their tenure more secure, their conduct less open to criticism and control, than is commonly the case in our federal or state governments in normal times.[4]

If a man's relation to his union is the important gain he has made in exchange for his loss of other individual rights, this picture of undemocratic tendencies within the union may lead to legislation establishing rules that will encourage union members to assert their rights.

Decreasing self-reliance on the part of individuals and necessary reliance upon a collectivist group to make all important decisions and supply protection and security—the tendency to blame others than yourself—may seem to some as the lesser of evils in an industrial state, but their moral consequences are difficult to calculate. It is a kind of spiritual anesthesia. "The brave new world" of which Kipling speaks "begins when all men are paid for existence and no man must pay for his sins."[5] But, over two thousand years before Kipling wrote, at the foot of the Temple of Apollo was recorded: "Give surety and trouble is at hand."

Our ultimate destination is too unpredictable, the values lost and the values gained are too unweighable and the years of experience under modern conditions are too few, to permit definite conclusions.   Who can tell what loss of individual right is offset by material gains or what sacrifice of material gains is offset by social or material gains?   Or what society will lose by sacrificing leadership or superiority to the ideal of equality?   The moral impact of all these changes on the personality of man is still unknown.

XVIII

Waves of Violence

A DETACHED OBSERVER surveying outstanding events and trends in labor relations in the last 50 years may seek a conclusion as to whether or not the prospect for goodwill, mutual understanding, and co-operation between labor and management and between society and labor is improving. Are unions and union leaders growing more submissive to the implications of private enterprise and to the will of democracy, or is there an increase in rebellious spirit and a growing unwillingness to recognize the rights of the public and the supremacy of government and the right of property to a profit? If one could confidently predict that labor unions would seek only to secure their share of the product whatever that may be, would not attack capitalism as an institution, and would not resist public laws, the forecast would indeed be welcome. It could then be hoped, for our time, at least, that an adjustment had been reached over the eternal controversy on the breadth of property rights.

The answer to such a question is, to say the least, difficult. The shift of emphasis in the manifestations of the rebellious spirit has been so great, because of the shift in objectives and controversial issues, that it is difficult to compare utterances and actions in the first half of the century with those in the latter half. I shall undertake, however, to make comments on this subject in a later chapter after I have reviewed some of the major events, which stand out like red lights on the horizon of 50 years.

The review is not gratuitous. History is never gratuitous. There is no desire needlessly to stir up the dead ashes of the past concerning the mistakes either of the unions or of the employers, except as it may be necessary to discern a trend throughout half a century and better to plot a future course. It is with this latter thought in mind that I write this chapter, reviewing all too briefly some of the spasms of organized lawlessness and violence in the course of these many years with the hope that the reader will find it easier to join with me in trying to answer the question of whether or not union sentiment reflects a greater willingness to accept existing institutions and to submit to the will and rules of democracy. Although it is not to be forgotten that the beginning of this century was marked by examples of antiunion practices that tended to provoke lawlessness, it should also be noted, as I unfold the picture, whether such lawlessness was aimed only at antilabor employers or whether it extended to the social-minded employer and to the later era when the more detestable antilabor practices had been largely exterminated.

The period immediately preceding our entry into World War I presented a picture of class conflict with brazen expressions of defiance of law and government, not only by spokesmen of the Industrial workers of the world, but also by important unions affiliated with the A. F. of L. and by the A. F. of L. itself. The decade following 1922, on the surface at least, was an era of co-operation, goodwill, and peace within American industry. Other countries marvelled at it. It was the depression commencing in 1929 that later destroyed it. Because of this debacle, which stagnated our industry in the early 1930's, employers as a group were condemned and hostility by workers was fed, notwithstanding the fact that the laws of the land prevented industrial leaders from agreeing upon a program that would have softened the blow. Out of this depression came the Norris-LaGuardia Law in 1932 and the New Deal program as embodied in the National Recovery Act of 1933, the National Labor Relations Act in 1935, and the Fair Labor Standards Act in 1938.

For the moment, the point is that class conflicts, colored with revolutionary threats, were at a notably high level before we entered World War I. Industrial peace and co-operation were at a high level for the decade following 1922 with the exception of the mine workers' unions, which carried on a civil war against nonunion or open-shop operations. In 1937, even after most of the pertinent New Deal policies had been entered on the books, came the wave of the sit-down strikes, and as late as 1946 came

mass violence even to the point of preventing executives from
entering their plants. Each of these waves of disorder had its
own background and its own motivations but the interesting fact
is that the extent of violence in any particular case was not always
the consequence of extreme mistreatment or extreme provocation—
quite the contrary. I review these cases briefly that the reader
may judge to what extent outstanding disorders were excusable
or inexcusable and whether they indicate a movement forward or
backward in our united desire to civilize industrial relations.
Moreover, an examination of trends in five decades ought to tell
us whether by education and adequate policies we are protecting
society against the recurrence of such lamentable developments
in the future or whether we are in effect inviting their recurrence.

The Dynamiting Conspiracy of 1910

Although personally I had nothing to do with the prosecution of
the dynamiting conspiracy against the open shop in the steel-
erecting industry, which reached its height in 1910 and 1911, I am
commenting on it as the outstanding example of industrial violence
in that period. Moreover I was familiar with these events, as I
successfully defended the industry from charges that it was resisting unionization by methods that violated the antitrust laws.
Those who are not old enough to recall the dynamiting program
may take some comfort from the fact that no such systematic
scheme for the use of explosives to fight the open shop on a nationwide front is ever likely to be repeated.

Thirty-eight union men, most of whom were officially connected
with the International Association of Bridge and Structural Iron
Workers, were indicted on February 6, 1912 for a conspiracy
unlawfully to transport explosives in interstate commerce, contrary to the criminal laws of the United States. The explosives
were bought, stored, and transported to demolish open-shop operations in the industry. The trial of these 38 men resulted in a
record of 25,000 pages of testimony and led to convictions
and jail sentences, which were sustained by the United States
Circuit Court of Appeals for most of them.[1] The longest sentence,
accorded Frank M. Ryan, the president of the international union,
was seven years.

With picturesque details eliminated, the summary of the facts
by the United States Circuit Court of Appeals is sufficient on re-

reading to shock again every normal person. From 1908 down to the time of the arrest of the McNamara brothers and McManigal in 1911, almost one hundred explosions, damaging and destroying buildings and bridges in the process of erection and killing people, had occurred. As technique improved, "infernal machines" were so set up that the explosion would occur several hours after the installation, when the person who caused it would be far away.

In the more active period, the headquarters of the union were at Indianapolis, where dynamite and nitroglycerine were stored in vaults and basements. In most instances these explosives were carried on passenger trains in suitcases and other types of hand-bags from Indianapolis to the points where they were to do their deadly work. On one occassion four explosions occurred in one night at the same hour in Indianapolis, and explosions planned to take place on the same night two hours apart at Omaha and Columbus, Indiana, did take place as planned. When the Times Building in Los Angeles was destroyed on October 1, 1910, 21 persons were killed, and immediately after this happening arrange-ments were made for an explosion in the east "as an echo in the east of what had occurred in Los Angeles." [2] All the cost of the explosives and equipment, including the expense incident to the stealing of some explosives, was paid by checks drawn against the international union funds and signed by the secretary-treasurer, John J. McNamara, and the president, Frank M. Ryan, both of whom were included in the convictions.

In generalizing over this entire picture, of which I have given only a few details, the Court of Appeals said:

that use of explosives for destruction of property as described embraced exclusively "open shop concerns" and was continuous and systematic from the commencement of such course up to the time of the . . . arrest. . . .[3]

James B. McNamara, when convicted, declared he did what he did "for a principle." Twenty-one of the convicted men were thereafter elected to office in the International Union or one of its locals. In March, 1913, after his conviction, President Ryan was re-elected president of the union and later from his cell endeavored to administer its affairs. At times our sense of civic decency has strange blind spots. Sam Parks, after serving a sentence in Sing Sing for corruption and racketeering in the New York building trades, was paraded up Fifth Avenue on a white horse.

In closing this dynamiting episode, it is interesting to note that it was not until July, 1937, that the big steel companies capitulated and placed their structural steel work in New York on a closed-shop basis.

Outcries against Public Authority

The second decade of the century, down to our entry into World War I, brought to the surface outspoken criticisms and challenges of government and the existing order. During this period, and earlier, it was the established practice for the district organizations of the United Mine Workers of America, encouraged by inflammatory statements of the national organization, to wage civil war against nonunion or open-shop operations in such states as Virginia, West Virginia, Alabama, Colorado, and Arkansas. The weekly journal of the national organization, year by year, led the miners to believe that every important industrial conflict in their industry, wherever its theater, whatever the issue, whoever the employer, was characterized by oppression and wrongdoing on the part of the police, constabulary, troops, and the courts. I doubt if one could find a single instance where the union, or its publication, encouraged the discipline or censure of any officer or member of the union for the lawlessness that took place, or made a single honest recommendation that law-breaking by union officials or members should be checked by union discipline. In some cases where these local battles broke out there were special provocations to promote resentment, but an examination of all instances shows that the same result followed even where there were no special provocations. The point of view was clear: The government was the common enemy as much as the employer, for it was the pliant and corrupt tool of the employer.

Here is a characteristic expression:

Why should we dodge the issue and rant about law and order and rights of citizens when law and order leagues, and citizens' alliances are murdering our brothers, desecrating our homes, burning our wives and children and are defended in their dastardly deeds by the powers of the state government.

It is fortunate for historical purposes and for the education of those who are inclined to regard these uprisings as unimportant that some of these battles led to lawsuits making it possible to document the charge.

As early as 1901 Mr. Lewis, speaking at a conference with the coal operators of Indiana, Illinois, Ohio, and western Pennsylvania, known as the Central Competitive Field, expressed the motivation that explains what followed. Mr. Lewis described the purpose of the conference:

As I understand it, it is for the purpose of wiping out competition between us as miners first, viewing it from our side of the question; next for the purpose of wiping out competition as between the operators in these four states. When we have succeeded in that and we have perfected an organization on both sides of the question, then as I understand the real purpose of this movement, it is that we will jointly declare war upon every man outside of this competitive field who will do anything in any way endangering the peace that exists between us.[5]

Skipping ahead a little more than ten years, we find that another representative of the union, speaking at a similar conference concerning a union resolution to end nonunion competition, said:

We have had men go to jail. We expect that more of us will go to jail. The penitentiary doors have no terrors for us so far as that is concerned. And if putting two or three hundred of our men in jail will organize West Virginia, we will send two or three hundred down.[6]

It was the reiteration of this theme to the miners through *The United Mine Workers Journal,* over a period of 15 years or more, that led the union membership and the district and local officers to believe that the law-enforcing officials of the country were the enemies of the coal miner and that inspired the practice of resistance to public authority wherever occasion arose. This was war on nonunionism in the coal industry.

In April, 1914, came the horrible Ludlow Massacre, growing out of the industrial battle between the United Mine Workers and the Colorado Fuel & Iron Co. Here was civil war on no mean scale. A battle was fought between the strikers and the militia over an area of some three square miles. It was charged and denied that the militia opened hostilities with machine guns and fired the tent that sheltered the strikers. Over 45 were killed and many wounded. Both strikers and militia had a full supply of guns and ammunition.

Whatever unfortunate blunders and lack of wisdom characterized the conduct of the strikers and the defenders of public order, it is all too clear that the clash grew out of a determined effort on the part of the union to prevent the mines from operating except on union terms.

I do not go into this incident in any detail because there is no adequate judicial review to which I can turn and I do not care to weigh the partisan statements of the day, but in two other instances involving coal miners we can look at sworn testimony for our guide.

The first of these began in a neighboring state only a few months after the Ludlow disgrace. The program of organized violence that destroyed the nonunion mines of a coal company in Sebastian County, Arkansas, in July, 1914, was shown to have been financed and directed by District 21 of United Mine Workers, which covered Arkansas, Texas, and Oklahoma. Shorn of too much detail, the judicial statement of the Supreme Court of the United States, in describing this situation, included the following:

. . . A large force of union miners of the local unions and of District No. 21, and their sympathizers, armed themselves with rifles and other guns furnished and paid for by the District No. 21 Organization, and before day on July 17th began an attack upon the men whom Bache had brought together, and proceeded to destroy the property and equipment. It was a battle, in which two of the employees of the mine, after capture, were deliberately murdered, and not only gunfire and bullets but also dynamite and the torch were used to destroy all the property on the premises of the Prairie Creek Mine and of three of the other mines of the plaintiffs.[7]

Following a suit for treble damages under the antitrust law in which the jury on the first trial returned a verdict that led to a judgment of over $600,000, the defendants escaped liability on the ground that their purpose was not to restrain interstate commerce. In a second trial and a further appeal, the international escaped on the ground that it was not shown to have authorized the violence. In all courts the evidence as to lawlessness and violence and direct participation of District No. 21 in the unlawful activities was never successfully challenged.

Of a like pattern was the attack on the nonunion operations of the Pennsylvania Mining Company in Johnson County, Arkansas, which led me to bring a similar suit in 1915. A judgment of over $300,000 was entered upon the jury verdict. Again the violent acts, including the attempt to dynamite a bridge on a railroad spur, were thoroughly established, but the verdict was set aside on the ground that there was no evidence of an intention to restrain interstate commerce.[8]

No discussion of this subject would be complete without reference to the horrible massacre that took place at Herrin, Illinois, on June 22, 1922. The inhuman barbarities that followed may be attributed largely to the passions that rise when mobs go into action. Nevertheless the attack was due solely to the determination of District No. 10 of the United Mine Workers of America to prevent the operation of strip mining by the Southern Illinois Coal Company during the coal strike of 1922. The historical importance of this incident is enhanced by the fact that the entire story can be told through the simple authoritative words of the Grand Jury.

Here is the story: In June, 1922, when a national coal strike was on, the Southern Illinois Coal Company decided to operate a strip mine owned by it and located in the vicinity of Herrin, Illinois. None of the men employed had any idea that they were strike breakers, the steam shovel men being members of a union that was not recognized by the American Federation of Labor. Apparently there was no objection to the stripping operations until the company started shipping coal into the market. Then serious trouble loomed on the horizon. The company employed guards. Colonel Hunter of the Adjutant General's office reviewed the situation and asked for troops, who were denied because the sheriff of the county, a member of the union and a candidate for public office, would not ask for aid.

On Monday, June 19, John L. Lewis sent State Senator W. A. Snead, President of District 10 of the United Mine Workers, a telegram, copies of which were posted and read in various places. It recited that the Steam Shovel Men's Union had been suspended by the A. F. of L. some years before and closed as follows:

Representatives of our organization are justified in treating this crowd as an outlaw organization and in viewing its members in the same light as they do any other common strike breaker.

From this point on, the words of the report of the Grand Jury tell the story:

Following the publication of the telegram from President Lewis preparations for an attack upon the mine were made. The hardware stores in all the cities of Williamson County were searched for firearms. The weapons were either taken by force or upon a verbal assurance that the local would pay for them.[9]

Bullets began flying into the mine on June 21st, and compelled the guards to seek cover. Return fire killed three union miners. McDowell, superintendent of the mine, asked Colonel Hunter for protection and the Colonel suggested a flag of truce. On the evening of June 21 the coal officials agreed with Colonel Hunter and the sheriff to discontinue the operations if the employees were allowed to depart in safety. Nevertheless, on the following day the attacking party crept closer and firing increased.

From this point on I return to the words of the Grand Jury:

A long range conversation was held and it was agreed by the spokesmen of the attacking party that safe conduct would be accorded the men if they laid down their arms and marched out with hands up.

This was done and from behind the earth embankments created by the shovel operators came a great number of unarmed men and more from the surrounding hills until the forty-seven surrendering men were surrounded by the many hundreds of men mostly armed.

The captive men were marched down the road toward Herrin in double file. After they had marched about one mile Superintendent McDowell, being crippled and unable to keep up with the procession, was taken by members of the mob and shot to death. The remainder of the captives were marched on the public road and were stopped at the powerhouse of the interurban railroad, about three miles from Herrin. Here a change in the leadership took place and the man who had guaranteed the safety of the men who had surrendered was deposed and another leader installed.

The new commander ordered the captive men to march into the woods adjacent to and around the powerhouse. Here the new leader directed that only those in the crowd who had guns should follow into the woods and those who were unarmed should remain without.

The surrendered men were then marched some 200 yards back of the powerhouse to the vicinity of a barbed wire fence, where they were told they would be given a chance to run for their lives under fire.

The firing began immediately, and thirteen of the forty-seven nonunion men were killed and most of the others were severely wounded.

The mob pursued those who had escaped and two were hung to trees, six were tied together with a rope about their necks and marched through the streets of Herrin to an adjacent cemetery, where they were shot by the mob and the throats of three were cut. One of the six survived.

The atrocities and cruelties of the murders are beyond the power of words to describe. A mob is always cowardly, but the savagery of this mob in its relentless brutality is almost unbelievable. The indignities heaped upon the dead did not end until the bodies were interred in unknown graves.[10]

The Illinois mine workers raised $875,000 to finance the defendants in the murder trials that followed, and under the influence of local emotions the particular defendants tried for murder were acquitted in the local court.   But when it came to civil suits in the federal courts it was a different story.   As I was considering the possibility of a suit for treble damages in behalf of the coal company, the claim was settled by the sale of the mining property to the union for $726,000.   I actually started a suit in the federal court for $3,000 on behalf of a woman who was deprived of her livelihood through a boycott, because her husband had been on the Herrin Grand Jury and because he refused to sign a protest against an injunction issued against the railroad unions.   The union settled that case in full.[11]

What would happen today if any attempt were now made to dent the monopoly of the United Mine Workers?   To this question there can be but one answer: Any attempt to carry on substantial coal operations anywhere in this country except according to the union formula would meet with organized violence, which the union would not seek to discourage.   If there is peace from time to time, it is the peace that comes from the nonassertion of independent rights.   Such is the inevitable result of the doctrines preached in *The United Mine Workers Journal*.   Strikes involving violence have contributed greatly to the mine workers' nationwide monopoly.

The epidemic of preachments against law and order was not limited to United Mine Workers.   In *The American Federationist*, the official organ of two million workers, it was constantly pointed out, that all courts and the military and the police were the tools of plutocracy, and in some cases defiance of law was counselled.

Thus an alarming number of citizens were brought to believe that the government was in league with capital to maintain a system of oppression and wrongdoing.   Statements against country and patriotism were not uncommon.[12]   "Don't run away with patriotism for your country," read one of these, "for it has been in hock to Rockefeller and Morgan."

During the period preceding World War I, the I.W.W. was permitted publicly to parade and prosecute purposes as lawless as the Molly Maguires, the Ku Klux Klan, and the Mafia.   "The tactics used are determined solely by the power of the organization to make good in their use," writes one of its leaders. Dynamite was officially advocated and "militant direct action" was urged, "for the going to jail en masse causes expense to the taxpayers." [13] Its publications urging violence and revolution were distributed through the mails without restraint. "No God, no Master," was the proud slogan of its banner. In prose and verse, in many ingenious forms, its official journal urged sabotage:

> Soap stops water from making steam in boilers,
> Asafetida keeps patrons from struck theatres,
> Oil containing emery makes machinery strike,
> Accidents often are an aid in winning strikes.
> Guerrilla warfare always gets the Boss's Goat.
> Ends that are revolutionary justify the means. [14]

With this preaching against authority came a dangerous collapse of government in the treatment of industrial lawlessness. Labor, with its resentment against industrial ills, employed the strong-arm method. Employers and even responsible communities adopted drastic measures. One evil begets another. The abandonment by the government of employers and nonunion men to these union outbreaks resulted in defensive methods, equally dangerous to society. It is not important to decide which was cause and which was effect. The outstanding fact is that the state was not performing its duty to enforce the rules of orderly society and that he who is not protected by society will resort to the primitive art of self-defense. That is the reason for the roughness of frontier justice. Necessity, the mother of invention, invented professional strike breakers and private guards. The results were satisfactory to no one. Leaving the enforcement of law and order to private citizens invariably leads to recriminations, reprisals, and other ugly results.

In some localities, particularly in the West, armed committees of vigilantes, established by indignant communities, were careless of the ordinary forms of civil authority. They found law enforcement inadequate and, taking their lesson from the disturbers, proceeded recklessly in the work of repression. They, too, argued that ends justify means. If freedom of speech is employed to arouse angry mobs to violence, then restrictions will be placed on the right of free speech and on the right of the entrance of such agitators into a law-abiding community. The persistent abuse of rights means a curtailment of rights by law or direct action. Free speech and free assembly will not be tolerated for lawless purposes, and he who carries the red flag should not appeal to the Stars and Stripes. That was the sophistry of retaliation.

Such was the experience of many cities. When drastic measures gained the upper hand, things turned a sommersault and those who had been the law-breakers began to invoke the law. By what warrant were they deported? Under what law were highways guarded to prevent their entrance to a city? Was it not contrary to the Constitution to repress their soap-box exhortations? And so it was again proved, as statesmen had often declared, that the guaranties of civil liberty are more important to the workers than to the employers, and the breakdown of these guaranties became a boomerang.

When war with Germany was declared in 1917, the labor conflict had become to such an extent a question of law and order that the struggle between public authorities and the union often overshadowed the dispute with the employer. We witnessed frequent contests between the union and the community, with the latter defending the good name and prosperity of the city. Paterson did not want to be the refuge of the I.W.W. The pride, not to say self-interest, of Indianapolis was hurt on seeing its streets decorated by pickets carrying "unfair" banners, for travelers would think it a city of unrest. Another city pasted gaily colored stamps on the backs of all letters: "Stockton, the Open Shop City." An appeal was thus made to civic pride, and the fight was on between the community and the labor leaders. Neither side missed the significance of the battle, for, said Mr. Gompers, "police administration is often the determining force in the struggles of the workers." [15]

The events that took place in Everett, Washington, during this period were as illuminating as they were deplorable. Trouble with the shingle weavers had been brewing for some time, and the I.W.W., imported to promote violence, finally organized a fight against the city. Physical combats followed, with the authorities indulging in brutal attacks. When the city commissioners prohibited soap-box orations on the most congested corners, where women and children passed, the I.W.W. defiantly sought the restricted places and challenged interference.

"We propose to have free speech on this corner," said one

speaker, "no matter what we have to do to gain it. To gain it we propose to use direct action. Direct action means what the scabs got in Los Angeles when twenty-one of them were blown to hell. Direct action means sabotage, arson, murder, or anything else that will gain our ends, and we propose to use it if we are not permitted free speech here."

The speaker was arrested, and that night the jail in which he was placed was surrounded until rumors of unpleasant action by the fire department scattered the crowd. Members of the I.W.W. then flocked to the city, and many were met at the outskirts and turned back. To avoid the deputies, some disembarked at Snohomish, ten miles to the east, and walked down the tracks to the city. One group hired a launch, which was intercepted two miles from shore, and the men after some resistance were temporarily placed under arrest.

The real climax came when hundreds of them organized an expeditionary force in Seattle, and after marching through that city fully armed and singing their war cries to the tune of "Onward, Christian Soldiers," prepared to embark for Everett on the steamer Verona. In Everett that night some emergency deputies gathered at the Commercial Club and were advised that the I.W.W. were coming 2000 strong to burn and kill and, in their own words, "make Everett look like Verdun." Preparations were made for armed defense. If news of the embarkation were received, a long blast was to be blown on the fire whistle, and only those prepared to risk their lives for the protection of their city were to respond. The tocsin was sounded, and over 130 deputies flew to the rescue. When they reached the wharf, the Verona was in the harbor, and the invaders massed on its deck immediately opened fire on the dazed deputies, who fell back, leaving their friends wounded on the wharves. The firing was soon returned, and the proprietors of hardware stores were hurriedly loading their automobiles with rifles and ammunition for more extended resistance when the ship's engine was reversed and she moved away. Some 72 of the disturbers were afterwards indicted for murder, but an acquittal in the first test case resulted in many releases.

Another example of hurried defense was in a city in one of the Dakotas where the citizens sawed up billiard cues into billies and proceeded to knock on the head, and drag off to prison, the street orators who persisted in violating the city ordinance. Many of these men, as one of the deputies later told me, were arrested without evidence, and the public authorities thereafter felt it necessary to convict them by any means whatsoever in order to justify their imprisonment.

In San Diego men speaking on forbidden corners were seized by vigilance committees of masked citizens and deported to the desert, where they were all ill-treated and warned never to return.

These methods of border justice menace the rights of all. But who is to blame, the apostles of disorder or the lawless defenders of the peace? As we review these incidents today, there was culpability on both sides.

Not only the I.W.W. but other trade unions have provoked such disorders. The strike in the Calumet & Hecla mines, fomented by the Western Federation of Miners in 1913, became a battle between law and anarchy, between the union and society. Violence openly ruled until the troops came and guerrilla methods followed. A deputy sheriff was slain on the highway, dynamite was exploded, and three nonunion men were murdered in bed on a Sunday morning. The restoration of civil order became a necessity. Only 100 soldiers were present in the district at this time. Government had collapsed and a private society had to rush to its assistance. Of this necessity was born a Citizens' Alliance, some 30,000 strong, and with its advent disorder rapidly diminished. Then came a great calamity. In Calumet a Christmas tree party was being given for the children of the workers when someone started a false cry of fire. About 80 people, chiefly children, were killed in the panic that followed. Moyer, the president of the union, wired rumors throughout the country that the mad rush was deliberately inspired by the Citizens' Alliance, and commanded the families of the victims not to accept a penny of the 30,000-dollar relief fund which was promptly raised. This capitalization of such a calamity first stunned the people, and then so incensed them that Moyer was summarily deported to Chicago without regard to law. There is no secrecy about this deportation. People boast of it today. "There may come a time in any community when the machinery of the law is too cumbersome to meet exigencies," explained a Detroit newspaper, which found that "the proceeding differed in no particular from that which is followed in handling undesirables the country over." [17]

San Francisco, that notorious closed-shop city, had long been waiting for *der Tag*, and in 1916 it came. The city's markets had been closed to some open-shop products, and so restrictive were union rules that its industries stood stagnant while those of other cities leaped ahead. A certain percentage on all brick contracts had to be paid into the union treasury. Policemen turned their backs when a scab was assaulted.

The unions at last threw the proverbial straw on the already overburdened back of the community. In May, 1916, the long-shoremen's union, which to a large extent controlled the commerce of the port, announced a strike for June 1st in violation of its written agreement. A telegram of protest from William B. Wilson, Secretary of Labor and a former officer of the United Mine Workers, was of no avail and the strike took place. Violence reigned and commerce was throttled. In June alone, it was estimated, two and one-half million dollars of imports were held up, and in about the same time nearly 50 men were sent to hospitals because of injuries from assaults. Only those who received permits from the union were permitted to pass the picket line to the wharves; and when the government desired to obtain U. S. Treasury funds it was necessary to secure such a permit, signed by the union president.

In total disregard of federal laws the union boldly proposed to interfere with the shipping of commodities which were classed as nonunion or unfair, in order to fasten closed-shop conditions not only upon the port of San Francisco but upon the entire Pacific Coast. Sugar landed on the docks was refused unloading because somewhere on its journey it had been handled by nonunion men. A shipment of shingles was embargoed because the shingles had been made in an open shop. Although information about this illegal scheme was formally transmitted to two members of the cabinet at Washington, and although the situation was legally identical with that which President Cleveland so promptly met in 1894, nothing was done by the government.

At this point the Chamber of Commerce of San Francisco determined to take a hand and adopted resolutions insisting upon integrity of contracts, the maintenance of law and order, and the open shop. Again a private society had to rush to the assistance of tottering authority. Within a short time the Chamber added 5000 new members, making it the largest Chamber of Commerce in the United States, and established a million-dollar fund for the fight.

On July 22 the "Preparedness Parade" was interrupted by the explosion of a bomb that killed ten and injured 50 people, most of whom were guests of the city. Men connected with organized labor were held responsible. This was a bugle call. Under the auspices of the Law and Order Committee of the Chamber of Commerce, 6000 men and women met at the Civic Auditorium to take part in the re-establishment of law and decency. The citizens took swift action. Eighty-seven injunction suits, started at one time, swept disorderly picketing from the streets, and damage suits and criminal prosecutions taught the primary lessons of law and order. Then came the political campaign for the enactment of an antipicketing ordinance to be voted on at the November elections. Four hundred telephone girls were employed in a single office to telephone every man and woman in the city who could be so reached and urge them to vote for this ordinance. The correspondence and circulation of propaganda surpasses belief. When the vote was counted it was found that the city had declared against picketing by a majority of 5000.

Struggles like that of San Francisco—political, social, and industrial—were kept alive by the agitators of opposing organizations and played a large part in the life of a number of cities during this period.

This poison of class conflict, this exaggeration of class interests, and the selfish rivalry for municipal and state control invaded the question of national preparedness. Some of our military companies were treated as private clubs, and this excited the suspicions of organized labor. The *Labor Review,* which was the official organ of the Trades and Labor Assembly, and the Building Trades Council of Minneapolis announced in April, 1916, that "the Assembly has not been misled into entering the preparedness campaign of the few millionaires who own this country," and that it was organizing "a citizens army"[18] to resist the companies formed by the property-owning classes. Two weeks later, the same paper, telling of the members' response, continued:

They seem to realize that no one could tell how soon the class struggle would become a matter of guns in the United States, as it already has in Ireland.[19]

The *Review* told of labor's plans for organizing an army, its steps towards the purchase of 1000 rifles and 1000 rounds of ammunition, and proceeded thereafter to advertise evening drills. This step was called "the beginning of Labor's third trench in Minneapolis."

Mr. James H. Maurer, president of the Pennsylvania State Federation of Labor, speaking in a public school in New York City, referred slightingly to the flag and declared:

I will never shed a drop of my blood, nor will I counsel the representatives of labor to shed theirs, unless I am certain that by so doing they are shedding their blood in the battles of their own class.[20]

As already pointed out in Chapter IV, the Baltimore convention of the American Federation of Labor held in November, 1916, went on record declaring that all judges who issued injunctions in labor cases should be impeached and that their orders should be defied and wholly disregarded, "let the consequences be what they may."

The implications of this action of the convention of the Federation were serious. Congress had refused to change the law and the people had refused to amend the Constitution but judges were to be impeached or defied for enforcing the law as unchanged. This convention was no secret meeting, no action of a few mad anarchists. Here were several hundred men, representing two million skilled and high-class workers, not merely asking for a change in the laws or the Constitution but publicly and deliberately adopting a program of concerted resistance to law.

The threatened railroad strike of 1916, which involved a union demand for an eight-hour day, gives another example of the prevailing labor psychology of that decade. Such a strike as was contemplated would be a devastating blow to society, yet the railroad unions, supported by the American Federation of Labor, declined arbitration and declared for a general suspension. They said that in all society it was not possible "to get neutral arbitrators"[21] and that they preferred "to trust their claims to the results of economic action."[22] President Wilson intervened and sought arbitration but to no avail. A strike was scheduled for Monday, September 4.

On the President's urgency a bill that would require the eight-hour day for a trial period during which a commission could study its consequences had been presented in Congress. The House passed the bill and finally at 6 P.M. on Saturday, September 2, the Senate did likewise. Even then the unions would not consent to call off the strike until the President signed the bill. With Secretary of Labor Wilson acting as his personal messenger, the President pledged his word to sign the bill and the strike was called off. On Sunday evening the President signed the bill, and fearing some question as to the validity of such a Sabbath-day act, he signed it again the following Tuesday. Only precipitancy by government saved the day. The unions held the whip hand.

Even after this crisis had passed and the unions had won, a representative of the trainmen, referring to the strike order, declared before a committee of Congress, "I wish to God . . . I never had recalled it." [23]

On another occasion Mr. Gompers, speaking for the Federation upon proposed legislation restricting strikes on public utilities, declared that "law or no law, President or no President, such a law would not be obeyed." [24] Under conditions such as these, is it strange that President Wilson should have felt the necessity of saying: "The business of government is to see that no other organization is as strong as itself; to see that no body or group of men, no matter what their private interest is, may come into competition with the authority of society." [25]

This spirit of defiance again reared its head in Bridgeport at a time when the manufacturers of that city were producing most of the small arms for World War I. Wage increases were demanded and strikes were threatened. The War Labor Board was hurried to Bridgeport to stave off the emergency. Everything happened quickly and no one was prepared. Representing the manufacturers, I advanced the proposition that wartime was not an occasion for social reforms but that wages should keep pace with the increased cost of living. I pointed out that there were about 110 different manufacturers involved in this dispute and that we had a fleet of accountants in the field gathering the figures that we would integrate into an over-all picture, but that we needed a week's adjournment to do this. Whereupon I noted a commotion among the assembled crowd and that a note was being passed up to the union spokesman. He read it: "If the Board grants the adjournment the men will go out on strike." The government surrendered and announced that it would appoint an examiner to

commence hearings the following day. When the award granting increases thought to be inadequate came down, a new revolt
started and President Wilson announced in effect that those who
went on strike would be routed to the trenches. That ended that
batch of strikes.

After the upset of the coal and railroad strikes in 1922, there
was comparative quiet, with the exception of a bituminous strike
in 1927, for a period of over ten years when labor legislation
granting immunities to labor was completed. The next wave of
trouble found its principal outburst in 1937.

The Sitdown Strikes

Although the total number of strikers set no record, there were
more strikes in 1937 than in any year in the nation's history [26]
down to that time. This was due in part to the rapid growth of
the trade union movement and the unions' consciousness of increased power. The passage of the N.L.R.A. in 1935, and more
especially the decisions of the Supreme Court in 1937, assured
hitherto unorganized workers of their right to swell the ranks of
organized labor without fear of discrimination and gave fresh confidence and courage. The very nature of the sitdown strike as a
new form of protest gave another outlet to suppressed feelings.
It enabled groups of dissatisfied workers, who were frequently
not even organized into unions, spontaneously to call strikes without much formal organization or preparation, and sometimes without guidance from trade union officials. It gave a new and satisfying sense of power.

The sitdown fever really began in 1936 but did not reach its
peak until 1937. In the earlier year there were 48 such strikes
out of a total of 2172 strikes of all types. In 1937 there were
477 out of a total of 4740. Nearly 400,000 employees were involved, although all of them did not stay in the plants. In March
alone 167,210 were involved in 170 sitdowns. The record length
of time was set by a sitdown of 100 workers in a New York cigar
factory from April to September. Both C.I.O and A. F. of L.
unions were heavily involved in these strikes. In 55 instances no
union was involved and in a few cases the protest was merely
against a rival union. Apparently the industrial atmosphere was
ripe for such an epidemic.

The most widely known of the sitdowns involved the General

Motors Corporation. On December 21, 1936, Homer Martin, president of the United Auto Workers, wrote to General Motors giving a list of grievances and asking for a conference to consider them. The conference was held on December 22nd, and William S. Knudsen, executive vice president of the corporation, informed the labor representatives that their demands should be taken up with individual plant managers.[27]

Between December 28 and 31 sitdown strikes were put into effect in several General Motors plants. Correspondence continued between the union and corporation officials, and the year ended with the strikers still sitting down in the plants.

On January 2, 1937, Judge Edward D. Black of the Circuit Court at Flint, on application of General Motors, issued an injunction ordering the strikers to leave the plant. Sheriff Thomas Wolcott ordered the evacuation of the plant, giving the strikers half an hour to leave. When they refused, the sheriff made no attempt to enforce the court order. On January 3, 1937, a union board of strategy was formed at Flint empowered to call strikes in all General Motors plants. On January 7 Governor Frank Murphy entered the picture as a mediator.

On January 11 the strikers in one of the plants, known as Fisher 2, thought they were to be ousted. The police assembled for a battle that lasted for seven hours; a tear gas shell was exploded in the plant by the police, but the strikers built a barricade of autos and held their ground. On the third rush the police fired and 14 strikers were wounded. More than 40 persons including policemen and sheriffs' officers were shot, beaten, or gassed in the prolonged rioting before this plant and some of the Chevrolet plants. The next day when the militia massed at Flint, the Fleetwood plant went on strike. From Washington, John Lewis announced that the auto strikers would have full support of the C.I.O.

Following an investigation of the rioting, some 21 warrants were issued by the prosecuting attorney of Genesee County, Michigan, charging some of the rioters with unlawful assembly and malicious destruction of property. Among these rioters were 14 who had been injured. Following a conference with Governor Murphy, the prosecutor announced that he was dropping charges against the 14 "in view of Governor Murphy's wishes and explicit request."

On January 15 Governor Murphy met with representatives of

the union and General Motors at Lansing, where after 17 hours of discussion an agreement was reached whereby the union would evacuate all plants and the company would not resume operations. To restate this amazing agreement of the Governor: It provided that the union would surrender the properties to their rightful owner on condition that the owner would not utilize them for the purposes for which they were erected. The union also agreed to waive its demand that it be made the exclusive bargaining agency. Following this Lansing agreement, the strikers left the Guide Lamp plant in Anderson and the Cadillac and Fleetwood plants in Detroit.

Then came the hitch. It was announced by the Flint Alliance, the organization of employees behind a back-to-work movement, that General Motors would deal with it. Informed of this, the union refused to evacuate Fisher 1 and Fisher 2 in Flint, and lawlessness flared again. The conferees met on January 18th but separated without results, and Governor Murphy went to Washington, presumably to see President Roosevelt.

Miss Frances Perkins, Secretary of Labor, endeavored to arrange a conference between Mr. Sloan, president of General Motors, and John L. Lewis and officers of the U.A.W., but Mr. Sloan refused to attend.

On January 27, when General Motors refused to negotiate while the unions had possession of their plants, Miss Perkins announced, "The American people do not expect them to sulk in their tents because they feel the sitdown strike is illegal. There was a time when picketing was considered illegal and before that strikes of any kind were illegal. The legality of the sitdown strike has yet to be determined." [28] This statement was certainly no discouragement to men who by violence seized the property of others and no encouragement to the strikers to end their unlawful seizure.

Governor Murphy informed General Motors on February 1 that he was authorized by the President of the United States to make a request that the corporation enter into negotiations with the C.I.O. committee, irrespective of the fact that that corporation's property was still occupied by sitdown strikers. Meanwhile on the afternoon of February 1 another serious riot brought injury to many and resulted in the seizure of the No. 4 plant of the Chevrolet division, despite the fact that more than 2500 National

Guardsmen were on duty in Flint, only a few miles from the scene of the bloodshed.

More than 25 persons were injured, two of them seriously, during the rioting, and another General Motors plant was in the possession of the strikers. The National Guard acted quickly. During the night it moved into the Chevrolet plant area and evicted all spectators, but made no move to oust those who had taken over the plant.

Aroused by the defiance of law and order, the Michigan Sheriffs' Association notified Sheriff Thomas Wolcott of Genesee County that the services of 1300 deputies were at his disposal in helping him to carry out the court's orders. This action was taken when the sheriff made it known that he had pleaded with the Governor for the use of state police or the National Guard during the rioting but had been refused assistance.

On February 2 Judge Paul V. Gadola issued an injunction at Flint giving the strikers 24 hours to leave the General Motors plants on penalty of a $15,000 fine. On February 5th Sheriff Wolcott received the court orders for the eviction of the sitdown strikers but, on reading it to the strikers, was met by boos and catcalls. The sheriff was unwilling to attempt forcibly to eject the strikers without the aid of the National Guard, but the Governor would not act. Fearing bloodshed, the Governor ordered the Guard, which had been on duty in Flint since early in the strike, to stand by.[29]

On February 11 a tentative agreement was reached, and on March 12 a final agreement was signed by U.A.W.A. and General Motors. Under this agreement the United Auto Workers was recognized by General Motors as the collective-bargaining agency for those employees who were members of the union.[30] The sitdowns were over by capitulation and not by triumph of law and order.

The scene now shifts to Philadelphia. What happened to the Apex Hosiery Company in that city can be told with a great degree of incontrovertibility, because the facts were judicially determined by the United States Circuit Court of Appeals and the Supreme Court of the United States. In April, 1937, the American Federation of Full Fashioned Hosiery Workers, Local No. 706, demanded that the company consent to a closed shop, although only eight of its 2500 employees were members of that union. The demand was rejected.

The relations of the parties at that time were described in detail by the United States Circuit Court of Appeals in a suit against the union and Leader, its president:

> The plaintiff has earnestly and persistently tried to negotiate with Leader for a settlement of this so-called strike and has offered to comply with any requirement except sign an agreement for a closed shop. This is practically all that was demanded of him, for there has never been any complaint as to wages, working hours, or conditions, or the treatment of employees.
>
> There was no strike or difficulty of any kind at the plaintiff's plant. Its payroll was about $70,000 per week and it did an annual business of approximately $5,000,000. There was a peaceful situation in this plant in which everybody was satisfied. The plaintiff alleges, without contradiction, that it was paying the highest wages and had the best and most desirable working conditions in the entire industry. No complaint of any kind was made by a single employee.[31]

On May 6 the management, having been informed that the union had called out all its members in union shops in Philadelphia in order to make a demonstration, sent home all of the Apex employees except about 60, consisting of the office and maintenance force and some foremen. The mob gathered, some 10,000 strong, and when the president of the local again demanded the closed shop and management again refused, President Leader shouted, "I declare a sitdown strike in Apex Hosiery Company!" Then followed the attack as described by the same court:

> . . . Immediately a volley of bricks, stones, and pipe was thrown through the windows, breaking practically every pane of glass; the sash were broken out and some of Leader's crowd were "tossed in" through the windows; the front door was battered down, and amid "the noise and yelling and crying and cursing and everything else that you can imagine" the crowd rushed in, broke down partitions, dumped out files, threw adding machines and typewriters around, and smashed up things generally. "Everything was overturned in the office, the offices were complete shambles, typewriters were broken, adding machines were wrecked, first floor mimeograph machines, everything was wrecked on the first floor." The Apex employees sought refuge in the wareroom to keep from being struck with bricks and to avoid bodily harm, but they were crowded out of there and finally forced up to the sixth floor. Meyer (company president) was struck on the shoulder with a brick and hit on the back of the head with an inkwell which caused "a tremendous swelling."[32]

Mr. Meyer, being backed up against the wall, shouted, "For God's sake, isn't there anybody around here who can stop this horrible situation!" And somebody responded, "Go get Bill Leader." Leader appeared with his committee, and again Mr. Meyer refused to sign the closed-shop agreement. The mob then again violently attacked the loyal employees; some of them were seriously injured and others were knocked down and beaten and kicked after they were down.

And now I let the Supreme Court of the United States tell the story:

The locks on all gates and entrances of petitioner's plant were changed; only strikers were given keys. No others were allowed to leave or enter the plant without permission of the strikers. During the period of their occupancy, the union supplied them with food, blankets, cots, medical care, and paid them strike benefits. While occupying the factory, the strikers wilfully wrecked machinery of great value, and did extensive damage to other property and equipment of the company. All manufacturing operations by petitioner ceased on May 6th. As the result of the destruction of the company's machinery and plant, it did not resume even partial manufacturing operations until August 19, 1937. The record discloses a lawless invasion of petitioner's plant and destruction of its property by force and violence of the most brutal and wanton character, under leadership and direction of respondents, and without interference by the local authorities.

For more than three months, by reason of respondents' acts, manufacture was suspended at petitioner's plant and the flow of petitioner's product into interstate commerce was stopped. When the plant was seized there were on hand 130,000 dozen pairs of finished hosiery, of a value of about $80,000, ready for shipment on unfilled orders, 80 per cent. of which were to be shipped to points outside the state. Shipment was prevented by the occupation of the factory by the strikers. Three times in the course of the strike respondents refused requests made by petitioner to be allowed to remove the merchandise for the purpose of shipment in filling the orders.[33]

On June 21 the United States Circuit Court of Appeals issued an order enjoining the defendants and requiring them to vacate the property. On June 23 the company regained possession of its factory.

The company brought suit for treble damages under the anti-trust law and secured a judgment of $711,932.55, which later was reversed by the Court of Appeals and the Supreme Court, on the ground that the disturbance was merely a local riot over which

the federal courts had no jurisdiction and that the effect on interstate commerce was purely incidental. A suit later started in the
state court resulted in a settlement, of which $125,000 was paid
by the union and $25,000 contributed by the city for its failure
to grant protection. So far as I am informed, there was no step
taken by the A. F. of L. or the international union to discipline or
punish Leader or the other moving spirits in this outrage.

Here was an assault as unprovoked as the dynamiting conspiracy
of 1910. The purpose in each case was identical: establishment
of the closed shop through violence. In the Apex incident, however, thousands of union men responded to the call to violence.
This is the question I ask myself: What is on the minds of the
workers that they should do this? How far have the vitriolic attacks on employers taken root and in how many industries and
localities must we be ever ready to "reap the whirlwind?"

Outstanding approval of this tolerance of organized violence is
furnished by Miss Frances Perkins, who in her book, *The Roosevelt I Knew*, includes this:

> The opposition of the public to the sit-down strikes was great, and they
> undoubtedly did a great deal to set public opinion against the automobile
> workers and the CIO. But the employers took a very intransigent attitude.
> They would not talk with a workers' committee until the strikers were out
> of the factory, and they continued to hold that position. No matter what
> happened, they would not give way on that. I never could see why
> employers should be so *stuffy* about it—Roosevelt agreed with me.[34]

This all adds up to the philosophy I have been discussing: Miss
Perkins and Mr. Roosevelt believed that employers should negotiate the terms under which they would regain their property. I
believe there should be no negotiations until the fruits of illegality
are surrendered. I do not believe in sanctioning violence as a
means of attaining social justice in the field of labor relations.

In the same book Secretary Perkins quotes President Roosevelt
on the sitdown strikes as follows:

> Well it is illegal but what law are they breaking. The law of trespass,
> and that is about the only law that could be invoked. And what do you
> do when a man trespasses on your property? Sure you order him off.
> You get the sheriff to order him off if he tries to pitch a tent in your field
> without your permission. If he comes on your place to steal, why, you
> have him for theft, of course. But shooting it out and killing a lot of
> people because they have violated the law of trespass somehow offends me.
> I just don't see that as the answer.[35]

The inappositeness of this statement is provoking. This was not a mere case of trespass. It started with a trespass and a violent seizure of another person's property, but in Michigan when the sheriff appeared with a court order to possess the property for the owners, he was defied and the chief executives of the nation and the state condoned the defiance. No one advocates "shooting it out" for any cause except as a last resort, but all except pacifists believe it is sometimes necessary at least to make a show of governmental force if order, national or international, is to be maintained. When men seize other people's property and defy the officers of the law and the law enforcement officers frown only upon the victims, "this bodes some strange eruption to our State."

The official publications of the C.I.O. give their own interpretation of the facts. In one place it is said "A sit-down strike swept the General Motors empire. Finally in 1937 the corporation yielded and another open-shop citadel had fallen." And again we find this statement, "From 1935 to 1940 thousands of workers in industrial unions braved clubs, tear gas and machine guns to build your CIO." [36]

It was not until February, 1939, in the case of the Fansteel Metallurgical Corporation, that the Supreme Court of the United States dealt specifically with the legal status of sitdowns. In that case the union had taken possession of the factory. On February 19 when the strikers were confronted with an injunction from the state court requiring them to surrender the premises, "a pitched battle ensued and the men successfully resisted the attempt by the sheriff to evict and arrest them. . . . " On February 26 the sheriff with an increased force of deputies made a further attempt and this time, after another battle, the men were ousted and placed under arrest. Most of them were eventually fined and given jail sentences for violating the injunction.[37]

Concerning the sitdown the Supreme Court said:

The seizure and holding of the buildings was itself a wrong apart from any acts of sabotage. But in its legal aspect the ousting of the owner from lawful possession is not essentially different from an assault upon the officers of an employing company, or the seizure and conversion of its goods, or the despoiling of its property or other unlawful acts in order to force compliance with demands. To justify such conduct because of the existence of a labor dispute or of an unfair labor practice would be to put a premium on resort to force instead of legal remedies and to subvert the principles of law and order which lie at the foundations of society.[38]

The most significant thing about the sitdown strikes, and particularly those in Michigan and Philadelphia, was the condonation extended them from President Roosevelt, Governor Murphy of Michigan and Secretary of Labor Perkins, and the complete collapse of governmental effort to maintain law and order or even to prevent defiance of court decrees. As an aftermath, President Roosevelt appointed Governor Murphy as Attorney General of the United States, the highest law-enforcement office in the country, and later elevated him to the Supreme Court of the United States.

The public reaction to these developments is important: Few people seemed adequately shocked, and unions must have begun to realize the extent of the immunities they enjoyed. On the other hand, the General Motors Corporation would not have been unionized in 1937 except for the collapse of government and the tacit sanction given to organized violence. From this point let the moralist and the social reformer take up the debate. The seizure of the factories by the workers in Italy in 1920 eventually led to less desirable results.

Other lawlessness in outstanding strikes was so common in 1937 that I can only take a few outstanding samples to portray its inexorable path. The details of the battle between police, National Guardsmen, and strikers in the little steel strikes in the middle of 1937—including the Republic Steel battle on May 30, 1937, where 16 workers were killed—I will not pause to recount. Let me comment, however, that these strikes are further evidence of the outstanding fact that a back-to-work movement in any large strike inevitably leads to violence, since the strikers feel that they own these jobs from which they have derived their livelihood. Accepting the inevitability of violence the Governor of Pennsylvania ordered one steel plant to close and the President requested Ohio steel plants to postpone their scheduled reopening, while the Governor of Ohio declared martial law. Organized violence was having a field day.

"But" interjects someone, "this is all past history. Why talk about it? There is better understanding now." That is just the question that thoughtful people are pondering and more recent events, which I will now review, do not permit us to dismiss the problem with complacency.

1946

As 1946 is not ancient history, let us see what happened in that year, which bears the flavor of resistance to the existing order rather than a lawful test of economic strength. According to the Bureau of Labor Statistics, more than 4,650,000 workmen were involved in strikes that year—the largest number in any year in American history, the previous peak being 4,160,438 in 1919. In analyzing this 1946 unrest, let us first examine the extent of general protest strikes against society and then the extent to which organized violence prevailed in the usual economic strikes.

In Pittsburgh an injunction secured by the Duquesne Power & Light Company against the United Electrical Workers, a C.I.O. union, led to a threat of a general strike in Pittsburgh, with the result that the injunction was withdrawn on September 26, 1946, because of that threat. That was a threatened strike against law and order—that was government by strike.

In Stamford, Connecticut, where some 3000 machinists of the Yale & Towne Company had been on strike for many weeks, a general strike of 12,000 workers tied up the city's industry on January 3, 1946, as a protest against the use of state police in breaking up the picket lines. That was a strike against law enforcement.

In Lancaster, Pennsylvania, where a strike against the Conestoga Transportation Company had been in existence since February 5, 1946, a general strike was called on February 18th by the Lancaster Central Labor Union. It involved some 12,000 members of 23 affiliated unions, which threw picket lines around bus stations and industrial plants and stopped all transportation. This general strike was ended only when 200 bus and trolleymen, members of the Street & Electrical Railway Employees (A. F. of L.), won their demands.

In Houston, Texas, where city employees had been on strike since about the middle of February, 1946, for an increase of wages that had been refused by the city council, the Central Trades Council (A. F. of L.) called a general strike on March 4th supported by all A. F. of L. and C.I.O. unions. The city yielded to this mass protest and appointed a committee to consider pay increases.

In Rochester, New York, on May 15 about 500 city jobs had

been abolished and union workers dismissed. In protest the A. F. of L. and C.I.O. unions called a general strike on May 28, 1946, which brought out upwards of 30,000 workers and tied up the city completely except for emergency services. The city yielded on the following day by re-establishing the abolished jobs and granted the right of city employees to join any organization that did not claim the right to strike against the public. The strike was then called off on May 29.

In Hartford, Connecticut, where strikes had been continuing for many weeks against Niles-Bement-Pond Company and the United Aircraft Corporation, a one-day general strike of 13,000 workers was called on July 23 to demonstrate their loyalty to the original strikers.

In Camden, New Jersey, a strike of 25,000 workers was called on November 22 in support of the striking employees of the Camden *Courier-Post* and as a protest against police brutality and restrictions on mass picketing. Restrictions on the number of pickets were removed as a result of this protest.

In Oakland, California, a work stoppage was called on December 3, 1946, as a protest against police action in connection with strikes that had been going on for about a month at Kahn's and Hastings' department stores. One hundred thousand employees responded and tied up all transportation and industry and closed all restaurants for two days. The retail clerks' union then reached an agreement with city authorities as to the future conduct of the police.

This list of such community strikes in 1946 is not supposed to be exhaustive. There may have been others. In every instance cited except Hartford and Stamford, where the strike was for one day only and automatically ended, the community surrendered. All these protesting groups were in effect informed that they had everything to gain by such protests.

In April, 1947, the A. F. of L. and the C.I.O. in Iowa joined in organizing a state-wide political strike of 100,000 workers as a one-day demonstration against labor legislation then pending in the state legislature. In June, 1947, 200,000 miners in the bituminous coal fields joined in a protest strike over the passage by Congress of the Taft-Hartley Act.

A national maritime tie-up in the fall of 1946 was the result of a strike by one of 17 maritime unions against an order of the National Wage Stabilization Board. This is not the only protest strike that lies at the door of the maritime unions.

In these political strikes, which were scattered throughout the country, the unions involved were deserting the democratic ideal and were drifting toward the European practice of trying to intimidate the government or society with which they were dissatisfied.

Without leaving 1946, the great strike year, let us now see how government handled the problem of maintaining civil order around strikebound factories. What actually took place in connection with the major economic strikes in 1946 has a curious analogy to the sitdown tactics of 1936 and 1937. In 1946 instead of taking forcible possession of the factories and thus excluding management from its property, as was the case with the sitdowns of 1937, the unions established solid phalanxes of pickets that excluded management. In both cases the rightful owners were kept out of their plants.

Because local police, sheriffs, and governors were unable or unwilling to protect management and its nonstriking employees in their right of access to the plants, it was necessary in many states to secure injunctions, which could only issue on proof of such inability or unwillingness. In these cases the burden of law enforcement often shifted from the executive to the judicial branch of the government.

The first nationwide strike of the United Steel Workers, involving some 750,000 workers in 30 states, started January 21, 1946. The union informed the Carnegie-Illinois Steel Corporation that after January 26, 1946, the pickets would not permit access to the plant, even to allow personnel to perform essential maintenance work. Superintendents of plants were forcibly detained and threatened with loss of their lives. Finally the union declared that it "had decided that no supervision below the level of department superintendent would be admitted to the plant and that the agreement . . . permitting free access to and from the plant by all supervisors was at an end." [39]

To make union control effective, 100 to 200 pickets, standing three deep, blocked all entrances. A few brave spirits who tried to pass were detained and later released. The facts being undisputed, the Supreme Court of Pennsylvania, which sustained an injunction, ruled that:

> Forcibly to deny an owner of property or his agents and employees access to the property for the purpose of protecting and maintaining it and its equipment or for any other legitimate purpose is in practical and legal effect a seizure or holding of that property.[40]

In the case of the S.K.F. Industries, employers of several thousand workers in Philadelphia, a strike was called in the latter part of 1945 by the United Steel Workers of America in violation of agreement. The alleged grievance, the transfer of a single employee, was one that both parties were obliged to arbitrate under the collective bargaining agreement. Issues broadened after the strike was called. For six weeks mass violence and physical obstruction kept officials and salaried employees from the plant. The vice president and general counsel of the company attempted without avail to enter the plant grounds in his automobile in the ordinary course of business, but mobs gathered around him. An American flag was laid on the ground in front of his car, and the men on one side of it started to turn the car over, so that he had no alternative but to retreat. Day after day these mobs gathered and prevented access to the plant. When I entered a cab at the railroad station and asked to be taken to the plant, the driver refused for fear of attack. An injunction, issued after exasperating delays, finally brought this anarchistic condition to an end.

The Mergenthaler Linotype Corporation of Brooklyn was also held in a state of siege and was obliged to open offices elsewhere for its officers and certain administrative workers. Like experiences were taking place in other cities. In October, 1945, the plants of the Timken Roller Bearing Company were shut down by a strike of 8200 employees in Canton, Ohio. This strike was conducted by the steel workers' union in violation of agreement. Company officers and directors, as well as office and maintenance employees, were barred from the plant by picket walls. The mayor of the city, instead of enforcing order, issued an open letter urging the company to agree with the union as to the names of company officers and employees who should be permitted by the union to enter the plant. Whereupon the company asked him, "Are we to understand that any employee not included on the proposed list would be denied any protection by the city police and would be subject to any violence which the union wishes to inflict on him?"[41]

To continue this survey, I summon Senator Joseph H. Ball as my witness. In a statement that appeared in *The New York Times* for October 28, 1945, he states:

I know of two instances, one in Toledo, Ohio, and the other in Hamtramck, Mich., where the management of such plants asked the local peace officers for protection for their employees who wanted to work (physical violence is the customary treatment for any individual with sufficient temerity to attempt to push through a mass picket line). In both cases the local mayors refused to act. Appeals to the governors of the two states brought delayed and irrelevant answers, but no action. The employees who wanted to work were prevented from working by clearly illegal means.[42]

In Whiting, Indiana, Governor Ralph F. Gates, confronted with a similar situation, alerted the state guard and informed C.I.O. leaders that unless the mass picket blockade was withdrawn it would be broken up. The pickets were withdrawn but C.I.O. leaders threatened to "get" Governor Gates at the next election as an enemy of labor. To remedy this is not impracticable. When during this same period Governor Martin of Pennsylvania made it clear that the law would be enforced, there was no mass picketing.

The General Electric Company had its difficulties when mass picketing in various cities barred access to its plants. Injunctions were sought to protect operations in Philadelphia, Cleveland, Fort Wayne, Bridgeport, Bloomfield, Pittsfield, Schenectady, Rotterdam, and Glenville. Not all these applications were successful, but in practically every case indisputable evidence showed that a physical barrier of mass pickets prevented access to the plant, and that local and state authorities were unable or unwilling to grant protection. Confronted even with such proof, the courts in some cases laid particular emphasis on the protection of the rights of nonproduction employees, as though production employees were not equally entitled to protection. In Cleveland, for an illustration, when it appeared that 1700 out of a total of 3800 employees were not production employees, the court emphasized the fact that "the company is not now in production" and provided that "if it should resume production for sale" either party might apply to the court for a modification of the order.[43]

In Philadelphia, where the General Electric Company had its worst difficulties, the strike started in violation of agreement. An

injunction was sought in the Court of Common Pleas and in March
the court found that massed pickets prevented all access and commented on the union claim that no one should be allowed to enter
the plant without a union pass:

> It is curious that the union officers seemed to think it meritorious on
> their part that they should give a pass, and do not recognize the arrogance
> and illegality in their demand that a pass should be needed. . . . The
> effect . . . was to lock the buildings against their owners and their
> employees.[44]

A union representative declared that anyone trying to enter the
plant without a pass "might suffer such serious bodily harm as
would cause them to be taken to the hospital."[45] The highest
management official of the plant was kept out. Trucks with fuel
were barred.

An injunction was issued late in February prohibiting mass
picketing and three days later the union organized a mass picket
line of 800 men in defiance of the order. The riot act, "disperse
yourselves and peaceably depart," was twice read, but without
avail. One thousand policemen then undertook to disperse the
pickets, and many heads were broken. The headlines of Philadelphia editorials reflected this. The Philadelphia *Inquirer* wrote
"Jail Law-Breaking Union Bosses"; the Philadelphia *Record:*
"There's Only One Answer to Defiance of the Law"; the *Evening
Bulletin:* "Unwise Labor Tactics." "The spectacle of mass defiance of a judicial determination is a disturbing one in an orderly
American community."

A substantial number of those riot leaders were arrested on
criminal charges and later tried but not convicted.

The Westinghouse Electric Corporation had a similar experience in Pittsburgh early in 1946. The union took possession of
the field and would not permit anyone, not even the manager of
one of the divisions, to enter the factories without a union pass.
A nurse of the medical department, a patent attorney, a research
engineer, a director of research, supervisors, and foremen were
all barred from entering because they had no union pass. Force,
violence, and mass picketing were resorted to when necessary, and
thousands of employees who were ready to report to work were
prevented.

In a proceeding under a Pennsylvania statute of 1939, which
allowed injunctions where there was an illegal seizure of a factory,

the union offered no denials of its illegal conduct but relied upon its contention that this conduct was not the equivalent of holding or seizing a plant. The Supreme Court of Pennsylvania disagreed with this contention and said:

Would defendants deny that, if they locked and bolted all the entrance doors and thereby prevented ingress and egress, such action would constitute a seizure and holding of the plant within the normal connotation of those terms and therefore within the meaning of the statute? But what difference is there between such a method of seizure and that of holding the gateway closed, not by mechanical devices but by a chain of human beings stretched across those gateways and thereby even the more effectively preventing access to the property and its use by the rightful owner? [46]

In this case the American Federation of Labor, Congress of Industrial Organizations, United Steel Workers of America (C.I.O.), United Railroad Workers of America (C.I.O.), United Mine Workers of America, Amalgamated Clothing Workers of America (C.I.O.), Textile Workers Union of America (C.I.O.), Industrial Union Marine & Shipbuilding Workers of America (C.I.O.), Transport Workers of America (C.I.O.), United Furniture Workers of America (C.I.O.), united in having their battery of lawyers seek to defeat this effort of the Westinghouse Corporation to regain access to its plant.

Early in November, 1945, the International Association of Machinists, traditionally an A. F. of L. union, instituted a strike at the Stamford plant of the Yale & Towne Manufacturing Company, where over 3000 people were employed. The strike lasted about 150 days and was settled early in April, 1946. During the entire period violence and obstruction, through mass picketing and other means, was actually or potentially present. For a long time access to the plant was denied to the president, general manager, and other representatives of the management, with the local police remaining passive.[47]

In the latter part of December the situation was out of hand and Governor Baldwin ordered the state police to assist in maintaining order. Whereupon, the C.I.O. and A. F. of L. joint committee, misrepresenting this action as an interference with peaceful picketing, wired the governor requesting the withdrawal of the state police because "we are fearful that failure on your part to do this will result in a united action on the part of labor in Stamford which will have national repercussions."[48] On January 3, 1946, as already stated, a general strike involving about 10,000 workers was called but continued for only half a day.[49]

An editorial in *The New York Times* for January 4 mildly describes the picture I am presenting:

> No realistic discussion of the present labor crisis can overlook the question of law enforcement in the states and localities. The situation yesterday at Stamford, where a general strike was called against ordinary law enforcement—that is against an attempt to permit people who wish to do so peacefully to enter and leave the plants of the Yale & Towne Manufacturing Company—illustrates the chaotic situation into which opinion on issues connected with labor problems has been allowed to drift.[50]

The General Motors strike, finally settled in March, 1946, involved the United Automobile Workers of America. It followed the same pattern of mass picketing, violence, and intimidation to bar access to many plants. Twenty-one injunction suits were instituted in courts of various cities in order to protect salaried nonproductive employees in their right to enter some 30 different plants. In two instances there were no employees involved except salaried employees who were not represented by the union. In a number of instances there appeared this distinction between the rights of officers and salaried employees and the rights of production employees who were eligible to union membership, which meant by implication that physical obstruction of production employees would be tolerated. The details of the violence, with assaults, property damage, and scuffles with police, and the manner of maintaining the picket wall are all interesting but would add little to my over-all picture.[51]

The rebellious spirit of labor and the established practice of resorting to organized violence whenever an attempt is made to resume operations in any large strike-bound plant, are illustrated here by strikes of the communist-ridden United Electrical and Radio Workers; the United Automobile Workers of the C.I.O., the largest union in the country; the United Steel Workers of the C.I.O., the second largest; and the International Association of Machinists, traditionally A. F. of L. but at times independent. Their activities are not confined to one state. As these instances could be multiplied, I do not think it unfair to conclude that they represent what is almost certain to happen in connection with strikes where nonstrikers try to work. What happened in 1949, when the union put up bail of nearly $400,000 during the Bell

Aircraft Company strike in Buffalo and when limited efforts were made to mine stripping coal during the coal strike, are later instances supporting this conclusion. Nor can the peacefulness of the steel strike of 1949 be regarded as an exception, since the strike-bound plants made no effort to operate. What would have happened if large-scale steel operations had been attempted is just as certain as death and taxes. If collective bargaining is to receive any laurels for the settlement of the steel strike one should remember that it is not the old-fashioned collective bargaining in a private contest between an employer and his employees but a kind of class battle between organized workers and society. Nor can we say that the possibilities of lawlessness if operations were attempted without a settlement did not affect the result.

Weighing the emotional attitudes of union men as cultivated throughout this half-century, it seems fairly safe to assert that public opinion and union opinion are more tolerant of organized violence during industrial combats now than they were at the beginning of the period. The reaction of the press to the lawlessness that characterized the coal strike of 1902 was quite unlike present-day comment on comparable situations. What paper today, in reviewing an arbitration award following violence in a strike, would comment as did the New York *Evening Post* in 1903:

We cannot help feeling a certain incongruity between this clear and high denunciation of the union methods and the practical granting of its demands.[52]

It would also be difficult today to match the utterances of John Mitchell, the labor hero of his day whose name is still honored by an anniversary date in the coal fields, when in 1903 he published these remarks:

Above all and beyond all, the leader entrusted with the conduct of a strike must be alert and vigilant in the prevention of violence. The strikers must be made constantly aware of the imperative necessity of remaining peaceable. . . . Under no circumstances should a strike be allowed to degenerate into violence. . . . No matter how just the demands of the men, no matter how unreasonable and uncompromising the attitude of the employer, the commission of acts of violence invariably puts the strikers in the wrong. . . . A strike or a lockout is coercion, but it is lawful, whereas a resort to physical force is both immoral and unlawful. . . . It is sometimes claimed that no strike can be won without the use of physical force. I do not believe that this is true, but if it is, it is better that the strike be lost than that it succeed through violence and the commission of outrages.[53]

The dynamiting conspiracy of 1910 was dealt with sternly and did not forward the cause of unionism. The lawless sitdowns of 1937 were encouraged by government and, temporarily at least, forwarded the campaign of unionization.

Unconsciously, in the field of labor relations, we seem to be developing a new type of social morality. If a man steals bread he is still regarded as a thief though sympathy and leniency might be extended to him if he were hungry. If a highwayman takes gold at the point of a gun, we do not judge him by the degree of his poverty. Thefts and holdups are looked upon as absolute wrongs not to be condoned or encouraged. Grievances by any type of social rebel are to be remedied by lawful means. This is a fundamental tenet of our social creed and it is supposed to mark progress toward a civilized society.

In the field of labor relations the condemnation of violence is less absolute. Holdups in interstate commerce are made criminal by the federal antiracketeering law, except holdups by labor unions to exact money for services not performed. Violence in labor disputes may only be checked by injunction when the injured party is willing to negotiate and arbitrate the grievances of his assailants.

But more important is the general demotion of law enforcement in labor disputes. If one may judge public sentiment by what appears in the press and magazines and by current performances of public officials, the impulse to condone labor violence and weigh the extent of its justification is quite prevalent. People seem more interested in social justice than in law and order. Thus violence is sanctioned as a ready means of flagging public attention. These bad habits will not cure themselves. The mischiefs of the minorities, if unchecked, develop into the mischiefs of the majorities. Personally, I think that maintenance of law and order should come first on the calendar of social progress and that in this respect conditions are more unwholesome than they were 50 years ago. When society sells out law and order for material gain, the price is "cruel high," and in the end there will be no gain.

Unionism is desirable, but buttressed by preferential laws as it is, it should seek its own promotion without resort to organized lawlessness. It should collaborate with public officials in maintaining order in connection with strikes it is conducting, instead of opposing public officials who perform this duty. Condonation and compromise on this elementary issue are having their moral impact on the entire future of civilization. When employers and government face industrial crises, they assume and expect that any movement on their part to cope with industrial conflict may mean organized violence and that the unions will not ally themselves with the law-enforcement authorities to prevent it. The result is disgraceful lawlessness and arrogant opposition to any form of social control such as we faced in 1947. Certainly the passage of the Taft-Hartley Act in 1947 should have taught labor that extreme misconduct will sometimes lead the public to reject the union desire to be let alone. Capacity for self-correction should be demonstrated before the public will assume its efficacy. Down to the present date it is not characteristic of the labor movement to oppose lawlessness in strikes.

Nor should the unions be surprised at the growth of leftism within their ranks when violence and hostility toward employers and law-enforcement efforts are regarded as essentials of their crusade. If we are to engage in an all-out effort to preserve the free enterprise system, here, in this nondebatable field of liberty and law, is one place to begin.

If, as I believe, there has been no lessening of class bitterness in 50 years and no less tendency to engage in organized violence around strike-bound factories, we must concede that among the prime causes of this unfortunate condition are the statutes, executive delinquency, and ill-conceived tolerance, which has been prone to sacrifice human freedom on the altar of sentimentalism. There has been too much compromise with lawlessness at a time when lawlessness is no longer excusable, for organized pressure groups are attracting and receiving special consideration from executives, legislatures and courts. Organized workers are no longer inarticulate; organized workers are no longer political stepchildren. Extenuations for violence or other revolutionary attitudes have grown thin. No longer is there occasion for desperate measures. For labor pressure groups, which deserve and now receive attention from all branches of government, to weaken support of law and order is sheer madness.

An outward appearance of peace when employers do not so impetuously try to resume operations in time of a strike is only a facade.   The nightmare of violence and disorder restrains them and restrains those who wish to work.   That, of course, is not progress toward the vindication of law and order; it is rather a recognition of the inevitability of tolerated lawlessness.

In a study entitled *Can Labor and Management Work Together?* is a section entitled "Steps Toward Peace," where I find this:

> Also, the bitterness of past years was gone from those strikes.   American industrialists, with few exceptions, made a significant decision: in the interests of good relations, no attempt would be made to operate during a shutdown in order to break strikes.   Thus, in one stroke, they removed almost all possibility of picket-line violence and a source of future bad feeling.[54]

That seems to suggest the incontrovertible fact that in most instances a "back-to-work movement" by those who do not wish to stay on strike usually results in violence.   In fact, this is so true that unless we cease to depreciate the importance of liberty and law, I see no present prospect of industrial warfare becoming so civilized, or of the laws against disorder being so effectively enforced, that nonstrikers may proceed safely to work.   The peace of coerced inaction, which the last quotation extols, may be socially desirable for a short period, but obviously such a concession to threats of violence is no cause for elation.   If, after a reasonable waiting period and some evidence that a substantial number of people desired to return to work, employer and employees could be confident that the law-enforcing authorities would protect them, there would at least be developed an affirmative step toward industrial peace.   No group should be encouraged to believe that violence pays.

Undoubtedly there are times when it seems good sense to avoid a showdown, but some compromises are like signing a note with usurious interest.   Someday the piper must be paid just as he is being paid in the coal industry.   There probably would never have been a world conflict in 1939 if the rape of Manchuria and Ethiopia had been prevented.   Today in industrial relations we often think only of an immediate settlement and too seldom of the violation of principles that may rise to plague us.   That is a growing vice of the day.   Employers shorn of defenses and left naked to violence, and merchants threatened with a secondary boycott, if they sell what the public desires, will not serve the public as it should be served.   They make antisocial concessions,

XIX

The Anthracite Lesson

No form of government and no set of principles fulfill their promise if, through repeated compromises in the interest of immediate expediency, they are subject to a process of erosion or attrition. It matters not whether such surrenders arise from employers thinking of immediate profits or government officials thinking of political popularity or the comfort of the public. In no phase of industrial relations with which I have had contact is this truism more conspicuously demonstrated than with the anthracite industry, a compact localized industry that about 45 years ago started with a promising form of industrial government. Those who believe that compromise and conciliation furnish the only solvent for industrial disputes would do well to study the record of labor relations in this industry, which has been led into the slough by too much emphasis upon settlement for its own sake. Peace at any price is just as much a menace as intransigence.

At the beginning of the century anthracite sales were about $100,000,000 annually and 90 per cent of the tonnage was controlled by coal-carrying railroads. The industry then employed about 150,000 people.

In the early part of 1902, the United Mine Workers of America, headed by John Mitchell, endeavored to arrange a conference with the leading anthracite operators in respect to conditions of employment. The operators refused to participate in any such meeting stating that at all times they were ready to talk to their own employees. In March a convention of the anthracite workers demanded union recognition, an eight-hour day, an increase in wages, and other items and served notice that after April 1 they would work only three days a week. The union then appealed for aid to the National Civic Federation, an institution organized in 1900 by such leaders as Mark Hanna, August Belmont, Samuel Gompers, and John Mitchell to promote industrial peace.

Senator Mark Hanna, chairman of the Civic Federation, prevailed upon the larger operators to meet officers of the United Mine Workers to discuss the miners' demands, but the meeting bore no fruit.

In May the union proposed arbitration through the industrial division of the Civic Federation or, as an alternative, a kind of fact-finding board composed of Archbishop Ireland and Bishop Potter and a third to be named by these two prelates. Mr. George F. Baer, speaking for the operators' group, of which he was the leader, rejected the offer saying:

Anthracite mining is a business and not a religious, sentimental or academic proposition. . . . I could not if I would delegate this business management to even so highly a respectable body as the Civic Federation, nor can I call to my aid as experts in the mixed problem of business and philanthropy, the eminent prelates you have named.[1]

To a skeptical stockholder who had misgivings as to the attitude of the operators, Mr. Baer wrote:

The rights and interests of the laboring man will be protected and cared for—not by labor agitators, but by the Christian gentlemen to whom God has given control of the property rights of the country.[2]

So Mr. Baer became known as "Divine Right" Baer or, as Clarence Darrow called him, "George the First."[3]

Faced with this impasse, the executive committee of the miners' union, carrying out authority previously given them at the Shamokin convention, ordered all men, except pump men, engineers, and others necessary to preserve the properties, to abstain from work on May 12th. Three days later a new convention of the mine workers hurriedly called to consider the crisis voted to continue the strike. In June the majority of the engineers, firemen, and pump men were also ordered to quit work, and 147,-000 people had abandoned their jobs.

The strike lasted from May 12th to October 23rd, a total of 163 days, during which period there was a great deal of suffering among the workers and much violence and persecution directed against nonunion workers.

In the latter half of 1902, President Theodore Roosevelt stepped into the picture and sought an agreement to arbitrate all questions at issue. The mine workers held a further convention, with John Mitchell as chairman and William B. Wilson as secretary, at which the union accepted the proposal. The operators at first refused to consider arbitration, but finally J. P. Morgan stepped into the picture and reversed their decision. The miners then returned to work pending the outcome.

To a commission of five that he appointed, President Roosevelt wrote:

You will endeavor to establish the relations between the employers and wage workers in the anthracite fields on a just and permanent basis.[4]

The commission met promptly in Washington on October 24th and elected Judge George Gray as its chairman. It made personal inspections of conditions in the anthracite field and held prolonged hearings involving over 500 witnesses, 10,000 pages of testimony and elaborate exhibits and documents. Its award, setting up a progressive and advanced form of industrial government which, on paper at least, promised well for the future, was transmitted to President Roosevelt on March 18th, 1903.

Out of fashion possibly, but still pleasant, is the following expression of the commission:

Fairness, forbearance, and good will are the prerequisites of peace and harmonious cooperation in all the social and economic relations of men. . . .

Where production is controlled despotically by capital there may be a seeming prosperity, but the qualities which give sacredness and worth to life are enfeebled or destroyed. In the absence of a trustful and conciliatory disposition the strife between capital and labor cannot be composed by laws and contrivances. The causes from which it springs are as deep as man's nature, and nothing that is powerless to illumine the mind and touch the heart can reach the fountainhead of the evil. So long as employers and employees continue to look on one another as opponents and antagonists, so long shall their relations be unsatisfactory and strained, requiring but a slight thing to provoke the open warfare which is called a strike.[5]

A wage increase of 10 per cent, a reduction of the working day from ten to nine hours, the establishment of check weighmen to be paid for by the miners, and the equal distribution of mine cars were among the advantages granted the miners.

Other provisions of the award were aimed at union abuses. It was declared that there should be no concerted effort "to limit the output of the mines or to detract from the quality of the work." [6]

The closed shop was condemned and the open shop was endorsed. Discrimination by either employer or employees was forbidden. The union was admonished that it "should strive to make membership in it so valuable as to attract all who are eligible, but in its efforts to build itself up, it must not lose sight of the fact that those who may think differently, have certain rights guaranteed them by our free government." [7] The commission then continued:

Abraham Lincoln said, "No man is good enough to govern another man without that other's consent." This is as true in trade unions as elsewhere, and not until those which fail to recognize this truth abandon their attitude toward nonunion men, and follow the suggestion made above—that is, to make their work and their membership so valuable and attractive, that all who are eligible to membership will come under their rule—will they secure that firm and constant sympathy of the public, which their general purposes seem to demand. [8]

Looking back from today, however, one sees that the most important feature of this award was the provision for a board of conciliation, with ultimate resort to an umpire, to deal with "any difficulty . . . growing out of the relations of the employer and employed." [9] On this question and the questions of grievance procedure the commission ruled:

That any difficulty or disagreement arising under this award, either as to its interpretation or application, or in any way growing out of the relations of the employers and employed, which cannot be settled or adjusted by consultation between the superintendent or manager of the mine or mines, and the miner or miners directly interested or is of a scope too large to be so settled and adjusted, shall be referred to a permanent joint committee, to be called a Board of Conciliation, to consist of six persons, appointed as hereinafter provided. . . .

The Board of Conciliation thus constituted, shall take up and consider any question referred to it, as aforesaid, hearing both parties to the controversy, and such evidence as may be laid before it by either party; and any award made by a majority of such Board of Conciliation shall be final and binding on all parties. If, however, the said Board is unable to decide any question submitted, or point related thereto, that question or point shall be referred to an umpire, to be appointed, at the request of said Board, by one of the circuit judges of the third judicial circuit of the United States, whose decision shall be final and binding in the premises. [10]

Since this procedure afforded an opportunity for impartial decisions of all disputes, the award logically forbade any resort to strikes or lockouts:

No suspension of work shall take place, by lockout or strike, pending the adjudication of any matter so taken up for adjustment.[11]

This provision, adopted and readopted by the parties over 43 years thereafter, was an unqualified covenant by the parties that no such stoppages would take place.

The commission, in addition to its reflections on discrimination, condemned lawlessness, boycotting, and blacklisting. It declared that:

No discussion of the conditions prevailing in the anthracite region during the continuance of the late strike, would be adequate, that did not fully deal with the disorder and lawlessness which existed to some extent over the whole region, and throughout the whole period. It is admitted that this disorder and lawlessness was incident to the strike. Its history is stained with a record of riot and bloodshed, culminating in three murders, unprovoked save by the fact that two of the victims were asserting their right to work, and another, as an officer of the law, was performing his duty, in attempting to preserve the peace. Men who chose to be employed, or who remained at work, were assailed and threatened, and they and their families terrorized and intimidated. In several instances the houses of such workmen were dynamited, or otherwise assaulted, and the lives of unoffending women and children put in jeopardy.[12]

Referring to the responsibility of the union to maintain law and order in such situations, the commission made remarks that, if heeded, would have been portentious in industrial history:

Surely this tendency to disorder and violation of law imposes upon the organization, which begins and conducts a movement of such importance, a grave responsibility. It has, by its voluntary act, created dangers, and should, therefore, be vigilant in averting them. It has, by the concerted action of many aroused passions, which, uncontrolled, threaten the public peace; it, therefore, owes society the duty of exerting its power to check and confine these passions within the bounds of reason and of law. Such organizations should be the powerful coadjutors of government in maintaining the peace and upholding the law.[13]

Concerning the boycott as practiced, the commission said, "It is a cruel weapon of aggression and its use immoral and anti-social." [14]

The blacklist was described as a system "as reprehensible and as cruel as the boycott, and should be frowned down by all humane men." [15]

The reaction of the leading metropolitan dailies to this award is truly significant. The award, commented *The New York Times*, "is without doubt one of the most important contributions ever made to the literature of the labor question." [16] Practically all papers united in featuring and praising its condemnation of union violence, boycotting, and the reviling of "scabs," and its support of the right of men to work. The New York *Evening Post*, as we have pointed out, questioned the propriety of condemning strikers for lawlessness and then granting them wage increases.

Today, over 40 years later, in times of industrial disturbance the metropolitan papers no longer emphasize such matters. For example, the sitdown strikes of Detroit would hardly have been tolerated in 1903 as they were in 1937, and certainly a governor who refused to try to enforce law and order would not have been elevated to the position of United States Attorney General. Today the protection of the right to work in times of industrial disturbances seems like a lost cause. Interference with the right to work is no longer news. Failure to protect the right to work is no longer news. At the most, organized lawlessness of this character is usually regarded as no more serious than a light attack of measles. Whether or not one thinks we have become numbed by what has happened or have developed a kind of practical wisdom in this respect depends on his viewpoint.

The anthracite award was pleasing to the American Federation of Labor, as well it might be, although it sponsored the open shop. In the May issue of *The Federationist* the editorial stated that "nearly every contention of the United Mine Workers of America has been fully sustained. . . . And thus ends one of the most interesting and eventful episodes in the history of industry; one which . . . will make for the good of the human family." [17]

As I review the events, I am convinced that the Federation was guilty of understatement. The award was, according to *The New York Times*, "the first arbitration ever brought about by a President of the United States in order to terminate an intolerable condition." [18] It certainly was the first arbitration of a dispute of such national significance. By its terms at least, it set a pattern for industry bargaining with a grievance procedure capped by arbitration, such as became more familiar 40 years later. If its principles had been defended and enforced by firm action, there would in all likelihood have evolved a model form of industrial government for this localized industry of national importance. But another fate awaited it.

The Roosevelt Award of 1903, which by its terms expired April 1, 1906, was extended without radical changes, by negotiated agreements, for a period of 14 years. The first two extensions were for three years each, and the second two covered four years each. Amazing as it seems today, not one of these extensions covering these long-term contracts provided for any reopening of wages or hours during the term of the agreement. The first increase in wages appeared in the agreement running from 1916 to 1920, which froze wages for that four years. But the coming of the war altered this stabilization. Four voluntary wage increases were made in conjunction with the United States Fuel Administration for the war period and the period of reconstruction that followed. The employees agreed to give the full co-operation necessary to maintain the production of the mines at their fullest capacity. Various improvements in grievance procedure were made during these years and the eight-hour day was recognized in 1916, but otherwise the provisions of the original award in 1903 were continued without substantial change. The 1917 increase of 10 per cent was granted on condition that the Fuel Administration advance the price of coal sufficiently to cover the increased cost of production.

In the latter part of 1919, when John L. Lewis appeared on the stage as acting president, the union attitude changed. It demanded the closed shop, the checkoff, a six-hour day, an increase of 60 per cent in wages and a contract for a period not exceeding two years. When negotiations resulted in no agreement, William B. Wilson, Secretary of Labor, intervened as a mediator, and proposed an agreement, which the union rejected. The union then presented some moderated demands, which the operators rejected, laying special emphasis on the provision of the 1903 award forbidding discrimination against employees on account of membership or nonmembership in a union.

Faced with this impasse in the anthracite coal industry, President Wilson, on May 21, 1920, wrote the parties that if they were unable to agree, "I insist that the matters in dispute be submitted to the determination of a commission to be appointed by me," [19] with the award retroactive to April first, the expiration date of the last contract. The miners yielded reluctantly, stating that they were "forced to accept" since "industrial legislation" and "the abuse of the writ of injunction, with the tying up of union funds and other repressive measures, makes it almost humanly impossible to wage a successful battle." [20] The acceptance of the operators came a few days later, and the commission, which consisted of one representative for the miners, one for the operators, and a third who was chairman, went to work in June.

The award, which came down in September, granted a 17 per cent increase in wages but denied the closed shop. It was altogether unsatisfactory to the union representative on the commission, who filed an emphatic dissenting opinion. The disgruntled mine workers, violating their agreement to abide by the award, engaged in a two-week "vacation strike" as a protest.

About this time President Wilson found occasion to express himself on this subject, in his usually effective way:

No government, no employer, no person having any reputation to protect can afford to enter into contractual relations with any organization that systematically or repeatedly violates its contracts. The United Mine Workers of America is the largest single labor organization in the United States, if not in the world but no organization can long endure that sets up its own strength as being superior to its plighted faith or its duty to society at large.[21]

When in 1920 the anthracite operators began to deal with the international union of mine workers, instead of the district unions, they did so on the assurance that anthracite problems would not be tied to bituminous problems. That action was a misstep of almost calamitous consequences both for the industry and the public. The entire coal industry, both bituminous and anthracite, was thus brought under the dominion of one union with one set of officers. The monopolistic power of the union to inflict privations upon the public was immeasurably extended.

In 1920 John L. Lewis became president of the United Mine Workers of America. He reported to the national convention of the union that "for the first time in the history of our organization there is a uniform date of expiration affecting all agreements in both the anthracite and bituminous industry. . . . The full measured influence and economic power of our great membership may thus be utilized to the advantage of our people for the achievement of our ideals." [22]

The union demands on the anthracite operators on this occasion again included the closed shop and the checkoff, and a disregard of the standards established by the conciliation board and the umpire in the disposition of grievances.

On March 20, 1922, when negotiations in the anthracite industry were in their initial stage and no final issues had been framed, the U.M.W. issued a national suspension order, covering both the bituminous and anthracite fields, to be effective March 31st, the date of the expiration of the agreements. The order covered 100 per cent of the anthracite field and the major part of the bituminous industry. The strike policy committee of the union also directed that "all power and influence of the international and district unions shall be exerted to bring about a strike in the nonunion coal fields of America." [23] The union avoided negotiations with the anthracite operators and refused to negotiate with union operators in various states because such negotiations would relieve public need for coal. An attempt by members of the shovellers' union to operate a stripping mine contrary to the orders of the strike policy committee led to the Herrin massacre in Illinois, described in Chapter XVII. The coal famine had to be made effective at any cost.

In May, 1922, the anthracite operators offered a five-year contract with annual reopenings for wages and a provision for arbitration if wage revisions were not agreed upon.

"The periodical adjustment proposed," said the operators, "provides for collective bargaining in the first instance and resort to arbitration only in case collective bargaining fails." [24]

When nothing came of these negotiations, the operators proposed that a commission be appointed by the President and that some practical way for resuming work pending its findings be found. This also the miners rejected. On July 10, 1922, President Harding called the parties to the White House, where he proposed that a commission be appointed to fix a temporary wage scale and to investigate and make recommendations as to all phases of the industry. This proposal was also rejected by the union, which thereafter boasted:

From time to time as the fight went on the operators changed their arbitration proposals and dressed them up in many disguises, but the mine workers refused to become parties to any arbitration or approach to arbitration. We refused arbitration from the President of the United States, notwithstanding that all pressure of the government was back of that proposal.[25]

Early in August the mayors of six anthracite cities sought to mediate, but the union refused to meet while the bituminous strike was unsettled. About the middle of August, President Harding moved again, stating that if there was any further delay "we shall be in danger of nothing short of a nation-wide disaster."[26] Accordingly, new conferences were held, but arbitration was again rejected by the miners.

Not belittling the result of its intransigence, the union described its work as "the greatest industrial dislocation in the history of the world" and "a domestic calamity."[27] In his report to Congress on August 18, 1922, President Harding declared, "The country is at the mercy of the United Mine Workers."[28]

On August 29, 1922, Senators Pepper and Reed of Pennsylvania proposed an immediate resumption of operations under the terms of the expired contract and that both operators and miners should unite in recommending that Congress appoint a coal commission to investigate all phases of the industry. In a few days this resulted in an agreement, along the lines of the Senators' proposals, extending the old agreement to August 31, 1923, and providing that after that date production should be continued "upon such terms as the parties may agree upon in the light of the report of the Commission."[29]

This strike had lasted 162 days, during which time the union was unwilling to make any settlement of the anthracite issues until it reached a settlement in the bituminous fields.

It was about this time that I entered the anthracite picture. To my great surprise my reputation for ability had far outrun the facts. "Mr. Lewis darkened up and began to storm," when he heard the news, according to Mr. Carnes, who wrote his biography.[30] Mr. Carnes then proceeds:

The perpetual shadow of another bitter strike in the anthracite fields played about the conference room the next day as Walter Gordon Merritt, the counsel for the operators, said that at the coming wage scale meetings, set for August 16th, the producers "must be plaintiffs and not defendants," and that the labor issue "was all one sided anyway." Now the miners could stand twice as much from almost any one else. It was a well-known fact that if Walter Gordon Merritt even stood up to breathe a cheery "good morning" to the mine workers it was like waving a matzoth at Herr Hitler. The vehemence of delivery shown by the New York lawyer-publicist who hurled each word like Walter Johnson used to pitch, caused impartial observers to see no other possibility but a strike in store after August 30th, when the agreement expired. Mr. Merritt's remarks left a bitter feeling when the miners read them in newspapers as the meeting closed.[31]

To carry out the settlement agreement the United States Coal Commission, which I will call the Hammond Commission after its chairman John Hays Hammond, was authorized by Congress and proceeded to work. It spent about $600,000 of the public funds, and although its work was voluminous, its results were nil.

In the early summer of 1923, when the commission was still laboring, the union again asked for the closed shop and the check-off and increases in wages in many forms. Conferences were held, but the union refused to discuss any other issues until such time as the operators yielded to its demand for the closed shop and the checkoff. The report of the Hammond Commission had not been issued when negotiations began and, when published, was of little aid in the negotiations. The commission contacted the parties for the purpose of mediation but to no avail. The operators again offered arbitration, and the unions again refused.

The governor intervened on August 25th and stated that "the safety and welfare of the people of Pennsylvania and the other anthracite-using states make it of vital importance that mining should go on." [32] But even while the intervention of the governor of Pennsylvania was pending, the strike was called for August 31st. The governor was deaf to the appeals of the operators for arbitration and rewarded the union with a 10 per cent wage increase. After a two weeks' stoppage the men returned to work with the 10 per cent increase under a two-year agreement that ran to September 1, 1925.

One of the results of these disturbing conditions was the growing boldness and frequency of outlaw strikes in violation of the collective-bargaining agreement. The union had covenanted that there would be no strikes during the term of the agreement and that all disputes would be settled by the conciliation board and the umpire, but in many instances it instigated and inspired these forbidden stoppages.

When I gathered the figures for presentation to the Hammond

Commission in 1922, one-half to two-thirds of the employees were annually participating in outlaw strikes, and a vacation strike against the arbitration award of the Wilson Commission had lasted two weeks in the late summer of 1920. The ideal form of government, with a conciliation board and an umpire, was not operating as it should, and the rights of the operators under the standard form of contract, which in its fundamental features had already lasted two decades, were being whittled down.

These outlaw strikes were so frequent and covered such a variety of causes that management was daily stalked by their shadow. "Button strikes" against men who went to work without union buttons violated the union agreement forbidding stoppages, as well as the agreement forbidding discrimination, but they were nevertheless openly and officially maintained by the union, sometimes by written notice to the employer. Even the constitutions of two of the three main district unions contained provisions calling for such violations of the agreement. Notwithstanding the fact that there was a provision in the agreement that "there shall be no concerted effort . . . to limit the output of the mines," [33] strikes were repeatedly called to hinder operations until some union member paid a union fine imposed for violation of union rules limiting output. In one instance, at least, the union struck to compel the company to pay the fine. In other words, where an employee was penalized for refusing to wrong his employer, the employer was forced to pay his union fine.

The subject of holidays was handled with a like disregard of the agreement, and in the case of one company at least, the union required the observance of 30 holidays over and above those recognized in the union contract. A union order issued in 1923 and selected at random reads this way:

Dear Sirs and Brothers: You are hereby officially notified to observe Monday, April 2, 1923 as a holiday by remaining away from work. This day is observed throughout the jurisdiction of our great union as the anniversary of the establishment of the eight-hour day.[34]

There were also local strikes for Old Home Week, Sunday School picnics, Polish picnics, and so on.

More serious than these were strikes protesting against discipline of employees for carelessness in connection with matters involving the safety and lives of the miners. The causes of such protest strikes are too many to enumerate.

Management was badly impaired by these outlaw strikes and the fear of them. Operators, believing they had no prompt remedy, frequently made concessions that they should not have made with no adequate attempt to adhere to the agreement and without even presenting grievances to the conciliation board. The union, taking advantage of this timidity, was gradually reducing the fundamental agreement to a mere shadow of its former self. As an instrument of industrial peace, it was failing. Thus the industry suffered all the difficulties of union recognition and collective bargaining, while allowing itself to be maneuvered out of its advantages. The Hammond Commission agreed in general with the operators' criticism of outlaw strikes but blamed them for lack of a central organization by which they could compel observance of the union agreement and by which they could maintain a fair bargaining power. The commission said:

So long as this disproportion in bargaining effectiveness exists, the process of attrition of the agreement will be likely to continue. . . . It will probably be the operators instead of the union who will be appealing to the public for fair play.[35]

And the commission went further when it found that:

The illegal strike and the threat to strike is used as a conscious and illegal policy by the union to obtain advantages which it is not granted under the agreement.[36]

As a remedy I suggested that the union should be held responsible in damages in the amount of one dollar per day per man for each unlawful strike. The commission adopted this recommendation to the extent of finding "that the agreements should include suitable clauses for penalities in case of violation."[37]

As nothing came of this I recommended that all operators unite in an insurance plan whereby they would consistently enforce their contract rights through the courts. By the terms of this plan each operator would be insured against damages due to stoppages in violation of the agreement. The insurance company would, in turn, be subrogated to the operators' claim for such damages and would prosecute that claim in its own name, in order to recoup itself for the money paid to the operator. At that time there was some limited experience in respect to strike insurance, and it seemed to me that limited payments covering only losses caused by strikes in violation of the agreement would be practical and would lead to the consistent firm prosecution of such claims since the insurance company itself would be beyond the reach of union attack. After all, this was but an effort to implement the recommendation I had made to the Hammond Commission, to the effect that the union should be held responsible for wilful violations of its agreement. The program, however, was considered too experimental. Conditions in this respect accordingly continued, with the final result, as we shall see, that union dictation has displaced collective bargaining and legal contract responsibility has been expressly eliminated.

In 1925 history repeated itself. The union demanded the closed shop and the checkoff, as well as wage increases, claiming that it was only through such a closed-shop system that it could accept responsibility and discipline its members. Arbitration was again offered by the operators.

In an address delivered in 1925 I warned against the dangers of undermining responsible collective bargaining and appealed for the principle of voluntary arbitration in industries of public importance. I said:

I believe the entire moral force of the nation should be marshaled to compel both anthracite operators and miners to settle their differences peacefully by arbitration, and without public injury. Where the tribunal of reason is available, there is no justification for resort to the tribunal of force; peaceful adjudication should supersede ordeal by combat and direct action. Periodic stoppages at the hands of those who control one of the most important of our natural resources constitutes a trifling with public interests which should not be tolerated.[38]

Again arbitration was refused by Mr. Lewis, and this time with a characteristic Lewis comment

We know that you think the medicine would be good for us, but frankly we have little faith in your diagnosis.[39]

So a strike took place on August 31, 1925.

Governors, mayors, legislators, clergy, and other important citizens intervened from time to time, and President Coolidge appealed to Congress for authority to act, but all without result. The strike continued for a period of 170 days, the longest in the history of anthracite, until settled by direct agreement in February, 1926.

I well remember the circumstances of the settlement. It had been a long night with protracted dickering, and the final dispute over the words "shall" and "may" was settled about dawn. This new agreement extended the old contract until August 31, 1930, and provided a procedure for interim wage adjustments "at any time after January 1, 1927 but not oftener than once in any year." [40] On such interim reopenings any disagreements were to be "referred to a board of two men with full power and without reservations or restrictions." [41] This board was "obligated within ninety days after appointment to arrive at a decision on all issues in controversy and to that end shall formulate their own rules and methods of procedure and may enlarge the board to an odd number, in which event a majority vote shall be binding." [42] This meant arbitration if the parties failed to agree.

On August 8, 1930, this agreement, with some amendments with which we are not now concerned but with the same provisions as to interim wage reopenings, was extended from September 1, 1930, to April 1, 1936. It was a long-term agreement with what seemed to be adequate provision for interim wage revisions. The intent was clear.

This is what actually happened to the reopening provisions: In 1932 the industry was dangerously on the wane through loss of markets to other fuels. Gross sales had fallen 30 per cent. Total employees had been reduced from 148,000 to 85,000, and the number of operating collieries had dropped from 188 to 113. Part-timing of work was common. It was apparent that the trend could only be reversed if prices were reduced to place anthracite on a more favorable competitive basis with other fuels. The operators felt that if unit labor costs were reduced this would result in such an increase in tonnage that annual earnings of the miners would not be impaired. To press their point they naturally turned to the contract provision for wage reopenings as it was embodied in their six-year contract. They proposed a 35 per cent reduction in wages, and when no agreement in this direction could be reached by direct negotiation, they called for the appointment of what was supposed to be an impartial and objective board. The operators named Mr. George Rublee, an outstanding attorney in Washington who had served in many public positions and whose disinterestedness and general liberalism was beyond challenge. The United Mine Workers chose Frank Morrison, secretary of the American Federation of Labor. When these two men were unable to agree on an award, Mr. Rublee called Mr. Morrison's attention to that part of the contract which read:

The board shall be obligated . . . to arrive at a decision on all issues in controversy . . . and may enlarge the board to an odd number, in which event a majority vote shall be binding.[43]

To carry out this provision, Mr. Rublee argued with Mr. Morrison that it was their duty to endeavor to agree upon a third person in order to perform their mandatory obligation to reach a decision. Otherwise, he reasoned, they would make a farce of the contract and obstruct its performance.

Mr. Morrison, acting under the mandate of those who appointed him, refused even to attempt to agree upon a third man and based his refusal upon the contention that he was not obliged to do so.

This certainly constituted a device to prevent a final determination by arbitration, as provided for in the agreement. I advised the operators that this wilful repudiation of one of the essential terms of the contract was adequate justification for a repudiation of the contract on their part, but of course such advice had no practical value.

Now let us stop, look, and listen. We have brought this anthracite history down to 1936. Since 1903 this industry had been operating under a form of industrial government whereby management surrendered such absolute powers as it might have had to decide disputes and had agreed that all of its decisions during the term of the labor contract might be reviewed by arbitration. Nor was this all. When differences prevented an accord in respect to new agreements, the operators laid aside all militancy by offering to arbitrate. Notwithstanding this abdication of power by management and this security of impartial adjudication for labor, this industry in the 1920's had a lamentable record for outlaw strikes during agreements and a lamentable record for terminal strikes at the expiration of agreements. From 1922 to 1926 the industry was shut down 351 days by strikes or more than one entire year's working time.

By May, 1936, a month after the expiration date of the agreement of 1930, the helplessness of the operators had become rather obvious. The union had made it clear that, by one method or another, it would avoid arbitration. The prospects of resisting a strike had become discouraging, and the market for anthracite had already been injured by repeated interruptions in supply. The upper hand of the operators had shifted to the miners, who had won prestige by stalwart endurance of strike privations. They had proved to be the better fighters.

In the spring of 1936, a two-year agreement that reduced the normal work week to 35 hours was reached. Provisions were included for the checkoff of union dues and initiation fees on individual assignments but not for the closed shop. Equalization of working time among the various collieries was to prevail, so far as practicable. To deal with outlaw stoppages, which were still a major problem, it was agreed that:

the District and International Officers of the United Mine Workers of America assume full responsibility for carrying out the provisions of this Agreement. To that end they shall use every power vested in them to require that grievances be taken up in the manner provided in the Agreement and to prevent illegal strikes in violation thereof; and for non-compliance with the instructions of said officers in this regard, upon the part of any member or members of the United Mine Workers of America, said officers shall impose such discipline as may be necessary to prevent violations and to secure compliance with the provisions of this Agreement.[44]

Although this provision did not prove to be much more than a pious utterance, it was nevertheless a reaffirmation by the parties of their conviction that a collective-bargaining contract should contain provisions for legal contract responsibility.

On November 13, 1937, this same agreement of 1936 was further extended to April 30, 1939. On May 26, 1939 a new agreement was reached to run until April 30, 1941. The 1939 agreement at long last overthrew one of the major provisions of the award of 1903 by agreeing upon the closed shop. A committee of 12, six from the union and six from the operators, was established to meet quarterly "or oftener on call . . . [to] consider and discuss all questions arising under this contract relating to cooperation and efficiency and the performance of the contract." [45] The committee was also given the power by majority vote to refer to the conciliation board any disagreement as to the interpretation or application of the contract.

Another agreement that did not alter the fundamental relationships of the parties was entered into on May 20, 1941, and was to run until April 30, 1943. The provisions for contract responsibility still survived.

On December 30, 1942, a strike involving about one-fifth of all the workers started in the anthracite industry as a protest against an increase in union dues that had been authorized at a union convention. As the strike continued, it developed into a demand for a wage increase of $2 per day, notwithstanding the fact that the wages were fixed by a union contract that did not expire until April 30, 1943. The strike was instigated and led by the officials of local unions, and there even developed a tri-district general mine committee to lead the rebellion.

On January 13th Mr. Lewis wired the secretary of this mine committee, calling upon him to retreat from this position. The War Labor Board called a hearing for January 15th and that same day Mr. Lewis sent a telegram to 350 anthracite local unions and Districts 1, 7, and 9 notifying them that the stoppage was illegal and stating that the president and secretary of the rump tri-district committee "and their outlaw associates on this alleged tri-district committee who are now engaged in this mad enterprise will be held to accountability under the laws of their own union." [46]

The War Labor Board hearing was held in Washington on January 15th, when Mr. Lewis recounted the facts and his determination to see that the collective-bargaining contract was respected. At the same time the acting chairman of the War Labor Board wired President Roosevelt suggesting that he proceed with such action as he deemed proper. Whereupon the President on January 19th issued a telegram to numerous presidents and recording secretaries of the local unions and to John Lewis, president, and Thomas Kennedy, secretary, of the United Mine Workers of America and other union officials. It directed the miners to resume work and stated that if his order was not obeyed within 48 hours "your Government will take the necessary steps to protect the security of the nation against a strike which is doing serious injury to the war effort." [47]

The cumulative effect of the telegrams from the President of the United States and the president of the United Mine Workers of America led to a collapse of the strike.

The lesson of this episode should not be overlooked: When men engaged in a strike against the authority of the union in raising dues, the top union authorities took steps effectively to squelch it by a wire that told the "outlaw associates engaged in this mad enterprise, they will be held to strict accountability under the laws of their own union." The outcome furnished some proof, if proof were needed, that decisive action by union officials some-times can be effective to end so-called outlaw strikes.

By 1943 our free economy had been forced to yield largely to a controlled war economy. What happened from then until June, 1946, involved a series of technical adjustments, processed through the War Labor Board, that are not material to the evolution of peacetime relationships which this chapter is designed to portray. So far as they are important they will be considered in Chapter XXII.

On June 7, 1946, something startling and discouraging hap-pened and collective bargaining suffered a bad blow. A new agreement that expressly stated it was to cover wages and condi-tions of employment of employees "during such term as they are able and willing to work" [48] was entered into. Instead of definite terms it provided a procedure whereby in a period of 30 days changes could be proposed and negotiated and notice of termina-tion could be served by either party in case of disagreement. This was a marked departure from the day when the public was pro-tected by an agreement that ran for six years. It left the union free to time its stoppages when the public need was the greatest. This agreement dealt with wages, overtime, and vacations and in-troduced an Anthracite Health and Welfare Fund. The bargain-ing status of foremen and supervisors was to be controlled by "the decision and procedure laid down by the National Labor Relations Board." [49]

Of outstanding interest was the abandonment of any contract obligation in respect to interim stoppages. The clause on this point read:

(a) In lieu of existing contractual obligations affecting the same subject matter, the United Mine Workers of America and the Anthracite Operators reaffirm their intention to maintain the integrity of this contract and to exercise their best efforts through available disciplinary measures to prevent stoppages of work by strike or lockout pending adjustment or adjudication of disputes and grievances in the manner provided in this Agreement. [50]

Thus, at long last, the entire legal theory of contract stability was tossed out of the window. The parties did just the opposite of what was recommended by the Hammond Commission in 1923 when it found that "the agreements should include suitable clauses for penalties in case of violation." [51] The contract existed only so long as the miners were "able and willing to work" [52] and the elimination of unlawful stoppages was made to depend solely on voluntary co-operation between the parties. The union moved further away from the standards of a business organization with contract responsibility.

On July 10, 1947, an agreement was entered into providing for some amendments that are not of importance in connection with the principles we are discussing. On July 3, 1948, another agreement, which extended the checkoff not only to dues but assessments and initiation fees and increased the tonnage tax for the Health and Welfare Fund from five to 20 cents, was adopted. This fund was put under the administration of three trustees, two of which were under the control of the union, with power to act by a vote of only two out of the three. Both in theory and practice the operators provided the money and the union disbursed it.

Early in March, 1949, Mr. Lewis and two of his associate officers called a strike in all bituminous and anthracite mines, designating it a "memorial stoppage" [53] under a provision of the bituminous contract that gave the union the right to "designate memorial periods." [54] No one believed that Mr. Lewis was motivated by any purpose which that provision of the contract was designed to cover, and in the anthracite field, where there was no provision for "a memorial stoppage," the violation of contract was not even camouflaged. It was a distinct act of bad faith against both the operators and the public. Again the anthracite industry was made a pawn in the bituminous game.

On March 23rd a statement was issued by Mr. Lewis:

. . . the present memorial period will terminate Monday, March 28th. Production may then be resumed. . . . The lessening productivity of the nation has encouraged powerful financial and mining interests to believe that your union and its wage structure and your living standards may be successfully attacked. Your welfare fund, which means so much in the alleviation of human agony in our industry, will also be placed in jeopardy.

Desperate efforts are being made by the employers and the banking interests of the nation to retain the infamous Taft-Hartley slave law on the statute books through the period of wage negotiations in the mining industry. They hope through the retention of this vile statute and the use of its injunctive and punitive provisions to hold you in irons, while the jackboots of American finance kick out your economic teeth.

We will not retreat. We will advance.[55]

The virulence of this statement is significant. Financial interests are the enemies of labor. The laws of the land are designed to hold labor in irons while American financiers kick out the economic teeth of the workers. Such vitriolics poured into the minds of miners by a man whom they revere do irreparable harm—no one knows how much harm. Although the statement does not advocate violence, it establishes a frame of mind that leads to violence. Just how long poison of this kind can be transfused into the blood of the workingman without unseating his native common sense is a question that worries many of us. Propaganda is potent.

As of July 5, 1949, John L. Lewis declared a policy of three days' operation a week, effective the day of the termination of the miners' vacation. All the vast competing corporations in both the anthracite and bituminous fields were forced by one centralized monopoly power to curtail production for the apparent purpose of reducing the supplies of coal available to the public in case of a strike. Again there was a clear repudiation of the terms of the anthracite agreement.

All bituminous and anthracite miners struck on September 19th, because the members of the Southern Coal Producers Association refused to continue their payments into the Welfare Fund, claiming that the contract calling for such payments no longer existed. Those who were not responsible for the act that created the grievance were included in the stoppage in order to injure the public with a coal famine. The anthracite industry, which was still operating under its contract and was continuing payments into its own welfare fund, was included in the stoppage regardless of its contract. The public must not have coal. The few nonunion operators in different states, largely engaged in stripping operations, continued to produce in their small way with the help of the police and the courts, notwithstanding interference by violence from roving pickets. Finally, on October 3, Mr. Lewis ordered the anthracite miners and the bituminous miners in the West to return to work, but all other operations had to remain closed. Why they were called out and why they were sent back is difficult to understand. But, stop or go, the fiat always works. The union control is effective.

Glancing over this picture of almost half a century exposes the contrasts of Then and Now. Prior to 1903 the power of the operators largely dictated terms, and it took a five months' strike to secure fair bargaining rights for the union. Today there is no collective bargaining because of union dictation. At the beginning it was George F. Baer who felt that divine wisdom had placed him in power and now it is John Lewis who feels the same exaltation.

In 1902 there was a more pronounced note of social-mindedness on the part of unions in the coal industry. *The United Mine Workers Journal* declared that the objects of the union were to maintain industrial peace "adjusting all differences so far as possible by arbitration and conciliation, that strikes may become unnecessary." For decades the miners' constitution provided for arbitration as one of its principles and objects. On June 26, 1902 John Mitchell had repeated the union offer "to arbitrate all questions in dispute." An editorial in *The American Federationist* for September, 1902, declared:

We have pointed out that labor is invariably willing to submit its demands to impartial arbitration.[58]

The Federationist further said:

These circumstances in connection with the strike are recounted so that the people of our country may place, where it properly belongs, the responsibility for all the suffering which the people may have to bear by reason of the impending coal famine. The cold blasts of winter confront us, the chattering teeth of young and innocent children; the shivering of the weak, poorly clad and underfed men and women; the stoppage of the wheels of industry and commerce; the health undermined and the thousands driven to untimely graves; the calamity threatening our entire social life and tranquillity with all the dire consequences which may follow, are all upon the heads of the mine operators.[59]

The great moral victory of 1902 was the success of the union, aided by the President of the United States, in forcing the operators to accept arbitration in order to bring to an end a stoppage that spelled disaster for the public. Today the shoe is on the other foot, and the problem of social control is complicated by the union's disregard of the public interest. John Lewis praises John Mitchell as "a very instrument of God," but repudiates his public-minded principles.

Now the union will take a strike of five or six months rather than arbitrate and boasts of its refusal of arbitration even when sought by the President of the United States. Then the practice was to continue work pending negotiation of a new contract. Now, contrary to the more civilized practice of the early labor movement, the slogan usually is "no contract—no work." Then the anthracite industry stood alone without being controlled by the destiny of the bituminous industry, and the union gave assurance that this independence would always be maintained. Today the union treats the anthracite industry as a mere pawn in the bituminous game. Then there was a real desire to observe terms of the contract. Now contract covenants are openly flouted by the union and at last the union has insisted that the customary no-strike clauses, which again are characteristic of the more civilized process of collective bargaining, shall yield to a clause that the men will work only so long as they are "able and willing to work." Long-term contracts have gone out of fashion. Contract responsibility, such as was intended by the award of 1903, has vanished. After 50 years of experience, we are further away from a proper sense of responsibility to the public. This fact shows, as always, that unchecked human power never stops at the portals of justice. One reads now with some nostalgia the statement of Philip Murray before the Anthracite Coal Commission in 1902:

Experience shows that the more fully recognition is given to a trades union the more businesslike and responsible it becomes.

Perhaps even Mr. Murray would now admit that there are some qualifications to such a statement.

The lesson to be learned from the experience in this industry is clear. It should be a warning that no system of industrial relations will prove satisfactory unless it includes as one of its facets a firm insistence on the observance of sound principles in the pubic interest and in the interests of the parties. Appeasement is not a remedy. This lesson is further emphasized by the fact that today the real difficulties in the anthracite industry arise not so much from conditions within the industry as from absentee dictation by the bituminous-dominated international union. There are many evidences that the district presidents and some local leaders in the anthracite field are ready to co-operate with the anthracite operators both in the conciliation board and in stabilizing production, and that the major friction arises largely when they too are made the puppets of outside interference. Of approximately 5000 grievances, which over a period of 46 years were not settled locally and were held for disposition by the conciliation board, about 60 per cent proved non-negotiable and were forced to arbi-

tration.   Although this is not a good record, it at least reflects
a revival of some degree of industrial order under the original
plan of 1903.   Without the Lewis leadership, it is my opinion
that contract responsibility and a better consideration of the public
interests would today dominate labor relations in the anthracite
industry.

XX

Unionism in Building Service
in New York City

THE HISTORY OF UNIONISM in the building service industry,
though in some respects of local interest, presents unique features
that make it an important case study. Having been general counsel for 15 years for the Realty Advisory Board on Labor Relations,
Inc., which functioned for the employers, I am in a position to tell
a story based on personal observations and experience.

The building service industry covers the employment of elevator
men, doormen, porters, handymen, and cleaning women in office,
loft, and apartment buildings. Skilled maintenance craftsmen,
such as carpenters, electricians, and painters, are excluded where
there is a cleancut demarcation, since the building service unions
must avoid a conflict with the well-organized and powerful construction trades. To be sure, handymen in apartment buildings
usually have craft skills, sometimes of a very high standard, but
for practical reasons their membership in the building service
union is tolerated on a live-and-let-live basis.

Building service employees in both commercial and residential
buildings on the island of Manhattan are embraced within the
jurisdiction of Local 32B of the Building Service Employees' International Union. This local excludes the cleaning women,
whose direct employment by building owners is largely confined
to commercial buildings of substantial size. They are eligible
to membership in Local 32J of the same international building
service union.

Except for the spur of low wages and long hours, which until recent years afforded a fruitful soil for organized protest, the organization of these employees by the union and the stabilization of their employment conditions as against chiselling owners seemed a difficult job. There was too much decentralization for effective organization; in each of some 4000 buildings, the average number of employees was less than ten. The problem of collective action for both the union and the employers was quite different from that presented by a single factory employing 500 or 10,000 employees, as the case might be. Then, too, many of these buildings were operated by managing agents on behalf of owners, who never entered the picture or approached the firing line except through the managing agent and who, even up to this date, have not experienced real exposure to the problems and social implications of collective bargaining.

In 1934, when my story begins, the industry had little taste of unionism and was substantially antiunion in its attitude—an attitude with which I had to struggle throughout the early years. My consistent advice to the owners and managers, even before the passage of the Wagner Act, was to do nothing to obstruct legitimate union activities. Such a platform, it seemed to me, was necessary as a matter of sound social policy and public relations. Advice of that character, as well as subsequent advice in favor of moderation and strike avoidance, finally led a growing number of supporters of the Realty Advisory Board to regard me, the "union-buster," as an appeaser. I well remember such a public denunciation from the floor at a general meeting of owners when I was tempted to remark, as President Roosevelt did, that when you are attacked by the two extremes, perhaps you are not far from right.

To meet the problem of securing collective action from these thousands of owners, jealous of their rights and profits and fearful of union encroachments, was difficult. A plan of operation was finally established whereby the Realty Advisory Board negotiated a collective-bargaining agreement, known as the "master agreement," which was binding on no employer unless and until he filed his assent with the union through the board. In practice, however, although there was often resentment over the concessions made to the union, this right to file became a valuable option that practically all members of the Realty Advisory Board who dealt with this union were eager to follow. They knew too well that if they did not exercise their right to adopt the open-shop master agreement before the deadline date, they would be attacked individually by the union in a demand for the closed shop. By this arrangement it was possible for a building with only a minority of union members, or none at all, to adopt this agreement and thus secure protection against strike action or picketing on the part of 32B. While raiding by another union was legally permissible where 32B did not have a majority, nevertheless the option, as well as the protection it afforded, was binding between employer and union. The option became so important that the union, when bargaining for the master agreement, sought to reduce the group that would qualify to enjoy it. The union aimed for broader privileges to attack individual buildings, which would be comparatively defenseless and would grant the closed shop.

With this preliminary explanation I proceed with the narrative.

In October, 1934, James J. Bambrick, president of Local 32B, threatened to tie up the elevator service in New York skyscrapers unless wage increases from 70 to 200 per cent were granted.

"If a strike is called," said Mr. Bambrick, "we will concentrate in the garment area between Fifth and Ninth Avenues and 14th and 42nd Streets." [1] He referred to the garment workers' unions as "impregnable allies" [2] and claimed that in that area the union had "8700 members out of a total of 20,000 employees." [3] In the meanwhile George Scalise, international vice president and a racketeer who had served four years in the federal penitentiary for violating the Mann Act, came to New York to direct the fight. Because of his inscrutable Italian smile we later nicknamed him after a famous portrait, "Mona Scalisa."

A strike was called in the garment area on November 1, 1934, and all loft buildings in the garment area were picketed. By noon the union announced that four-fifths of the buildings in the zone were tied up. "Flying squadrons of 100 men each," said the union, were "being sent to each building," [4] and soon 6000 employees were claimed to have joined the strike. The mayor received reports of disorder and violence, and arranged for a conference between the parties at the City Hall. Mr. Bambrick declared, "On the question of union recognition we stand absolutely firm, as we do on the closed shop." [5]

The tenants in these garment center buildings were largely garment manufacturers operating under closed-shop agreements with the garment workers' union. The employees of such tenants could hardly be expected to cross a picket line. The building owners in this large and important industry were helpless because no employers' organization as yet existed to cope with such a situation. The result was a precipitate settlement at 2 A.M. through the adoption of a printed form of agreement presented by the union. The owners signed on the dotted line. The agreement was to run until June 30, 1935, and provided for (1) the closed shop; (2) an immediate wage increase; and (3) the future arbitration of wages, hours, and working conditions.

That happened on a Saturday, and Mr. Bambrick, elated by success, announced:

About next Wednesday the strike will hit apartment houses on the east side up Park Avenue from 60th to 96th Street. It might involve 25,000 more employees. Within ten days the financial district will be reached.[6]

Vice President Scalise of the international declared:

The entire resources of the international organization will be thrown into the campaign of the Greater New York Council for the definite purpose of making New York City 100% unionized in the building service line.[7]

While these rapid events were taking place, the Real Estate Board of New York, of which Lawrence B. Cummings was president, took a hurried look at the situation. Mr. Cummings pointed out that this was a new field for the board, which was in no position to bind its members to any course of action. At best, he said, the organization "could only recommend and use its good offices in bringing about agreement."[8] He asked for time to make a survey of the working conditions maintained by the board members, but the union refused, calling this "the old run-around."[9] From the union viewpoint only a stampede could win.

Violence was generally feared in hotels, apartment houses, and business buildings, including the financial district, and the union cleverly kept the city in the jitters by holding the strike club poised without actually striking the blow. As one union official expressed it, "Only God and Mr. Bambrick know when the strike will be called."[10]

Meanwhile, the hastily organized committee representing owners and managers placed an advertisement in the New York dailies, which read as follows:

A CRISIS CONFRONTS US

The City of New York is faced with a crisis. The recent strike of elevator operators and other building employees in one of our manufacturing sections is now, according to the public announcement of those in control, to be carried to all office buildings and to apartment houses which are the homes of our citizens.

We wish to put property owners and the public on notice that if the strike is carried to these sections it undoubtedly will be accompanied by the same sort of violence that marked the original strike.

It will result in loss of employment for thousands of men happily employed, disruption of our city's commerce and violence in our homes.

We are making this as a public statement so that the public may be apprised of the situation as it is. If it is not checked at the outset the city authorities may have difficulty in quelling it later.[11]

As the clouds of conflict grew blacker, Mayor LaGuardia stepped into the picture and issued a telegram to the New York representative of the A. F. of L.:

The public is now concerned. The safety and comfort of residents of apartment houses requiring elevator service are at stake. People living in apartment houses over six stories high cannot be left with uncertainty as to whether they will ride or walk. I shall insist that these differences be immediately submitted to arbitration.[12]

He summoned the parties to the City Hall on November 20th.

At the outset the union refused to discuss any settlement unless the closed shop were first granted. The owners agreed to arbitrate hours, wages, and working conditions but would not consider the closed shop. The union then moderated its position and offered to arbitrate all issues. Confronted with this predicament, the Mayor then appointed a settlement committee composed of the attorney for the union, the attorney for the Real Estate Board, and Raymond V. Ingersoll, president of the Borough of Brooklyn and a man of broad experience in labor relations. The union then agreed to postpone the strike at least 24 hours.

The committee labored with the parties. The Mayor insisted on arbitration of all issues, and Mr. Cummings for the owners' group declared that he was specifically forbidden to arbitrate the closed shop. At four o'clock in the morning the parties reached an agreement, which took the form of a letter from the committee to the Mayor.

It provided for a committee of arbitrators, one to be selected by

Mr. Bambrick, one by Mr. Cummings, and a third to be selected by the two so chosen and to act as chairman. If agreement was not reached on this chairman, the original committee was to appoint him. For all practical purposes this meant that Mr. Ingersoll would name the chairman.

The arbitrators were to establish "reasonable minimum standards of wages and hours in the several kinds and classes of buildings in the Borough of Manhattan," and these were to take effect at such time after their announcement "as the [arbitration] Board may deem reasonable, not exceeding one year." [13]

The committee of arbitrators was also to set up agencies "for the adjustment of all complaints and grievances arising from alleged violations of such standards . . . and for the proper interpretation and maintenance of these standards." [14]

Then came the clause that recognized these standards could only be imposed on those who accepted them. The clause reads:

> During the period for which such standards are to take effect, there shall be no lockout by, and there shall be no strike against, any owner who shall have signified his acceptance of this plan and agreement by written notice to the Committee on Arbitration. [15]

In this way every owner was given the option to accept the standards and to receive the protection of this no-strike clause, or to reject the standards and be open to attack. A practical basis of operation, which still functions, was established.

On the subject of union security, the union yielded and the employers won by the adoption of the following:

> Building owners shall not in any case discriminate against any employee because of membership or activity in the union. On the other hand, employers will not be called upon to discharge any employee because he or she is not a member of the union. In the event of a vacancy in a position previously held by a union man in good standing the employer shall replace such employee only by another member of the union in good standing who is competent and qualified for the position. [16]

This came to be known as the "replacement clause."

Here was a provision designed to maintain an honest open shop. The union was protected against discrimination; the employer was relieved of the temptation to discharge union men in order to increase his percentage of nonunion men.

This short agreement was another tribute to the sagacity and fairness of Mr. Ingersoll and proved of lasting value for the basic relationships it established.   The general stoppage of vertical transportation, carried on by approximately 30,000 elevators traveling over a hundred thousand miles a day and conveying as many as 10,000,000 passengers a day, was averted largely through the skill of one man.   Meanwhile, since it did not seem advisable to involve the Real Estate Board with labor issues, the Realty Advisory Board on Labor Relations had been organized to deal with such matters in the future.

A comparison of the agreement of November 21st with the stampeded garment-center agreements of November 3 establishes the advantages of organization and sustains the truism that "before the organized, the unorganized go down."   The garment-center agreements of November 3 constituted an unconditional surrender, but the agreement of November 21st reflected collective bargaining.   The latter was an open-shop agreement and provided merely for the arbitration of reasonable minimum standards of wages and hours, such standards to become effective at some future date to be fixed by the arbitrators.   The garment-center agreements of November 3 provided for the closed shop and immediate wage increases and submitted to arbitration the broader questions of still better wages, hours, and working conditions. Moreover they were for a comparatively short term, thus opening the door for further disagreement on June 30, 1935.

In the latter part of November the union agreed that the arbitration board, which was to set up reasonable minimum standards of wages and hours pursuant to the Mayor's agreement of November 21st, should function also to carry out the arbitration provided for in the agreements of November 3.   Thus this committee was to arbitrate under both sets of agreements.

To carry out the purposes of these agreements, the Realty Advisory Board appointed Mr. Clarke Dailey as its representative on the arbitration committee, and the union appointed Mr. Bambrick.   Mr. Henry H. Curran, formerly borough president and once an unsuccessful candidate for mayor, was jointly chosen by these two to be the chairman of the arbitration committee.   Meanwhile, by continuous effort, the Realty Advisory Board induced the owners of several thousand properties to agree to be bound by this arrangement.

The arbitration hearings were closed about January 24th but were followed by long and extended discussions among the three arbitrators, supplemented by conferences with real estate owners and others in an earnest effort to secure a unanimous award. In addition to increasing wages and shortening hours, the award provided for an Administrative Board of three, composed of a representative of the union and one of the employers with Mr. Curran as chairman. The board was to interpret and maintain the new standards and to prescribe procedure for the settlement of grievances. For a time it appeared that the chairman would be able to accomplish this. At the eleventh hour, however, Mr. Bambrick refused to sign the award he had agreed to accept, because it did not extend the wage increases agreed upon to the more high-paid employees of office and loft buildings. He stated that in all other respects he was prepared to concur.

When the Curran award was submitted to a meeting of Local 32B on February 15th, the union voted to reject it. Bambrick, the president of the union, who had been one of the arbitrators, announced his readiness to lead a strike in protest against it, because it did not provide increases for the more highly paid office and loft employees—and this despite the fact that within the prior 48 hours he had assured the chairman he would abide by it.

A protest strike was organized to take effect on Monday morning, February 18th, at 10:30. At that time various buildings that came under the Curran award were struck, as well as garment-center buildings coming under the closed-shop agreements of November 3. Both agreements were violated, and some violence followed.

The Mayor issued a statement:

I have conferred with officials of the American Federation of Labor and they agree with me that the arbitration having been accepted, there is no reason for a strike and the terms of the award should be put into effect.[17]

The parties were summoned to the Mayor's office for a conference that lasted until the early morning of February 19th. During the conference reports were received by the owners' representatives that additional strikes were taking place. Thereupon, speaking for the owners, I refused to continue negotiations until all strikes were declared off. The Mayor agreed with me, and when the union leaders accepted this condition, the conference resumed.

During these negotiations in the Mayor's office our representatives stood firmly by the contention that every property owner they represented had a vested right in the Mayor's agreement of November 21st, which forbade strikes, and in the Curran award, which had been rendered pursuant to that agreement. They pointed out that since each owner individually had signed such an agreement, and the Realty Advisory Board represented them solely for the purpose of carrying out that agreement, no proposition that took away the rights of any of these owners without their individual consent could be considered. In the protracted conference to settle this unlawful strike were Edward F. McGrady, then representing the A. F. of L., Henry H. Curran, Raymond V. Ingersoll, and my own group. I well remember the Mayor, with the blood surging up his neck, slamming his fist on the table and shouting, "Merritt, I will not let you ruin my city!" But all we were trying to do was to induce 32B to abide by the Mayor's agreement of November 21st and the arbitration that took place under its terms. The owners had not liked that agreement. The union had acclaimed it as a great victory. It should surely have abided by it.

A memorandum, whereby it was agreed as follows, was finally entered into in the small hours of the morning:

1. The award was to be respected and observed;
2. The Realty Advisory Board was promptly to propose to the signatory owners of loft and office buildings, that the award be amended to
   (a) Shorten its duration to months and
   (b) Empower the administrative board under the Curran award to study classification of buildings and occupations, with a view to making such study available for the basis of negotiating a new agreement at the end of the six months' period.

Then I was whirled home in the Mayor's car about 5 A.M.

The settlement memorandum was signed by various public officials, as well as the parties. It then remained for the signatory owners of office and loft buildings, who alone were involved, to decide whether they wished to assent to a proposed amendment to the Curran award. The Realty Advisory Board proposed this amendment to them for their consideration and they rejected it.

As a matter of fact, this settlement proved merely a union face-saver and nothing ever resulted to change the original award. Ultimately there was general acceptance of the Mayor's agreement and the Curran arbitration by most of the important office, loft, and apartment buildings in Manhattan.

After the settlement in the Mayor's office on February 19th, the union concentrated on the fur and garment areas where the agreements of November 3rd prevailed. Strikes were called and others threatened against the members of the Midtown Realty Owners' Association and the Penn Zone Association, but meanwhile those organizations had become affiliated with the Realty Advisory Board and were therefore in a position to command some respect for their rights. Acting through the Realty Advisory Board, the owners twice rejected the union ultimatum and finally refused to negotiate further until all threats of strike were withdrawn. The union thereupon withdrew its threats of strike, with the result that through mediation an agreement was reached in the small hours of the morning on February 26. This agreement was drafted in final form and signed in the Mayor's office on March 1. Again in marked contrast to the agreement for the entire borough, it continued the closed shop which had already become *fait accompli* for that group.

With the signing of this last agreement peace seemed to have been established in the building service industry in Manhattan for some time to come. The garment-center agreement of March 1 did not expire until January 31, 1936. The Curran award and the agreement of November 21st, covering apartments, lofts, and offices, continued until March 1, 1936.

But peace is not everything. Nothing is ever settled until it is settled right. One of the great accomplishments of that peace was that it had eliminated substandard conditions in the building industry, where chiseling owners had taken advantage of the distress then prevailing to employ labor under oppressive conditions. From the outset the Realty Advisory Board had been opposed to such conditions and had been resolute to correct them. It was now possible more effectively to accomplish this result. The agreement provided minimum wages and maximum hours for apartments, lofts, and offices and thus prohibited a return to the former abuses, which were the main cause of the unrest with which the industry had been confronted.

On the other hand, it must be admitted that these union agreements, at best, were treaties for a limited time. Before their expiration date the negotiators again would have to convene, and if new treaties could not be effected, new difficulties would arise. None of these problems could be approached properly unless the owners were in a state of preparedness to meet all possible emergencies, whether it was negotiation based on collected facts, arbitration proceedings where the parties must support their respective positions by intelligent data, or the organized defense of right and justice, where one of the parties proved overbearing and unreasonable or seemed determined to embark on strife.

For these and other reasons, the Realty Advisory Board realized that its problems were not at an end. The permanent administration board, set up in the Curran award with Major Curran as chairman and set up in the garment-center agreement of March 1 with Judge Jeremiah T. Mahoney as chairman, had difficult questions to decide, and the presentation of these issues had to be handled under organized direction from the Realty Advisory Board. Likewise the realty owners were compelled to attempt to guide and shape industrial relations in the industry along fair and reasonable lines. To meet its future responsibilities the Realty Advisory Board established permanent offices and a permanent staff.

The garment-center agreement, known as the Mahoney agreement, was scheduled to expire on January 31, 1936. Just prior to that date rather extensive strikes were instituted against buildings that had not adopted this no-strike agreement in order to bring them within the scope of the oncoming negotiations. It was union policy at this time—but later changed—to bring as many buildings as possible under the master agreement. When the end of January arrived with no agreement for the future, Mr. Bambrick declared a fight to the finish. He announced that reception committees "would consist of men six feet tall and taller." [18] Such a contemplated stoppage, involving as it did tens of thousands of employees of tenants in the unionized garment industry, was of public importance. With the intervention of the Mayor, strike action was held off from day to day until he could meet the parties at the City Hall. On February 5, with the help of the Mayor and others, a new three-year agreement was reached providing for a two-dollar increase and running to January 31, 1939, with provisions for annual wage adjustments to meet the increased cost of living, if any.   At that time Mr. Scalise and Mr. Bambrick, both later imprisoned, were still in the picture.

In the meanwhile, the Mayor's agreement of November 21, 1934, supplemented by the Curran award of 1935 and affecting both residential and commercial buildings outside of the garment center, was due to expire on March 1, 1936.   Mr. Bambrick insisted that everything granted by the owners in the union-controlled garment center would have to be granted for the rest of the city and announced that a strike was scheduled for some time after March 1 to enforce the closed shop.   While claiming that 75,000 building service workers were prepared to respond to a strike call, he kept secret the exact date of the call.

On Sunday, March 2, when many people were at church, the storm broke.   Apartment-house dwellers still in their apartments were marooned in high stories, and those who had left to seek their place of worship or for other reasons found themselves separated from their homes.   Flying union squads spread terror, assaults took place, property was damaged, and there were many arrests. Mr. Bambrick made the extravagant announcement that before the end of the day 125,000 building service employees would be on strike.   He threatened "to tear down the whole town." [19]

A city emergency was soon declared by the Mayor, who called a peace parley and urged arbitration.   Still the employers refused to arbitrate the issue of the closed shop.   In the meanwhile, notwithstanding violence, skeleton service was being furnished the public, and the number of people applying for building service jobs increased.   Tenants organized in self-protection.   Violence increased and nonunion elevator operators were slugged by ruffian bands.   Another fruitless conference at the Mayor's office broke up at 4 A.M.   Again the union offered to arbitrate all issues, but the employers refused to include the closed shop.   One responsible city official, speaking to me alone, suggested a form of settlement whereby the employers would agree to arbitrate the closed shop, with a secret pledge from the arbitrator that he would decide against the closed shop.   This proposal constituted such a double cross that I was struck speechless.   Finally regaining my control, I merely answered in a mild voice, "We do not do business in that way."   I am afraid, however, judging from what has happened in other crises, that this was neither the first nor the last time such a ruse has been employed.   Well-intentioned people suggest startling compromises to attain laudable ends, forgetful that the maintenance of principles of straight dealing is of more enduring importance to the community than the immediate settlement of a strike.

During one of these tense days Mr. Bambrick broadcast about me over WEVD and, referring to an article entitled "Wings Over Africa," said: "The story dealt with those buzzards who sweep down upon a dying man, pick his eyes out and then in a space of twenty minutes actually devour ever part of his body and then swing away to the next victim.   That is Mr. Merritt.   His victim is labor.   His victim is the average everyday human being." [20] The following Christmas I received his card proclaiming "Peace on Earth, Good Will Towards Men."   It all sounds very amusing, but the fact remains that the rank and file who heard about the buzzards never knew about the Christmas greeting.   The sentiment of "hate the employer," which characterizes the public utterances of so many union men, is all too prevalent and finds itself growing like a rank weed in the hearts of too many union members.

After this digression, let us return to the strike crisis of 1936. As the month of March advanced, Mr. Bambrick began to qualify his closed-shop demand, and the Mayor, realizing that the owners were adamant in this respect, proposed a scheme for preferential hiring.   The owners in return offered to execute a basic agreement similar to the one that had just expired but which would run for three years and would provide for annual reopenings of wages through arbitration.

As time went on a new obstacle to settlement developed.   What would become of the increasing number of replacements when the strike was settled?   These men had been employed for permanent jobs and in the usual sense could not be properly regarded as strike breakers.   To the union, however, they were scabs.   After various meetings with public officials, lasting until dawn or nearly dawn, at which efforts to solve this issue had no results, the Mayor on March 14th appointed a Board of Survey of five distinguished citizens to facilitate arbitration.   The closed shop had now faded out of the picture and the vexatious question was how to handle returning employees whose jobs had been filled by legitimate replacements.   The union felt it could not desert any of the strikers and the employers felt they could not desert the new employees. The Mayor's Board of Survey met with the parties at the Bar As-

sociation for most of the night of March 14 and 15.   They feared
dire things for the city and talked of a rumor that Mr. Lewis would
see that no coal reached the city.   The atmosphere was tense.
The board finally persuaded the parties to sign an agreement,
which can be briefly summarized:

1. The previous agreement was to be continued for a period
of three years;

2. An immediate arbitration was to take place covering
minimum standards of employment and a like arbitration was to
be held annually thereafter, upon the application of either party;

3. Striking employees were to be restored to their previous
positions, but if any question arose as to such restoration (meaning
that the position had been filled by a replacement or that the
striker seeking his former job had been guilty of improper conduct) the question was to be arbitrated by Hugh Robertson of
Rockefeller Center;

4. Ferdinand A. Silcox of the Forestry Service to act as the
wage arbitrator.

So ended this two-week strike of building service employees,
which was the most disastrous New York ever experienced and
which threw the citizens and the public fathers into a state of
confusion and alarm.   People felt particularly touchy about
labor relations in those days.   It was less than a year before the
extraordinary collapse of government in connection with the sitdown strikes.   In fact, some building service employees practiced
sitdown strikes early in 1937.

Mr. Silcox rendered his award on April 20th and, against the
vehement protest of the members of the employer group, who felt
that he went beyond the issue submitted to him, when he classified
both office buildings and loft buildings into three groups, depend-
ing on their rental space.   For each of these groups he fixed a
different minimum wage.   Over-all increases were granted to all
groups except the highest-paid.

With the garment-center agreement running until January 31,
1939, and the Mayor's Board of Survey agreement running until
April 20, 1939, labor relations for the building service industry
in Manhattan were temporarily stabilized by no-strike covenants.
Under each agreement there were two annual reopenings of wages,
that in each instance led to arbitration with awards of wage in-

creases. By and large, despite many irritations, occasional flamboyant threats to tie up the city with general strikes, and some
actual stoppages in individual buildings, the parties were learning
to live together under these long-term agreements. In one instance at least, an impartial arbitrator under the garment-center
contract imposed monetary penalities on a high union official for
permitting a strike against handling merchandise delivered by
nonunion teamsters. Mr. Bambrick claimed that this strike was
spontaneous co-operation without organized direction, but the
arbitrator asked him whether he was running a mob or a labor
union. As most of the details of administering the three-year
agreements are of little importance or interest to the average
reader, I pass on to 1939.

In January, 1939, the committee on unlawful practice of the
law of the County Lawyers' Association, acting on the complaint
of some unnamed person, raised the old ghost as to the unlawful
practice of law by the Realty Advisory Board on Labor Relations,
Inc. The complaint was based primarily on the contention that
the board paid counsel who acted for the membership within the
scope of the board's business, the result being that the members
paid no counsel fee except through their membership dues.

Through conferences and correspondence the position of the
Realty Advisory Board was developed. The board insisted that
its counsel had the right to act for one, any, or all of its members
in collective-bargaining and all its incidents, as well as in all disputes involving the interpretation and enforcement of the union
agreement.

I argued to the committee of the County Lawyers' Association
that these matters were all an integrated and necessary part of
the collective-bargaining process as recognized by every labor
union, and that equality of bargaining rights made it desirable
that the collective activity of the employers should be equally
broad.

I called the committee's attention to the monthly journal of 32B,
which advertised to its members "free legal advice on personal
problems" and "Office Hours—Legal Department at General
Headquarters," and also to a general report on this subject in
the union magazine, which began as follows:

Counsel for the union has advised that the members in increasing numbers are attending union headquarters during consultation hours on

Monday, Wednesday and Friday of each week to seek advice pertaining to the personal problems that confront them in daily life.[21]

With this evidence before me, I asked the committee why it picked on the employer, and suggested that if the committee decided to prosecute the Realty Advisory Board it should also prosecute this union, which was clearly violating the law. The reply was, "But we would find ourselves in a hornet's nest." Needless to say, the committee decided to do no prosecuting. I was greatly amused at the attack on the employer while this union was making no pretense of observing this law and was enjoying comparative immunity. Later I took our own situation up with the Bar Association of the City of New York, which saw no impropriety in our setup.

Towards the end of January, 1939, when the garment-center agreement was about to expire, negotiations took place, with the aid of the New York State Board of Mediation, upon the terms of a new agreement. There was no issue of union security, as this was a closed-shop area, and the employers offered arbitration of all issues. The union wanted a fight. These conferences, as well as conferences with the borough president, produced no results, and a strike was called on February 1.

The following day the Realty Advisory Board published an advertisement, which, in referring to the stoppage, noted:

It was a ruthless act. It threw out of employment at the height of the manufacturing season tens of thousands of workers employed by tenants. The same union opposes a three-year contract, so that it can annually repeat this performance. There is the problem. The operation of elevators is a transportation service upon which millions of people depend. It must not become a football of industrial strife. The employers should receive a mandate from public officials and private citizens that where unions reject arbitration in an industry of such public importance, the employers must not yield to the coercion of a strike.[22]

As a matter of fact, the number of employees made idle involuntarily and indirectly by virtue of this strike of some 1400 employees was said to reach about 100,000; this illustrates how the stoppage of strategic services by a few inflicts privation on a far greater number of noncombatants. Again the Mayor sought to aid the city. He conferred with the two groups and told the union it must accept arbitration or, in the alternative, a wage increase of one dollar and a reduction of hours from 48 to 47,

When these alternatives were submitted to the union membership, they voted to accept the wage increase and hourly reduction, and on February 4, 1939, a new three-year agreement, patterned after the previous one, was executed.

The next crisis related to residential and commercial buildings outside the garment center and covered by an agreement with 32B that expired April 20, 1939.   Again the union insistence on the closed shop made negotiations difficult.   Mr. Arthur S. Meyer, chairman of the State Mediation Board, entered the discussions. The owners again agreed to arbitrate wage demands but the union refused to discuss any other issues until the closed-shop question was settled.   That position definitely prevented progress.   On April 17th the Mayor summoned the parties to the City Hall.   "If the owners think to make this a war of extermination," declared Mr. Bambrick, "we are ready to meet the challenge and fight to the end." [23]   The Mayor was particularly apprehensive, because the New York World's Fair was about to open.   On April 20th, the date when the strike was to take effect at midnight, the Mayor again appointed a committee of four citizens to find a solution. Again, as on previous occasions when contracts had expired, the issue of peace or strife hung in the balance.   Again the strike call was postponed to some future date, but this time subject to a notice of 48 hours.

On April 22nd the parties accepted the recommendations of the Mayor's committee as the basis of a new agreement.   The issue of union security was not fundamentally changed; a weekly increase of wages was granted, and minor details were to be worked out with an arbitrator.

By August, 1939, the union developed a factional fight. Charges were made by members of the union against Mr. Bambrick for malfeasance, misfeasance, neglect of duty, misuse of union funds and the use of dictatorial methods.   Mr. Bambrick obtained an injunction against holding rival meetings to displace him.   A meeting nevertheless took place, and those present voted to sustain the charges and to elect a trial board.   The court action was then withdrawn, and on December 11th a union board, including the unsavory Mr. Scalise and appointed by President Green of the A. F. of L., dismissed the charges in a palpable and shameless whitewash.

On April 22, 1940, Scalise was indicted and arrested under the

Dewey investigation for a plot to extort $100,000 from hotel owners and cleaning contractors. He was forced to resign as president of the international. Indictments for larceny and forgery followed. In September, 1940, he was tried and found guilty of one count for larceny and four counts for forgery in connection with the handling of union funds. Frank Gold, an official of Local 32B, was found guilty of extortion in February, 1941. On March 20, 1941, Bambrick himself was indicted and arrested for stealing $10,000 of union funds. In April he pleaded guilty and was sentenced to serve from one to two years in Sing Sing. In July, 1941, Robert Conroy, another union representative, pleaded guilty to extortion.

In June, 1941, David Sullivan, who for two years had been secretary-treasurer of 32B, was elected president. From that date on, despite some mistakes, which I will recount, the parties gradually developed a sounder basis of collective bargaining and, generally speaking, began to learn that in this industry the public interests must be respected.

On February 17, 1942, after some tension and with the help of Mr. Arthur S. Meyer, chairman of the State Mediation Board, a new closed-shop and no-strike agreement was signed for the garment center. Again it ran for a three-year term with annual reopenings for wages. This time the men received a 10 per cent wage increase. The main difficulty arose from the decision of the United States Circuit Court of Appeals, which had just ruled that these loft buildings, housing tenants engaged in producing goods for commerce, came under the Fair Labor Standards Act and were obligated to pay time and a half for all hours worked in excess of a 40-hour week. The owners felt that they should not be required to pay wage increases with this liability hanging over their heads. They argued that the men had received the full wage they had agreed to accept and that any additional amount imposed by statute, beyond the agreement, should be credited to a wage increase. But this argument did not prevail, although some of the union officials admitted the justice of it.

This particular negotiation marked a new atmosphere. Criminals were no longer sitting in the driver's seat. A new era had arrived. An agreement was reached. In fact, the negotiations were on the whole conducted with amazing good temper and some show of mutual understanding. The future for collective bargaining with these groups looked brighter.

In March, 1942, the parties opened negotiations for a new agreement for Manhattan as a whole, to succeed the agreement that would expire on April 20th. The Realty Advisory Board flatly rejected all demands for wage increases, as well as the union demand for the closed shop and union hiring halls. Of fresh interest was the union demand that when a signatory to the union contract sold his property, the seller should guarantee that the new owner would abide by the terms of the union agreement. They described this as a demand for "a covenant running with the land." The owners were not willing to encumber the sale of real estate by any such requirement.

As the day for the expiration of the old contract approached without any real show of progress, the Mayor invited the parties to a conference at the City Hall. Again strike action was deferred pending conference, and all proceedings were carried on under the threat of strike. Again it was the closed-shop issue that prevented an accord.

On May 1, according to union reports, 8000 employees started striking in the early morning. The Mayor denounced the strike as premature. The garment center was unaffected. The War Labor Board then called upon the parties to submit the case for hearing at the earliest possible moment. The union accepted but the owners again placed some reservations on the arbitration of the closed shop. Off to Washington the parties went. The strike had been called in violation of the no-strike pledge that had been given by the unions throughout the country and in violation of an agreement with the Mayor. It lasted 13 hours.

A panel of the War Labor Board began hearings, with the final result that on July 29, 1942, the board itself in most particulars unanimously adopted the recommendations of the panel. These recommendations included maintenance of membership (the board's favorite brand of union security), wage increases that averaged about 13 per cent, and reduced hours of employment in all buildings. The decision had direct application to about 2225 buildings and about 21,000 employees and indirectly included more. One part of the panel's report that the board did not modify said:

We do not condone the strike of May 1, 1942. It was a violation of the no-strike pledge between management and labor; a violation moreover which was apparently approved by the union's international officers.[24]

Nevertheless the panel decided to grant maintenance of membership in order to give the offending officers greater power, and the board followed the recommendation.

Based on the board's directive, a new three-year agreement running until April 20, 1945 was executed on September 1. Wage increases were retroactive to April 20th, and the usual annual reopening as to wages was required.

At this point industrial peace in the industry was stabilized under the terms of the garment-center agreement expiring February 3, 1945 and under the terms of the general agreement expiring April 20, 1945. In the next two years reopenings brought wage increases won by arbitration but controlled by the War Labor Board, which was administering wage stabilization policies. These increases continued to give the employees improved working conditions.

The next crisis arose early in 1945 because of the need of negotiating an agreement to take the place of the garment-center agreement expiring February 3, 1945 and the agreement for the city at large expiring April 20th. Voluntary agreements were made doubly difficult because of wage-stabilization laws and regulations. To comply with the Smith-Connolly Act, notices were filed by the union with the Department of Labor scheduling a strike in the garment center for April 11th and another strike for the remainder of the borough for May 19th.

On March 29th the Secretary of Labor certified the garment-center dispute to the War Labor Board. The union men in the respective buildings then voted for a strike by large majorities. Meanwhile, a regional panel of the War Labor Board was hearing the dispute. The union announced there would be no strike until the regional panel had heard the case and made its recommendations and these recommendations had been approved or rejected by the employees. When the panel finally submitted its recommendations to the regional War Labor Board, they were so favorable to the union that on July 1st they were promptly approved and accepted by the union membership. To the employers, however, they not only seemed unjust but contrary to the laws then prevailing on wage stabilization. They accordingly announced that they would oppose the adoption of the panel recommendations on appeal before the regional War Labor Board.

The regional War Labor Board held that much the panel had recommended went beyond the limits of the national wage-stabilization policy and thereby reduced the benefits that the panel had recommended. From this decision the union could appeal to the National War Labor Board, but President Sullivan defiantly announced: "We will not accept the War Board directive as handed down, and we have no intention of appealing to the National War Labor Board." [25]

In this manner was the War Labor Board rewarded, even though it granted maintenance of membership in order to give the union the fullest opportunity to show its responsibility. The Realty Advisory Board chose the opposite course. It announced: "The W.L.B. has made its decision and the employers have no intention of defying it."

The union called a strike against the business buildings, including those in the garment center. The strike paralyzed the garment industry, and the union continued to brandish the big stick by threatening to extend it to apartment buildings. In the garment center alone it was said that 300,000 workers were thrown out of work. There were threats of a general strike throughout the city, which the press did not ignore. All this was an irresponsible attack on the War Labor Board.

To a meeting of building owners at the Commodore I said:

> It is more important to vindicate the rights of the public in this present crisis than to settle the particular issues. The only sound objective is a durable peace, not a temporary peace. The union must be resisted in the present holdup so that it knows for all time that the people have the courage to defend themselves. . . .

The regional War Labor Board sought to mediate, but without success. The only issue was the enforcement of its own decision. The State Mediation Board intervened through its chairman, and the Realty Advisory Board suggested the establishment of a three-man commission with power to rule in such crises.

Finally on Saturday, September 29th, Governor Dewey wired each of the parties:

> As Governor of the State of New York I call upon your organization to resume operations of the struck buildings on Monday morning and to submit your differences to an impartial arbitrator. If you cannot agree

upon an arbitrator I will name one directly to proceed immediately and hand down findings within ten days.[26]

And so, after all, the employers were being told to rearbitrate a case that had already been arbitrated by an agency of the federal government. The Governor cut behind the decision of the War Labor Board by forcing a new arbitration. Of course the union immediately accepted the Governor's edict. The owners also accepted, because of lack of unity in their ranks, and the Governor appointed the Honorable George Frankenthaler to retry the case.

Mayor LaGuardia made this comment:

A dissatisfied party, either one, should not be permitted to reject the decision and shop around for another agency. . . . In this instance, in all likelihood, it is a foregone conclusion that a better award will be obtained by the employees. We should stop to consider, though, if this is really rendering a service to organized labor, for when conditions change, as well may happen, it may be the employers who will reject decisions. . . .[27]

On October 11th the expected happened, as the arbitrator handed down his award. The award contained no word of reproof for the union's misconduct and practically gave it that for which it had been striking, except that in substance the award was made effective as of October 1st instead of April 20th. In response to the arguments of the employers, who tried to save some hope of industrial order for the future by urging a long-term contract with arbitration, the arbitrator inserted a so-called "Peace Plan," which, when the expiration date of an agreement approached, called for negotiations and conciliation through the State Board of Mediation and finally fact-finding by a board to be appointed by the Governor. To provide opportunity for such peaceful processes stoppages were forbidden for a period of 45 days following the expiration of the agreement.

The award applied to both the garment center and the rest of the city and extended these two agreements, with appropriate changes, for another period of three years from their respective expiration dates. So government officials rewarded labor for resistance to orderly procedures, and the public showed no disapproval.

My story then follows the old theme. The three-year peace was fairly uneventful, with interim arbitration awards continually pushing wages upwards. As 1948 approached, and with it the expiration dates of the two contracts, everybody wondered whether the parties were girding themselves for another battle.

By February 26, 1948, President Sullivan was able to announce that for the first time since the parties began negotiating 14 years before they had reached an agreement for the garment center without a strike or threat of strike. Our price of peace was a five-dollar weekly increase. Business was booming, and the union's bargaining position was strong. The union shop, as provided for under the Taft-Hartley Act, was substituted for the closed shop, but this required separate elections for each building, which were held under the auspices of the National Labor Relations Board.

Difficulties arose, however, when it came time to negotiate a new contract for the office, loft, and apartment buildings outside of the garment center to take the place of the contract scheduled to expire on April 20, 1948. The five-dollar increase granted the employees of the business buildings in the garment center seemed to be a logical pattern for the workers in business buildings outside that area, particularly as the owners were enjoying comparative prosperity. But with residential buildings it was a different story. These owners were confronted with rising costs, rents frozen by rent controls, and diminishing profits, if not actual losses. The return on investment was grossly inadequate. The owners of those buildings operating under strict rent control did not feel that they could absorb a further wage increase, nor did they feel that they could trust their precarious destiny to arbitration. On the other hand, the union, with about an even division of membership between business buildings and apartment houses, could hardly accept a smaller increase for those working in residential buildings than they were able to obtain for the employees of commercial buildings, who were working shorter hours. The parties were bargaining within narrow walls that confined both of them, and some novel solution had to be discovered.

It was for this reason that the apartment-house group bargained separately from the commercial-building group and finally accepted the inevitable five-dollar increase under a three-year agreement. Both parties, however, had the privilege of cancelling, rather than arbitrating, if they were unable to agree upon wages

at the time of the annual reopening.   The commercial buildings
followed the usual pattern by agreeing to arbitrate on the reopenings.

The reasons for this change of policy concerning apartment
buildings was expressed in the agreement itself as follows:

The Employers have insisted that apartment buildings faced with regulated rents and mounting costs are in a depressed financial condition and
unable to meet any increase in operating costs.   The Union has listened to
these representations of the owners but feels that such a hardship, if it
exists, should not be borne by apartment house Employees, to the extent
of denying them an increase at least equal to that granted to like classifications in loft and office buildings.   The parties have accordingly accepted
the Mediator's proposal as to apartment buildings that if an agreement
cannot be reached through negotiation in connection with any annual
reopening in December, as herein provided, either party may cancel the
agreement in respect to apartment buildings effective April 20th of the
following calendar year.   The purpose of this option to cancel is to give
the rent control authorities full opportunity to consider this matter and to
give either party the opportunity to escape from the obligations of a
contract negotiated in the face of present obstacles.[28]

When 1949 came around, the date of reopening for commercial
buildings outside of the garment center for the first time preceded
the reopening for the garment center.   The former group therefore
had to carry the burden of the arbitration, which, after contested
hearings with economic experts on each side, resulted in another
increase of $3.50.   To this was added the Blue Cross Hospitaliza-
tion Plan, which had been arranged through direct negotiation.

Meanwhile no agreement had been reached covering apartment
buildings, and neither party was required to arbitrate.   The union
served the required notice of termination.   As April 20th arrived
the old agreement expired, and there was no new agreement on
wages.   The issue was wide open.   There were many awkward
and anxious moments, for each group recognized the problems of
the other.   There was no leeway for compromise.   After various
conferences with the chairman of the State Mediation Board, however, the committee for the apartment-house owners signed an
agreement on May 5 granting the $3.50 increase and the Blue
Cross Hospitalization Plan, but it was an agreement for only one
year.   More than ever before it looked like an armistice rather
than a peace.

With the rise in wages came still another problem.   To economize, building owners reduced their staff and curtailed the service available to tenants, and more and more apartments installed self-service elevators.   To this trend labor reacted by repeated demands that the collective-bargaining agreements should contain a clause against any reduction in the number of building service employees.   It is a familiar story: With wages at their present levels, neither subways nor railroads can afford to have trainmen on every platform, and many young women can no longer afford to employ domestics.   The public, whether they are maintaining a home, travelling on a public conveyance, or living in an apartment, must learn to expect less service for their dollar, for service costs too much.   To that extent labor is in danger of pricing itself out of the market—or at least, that was the fear of the building service union.   Of course responsible managers would not yield to such a full-crew demand of the union for building service.

Now we turn back to the time when comedy entered the picture. In this business each building is a separate unit for collective bargaining; each owner is a separate employer operating under an individual agreement, if he elects to adopt the master agreement. Each building is a competitor of other buildings in its class.   The average apartment building employs about ten building service employees and a resident manager, called a superintendent, who hires, fires, and directs, and who is the owner's sole representative on the job.   In principle he may be compared to the chief executive of some factory within a large corporation.

What was our astonishment, therefore, when in 1943 Local 219, a sister local of 32B, asked that it be certified as the collective-bargaining agent for a superintendent in a large apartment house. Thus the union claimed the superintendent as a one-man unit for collective bargaining and sought to throw management's sole representative into a building service union affiliated with a union of the rank and file.   Such was the issue presented in three separate petitions filed by Local 219 for three separate buildings.

In opposing these petitions we argued: (1) that it was a contradiction in terms to call one man a collective-bargaining unit; and (2) that the superintendent, being the sole representative of the owner on the job, was for practical purposes the employer.   We urged that the superintendent could not properly function if he transferred his loyalty to a union which acted in concert with a union of the rank and file.   On all these issues, we lost.

The National Labor Relations Board had held that one man could not constitute a separate unit for collective bargaining.[29] The state board held otherwise, and in 1946 the New York State Courts upheld its ruling.[30]

A labor board election had to be held for each building. Under the law it had to be by secret ballot, so that no one in these cases would know how the superintendent voted. There were no short cuts. A comedy of Gilbert and Sullivan proportions began.

Notice of election with a sample ballot was sent by mail to the lonely voter and was posted on the premises. The notice announced that a majority vote would control. At the voting place the voter received the official ballot. A representative of the N.L.R.B. was present at the voting place to guard the ballot box from being packed by ineligible voters. The union and the employer had representatives as watchers to see that there was no foul play or irregularity. The lonely voter was instructed to fold his ballot so as to conceal how he voted and then to deposit it in the ballot box in the presence of the N.L.R.B. representative. The ballot was then "counted and tabulated" under the supervision of the representative of the Board, duly watched by representatives of the employer and the union. The agent of the Board then formally reported to the Board that "the ballots were duly and fairly counted" and the report, in the three cases of the superintendent elections, showed a unanimous choice, 1 to 0. The mountain labored and brought forth a mouse.

Such is the story of unionism in building service down to 1950. The industry was frontier land for unionism when it embarked on its first major venture in 1934 and its relation with several thousand individual owners involved many problems for which practical solutions had to be discovered. Long-term contracts, with arbitration of annual wage reopenings and of grievances arising during the term of the contract, were the practice until apartment houses faced the restrictions of rent control. Political mediation or voluntary arbitration was necessary to protect the public because of the strategic nature of vertical transportation in a city of skyscrapers. The wage scale and other conditions of employment were the resultant of collective bargaining between a strong union and an employers' association, plus political pressures. The importance of the service involved, coupled with the readiness of public officials to seek peace at any price, has been instrumental in creating a generous wage scale with job security. Employment relations have become sounder than might have been expected. An examination of the various agreements outside the garment center will disclose an absence of such embarrassing features as the closed shop, extreme seniority, restrictions on promotions, and other familiar encroachments on management. As a later development, an over-all informal grievance committee was established to handle all disputes not settled at the local level before they were permitted to go to arbitration. The administration of the agreement has been satisfactory. Between the leaders in the two groups, there has evolved, notwithstanding occasional outbursts, a creditable feeling of good nature, goodwill, and mutual understanding. On the employers' side a large part of the credit is due to William D. Rawlins, the executive secretary of the Realty Advisory Board until the summer of 1949. Considering the pressure for more radical leadership within the union, the results attained by President Sullivan show a broadening viewpoint.

Experience with collective bargaining in the building service industry in New York City is in marked contrast with experience in the anthracite industry. Anthracite started with John Mitchell, who, recognizing his responsibilities to the public, pledged himself and his union to the principle of voluntary arbitration and the faithful performance of union agreements. In its first battle the union won an advanced type of industry-wide government, but, despite the intoxicating victory, kept its head. From this early standard, collective bargaining in this industry ultimately sank lower and lower—particularly after the advent of the Lewis leadership—until the principle of arbitration was spurned with scorn, even when urged by the President. Contract violations were at times deliberately fostered. Contract responsibility was discarded. The closed-shop monopoly displaced the principle of no discrimination, and nationwide stoppages and curtailments were maneuvered to inflict maximum privations on the public. Collective bargaining between employers and unions gave way to collective bargaining between the unions and the government. Strategy that formerly depended, and which in a free economy must depend, on the economic pressures either side may apply to the other gave place to a revolutionary strategy to high-pressure society.

In the building service industry the trend has been otherwise.

Local 32B started with a low level of racketeering leaders, some of whom have since been behind prison gates. The very first arbitration that took place under the Mayor's agreement in 1935 led to a protest strike in that year. In 1942, to be sure although the racketeers had been eliminated, a strike took place in violation of the nationwide no-strike pledge and in violation of an agreement with the Mayor. Again in 1945 a further strike against the War Labor Board was sanctioned and rewarded by the Governor.

Despite these bad beginnings and the indefensible incidents of 1942 and 1945, a time when appeasement by government was an outstanding policy, the record of collective bargaining is on the whole one of continued improvement and increased consideration of the public interests. The parties have learned to live together under the terms of their agreements.

The mine workers' slogan of "no contract, no work," their adamant refusal to arbitrate, and their aim to inflict maximum suffering on the public have no counterpart in the building service industry in New York. The over-all long-term building service agreements with no-strike covenants have usually been respected. Union leadership has shown improved statesmanship, and I believe it would not at the present time question its responsibility to resort to arbitration rather than throw metropolitan life into confusion.

The reasons for these contrasting pictures of progression and retrogression are several and the lessons are obvious. Firmness for right principles on the part of any group, whether it be employers, unions, or the public, constitutes one indispensable factor for the promotion of industrial self-government. Incidents like governmental tolerance of lawlessness and tolerance of strikes against a government or government agencies are examples of social retreat from which it takes long to recover. The journey back recalls the Chinaman's comment on the toboggan slide, "Swish—walkee half a milee." The over-all picture of labor relations in this country is unfortunately cloudy, and largely because there is too great a tendency to compromise principles without which liberty and order cannot survive. Our attitude in this respect was more courageous 50 years ago. The doctrine that the ends justify the means is receiving growing sanction from those in high places as well as from those who must be satisfied with a narrower horizon.

PART II

XXI

Injunction Phobia

IT SEEMS TO BE POSSIBLE by persistent propaganda to put over almost any idea. That has been proved to be true to an incredible degree where censorship has prevented presentation of competing or corrective views. It is importantly true with growing class consciousness, where the acceptance of any idea depends, not upon its inherent merit, but upon the background of the person who advances it.

The injunction phobia, planted by persistent propaganda, is typical of the waves of public opinion that have carried us off balance. To deal with it intelligently is political dynamite. The propaganda on which it was fed began in the opening of the century, as we have shown, with statements by Samuel Gompers that the injunction was the "outrageous, impudent, revolutionary invention of lawless plutocracy."[1] This propaganda, meeting little resistance, has resulted in blind acceptance of assumptions that are not well founded. I know of no other controversial subject where open-minded discussion and intelligent treatment are more impossible than the subject of labor injunctions. The wave of injunction phobia is so powerful that it is a political risk for anyone in public office to discuss the subject on the basis of an informed analysis. It took us so long to correct the abuse of injunctive power that labor still persists in its blind and undiscriminating attacks on all labor injunctions, whatever the circumstances or occasion for their consideration. The tidal wave of propaganda made the most of this. Half the states passed anti-injunction laws before it expended its full force. Any fair reconsideration of this subject still seems almost an untouchable.

239

George Meany, secretary of the A. F. of L., writing for *The American Federationist* of May, 1949, under the title "Why Labor Hates Injunctions," is unable to make any case against them except by referring to conditions and circumstances that are gone, never to return.   He says that in the past "the employers having a powerful ally in the court, would quickly confront the strikers with an injunction" and that "in a fit of hysteria the reactionary Eightieth Congress turned the clock back." [2]   I submit that it is labor that views this problem with hysteria and that no sound argument has been advanced against the use of the injunction, either to protect private rights or to uphold public policy, when the process is properly regulated.   Certainly it is only those who are fighting against the existing order who can truly feel that the courts are now pro-employer and antilabor.   Theodore Roosevelt in an annual message to Congress in 1907 declared, "The process of injunction is an essential adjunct of the court's doing its work well; and as preventive measures are always better than remedial, the wise use of this process is from every standpoint commendable." [3] What man in public office today would endorse this statement in connection with labor injunctions?

The time has come to get this controversial issue on an even keel: to safeguard labor against injunction abuses and to safeguard the public against blind opposition to all labor injunctions. There is no difficulty in steering such a course.   If we will start from scratch and revaluate this problem and the possible solutions, if we will live down the powerful political prejudice on this subject, which draws an iron curtain against a sober scrutiny of the problem, we shall perform a national service.

To do this let us now re-examine some fundamentals.

For the protection of rights, public or private, there are only a few major legal controls: injunctions, compensation for injuries, fines or imprisonment, and in a more limited group of cases, forfeitures.   Notwithstanding present distorted notions on this subject in the labor field, each of these remedies is fundamental and prevalent in the administration of justice in this country.

Of all these controls, the injunction is the most benign, because it warns the wrongdoer to cease and desist from a particular course of conduct before otherwise proceeding against him.   If the injunction is obeyed, no other consequences need follow.   The businessmen of this country would be thankful indeed if, in dealing with the twilight zones of the antitrust laws, they could feel sure that they would always have the benefit of the injunction proceeding before they could be mulcted in damages or adjudged to be criminals.

In the last half-century, except in dealing with unions, the injunction has become a nationally accepted instrument of justice for the purpose of effectuating social policies. By the Clayton Act Congress deliberately extended to private parties the right to secure injunctions against economic combinations while at the same time seeking to limit injunctions against labor. Mr. Justice Frankfurter in a recent opinion speaks of the "increasing use of injunctions for the enforcement of administrative orders and statutory duties." [4] Injunctions are provided for in the antitrust laws, the Interstate Commerce Act, the Federal Trade Commission Act, the Securities & Exchange Commission Act, the Fair Labor Standards Act, and numerous others. Thousands upon thousands of injunctions, in the form of cease and desist orders, were issued to protect labor under the Wagner Act. Moreover when a local union comes into conflict with a rival union or a local union comes into conflict with its international, and in many other situations, the unions seek injunctions. With the growing popularity and acceptance of this remedy to deal with problems in so many walks of life, including the protection of labor itself, I see no reason why legislators should not have the resourcefulness to write reasonable rules and regulations safeguarding labor from the misuse of injunctions but permitting the courts to issue injunctions to protect private and public rights in labor disputes.

The idea that the courts cannot be trusted to deal fairly with labor, I dismiss as unworthy of notice. If our courts are untrustworthy, we should stop passing regulatory laws giving them more and more power over the lives and liberties of all of us. In a democratic country such as we have today, it cannot be demonstrated that courts are antilabor and pro-employer. Ours has become a laboristic society and there is no government institution that has more completely yielded to this trend than the courts. What I have already written is incontrovertible proof of this assertion.

Why has the injunction remedy been included in so many of our statutes? Why have 14 states or more included it as an instrument to enforce labor policies? The answer is that it is an effective instrument of social control.   Why do so many people oppose the injunction in labor disputes?   I think it is for exactly the same reason.   If the boundaries of right and wrong are carefully set forth by our popular assemblies, there would seem to be no reason why a remedy that is both effective and benign should not be applicible here as elsewhere to guard such boundaries.   Mr. Gompers, who bitterly fought certain injunctions against labor, seemed to have entertained the same thought when in writing for *The Federationist* in February, 1922, he declared:

Labor has no objection to the writ of injunction when properly used.   It is when the injunction commands the doing of things which the workers have a lawful right not to do, or when the injunction forbids the doing of things which the workers have a lawful right to do, that labor protests.[5]

That is exactly my point, but let me be more specific: It is not a question of vesting the judiciary with authority or discretion to determine what shall be lawful and what shall be unlawful.   That is a legislative function.   It is merely a question of looking to the courts to enforce the legislative will through the usual remedies and penalties.   To distrust the courts and to deny them their normal and usual functions in this particular field is to go contrary to the fundamental structure and purposes of our government and the realities of the present.   When the popular will has defined the boundaries of legality and illegality in connection with industrial strife and the methods by which it may be carried on, the only remaining question for judicial determination is the application of the remedies or controls to enforce the democratic will. It is as simple as that.

The constitutional right to quit work is not controverted.   The right of men spontaneously to quit work singly or in groups would not be restricted by anything I am now advocating.   It is only with the organized incitement and support of stoppages for illegitimate ends and unlawful interference with the rights of others that I deal.   Spontaneous nonco-operation by the workers without inducement or aid from others would be allowed to run its course. If government decides that under certain extreme or special situations men engaged in unorganized and irresponsible stoppages shall forfeit some special statutory privileges, that is another matter, which I am not discussing.   I speak only of organized action for unlawful ends or organized action aided by unlawful means and the best method of protecting the community against it.

In evaluating any proposal in this highly controversial field, it is important to distinguish between the strike as a constitutional right to quit work and the normal pattern of a strike where employers and nonstrikers may wish to continue, or resume, operations and are prevented from so doing.

Not enough attention has been given to isolating the word "strike," which need not connote more than a peaceful quitting of work without organized leadership or support or without otherwise obstructing the operations of a business. Speaking of his understanding of a strike, Mr. Gompers declared in 1913, "Strike is not an aggression act, it is not an affirmation act, it is negation. It is expressed by nonresistance. It is the state of doing nothing." [5a] Realistically a so-called "strike," as the word is used today, is usually a package with additional and varied contents.

Any prohibition of stoppages by those directly involved in a labor dispute is contrary to our free institutions, except where exigent public interests require protection, but when we so frequently euphemize industrial disturbances, including those which involve civil rebellion, by calling them strikes, we are immediately involved in confusion. Where a strike—perhaps of a small minority of the employees—is followed by mass picketing, organized violence, boycotting, sympathetic extension of the strike against noncombatants in order to pressure the public, and demonstration strikes against police interference, it is far more accurate to call it industrial strangling or industrial war. It is no longer just nonco-operation. It becomes aggression. The right to abandon jobs in concert with others is quite different from the asserted right to prevent others from taking the jobs, to strangle the employer's business, and to inflict maximum injury upon the community by positive attack. We should long since have coined a word to distinguish more clearly between such activities and the right to strike. The promiscuous use of the word "strike" has been the cause of much confusion. To use it interchangeably when speaking of the constitutional right to quit work and when speaking of organized strangling of a business misleads the public.

The labor injunctions I would propose are not even remotely

suggestive of compulsory work or involuntary servitude.[6] They restrain the mechanics of promoting or maintaining an illegal strike by enjoining leaders from instigating, guiding, or supporting such a strike or picketing or boycotting in furtherance thereof, but they do not chain workers to their jobs. The injunctions might even go further and require the leaders to cancel strike orders and otherwise to take all reasonable steps to prevent or end an illegal stoppage. Reaching the leaders who direct and control such concerted movements is usually all that is necessary to deal with such situations. Large groups do not act together without a binder, usually a spellbinder. Spontaneous combustion is rare. In the case of lawful strikes an appropriate injunction might require union officials to take all reasonable steps within their powers to keep picketing within lawful limits.

By what courts and subject to what procedures such orders should be issued and by what procedures such orders, if defied, should be enforced are matters of legislative determination. I do not discuss them here, because I wish to drive home the simplicity of my point that court orders or administrative orders to prevent the promotion of industrial stoppages that are wholly unwarranted should not be discarded as something impracticable or undesirable. In fact I am convinced that there can be no such thing as the social control of industrial warfare except through the use of the injunctive process. The fact that society has adopted it as a remedy in connection with the enforcement of so many other social policies is certainly presumptive evidence that the majority of people, when not bitten with the "injunction phobia," agree with me. Evidently Congress had something of the same feeling when in the Taft-Hartley Act it gave authority to the Attorney General, on direction of the President, temporarily to enjoin national emergency strikes. It also vested the N.L.R.B. with power to issue cease and desist orders against unfair labor practices and against strikes that conflict with Board decisions, jurisdictional strikes, and strikes used as a means of boycotting products.

To show that my underlying idea as to injunctions is not so far removed from reality, I quote a clause from an A. F. of L. contract with a large employer:

If any strike or stoppage occurs in violation of this agreement, the Unions agree immediately and publicly to disavow such strike or stoppage: to use all reasonable means to prevent the conduct and continuance of such strike or stoppage by their officers, agents or members; to take prompt and adequate action, disciplining and penalizing any of its members or representatives who abet, or participate in such a strike or stoppage; to use its best endeavors to prevent picketing, boycotting, payment of financial aid, and any kind of propaganda or advertisement against the Employer, in connection with said strike or stoppage.[7]

To be sure, these are self-imposed contractual obligations, but they are assumed and, if not carried out, should be enforceable in court. By a like token, if a proposed stoppage is contrary to the law of the land, I see no reason why comparable obligations should not be imposed by law and enforced by injunction. Obligations voluntarily assumed by contract cannot be deemed too unreasonable and onerous in character to be imposed by law when public interests are involved.

In contending for the right to restrain organized promotion of antisocial strikes, I am not unmindful of the importance of protecting the right to strike for legitimate ends. The strike is socially desirable as a weapon of last resort to secure justice and to promote social reform. The value of that right is in direct proportion to the power it carries. As a lever for social improvement it has few compeers, but by like token it becomes an implement of tyranny and injustice when employed for antisocial ends. The right to strike and strike effectively is one of the indicia of freemen and a free economy, and in its normal use it is better to endure its evils than to pay the price of alternatives. This does not lead to the conclusion, however, that such a devastating power should not be confined to its proper sphere, and it does not refute the conclusion that the injunction is the most benign and effective means of securing that desirable result.

The unique nature of the right to strike supports this viewpoint. The strike is not comparable to any other civil right recognized by law. Just as revolution is a sacred right of last resort to correct wrongs not otherwise remediable, so the right to strangle business and injure the community should be appraised as a radical surgical operation not lightly to be undertaken. Laws requiring a union to deliberate before embarking on such a destructive enterprise should be helpful to everybody. Strikes should not continue to be commonplace.

The public is fed up by industrial strife. It does not believe in violence or the resort prematurely or unnecessarily to industrial strife. It does not approve of strikes in violation of contract or for illegal or political purposes, and since industrial strife has a disastrous impact on the community, the public believes that it is justified in establishing a legal code that confines industrial strife to a necessary use. In doing this, however, it does not wish to destroy important individual rights.

Let us further fortify our conclusion by illustration. Over 50 years ago the Supreme Court of the United States, in commending the action of the federal government for seeking the peaceful settlement of the Pullman difficulties through appeal to the Court for an injunction, quoted from a speech by Mr. Debs, as follows:

Once we were taken from the scene of action, and restrained from sending telegrams or issuing orders or answering questions, then the minions of the corporations would be put to work. . . . Our headquarters were temporarily demoralized and abandoned, and we could not answer any messages. The men went back to work, and the ranks were broken, and the strike was broken up, . . . not by the army, and not by any other power, but simply and solely by the action of the United States courts in restraining us from discharging our duties as officers and representatives of our employees.[8]

Since the Debs Case provoked the bitterest diatribes against the injunction and since the foregoing is Mr. Debs' own description of its horrors, it behooves us to take a second glance at the picture painted by him. It was the order against the activities of the leaders and officers, and not against the rank and file, that was presented as a grievance. As the Court said: "The right of any laborer, or any number of laborers, to quit work was not challenged."[9] It was the control of the rank and file by the leaders that could start or stop the disturbance. To deal with this control and direction does not in any way impinge upon the right of each worker to determine whether or not he will continue at work. Mass action is difficult to start, and even more difficult to maintain, in the absence of guidance and direction from on top. It will be remembered that in 1920 the mine workers, responding to the insistence of the President, felt "forced to accept" arbitration because this "tying-up of union funds" and other things made it "almost humanly impossible to wage a successful battle."[10] But why not, if the issue is merely the protection of public or private rights from combinations that the people's legislature has declared to be against the public interest?

One amusing incident showing the effectiveness of union control and the injunction process I shall never forget. A strike was about to be called in violation of contract and I secured an injunction. The court order was then served on the president of the union as he was presiding over a mass meeting of members. The president paused to glance at the papers and then shouted, "Boys, we are enjoined, the strike is off!" Nor did there seem to be anything loath in his announcement.

The story has significance. There are many times when union officials, driven by the demands of union politics, welcome an opportunity to escape from a position into which they have been pushed by the leadership of some clamorous rival. So often is this true that I sometimes wonder how much ground has been lost by the failure of government to support conservative union leadership with adequate laws that would furnish them with alibis when radicals shout for something the conservative leader thinks is unwise. With violence and indefensible stoppages condoned by the government and, to an important extent, by the laws of the land, the conservative leader has been in no position to raise the banner of social righteousness when the radical takes the floor. To be sure at times he may not openly seek to remedy this situation but sometimes he might secretly welcome the change.

To order union officials to employ their official influence and authority to minimize antisocial strife is consistent with our policy to look to union officials to govern union members within the limits of union bylaws. We would but follow the trends if we looked to the unions and their officers for co-operation in establishing a proper relationship between the workers and the public. Unions should be something more than collective-bargaining agencies. They are, or should be, public agencies—still treated as too private. Society should be able to look to them for protection from irresponsible action. Unions have asked for authority and control and have been given it. They must accept responsibility, not only for the behavior of their membership to the employer, but for their behavior toward the public. They must utilize their power not only to make gains but to promote adherence to the laws of the land.

We should not close this chapter without emphasizing the beneficial effects of an injunction against picketing for unlawful ends. Probably the greatest contribution to industrial strife, with all its distressing incidents, is picketing, particularly mass picketing. If picketing were enjoinable in connection with unnecessary and illegitimate strikes, we would be taking a long step forward in creating a better state of industrial order.

The experience of the government in restraining national emergency strikes by injunctions issued under the Taft-Hartley Act has demonstrated the efficacy of such a social control. A possible exception was the coal strike of 1950, which was so mishandled by the government that it proved nothing. Union responsibility for the uniform conduct of its several hundred thousand members scattered throughout many states can certainly be established by statute. In nearly every instance under the Taft-Hartley Act, the injunction order was observed and the strike was postponed. In the case of the coal strike in 1946 an injunction, issued before the passage of the Taft-Hartley Act, was ineffective partly because of the speed of events but was finally vindicated by heavy fines against the United Mine Workers and John Lewis. From the angle of experience as well as theory, it would seem that the injunction, as one of the remedies in the arsenal of jurisprudence, should be employed in industrial disputes wherever appropriate to secure compliance with established social policies.

The Supreme Court, in upholding an injunction to require the Brotherhood of Locomotive Engineers to represent minority groups without discrimination (in this case, Negroes), rejected the claim that the Norris-LaGuardia Act was a bar and said, "To depart from those views would be to strike from labor's hands the *sole judicial weapon* it may employ to enforce such minority rights." [11]

I have never heard a sound argument against the labor injunction, as such, that cannot be met by proper regulation. I have heard many good arguments against particular labor injunctions as going too far, or as being improvidently granted. But why deprive society, or the administration of justice, of a useful weapon of defense against destructive strife because it was once misused? Why not aim at the misuse? It does not make sense to say that the injunction is a useful and permissible remedy in connection with all human activities except labor disputes.

I endorse the statement of the late Justice Louis D. Brandeis when he said:

The plea of trades unions for immunity, be it from injunction or from liability for damages, is as fallacious as the plea of the lynchers,[12]

Labor's emotion over the injunction distorts its reason, probably because in this field it has been shown such outstanding and unreasoning favoritism. A resolution passed at the C.I.O. convention in November, 1946, entitled "Anti-Labor Injunctions," condemns the injunction against the United Mine Workers, as well as the one obtained by the city of Pittsburgh when the city was thrust into darkness. Then, in language which smacks of revolutionary fervor, the resolution declares, "The attempts by judges to nullify existing anti-injunction laws must be smashed." [13] Again there is heat but no light. Social control there must be, if democratic order is to prevail. It is far better for unionism that this control be through injunction, or cease and desist orders, than through criminal prosecutions and suits for damages. Feeling as strongly as I do on this subject, I can but exhort the public:

> On fires that glow with heat intense
> Let's turn the hose of common sense.

XXII

Industry-Wide Bargaining and Stoppages

THE LURE OF PAPER THEORIES is strong. So is it with industry-wide bargaining or multi-employer bargaining, which seems to offer a real opportunity for industrial self-government. One can envision a labor agreement blanketing an entire industry, with broad areas of bargaining reserved for local levels, but with a joint industry-wide board of mediation and arbitration to deal with disputes not settled at the local level. A few industries like the clothing and glass industries have approached such a pattern of self-government, and English and Scandinavian experiences along similar lines have yielded favorable results. On the other hand, the power developed by such an extension of collectivism raises serious problems of individual rights and public welfare.

One of the unfortunate results of industry-wide bargaining is its adverse effect on democratic procedures. It spells the death knell of local bargaining. In most cases where industry-wide standards or their equivalent are determined by collective bargaining, the great majority of employers and local unions have little or no voice in what takes place. A pattern is offered them by an absentee power they do not control. Thus local collectivism is swallowed by national collectivism and individual control or responsibility is elbowed still further into the background. Then there is the public problem of self-protection. In coal production, for illustration, industry-wide agreements controlling an entire industry have led to nationwide stoppages, which are intolerable.

In industries or functional groups where the public is not seriously and suddenly injured by industry-wide stoppages and where capacity for self-government and self-restraint is indicated, it may be that labor and management should be trusted to establish a *nisi prius* self-government for the industry as a whole, with the right of review lodged with some public board when the interests of the community are endangered.   Such a development might be one of the alternatives to more bureaucracy, or British Socialism, and might promote a greater degree of acceptance and co-operation from those who are regulated.   In principle that was the underlying theory of the Swope Plan and the N. I. R. A. in the 1930's, when the government adopted the theory of self-rule but made the mistake of intervening too much in the administration of the plan, instead of confining itself to the function of a review board on complaint.

The obvious economic consequence of industry-wide bargaining, like the fundamental philosophy of unionism, is the removal of wage standards from competition.   It may permit wage differentials as between different regions where variations in living costs and other costs justify differentials, but, by and large, it means that no employers and no group of employees will be permitted to profit by breaking wage standards.   This is the very essence of unionism, and notwithstanding its risks, we enforce it by laws that require minority groups to refrain from competing in wage rates with the majority group within the bargaining unit. In principle our common law has recognized the right of labor to a protective monopoly by permitting the boycott of goods made under substandard conditions.   The Webbs in their book on industrial democracy [1] said "It is a necessary incident of the collective bargain that one man should not underbid another."   The debate over industry-wide bargaining or multiple bargaining is whether or not groups of employees in competing factories are warranted in extending this protection to cover employees of many different employers.   Evidently there were many in the House and Senate in 1946 and 1947 who thought that by legislative fiat we could enforce competition between groups of workers in different factories and could substitute factory solidarity for class solidarity by forbidding multiple bargaining, for a provision to that effect barely escaped being included in the Taft-Hartley Act.

If, on the other hand, we accept the class-cleavage concept of noncompetitive wages, with all its implications, we necessarily have to face the alternatives of industry-wide bargaining, a realistic fair labor standards act, or possibly secondary boycotting of goods made under substandard conditions. Under no circumstances, it is urged by those who uphold this philosophy, shall labor become the victim of a competitive battle.

Bearing in mind the logic of economic facts and policies, as well as world trends with which we are contending and our limited and varying experiences with large-scale bargaining, I believe its unqualified condemnation either by law or public opinion is not warranted by the present record. The size and far-flung character of existing units, which are the dynamic results of modern industrialism, reflect changes and forces difficult to check by legal edict.

Twenty-two national unions have a combined membership of nearly 10,000,000 or an average of 450,000. Ten large employers, including subsidiaries, employ about 2,200,000 workers or an average of 220,000. It is these units that to a large extent determine the industrial relations pattern of the nation, and there seems to be no tendency toward the contraction of their size or influence. When clouds of war lurk on the horizon national preparedness does not permit the disintegration of these units. On the other hand, no one who wishes democracy and a free economy to prosper under the most favorable climate can fail to discern with anxiety the frightening social problems and class stratification that follow this trend.

In weighing the practicability of any form of social control where democratic government is called upon to cope with domestic giants, the underlying dynamic forces and the attitudes, emotions, and allegiances that have developed, cannot be ignored. To attempt to fragmentize or localize collective bargaining between nationwide combinations of both capital and labor or under an economy predicated upon freedom of commerce and communication throughout a nation is like attempting to fragmentize a class —a discouraging task to say the least. The crystallization of class solidarity seems too strong to be atomized. "The moving finger writes and having writ moves on."

I do not believe it is practicable by a legislative broom to sweep back this tidal evolution that brings us big business, big unions, and nationwide patterns of industrial relations, and I am, therefore, opposed to a general law outlawing industry-wide bargaining or its equivalent in the usual type of industry. If through the operation of economic forces and the wise administration of business it can be stopped or deferred in some industries, democratic forces will have freer play, but I am satisfied it cannot be done by legal fiat. Those who think otherwise must assume that workers in one community or of one corporation will be content to accept something less than is known to have been attained by comparable groups in other localities, or that workers will place allegiance to a particular company above allegiance to their class—all of which seems chimerical. Willy-nilly the results of broad-scale bargaining are here to stay so long as our industrial institutions follow present trends, and sooner or later the problem of protecting the public from the overreaching of these institutions will have to be faced. Perhaps the answer will be some new approach, emerging from the surging forces now operating in this country, but it is not likely to be decentralization. In this transition era we know too little of what the future has in store to be able to justify final conclusions.

Progressing from these general comments, I turn to a discussion of some underlying factors and principles together with some concrete suggestions.

Our public policy and our economic philosophy are predicated on free and unobstructed competition. Under a system of free enterprise, competition—so runs the argument—protects the public without resorting to governmental regulation. If the public protects liberty, liberty will protect the public. The exceptions prove the rule: Industries like public utilities and railroads, where monopoly, and not competition, is inherent in the enterprise, are not trusted to respect the public interest. They are regulated and their charges are usually fixed by law. All industry, it is believed, must be regulated either by competition or by statute in order to insure fair treatment of the public. Related to this subject we have several kinds of statutes: antimonopoly statutes, designed to protect the liberty of the trader to compete; patent laws, giving the patentee a monopoly grant for a limited number of years in order to stimulate invention; and lastly, regulatory laws fixing the rates that may be charged by public utilities and other industries where monopoly is the only practical scheme of affairs.

Prior to the Norris-LaGuardia Act and New Deal legislation, as we have seen, labor was subject to these antimonopoly laws when, through boycotting or other means, it attempted to exclude certain goods from the market place, and thus to deprive the public of the advantages of competition. For illustration, it was a violation of the antitrust laws for the United Mine Workers to make agreements with the operators of the central competitive field based on the understanding that the union would employ its usual methods to prevent the operators of Virginia and West Virginia from shipping coal into markets the central competitive field wished to supply. The legislation of the 1930's changed this. Exempting unions from the antitrust laws opened a Pandora's box and left the public without protection, either through competition or statutory regulation. Through industry-wide bargaining, or its approximation, and a monopoly enforced by violence, it is now possible for the United Mine Workers to say when the public shall receive coal and likewise to say that the public shall receive no coal at any time, or from any place, except at a price built on a floor of labor cost dictated by that monopoly.[2] The public is defenseless. Even the anthracite industry, which once was in an independent position, is drawn into the vortex. Now even a return to the antitrust laws would not solve the problem, for it has never been the law that industry-wide bargaining or an industry-wide stoppage, arising from a dispute over working conditions, was a violation of our antitrust laws. Our fundamental public policy, calling for public protection by either competition or statutory regulation, is swept aside. Obviously that situation will be changed some way, somehow, somewhere, and obviously the existing antitrust laws would not meet the issue.

In the case of railroads and public utilities the problem of protecting the public reappears in a different garb. In the sale of such services, antitrust laws are deemed to be inadequate or inappropriate. To protect the public, we usually establish regulatory commissions such as the Interstate Commerce Commission and public service commissions to fix the rates that may be charged the public. In the performance of such duties, the commissions usually reserve the right to pass upon the reasonableness of every item of cost, except the labor cost fixed by the labor monopoly. The question is whether or not this exception should be eliminated so that the public policy of protecting the public, either by regulation or competition, will fully apply.

Stoppages of coal production, railroad, transportation, or the services of public utilities are illustrations of what I regard as national emergencies, against which society must protect itself either by wage regulation, compulsory arbitration, or the pro-regulation and the abolition of labor stoppages in public utilities. We also have had experience with far-flung wage regulation under the Fair Labor Standards Act, which deals with minimum wages and overtime rates. Is it therefore such a long leap now to fix maximum as well as minimum wages in connection with railroads and public utilities operating under a system of price regulation?

To recapitulate: the experiences we have had with fact finding, cooling-off periods, governmental seizure, and efforts to secure voluntary arbitration should convince us that when such postponements and temporizings fail, as they often do, society must intervene, in a few strategic industries upon which it is most dependent, to protect itself from the disasters of national or community stoppages.

Society's problem of self-defense against a labor dictatorship calls for fortitude and delicacy. Its most essential implement of defense is the injunction. But even with the use of injunction, it is essential that the public suffer minor discomforts and dislocations as incidents of a system of free enterprise rather than to curtail important liberties: The public should confine its controls to situations of pressing necessity. What I have suggested is based on the hope that unionism and collective bargaining may reach a livable and stable adjustment without destroying the essentials of a system of free enterprise. The turbulence of recent years is discouraging, but it should not lead to despair.

XXIII

Legislative Experiments with Union Regulation

How THE WINDS OF PUBLIC OPINION have blown, shifted, and turned back, and how the character of labor legislation veered with these shifts is almost as dramatic a story as our treatment of prohibition.

In the first part of the century, our traditions of individualism and the inviolability of property rights led us to look upon unions as a danger against which society must be protected. Later, with more enlightenment and understanding, this attitude yielded to the conception that unions were desirable institutions, indispensable to the proper development of a democratic society. Accompanying this changed viewpoint was the enactment of a new set of laws, based on the general philosophy expressed in the Clayton Act of 1914, which gave a more hospitable reception to the labor movement but entirely overlooked the problem of adequate regulation of mounting union power. Roughly speaking, this second era, which was one of unbalanced liberalization, began about 1913 and continued to the time of the sitdown strikes of 1937.

The third era, when the public began to take a more discriminating view of the conduct of both labor unions and employers, began in 1937—the year of the sitdown strikes and the year when the National Labor Relations Act, upheld by the Supreme Court of the United States, actually got under way. From that time on, except for the enactment of one-sided labor relations acts in five states in 1937 before the new and broader opinion gathered strength, the trend changed, and with few exceptions legislation

302

dealing with labor relations looked to the regulation of the conduct of both groups. Then the union excesses of 1946, which have been in part reviewed earlier in this volume, further accelerated the enactment of regulatory laws. Probably it is no exaggeration to say that over 75 per cent of the legislation passed by federal and state legislatures to regulate labor unions followed directly upon public shock and fright caused by the dramatic labor disturbances of 1937 and 1946. Cause and effect are very clear.

Starting with the first of these three eras, which extended somewhat beyond the first decade of the century, we find that there was less understanding of the significance of the labor movement or the social need for some degree of collectivism. Statutes and court decisions, state and federal, recognized a broad area of absolutism for property and a narrow area for concerted action by workers.[1] Two-thirds of the states had laws prohibiting violence, intimidation, or coercion against either employer or fellow employees. About 20 states had laws against criminal syndicalism.[2] Boycotting was outlawed by the statutes of a few states, and the decisions of many state courts severely restricted picketing. Ten states had special laws forbidding interference with the operation of railroads or mines. Injunctions were freely issued as a matter of general law to protect persons and property from practices forbidden by statutes and by the general principles of conspiracy law. Even antiunion employment contracts forbidding an employee to join a union received judicial protection by injunction against union interference. The end of this era was largely brought about by the ceaseless agitation of the American Federation of Labor.

In the second era the tide turned. Both legislatures and courts reacted to changes in public psychology. Beginning about 1913, when Congress was considering various statutes of a prounion character and passed the Appropriations Act of 1913[3] and the Clayton Act of 1914, headway was made with state legislation to protect and encourage the growth, and strengthen the privileges and power, of labor unions. Anti-injunction laws were urged upon state legislatures and in many instances found ready adoption. Labor unions were exempted from antitrust laws and conspiracy laws by special legislation, and some states provided that acts done in concert should not be deemed illegal if they were acts that might be lawfully done by an individual. Some states declared that business or the right to do business was not to be regarded as property, and others declared no union or union member should be liable for the acts of its officers and agents except when expressly authorized or ratified. Twenty-five states outlawed blacklisting, and nearly as many outlawed the yellow-dog contract or any form of discrimination against employees on account of union membership or union activities. Then followed more positive recognition and protection of union rights.

By "union rights" I mean the rights of employees to organize and bargain collectively through representatives of their own choosing; the right to be free from domination, interference or discrimination in the exercise of those rights; and the right to engage in concerted activities for the promotion of these rights. Union rights received genuine acknowledgment in the Norris-LaGuardia Act of 1932, which imposed severe restrictions on the power of courts to interfere with their exercise. The following year their definite and positive recognition was asserted in the National Industrial Recovery Act. Then followed the National Labor Relations Act of July, 1935, which established a National Labor Relations Board empowered to issue cease and desist orders enforceable in the courts against interference by employers with such union rights. As construed, this Act also required the employer to recognize and deal with a union of executives as well as a union of the ordinary type of worker. One provision declared that nothing in the Act "shall be construed so as to interfere with or impede or diminish in any way the right to strike." This provision, wholly indefensible and unmoral, permitted a union to invoke the services of the Board and, if not satisfied with its conclusions, to combine by strikes, picketing, and boycotting to injure the business of the employer because, as required by law, he complied with the Board's decision. There was thus created a labor dispute that the employer was not legally free to settle—an absurd result, which I believe the Court could have avoided by a wiser and more logical interpretation of our federal statutes.

The aim of the Wagner Act was to prevent the worker from being influenced or pushed around by the employer in connection with his rights to organize and engage in collective bargaining, although giving the union complete freedom to push the employee around, even to the point of conscripting him through various applications of economic coercion. The union could discriminate against communist members or expel a communist local, but an employer was forbidden to do the equivalent. The nonunion status was denied the protection extended to the union status so that the push would be in one direction.

In considering the date of the impact of this National Labor Relations Act, one must remember that the validity of the Act was generally doubted, and its application was rather generally frustrated, until the Supreme Court in 1937 proclaimed its legitimacy and gave it a blessing.[4]

In 1937 "little Wagner Acts" were offered in at least 17 state legislatures but were adopted by only five: Massachusetts, New York, Pennsylvania, Utah, and Wisconsin. Utah was the earliest, its act becoming effective on March 22, 1937. A measure, approved by both houses of the Michigan legislature, contained limitations of the right to strike and was vetoed by Governor Murphy on that account. Not one of these labor relations acts requiring the employer to deal with unions and forbidding interference with union activities by unfair labor practices contained any substantial provisions protecting employers, the public, and the individual worker from unfair conduct by the union.[5]

The "state Wagner Acts" of 1937, as well as the still more numerous efforts to secure such acts in other states, were the result of the general trend, strengthened by the National Labor Relations Act of 1935 and the affirmation of its validity by the Supreme Court in 1937. But that marked the end of the trek. Before 1937 had passed, the sitdown strikes and other excesses of unionism turned the tide. The public set out to socialize labor unions.

When the orgy of unbalanced legislation of the second or middle era was terminated, it is specially interesting to note that certain states, rather than the federal government, first sensed their mistakes. Awakened by the sitdown strikes of 1937 and other frightening stoppages affecting the public welfare, the states first went into action long before Congress moved. The trend toward more symmetrical legislation became a wave of no mean proportions. Elected officials or those seeking election were made to feel the impact of public apprehension. The argument was a familiar one. Organized labor was no longer a struggling child that needed protection from employers. It was on the way to represent 50 per cent of what might be called the organizable nonagricultural workers. Having given it a helping hand to tide it

over its years of infancy, the general public demanded that in its
days of maturity organized labor should recognize its social responsibilities.   In expressing this conviction the rural vote played
an important part.

To demonstrate—what hardly needs demonstration—that legislation regulating unions immediately follows a wave of antisocial
conduct by the unions, I first invite attention to the labor legislation
that followed the major disturbances of 1937, outlined in Chapter
XVIII, and then to the still more voluminous legislation enacted
in 1947 as the immediate result of the labor disturbances of
1946.   The output of the first of these two periods may well be
called "the crop of 1937," although that harvest extended over a
series of years, and the crop of 1946 was harvested almost entirely
in 1947.

So I first appraise the crop of 1937.

In 1938 Massachusetts repealed its one-sided labor relations act
and substituted a more balanced act.   The Wisconsin legislature
in its 1939 session, which was the first session to follow 1937,
repealed its act of 1937, which had recognized no wrongdoing by
unions.   It substituted the Wisconsin Employment Peace Act, listing a series of union activities that were declared to be unlawful
or unfair labor practices.   That same year Michigan and
Minnesota enacted laws following this new pattern, and by amendment, Pennsylvania did the same.   Only New York failed to move
forward.   Thus these states, the leaders in the movement toward
balanced labor legislation, adopted this enlightened viewpoint
eight years before Congress corrected its mistake by the enactment
of the Taft-Hartley Act.

Since Wisconsin has been one of the states most notable in its
contribution to progressive understanding of labor relations and
has furnished us with some of the most notable scholars in this field,
and since its statutes have led others to the recognition of collective
bargaining and the right to organize, it seems desirable to deal
more at length with its labor relations act, as an example of advanced thinking.   As early as 1931, its statutes had enunciated the
rights of employees to freedom of association, self-organization,
and the designation of representatives to negotiate terms and conditions of employment.[6]

In changing its one-sided labor relations act of 1937 to a

balanced program, the Wisconsin Act of 1939 begins with a declaration of policy that includes this:

It is the policy of this state in order to preserve and promote the interests of the public, the employee and the employer alike, to establish standards of fair conduct in employment relations and to provide a convenient, expeditious, and impartial tribunal by which these interests may have their respective rights and obligations adjudicated. While limiting individual and group rights of aggression and defense the state substitutes processes of justice for the more primitive methods of trial by combat.[7]

By this it will be seen that Wisconsin aimed to substitute adjudication for combat in certain disputes and thus to narrow the field of strife. Unlike the original Wagner Act, the Wisconsin Act did not provide that nothing in it shall be construed to limit the right to strike, and unlike the Taft-Hartley Act, it did not propose to give the unions a dual opportunity, in some cases, of securing a decision from the board and then striking against it.

In addition to the usual provisions forbidding an employer to interfere with the right of employees, it is also made an unfair labor practice for the employer to do any of the following:

1. To execute an all-union agreement unless it is first approved by two-thirds [8] of those voting by secret ballot conducted by the board. In the case of an employer who has a contract or is negotiating a contract, such union shop vote shall be taken only after the employer has agreed to accept the outcome.

2. To bargain with representatives of less than a majority.

3. To violate the terms of the bargaining agreement, including an agreement to accept arbitration.

4. To refuse or fail to recognize or accept as conclusive of any issue in any controversy as to employment relations the final determination (after appeal, if any) of any tribunal having competent jurisdiction of the same or whose jurisdiction the employer, the employees or their representatives accepted.

5. To deduct dues except under an individual authorization terminable in a year by 30 days' notice.

6. To discharge or discriminate against an employee because he has filed charges or has given information or testimony under the act.

7. To employ persons to spy on employees or their representatives.

8. To circulate a blacklist.

9. To commit any crime or misdemeanor in connection with any controversy as to employment relations.

On the other side unfair labor practices by employees include the following:

1. To coerce an employee in respect to his labor rights, to intimidate his family or picket his home, or to injure his person or property or that of his family.

2. To take unauthorized possession of property of the employer or to engage in any concerted effort to interfere with production except by leaving the premises in an orderly manner for the purpose of going on strike.

3. To induce an employer to interfere with labor rights of his employees, or to induce him to engage in an unfair labor practice.

4. To violate terms of a collective-bargaining agreement, including an agreement to accept arbitration.

5. To refuse to accept a decision from a board of competent jurisdiction (as already quoted in respect to employers).

6. To fail to give the prescribed notice of intention to strike.

7. To promote or induce picketing or boycotting or any other overt act in connection with a strike that has not been authorized by the required secret ballot.

8. To hinder or prevent anyone in pursuit of lawful work, either by mass picketing, force, threats, obstruction of entrances, highways, or any method of travel or conveyance.

9. To commit any crime or misdemeanor in connection with any controversy as to employment relations.

10. To engage in, promote, or induce a jurisdictional strike.

11. To engage in a secondary boycott or, by threats, force, or sabotage, to hinder or prevent anyone from obtaining, using, or disposing of materials or equipment, provided that sympathetic strikes in support of those in similar occupations working for other employers in the same craft shall not be forbidden.

Here is an important provision preserving the right to go to court for an injunction:

Any controversy concerning unfair labor practices may be submitted to the Board in the manner and with the effect provided in this chapter, but nothing herein shall prevent the pursuit of legal or equitable relief in courts of competent jurisdiction.

The Wisconsin Act further provided that the union shall keep a record of financial transactions and shall present annually to each member within 60 days after the end of its fiscal year a detailed written financial report thereof. Any member was given the right to petition the state board to issue an order compelling compliance.

The board may appoint a mediator, and where the parties to a labor dispute so agree, he may act as arbitrator or appoint arbitrators.

Employees producing, harvesting, or initially processing farm products must give the board ten days' notice of strike, if the stoppage would result in destruction or serious deterioration of the product. In such cases the board must undertake mediation and attempt to induce the parties to arbitrate.

One illustration of the way in which this state law met unfair activities that could not be met by the Wagner Act of 1935 is illustrated by a case that went to the United States Supreme Court.

In November, 1945, the union leaders representing the employees of Briggs & Stratton Corporation, who were about 2000 in number, embarked upon a program of repeated surprise stoppages, under the guise of attending union meetings, for the purpose of coercing the employer, but without giving notice or presenting demands. In a period of about six months 26 such stoppages took place. The employer, instead of attempting to retaliate, sought relief from the Wisconsin Employment Relations Board, which, in turn, directed the union to cease and desist from such practices. This order was sustained by the Supreme Court of Wisconsin and later on appeal by the Supreme Court of the United States.

In the course of its opinion the Supreme Court said:

> The Union contends that the statute as thus applied violates the Thirteenth Amendment in that it imposes a form of compulsory service or involuntary servitude. However, nothing in the statute or the order makes it a crime to abandon work individually (compare *Pollock* v. *Williams*, 322 U. S. 4) or collectively. Nor does either undertake to prohibit or restrict any employee from leaving the service of the employer, either for reason or without reason, either with or without notice. The facts afford no foundation for the contention that any action of the State has the purpose or effect of imposing any form of involuntary servitude.[9]

Elaborating on the nature of the right to strike the court said:

The right to strike, because of its more serious impact upon the public interest, is more vulnerable to regulation than the right to organize and select representatives for lawful purposes of collective bargaining which this Court has characterized as a "fundamental right" and which, as the Court has pointed out, was recognized as such in its decisions long before it was given protection by the National Labor Relations Act.[10]

In 1943, both Colorado and Kansas and, in May, 1945, both Hawaii and Puerto Rico adopted what I call a balanced labor relations act, including restrictions on both employers and employees, but contrary to the trend of these years, Rhode Island in 1941 and Connecticut in 1945 adopted one-sided statutes like the original Wagner Act.

Other illustrations of the legislative crop of the 1937 tillage—whether the restrictions are listed as unfair labor practices to be embodied in labor relations acts or are designated as unlawful acts—reveal to some extent what the voters regarded as abuses to be remedied. Regulations extended to sitdown strikes, excess picketing, violence, jurisdictional strikes, strikes not authorized by the democratic vote of union members, and strikes called without following the prescribed procedure for a cooling-off period. They covered also boycotts, the closed shop, discrimination against non-union men, the checkoff, work permits, and internal regulations requiring registration, financial reports, regular elections, procedure for determining amount of dues, and union discrimination on account of race, color, and so on. Practically all the state legislation of this character within this period is summarized state by state in Appendix A of this volume.

Now let us turn to the legislative crop following 1946: As pointed out earlier in this volume, the industrial disturbances of 1946 were the greatest in our history. More than 4,650,000 workmen were involved in strikes—the all-time peak. Protest strikes, political in nature, and mass picketing that prevented even executives from entering their factories were familiar developments throughout the country. The soft coal strike, which had forced the government to take possession of the mines in May, and a subsequent stoppage in November after the government was in possession had led to a situation in which 80 per cent of the railroads, 60 per cent of the public utilities, and the entire steel industry would be shut down within 60 days if the stoppage were continued. In May the government was compelled to seize and operate the railroads because of a threatened strike, but notwithstanding this, 250,000 railroad employees quit work and completely paralyzed an important part of the nation's transportation system.

President Truman declared that this situation "vitally concerns the well-being and very life of all our people" and was about to ask Congress for a bill authorizing him to draft strikers into the armed services wherever necessary to break strikes against the government when the unions capitulated.

The tugboat workers in New York harbor, by their stoppage, curtailed the distribution of food products. Various strikes occurred on public utilities, and others were threatened. Stirred and startled by these developments, the public demanded protective legislation both from Congress and from various state legislatures.

In April, 1946, Congress, when working on the Case Bill, passed the so-called Lea Act, aimed at the activities of James Caesar Petrillo that forced the employment of stand-by musicians and prevented the use of records and transcriptions and the broadcasting of the performances of high school bands. This Act made it unlawful to coerce a broadcasting station for the purpose of compelling it to employ more persons than it needed; to coerce the broadcaster to refrain from broadcasting noncommercial, educational, or cultural programs by performers who served without compensation; to refrain from broadcasting a program originating outside of the United States; and to force any person to make any payment for the privilege of producing, buying, or using recordings or transcriptions. When Petrillo was prosecuted, despite his threats, the Supreme Court upheld the statute.[11]

In July, 1946, right after the veto of the Case Bill, Congress, faced with a decision of the Supreme Court that union activities were not covered by the Anti-Racketeering Act of 1934, amended that Act to cover them.[12] This change was also made in the midst of the disturbances of 1946. These two statutes and the Labor Management Relations Act, popularly known as the Taft-Hartley Act, which followed a few months later, constituted a significant reversal of policy. Congress had heard from the electorate and, notwithstanding intense opposition from pressure groups, undertook for the first time in this century to pass laws looking to the social control of union activities in industry. Collective bargaining, under orderly procedures consistent with its true function, was reaffirmed, but the philosophy of class conflict was rejected.

The belated Taft-Hartley Act was the most important part of this crop of 1946. But for the opposition of the President through his veto power the legislation would have come earlier. The unions felt the Act flowed from the grapes of wrath, but it would be fairer to say that it flowed from public fear. In passing this law Congress was not in the vanguard. Rather did it follow the examples set by various states, some of them eight years earlier. As in the case of these earlier state acts, the aim was to correct the mistakes, injustices, inadequacies, and impracticabilities of unbalanced legislation.

The Taft-Hartley Act continued to protect the fundamental rights of labor to organize and engage in collective bargaining, as recognized in the Wagner Act, but added new provisions specifying unfair labor practices on the part of employees. If this Act, rather than the Wagner Act, had been passed in 1935, it would have been regarded as a great victory for labor instead of a slave-labor act. In brief, its pertinent provisions may be summarized as follows:

1. *Discrimination.* It is an unfair practice for a union to restrain or coerce an employee in the exercise of his right to organize and to cause an employer to discriminate against an employee on account of nonmembership in a union, except that such discrimination is permissible where a union shop has been endorsed by a majority vote of the employees in the bargaining unit in an election held under the supervision of the Labor Relations Board. Where such union shop has been so approved and the employer agrees to it, an employee may be discharged for "failure to tender the periodic dues and initiation fees uniformly required as a condition of acquiring or retaining membership." [13] Discrimination for nonmembership for any other reason is forbidden.

2. *Refusal to bargain.* The union, like the employer, must not refuse to bargain. Where there is a collective-bargaining agreement, the duty to bargain collectively requires that no party to such agreement shall terminate or modify it without serving 60 days' notice with an offer to confer and, after the lapse of 30 days if no agreement is reached, without giving the Federal Mediation Service 30 days' notice of failure to agree. Meanwhile, conditions

shall remain unchanged and neither party shall resort to a strike or lockout. The wedlock of a collective-bargaining agreement is not to be dissolved carelessly without proper divorce proceedings. Any employee who violates the requirements of such a 60-day period by striking loses his status as an employee unless the employer elects to re-employ him.

3. *Unlawful strikes and boycotts.* It is unlawful to engage in a strike or a refusal to handle or work on goods for the purpose of forcing an employer (1) to join a union; (2) to cease handling products of another producer; (3) to cease doing business with any other person; (4) to recognize a union that has not been certified by the Board; or (5) to assign particular work to the members of a particular union, except where the employer is failing to conform to a certification of the Board.

It is also an unfair labor practice for a union to require employees working under an authorized union agreement to pay an excessive or discriminatory initiation fee or to require the employer to pay for services that are not performed or not to be performed.

The Act does not require the employer to recognize a union of supervisors but does not prohibit him from so doing. It concedes the right of free speech to all parties. It provides new specifications for determining the bargaining unit, all designed to protect professional and craft groups in their right to have a bargaining unit of their own if they so desire, and requires that guards be not included in any unit containing other classes of employees.

As a condition to the enjoyment of full rights under the Act, the union must file with the Secretary of Labor detailed information as to its name; place of business; names, titles, and compensation of its principal officers and compensation of all officers receiving more than $5000 a year; the manner of electing officers; the amount of initiation fees and dues required; detailed provisions of its constitution and bylaws relating to certain enumerated matters; and a financial statement with a showing that it has been furnished to members. As a further condition to the enjoyment of the major statutory protections of the Act, there must be filed an affidavit by each union officer disavowing any communist or revolutionary association.

Nothing in the Act is to be construed as authorizing the making of any agreement "requiring membership in a labor organization as a condition of employment in any state or territory in which such execution or application is prohibited by state or territorial law." [14] In view of state legislation against the closed shop, this provision is of great importance.

The union is declared to be bound by the acts of its authorized officers and agents and may sue or be sued in its own name as an entity, but judgments for damages obtained against it shall be satisfied only from union funds and shall not be enforceable against the individual assets of its members. Thus the provision of the Norris-LaGuardia Act to the contrary is repealed to that extent. There seems to be no prohibition against suing union members directly as in the Hatters Case.

It is made unlawful for an employer to pay money to the representatives of the employees and for such representatives to receive money from the employer with certain exceptions, including a checkoff for dues under a written assignment. Payments to a trust fund for employee benefits are permitted, subject to specified regulations. Violations of this section are subject to extreme penalities and injunctions.

Political contributions by a union in connection with federal elections are forbidden and subject to severe penalities.

Secondary boycotts enforced by refusal to work, but not secondary boycotts enforced by withdrawal of patronage, are made unlawful, and suits for damages may be maintained on that account. Injunctions against such boycotts are to be sought by the N.L.R.B. but not by the injured employers. Jurisdictional strikes are forbidden and when not otherwise settled the dispute is to be resolved by the Board. Suits for damages growing out of such strikes may be maintained.

Strikes of employees of the United States or any agency thereof are forbidden and any individual who engages therein "shall be discharged immediately from his employment and shall forfeit his Civil Service status, if any, and shall not be eligible for re-employment for three years by the United States or any such agency." [15]

In case of national emergency strikes, power is given to the President to appoint a board of inquiry and to direct the Attorney General to secure an injunction to last for 80 days. This procedure has already been described in Chapter XXII. In the last analysis, after the termination of the 80-day injunction, emergency strikes may take place notwithstanding the fact that they may spell national disaster.

In comparing this statute with the provisions of state laws, which we are about to examine, it should be noted that, although it forbids organized attack on an employer to compel him to repudiate the decisions of the Board involving certification, it does not forbid union activities to compel an employer unlawfully to reject other decisions of the Board.   It does not prohibit secondary boycotts through the withdrawal of patronage, such as the boycott involved in the Danbury Hatters Case, and does not authorize the employer or a union member to seek relief in the courts from unfair labor practices.   The rights in that respect can be enforced only by appealing to the N.L.R.B.   Upon the whole, the federal act is moderate in its regulation of unions, as compared with corresponding state acts.

The crop of state legislation harvested in 1947 covers the same general field as did the laws passed in the period from 1937 to 1946.   It extended to intimidation, union security, strikes, boycotting, political contributions, and internal regulations, but the emphasis was different.   Sitdown strikes and general labor relations acts did not come in for much attention, but the closed shop and the regulation of strikes of public employees and strikes on public utilities were marked for special treatment.

An inventory of this legislation, except that relating to strikes of public employees and strikes on public utilities, which are reviewed in the main text of this chapter, is set forth in Appendix C.

Measures taken to regulate or forbid the closed shop or to forbid discrimination on account of nonmembership in a union or on account of membership or nonmembership were enacted in 1946 and 1947, but almost entirely in 1947.   Four states require a vote of approval, running from a majority in one state to three-fourths in Colorado, as a condition to the adoption of the union shop.

Massachusetts in its Labor Relations Act of 1947 provided that any employee who is required as a condition of employment to be a member of a union may file with the Labor Relations Commission a charge that he has been unfairly denied admission or suspended or expelled for reasons other than malfeasance in office or nonpayment of fees, dues, or assessments.   If the commission sustains the charges on the ground that the union action was contrary to the union constitution or bylaws, or that the penalty was imposed without a fair hearing, was not warranted by the offense, or was inconsistent with the public policy of the Commonwealth, it issues an order requiring the union to restore the employee to good standing with full voting rights or to refrain from any discrimination against him. Such an order is reviewable in court, but during such review the employee must continue to pay dues. Thus under the Massachusetts Act, it is an unfair labor practice to discharge a man for nonmembership unless the union certifies to the employer that the member was deprived of membership because of occupational disqualifications or discipline, and has exhausted his rights of appeal within the union and to the Labor Relations Commission, and has had his appeal denied.

The New Hampshire statute of 1947, like that of Massachusetts, came nearer to some of the more advanced thinking on this subject than did the other statutes. It prohibited arrangements that made union membership a condition of employment, except where the employer employed more than five persons and two-thirds of them had voted by a secret election conducted by the labor commissioner in favor of such union security. Even then the union must satisfy the commissioner that its entrance fees and dues are not excessive, an initiation fee in excess of $25 being deemed excessive. Furthermore, every union security agreement must contain a clause binding the union not to discriminate against applicants for membership on the basis of race, color, religion, sex, age, and so on and to grant equal voting rights to all. And here follows the most interesting condition of all: The union security agreement must also provide that no member will be expelled except for just cause and only after appeals within the organization and to the labor commissioner, who may order reinstatement. This law, being subject to enforcement by damage suits, injunctions and criminal proceedings with penalities ranging from $200 to $1000 or nine months' imprisonment or both, was given teeth.

Massachusetts and New Hampshire, as well as Puerto Rico in 1946, thus chose the alternative of regulating a labor monopoly rather than abolishing it, but in 1949 New Hampshire repealed its act.

Early in 1949 the Supreme Court of the United States had occasion to pass upon the validity of laws and constitutional provisions of North Carolina, Nebraska, and Arizona that forbade discrimination against nonunion men or discrimination against either union or nonunion men.[16]   The Court sustained all of them with Justice Murphy dissenting in one case.   In the first case the court rejected the argument "that the Federal Constitution guarantees greater employment rights to union members than to non-union members." [17]   The Court reasoned that just as it had previously upheld the power of Congress to give legislative protection to union members, "we now hold that legislative protection can be afforded to non-union workers." [18]

The Speakers Book of Facts, prepared by the Political Action Committee of the C.I.O., conveys the same notion that a nonunion status has no legal standing.   It declares that the Taft-Hartley Act, in giving protection to the liberty of both the union and the nonunion man, straddles "mutually hostile concepts." [19]   This Act, says the P.A.C. book of instruction, "creates a new federal right— the right not to engage in union activity." [20]

The second case, decided by the Supreme Court on the same day as the case just mentioned, involved the Arizona law, which merely forbade discrimination against nonmembers of a labor organization.   Replying to the contention made in behalf of the union that the act was unconstitutional because it did not afford equal protection to union members, the Court pointed out that other laws in Arizona protected the union membership.

Justice Frankfurter, in a masterly concurring opinion for both of these cases, said:

The right of association like any other right carried to its extreme encounters limiting principles.   At the point where the mutual advantage of association demands too much individual disadvantage, a compromise must be struck.   When that point has been reached—where the intersection should fall—is plainly a question within the special province of the legislature.[21]

Interesting is it to observe that these laws arose in less populated areas and that no state in the northeastern industrial area and no state on the Pacific Coast broadly forbade union security agreements.

The bewildering implications of union security and laws to correct the abuses of union security are reflected in the varying responses of the electorates and legislatures.   In the fall of 1948 on referenda the voters of Maine, Massachusetts, and New Mexico frowned on laws forbidding the union shop, while the electorate of Arizona and North Dakota approved them. This same conflict also appears in the acts of the legislatures. The number of state legislatures that have rejected such laws is almost equaled by the number that have enacted them.[22]

In 1947 Delaware enacted an over-all labor relations act, which it proceeded to repeal in 1949. This short-lived act, however, is significant in its totality, because it included nearly every idea of union regulation contained in the other laws except those relating to public employees and public utility employees and also included unique provisions not elsewhere found. I have, therefore, summarized its important requirements in Appendix B. Its comprehensive and detailed provisions were dumped into the lap of the courts for enforcement without the aid of any administrative agency like a labor relations board. On the other hand, those who believe that unions should be regulated extensively in their relationships to their membership, as well as in their relationships to the public and the employer, cannot afford to ignore this unique statute. Its range is suggestive.

No other state passed a state-wide labor relations act after 1945, but in September, 1949, Alabama passed a "little Taft-Hartley Act," *applicable only to Wilcox County*. It followed the Taft-Hartley Act even to the numbering of subsections. A state judge has the duty of performing the many-sided functions of a labor relations board, a general counsel, the trial examiners, and the mediation and conciliation service.

Wilcox County has a population of about 30,000, and Camden, its county seat, has a population of about 1000. It is said that the state senator for Wilcox County introduced this "little Taft-Hartley Act" in the legislature as a means of attracting industries to the area. At the last report the only industries in the county were one shirt factory, two sawmills, two cotton gins, and a stockyard.

No branch of this subject indicates more decisively how the public reacted to the industrial disorders of 1946 than does the legislative activity of 1947 in respect to strikes of public employees and strikes on public utilities. I deal first with public employees.

Prior to 1946 neither the federal government nor any state had enacted legislation specifically outlawing strikes of public employees, but the statements of various governors following the Boston police strike clearly condemned them.

In legislation Virginia led off in 1946. The Virginia law provided that strikers against the state government shall forfeit their jobs and shall be ineligible for re-employment for one year.

In 1947 New York, which ranked high as a pro-labor state, led off by amending its Civil Service Law. This amendment prohibited strikes of those holding governmental positions and prohibited action by any person having power to authorize or consent to such a strike. One who violates this Act terminates his employment. He may, however, be re-employed at the same compensation as before, but such compensation may not be increased for three years thereafter. For a period of five years, he is on probation and serves without tenure. Any employee absenting himself without approval of his superior is deemed on strike, but within ten days he may request an investigation as to whether his conduct constituted a violation. Within four months after New York acted, Michigan, Missouri, Nebraska, Ohio, Pennsylvania, and Texas followed suit.

The laws passed by Michigan, Ohio, and Pennsylvania were of the same character as the New York law, except that Michigan made it a misdemeanor for anybody to incite a public employee to strike. Pennsylvania added a provision for a mediation panel to be formed at the request of state employees. If the panel is unsuccessful in avoiding trouble, the governor or the head of the agency of government where the men are employed, "may then take administrative measures accordingly or refer the situation to the legislature for correction." Missouri, like Michigan, made strikes of public employees a misdemeanor.

Nebraska forbade strikes of public employees and forbade all acts to induce or abet them. A court of industrial relations was created to settle industrial disputes in public service and may be invoked by either the employer, the employee, the union or the Attorney General. Its decisions are binding and enforceable in court.

Texas declared that such strikes are against public policy and forfeited the civil rights and employment rights of the strikers. The state and any subdivision thereof are forbidden to recognize a union as a bargaining representative or to enter into a collective-bargaining agreement. Discrimination in public employment on account of membership or nonmembership in a union is prohibited.

Already we have had one important experience under such a law, and that was in the City of Cleveland during Yuletide, 1949.

The Ohio Act of June, 1947, like the New York Act, provides that no public employee of the state, city, or any other political subdivision of the state or of any commission or board or of any branch of public service, shall strike and that no one having authority shall induce or consent to such a strike.

On December 22, 1949, the rapid transit system of the City of Cleveland, operated as it was by the city rapid transit board, had occasion to put this law to the test. About one-fifth—some say one-eighth—of the 4200 members of Division 266 of the Amalgamated Association of Street, Electric Railway and Motor Coach Employees of America voted to strike, and the operating employees of the transit system, of which there were about 3200, quit work. The strike constituted a violation not only of the statute but of the employment agreement, which forbade stoppages and provided for an impartial chairman to whom either party could refer disputes. In this instance the dispute, which was over a vacation formula, had been referred to the impartial umpire, and the strike was called because of dissatisfaction with the umpire's award. The principal union leaders, including Robert Stack, international representative, had disapproved the strike, but backed it after it was called. Stack immediately announced, "We will give them all the aid necessary until the dispute is settled along their demands."

On December 26, 1949, the City of Cleveland instituted a suit for an injunction against the union officials as representing the union and its members. The court in granting the injunction held:

> Under the common law there is no right to strike in behalf of public employees. . . . The right to strike if accorded to public employees is one means of destroying government. And if they destroy government we have anarchy, we have chaos.[23]

The injunction, issued at 8:30 P.M., directed a termination of the strike as of 2 P.M. Tuesday, December 27. It forbade any interference with the car lines or buses and inducing, counseling, or advising employees to abstain from the performance of their duties. It directed Thomas P. Meaney, the president, and Harry C. Lang, secretary-treasurer of the union, and the members of the Board of said union:

To issue an order upon the members of Local 268 to cease striking, to cease abstaining from their public employment in whole or in part and to return to their respective duties as public employees of the Cleveland Transit System in order to resume operation of its vehicles and to resume normal operation of the Transit System of the City of Cleveland.[24]

To protect the individual rights of the strikers, the injunction further provided that nothing in the court order "shall be construed as affecting the right of any individual employee of the Transit System *to abandon* or *to resign* his employment." [25]

President Meaney of the union and Secretary Lang promptly complied with the court's order by directing the membership to resume normal operation, and Meaney warned the members that their noncompliance might result in fines against the union of $100,000.

When the men returned to work on December 27, the suit was dismissed on the motion of the city, pursuant to an understanding reached the previous day that such a course would be taken and that no penalities would be pursued if the membership returned to work on the date specified.

Leaving now the subject of strikes of government employees, I turn to the equally decisive action of the country in dealing with strikes on public utilities.

Our first experiment with strike bans coupled with compulsory arbitration was the Kansas Industrial Court Act of 1920. In 1922, South Carolina enacted a law for compulsory arbitration of city railway disputes in cities of a specified size, which was never enforced. The Kansas Act, which was limited to certain industries, including utilities, declared to be affected by the public interest, gave the Kansas Court of Industrial Relations the power, on its own initiative or at the request of others, to adjudicate labor disputes. Strikes and picketing were prohibited and violations were punishable as criminal offenses. In 1923 the Supreme Court of the United States declared the law as applied to industries other than public utilities to be unconstitutional because it purported to require the business to continue to operate. The Court found that it was not a law generally regulating wages and hours.[26] No longer being applied, this law is still on the statute books and it is conceivable, though unlikely, that the Court of

Industrial Relations might be recreated to apply its stringent provisions to the more limited field of public utilities. Meanwhile,
various other acts reaching into this same field have been passed.

In Colorado a statute providing for compulsory fact finding in
industries affected with the public interest and prohibiting stoppages until 30 days after filing of notice or 30 days after completion of a hearing before the Industrial Commission has been
on the books since 1915. That is the law that aroused Mr. Gompers' ire.[27]

In 1939, Michigan and Minnesota enacted laws requiring advance notice of any intention to alter terms of employment and a
waiting period before a strike or lockout could take place in connection with industries affected with the public interest.

As of 1941, the Minnesota Act embracing utilities authorized the
governor, on receipt of notice of a dispute from the state conciliator, to appoint a commission representing employees, employers, and the public to report on the issues and forbade strikes
or lockouts for a period of 30 days after the governor received
such notification. On the other hand, the parties were left free to
act if the governor did not appoint such a commission within five
days of notification.

North Dakota acted under its military law. As of 1941, the
state law authorized the governor, in case of threatened stoppages
of coal mines or public utilities that threatened the life and
property of the people, to commandeer facilities and equipment
and to operate the business.

It will be seen, therefore, that, down to the events of 1946 and
the repercussion that immediately followed, this country had
little legislation and experience of significance in this particular
field. In 1947, the year when Congress enacted the emergency
strike provisions of the Taft-Hartley Act, 14 states [28] and the
Territory of Hawaii, which merely provided a cooling-off period,
dealt with strikes on public utilities. The impact of the events of
1946 was that sudden. Nine of these states clearly provided compulsory arbitration or its equivalent.[29] Four provided for
seizure.[30] New Jersey and Missouri provided for both. All
except Mississippi forbade stoppages and all provided for severe
penalities by way of fines and imprisonment or injunctions or both.

New Jersey tackled this problem of public utility strikes early in 1946 in a timid and cautious manner, but 1947 brought stringent regulation. The 1946 Act required 60 days' notice of proposed changes in employment conditions and, if negotiation and mediation failed, called for the appointment of a public hearing panel, the recommendations of which were to be submitted to the governor. If this fact-finding process failed to secure an adjustment, the governor was empowered to seize and operate the properties in order to insure continuity of service. The Act contained no sanctions and entrusted its hope to the force of public opinion. Since this hope proved illusory to a considerable extent, the law was amended in 1947 primarily as a result of the telephone strike in April of that year, and this time contained teeth. It specifies that upon the seizure of a plant by the governor the employees become employees of the state and are therefore forbidden to strike. Within ten days after seizure, the issues are to be submitted to a tripartite board of arbitration, the award of which is final and binding for one year unless modified or reversed on appeal to the Supreme Court of New Jersey. Failure to abide by the award subjects the union to a penalty of $10,000 for each day of violation.

The first arbitration under this amended Act involved employees of the New Jersey Telephone Company, where the governor had taken over the facilities. Subsequently arbitration boards were set up in 13 other situations involving utilities. In two of these agreement was reached before a hearing; in two others agreements were reached during hearings and in the remaining instances awards were made. In nine of the 13 cases the parties waived the preliminary steps of a public hearing panel and seizure of the property and requested the immediate appointment of the arbitration boards. Experience in this state does not fully support the popular contention that a provision for ultimate resort to compulsory arbitration necessarily discourages agreement without resort to such compulsion.

In May, 1949, the Supreme Court of New Jersey declared the law unconstitutional on the ground that its provisions in respect to compulsory arbitration did not sufficiently establish standards to govern the arbitrators in their decisions. Other contentions to the effect that the police powers of the state did not extend to regulations of this scope and character were rejected.

In this connection the court said:

> Where by reason of a strike, work stoppage or lockout, the flow of the services of any of these essentials of community life is halted or impaired, the state has not only the right but a pressing duty to step in and prevent the continuance of such stoppage or impairment and to take appropriate measures to restore them. If instead of a stoppage or curtailment of essential services there is an imminent danger of their being halted or curtailed, the state has the right as well as the obligation of preventing the occurrence of any such catastrophe.[31]

In 1949 New Jersey sought to remedy the defect of this statute by including specified standards to control the arbitrators, a provision that is highly important, for social as well as constitutional reasons, if wages fixed by compulsory arbitration are to keep pace with wages fixed by unregulated industries.

Early in 1950 an arbitration board of five, three representing the public, one representing labor, and one representing the employer, was appointed by the Governor of New Jersey pursuant to the laws as amended in 1949 and 1950 to settle the issues between the New Jersey Bell Telephone Company and the Communication Workers of America, New Jersey Traffic Division No. 55, C.I.O. On April 20th the public members of the board rendered an award granting among other things a union shop and a $2.50 weekly wage increase. Both union and employer arbitrators dissented. A few weeks later the public members rendered an opinion in support of its conclusions.

The company challenged the award on the ground that it took wage trends into account, whereas the statutory standards included no such trend. It accordingly obtained from the courts a stay of the wage increase and a portion of the union shop sections of the award until the validity or invalidity of the award was determined. The state Supreme Court returned the award to the arbitrators for further hearing. The union threatened to strike and early in October the dispute was ended by direct agreement between the parties.

For an outstanding example of a state act dealing with labor disputes on public utilities, again I turn to Wisconsin and its law of 1947, which begins by providing that it shall be the duty of public utilities and their employees "to exert every reasonable effort to settle labor disputes by the making of agreements through collective bargaining." [32] It requires the labor relations board to maintain a panel of conciliators and arbitrators, but the same person shall not act as conciliator and arbitrator.

If a conciliator appointed by the labor relations board is unable to effect a settlement within 15 days after appointment, he shall so report to the board, which shall submit to the parties the names of three to five persons to act as arbitrators. Each party shall strike one name from the list and the remainder shall be appointed arbitrators "to hear and determine the dispute. . . . During the pendency of proceedings . . . existing wages, hours and conditions of employment shall not be changed by action of either party without the consent of the other." [33]

Factors which the arbitrators must consider in passing upon wages are enumerated in the Act. If there is a valid existing contract involving the dispute in question, the arbitrators shall have the power only to pass upon its interpretation. A further restriction on their powers is this:

The arbitrators shall not make any award which would infringe upon the right of the employer to manage his business or which would interfere with internal affairs of the Union.

No award as to wages shall be retroactive beyond the expiration date of a pre-existing contract or beyond the date of presentation of demands. The award shall be furnished to the parties and the Public Service Commission. Either party may petition the court for review on prescribed grounds, such as those that are usually reviewable in arbitration proceedings, but not for a review on the merits. The award shall be binding for one year unless changed by mutual consent.

Strikes or lockouts causing an interruption in essential services are a misdemeanor. The board has power by court proceedings "to restrain and enjoin such violation and to compel performance of the duties imposed." Nothing is to be construed to forbid an individual from quitting "unless done in concert or agreement with others. . . . It is the intent . . . only to forbid employees of a public utility employer to engage in a strike or to engage in a work slowdown or stoppage in concert and to forbid a public utility employer to lockout his employees where such acts would cause an interruption of essential service." [34]

The Massachusetts Act of 1947 is a different model.[35] By its terms the governor may require the parties to appear before an impartial mediator to show cause why they should not arbitrate, or in the alternative, he may request arbitration. If an impartial mediator is called upon to function, he shall make public his findings. If such procedure proves fruitless, the governor (1) may contract with either or both parties for resumption of work or (2) may seize the properties.

The Act provides that no one shall aid or encourage cessations of work during any of such proceedings, and that injunctions may be sought to secure compliance.

In 1947, Michigan amended its Labor Relations Act of 1939 to provide for compulsory arbitration of labor disputes in hospitals and public utilities, the chairman of the arbitration board to be a circuit judge designated by the presiding circuit judge. This Act was declared unconstitutional in 1948 because the state constitution made the circuit judge ineligible.[36] An amendment in 1949 eliminated the constitutional objection and the provision for compulsory arbitration. What remained of the Act merely provided for a cooling-off period with fact finding. Pending mediation and fact finding, strikes are forbidden. As sanctions the Attorney General may secure an injunction, and fines and imprisonment await violators.

In 1947, Minnesota provided for compulsory arbitration of disputes in hospitals.

The Pennsylvania Act of 1947[37] requires negotiation and mediation and then calls for a vote on the last offer of the employer. If the vote is for acceptance, the terms of the offer are binding for one year. If the vote is adverse, it shall be interpreted as a vote to arbitrate. The award of the arbitrator under such circumstances is binding for one year. Anyone adversely affected by any stoppage may seek an injunction, and anybody violating the Act is subject to fines from $500 to $2500 and six months' imprisonment.

The Virginia law passed in 1947 is unique.[38] It requires a five-week notice of a strike or lockout following failure of mediation, during which period the governor may poll the employees to find out how many will stay on the job after the state has seized the plant and may mobilize new workers to replace those who insist on striking. Under state operation a share of the profits is retained by the state as compensation for its services. Wages and working conditions are to remain intact until the parties themselves come to an agreement and the utility notifies the governor that it is in a position to resume operations.

When the telephone strike took place in 1947, the governor of Virginia directed the state commision to prepare for seizure and when the commission polled the employees 88 per cent indicated their willingness to work for the state. The commission then mobilized several hundred additional employees to provide replacements for the prospective strikers. In the end, however, very few workers went on strike, and the state continued in possession for only three days.

Nebraska established a court of industrial relations empowered to order the parties to begin or resume bargaining and to make any order governing the situation during the bargaining. The court further has authority to establish conditions of employment comparable to those maintained for the same or similar work. Any acts guiding or supporting stoppages or slowdowns are forbidden, and anyone violating an order of the industrial court is guilty of contempt.[39]

Texas authorizes injunctions against picketing of public utilities and specifically authorizes the governor to exercise all his powers to protect the public from dangers incident to interruption. Any sabotage of utility operations is made a felony.[40]

This harvest of public utility legislation from the soil tilled in 1946 is arresting in its contrast with federal legislation. Under the Taft-Hartley Act the ultimate right to strike is preserved even on railroads, atom bomb production, federal power plants, and the like, regardless of public danger and privation. The states I have listed have seen the problem otherwise. They have subordinated the right to strike to public interests where the health and safety of the public are threatened.

1948, an off year for state legislatures, saw little action in this field. In 1949, when the repercussions of 1946 had spent themselves, there was some slight reaction. Delaware, Missouri, and New Hampshire repealed their restrictive laws and Michigan abated its restrictions, including, as already pointed out, its requirement of compulsory arbitration for public utilities. Massachusetts required unions of more than 50 members to file financial reports and provided for court enforcement of arbitration awards where arbitration was agreed upon. Nebraska restricted picketing.[41]

The aggregate of all legislation regulating union activities after the upsets of 1937 and 1946 follows a few preponderant conceptions, and these few indicate what the public regarded as objectionable union activities. Starting with violence, intimidation, and excessive picketing, legislation proceeded to deal with the illegitimate use of economic power, such as strikes for improper purposes or in violation of contract, premature strikes, jurisdictional strikes, strikes of public employees and public utility employees, secondary boycotts, and closed-shop discrimination. Of a different nature are regulations forbidding political contributions and legislation designed to promote the democratic administration of union affairs; such regulations are very spotty. Excepting laws dealing with picketing and violence the over-all targets of the Taft-Hartley Act are much the same as those of the states that have entered this field, albeit there is disagreement on remedies.

The importance of regulating the internal management of unions in order to insure democracy and fair play in respect to its membership has not been fully recognized. As I pointed out in Chapter XVII, it is not a class question and should not be highly controversial. The interests of the employer do not hang heavily on its solution. It is because of these considerations and the experience of many years, I repeat, that the employing class as such has no direct, immediate self-interest in promoting the democratization of the union.

This problem of union administration should be placed on a much higher level than any possible controversy between employers and union leaders. With the growing importance of what I may call union citizenship, more states, particularly in 1943 and 1947, and Congress, in 1947, have passed some regulatory laws in respect to the internal affairs of unions just as in the past, under provocations no more compelling, corporation laws were enacted to protect the rights of stockholders. But these laws have not been as complete and well rounded as they should be. Too often they have stressed unimportant problems and overlooked important ones.

Union membership, where necessary to the pursuit of a livelihood, is certainly as much in need of protection as the ordinary stockholder's investment in a corporation or political suffrage. If union membership is to become what it already is in many cities and occupations, an eligibility requirement for the exercise of the essential right of pursuing a trade, then that individual right of a citizen to contract in respect to his livelihood has largely yielded to the diluted right of discussion and voting in the union hall. Since in the field of economic citizenship, which for all practical purposes may often be of more immediate direct importance than political citizenship, a man's relation to the union thus becomes one of the last citadels of individual expression, action, and democracy, we must not allow it to be displaced by bossism, racketeering, or repression.   Individual development of such a citizen may depend importantly on the extent to which he feels, and is permitted to exercise, responsibility for the action of his group.   If he feels, as he often does politically, that individual action in the union is futile and ineffective, we will again be adding to his sense of frustration and irresponsibility, which leads him to look to others to make the decisions of his life and to provide for his security.

As one weighs the profound importance of these changing relationships, one is shocked at the lack of an adequate over-all legislative program for this phase of our reconstructed society.   It seems clear that no union should be allowed to instigate or conduct strikes or to act as a bargaining agent unless it provides for democratic control and the fair protection of the membership status of those who wish to join the union or remain in it.   A model bill to that effect would, I believe, be welcomed by the public and certainly its advancement should carry no implications, for the reasons I have already stated, that its proponents have a special interest in the employer class.

There is room for a great deal of thoughtful consideration in the New Hampshire approach, which limited internal regulations to closed-shop unions on the theory that unions operating under monopolistic practices, involving as they do a greater menace to the civil liberties of individuals and the interests of the public, should be subject to greater restrictions than unions that do not discriminate against nonmembers.   If a man must join a union to pursue his trade, he must be protected in his union rights.   If the open shop is practiced and union membership is not essential, regulation may prove unimportant.   It is the difference between voluntary associations and involuntary associations.   If this distinction underlying the New Hampshire approach is sound, it might be extended to many areas of union regulation.   Regulation is the price of monopoly.

The controversy, between those who believe that all legislation dealing with collective bargaining and labor relations should be heavily weighted in favor of unions and those who believe that there are basic moral factors on both sides and that the rights and obligations of both should be defined as a means of promoting co-operation or a *modus vivendi,* is still with us.   As the struggle between these conflicting forces—if not conflicting ideologies— has run its course, the score to date in respect to labor relations acts is interesting to note.   Twelve states, the federal government, one county, and two territories have enacted labor relations acts enumerating unfair labor practices and in most cases creating a labor relations board to administer its provisions.[42]   All the acts, except those in three states [43] that follow the original one-sided pattern, have extended their controls to unfair practices by em-ployees as well as employers.   Of the original five states that in 1937 followed the one-sided pattern of the Wagner Act, New York alone remains, the other four having adopted the rounded-out con-trol either by amendment or substitution.   Only Rhode Island in 1941 and Connecticut in 1945 have pushed affirmatively against the tide by enacting the original lopsided pattern, but both acted prior to the excitement of 1946.   So the score is 13 to three in favor of balance.   The repeals by Delaware and New Hampshire are of a different significance whatever their cause, for they did not give place to one-sided legislation.

In writing the Wagner Act of 1935, compelling employers to recognize and bargain with representative unions and enforcing this obligation through an administration board, Congress had been a leader in a new and outstanding venture.   In discerning and correcting its mistakes and providing a more balanced control of labor relations, Congress proved a laggard.   Various states out-stripped the nation in meeting the realities of the situation.   While Congress slumbered, the states went into action.

This aftermath of the disturbances of 1937 and 1946 should be a lesson to special interests that indulge in antisocial conduct. Capital had to learn the hard way—by experience.   It had been warned from historic sources that it is easy for a special group to commit suicide by excesses, even though they be the excesses of minorities.   Failing to heed that warning, it met not only with so-cial controls from many directions but with the Wagner Act of 1935 with its extraordinary one-sidedness.   For this reason the employers of today fully understand the fears of labor unions when confronted with regulation, however fair at the outset. If labor leaders will frankly connect the many-sided regulations of labor unions and the unwillingness of Congress to repeal the Taft-Hartley Act with their antisocial conduct in 1937 and 1946, they will be more likely to pause before again provoking the public to action. As I have said elsewhere, they now find themselves pitted against something far more formidable than mere employer opinion or the desire of employers to preserve private management and the opportunity to make profits. They are pitted against the public.

It is difficult to convince any reasonable person that a program of balanced legislation, supported as it is by logic and reason and by various electorates and legislatures, is entirely unsound. It is difficult to understand why anyone, believing in a balanced program, should be put on the defensive by mere denunciations and epithets. Until labor leaders are willing to break their silence and openly and frankly discuss the most reasonable solution of the problems with which they have confronted society, no stable equilibrium can be reached.

XXIV

The Onward March of Collective Bargaining

ALL THE ISMS OF DISCONTENT growing out of the class struggle, whether they be titled Socialism, syndicalism, communism, statism, or unionism, are galvanized by similar emotional attitudes toward property rights and the inequalities in wealth that characterize industrial life under a system of free enterprise. Some of these "isms" resort to organized violence to promote their ends whenever they believe that the needs of the emergency require it. In the case of unionism, as distinguished from others, the workers in the United States, for the time being at least, are practical enough to believe that their greatest satisfactions can be secured through toleration of private capital and private management and the process of collective bargaining. Carried to its extreme, this system, through the broad exercise of the right to strike and otherwise attack business, may result in a back-door attack on private management that will be separated only by a thin partition from important features of the other isms. Some people characterize the onward march of collective bargaining as "creeping Socialism." Others call it merely a transitional step, and others "a step in the process of control."[1] The goal or destination is undefined. The one essential is advancement. "The possession of power by a class or organized group," says the editor of the official organ of the Amalgamated Clothing Workers of America, "compels action in the interest of further expansion or doom is the inevitable alternative. . . . Thus driven by the logic of its own development trade unionism proceeds from the prosecution

332

of its immediate objectives to positions from which it menaces, if it does not entirely attack, the balance of social power which is the foundation of the present Social order." [2]   Certainly where the union movement proclaims that industrial workers are a group that the employer is determined to abuse, it would be politically impossible for union leaders to accept the *status quo* without giving rise to a new political faction that would demand more rapid progress.

However, practical restraints on radicalism through collective bargaining are perfectly obvious.   How far will private capital and private management, still operating under a system of semi-free enterprise, yield to demands that deny them a large part of the very privileges that entice them into this field?   How far can this trend go without impairing efficiency and material standards? How long will private management and property owners, if shorn of too many of their prerogatives, consent to be harnessed for the benefit of the masses?   Society needs enthusiastic co-operation from all groups and particularly industrial leaders.   These are considerations that should lead both unions and management to stop, look, and listen but that conceivably may be taken out of the control of union leaders of the present type because of the emotional attitudes they are recklessly cultivating among their constituencies.   Among union leaders as well as public men there is always severe competition in promise making and slogan slinging.

With these cogitations in mind, I write this chapter on the scope and possibilities of collective bargaining, or rather on the ability and capacity of the management-union relationship to establish a permanent stabilized basis for the conduct of business.   In such a survey I am not concerned with details, the present customary line of demarcation of management rights, or the exact wording of the Taft-Hartley Act, which may be changed.   I am concerned with the broader contours that indicate whether or not unions in this country will be satisfied with anything short of too large a measure of joint responsibility over many important aspects of management.   Will unions underestimate the importance of special talent and disciplinary authority and overestimate the benefits of industrial democracy?

Russia soon discovered that business could not be conducted efficiently without delegating full authority to a factory manager, and it seems equally clear in this country that the price of real management-sharing would inevitably spell a lower standard of living. Business cannot be operated by debating committees. Experience tells us that it is not practicable really to democratize the administration of industry and maintain efficiency any more than it is possible to democratize an army, and it is not likely that the results of the future will prove otherwise. On the other hand, if the workers through collective bargaining, with its ever-expanding scope, cannot secure satisfaction, they may do as the English unions have done and turn to a Socialist commonwealth as an answer to their sense of frustration. They must be sold not only the free enterprise system but all the incidents of that system.

Perhaps I am making a mistake in calling this chapter "The Onward March of Collective Bargaining," when in fact I am thinking in terms not only of the statutory obligation to bargain but of the entire subject of union intrusion into the field of management, whether it be based on statutory compulsion to bargain, the lure that flows from promise of co-operation, or the economic compulsion that flows from the threat of industrial warfare.

In the legal field many able and disinterested minds are alarmed over the expanded field of bargaining. This alarm is accentuated by recent developments, such as the decisions of the courts that require the employer to bargain over pensions, welfare funds, and merit increases; the insistence that foremen unions be recognized; and the Taft-Hartley Act, which imposes the obligation on both unions and employers to bargain over "wages, hours and other terms and conditions of employment." To be sure, the Taft-Hartley Act, unlike the Wagner Act, explicitly rejects the idea that the employer is obligated to recognize unions of supervisors, but that may not be the last word on this subject since the unions are free to enforce such a demand by industrial war waged jointly by the foremen and the rank and file.

Regardless of whether or not a particular demand or grievance comes within the scope of the statutory obligation to bargain, there is always the question as to whether it comes within the broader scope of objectives that the union is free to further by means of industrial war. For illustration, it can hardly be questioned that it would be lawful to wage a strike, enforced by the picket line, to compel the discharge of an objectionable superintendent or even an objectionable general manager if the effect is not to restrict the employers' choice of representation to deal with grievances or collective bargaining. Whether that would be an issue concerning which parties would be compelled to bargain within the meaning of the Taft-Hartley Act has not been determined. Under extreme circumstances I can conceive of such a demand as morally and legally justifiable. At any rate the present law leaves the door wide open for the courts to define the area of compulsory bargaining.

In well-unionized industries, of which there is an increasing number, it might be of more practical importance to define the breadth of the issues that unions may enforce by industrial combat than to define the legal field of interests concerning which both unions and employers are under statutory compulsion to bargain. The purpose of labor relations acts was not to limit the subjects over which the parties might bargain but to define the subjects over which they must bargain. The pressure to bargain under threat of industrial warfare may often be greater than the pressure to bargain because of the statutory mandate. Under the development of federal legislation in the last decade, as pointed out in previous chapters, the right to force terms by industrial war is not coterminous with the statutory obligation to bargain. The former is broader. Ever since the Supreme Court in effect declared, prior to the passage of the Taft-Hartley Act, that the lawful or unlawful nature of the purposes labor seeks did not qualify its absolute rights to engage in normal activities to obstruct business, there would seem to be few, if any, limits—in the absence of statutes to the contrary—on the right of a union to compel bargaining on any issue in which it had even an attenuated interest. Labor was thus guaranteed the same freedom to injure business for antisocial or illegal purposes that it enjoyed for legal and commendable purposes. Thus the freedom to wage warfare is broader than the freedom to make a collective-bargaining agreement, since labor, by virtue of its exemptions from the antitrust laws, may alone perform acts that are illegal for it to do in combination with a nonlabor group. Of course this sounds silly, but it is true. If the limits of the bargaining area should be fixed by statute, they could hardly be made effective unless at least the statute banned the picket line to enforce purposes outside of the statutory bargaining area. The frontier lines of the legitimate bargaining area have not as yet been located.

On March 28, 1945, Eric Johnston, president of the Chamber of Commerce of the United States; William Green, president of the American Federation of Labor; and Philip Murray, president of the Congress of Industrial Organizations, signed a labor-management charter, which undertook to outline in general terms the broader concepts of labor-management relationships. The charter declared: "We dedicate our joint efforts for a practical partnership" under a code which recognizes that "improved productive efficiency and technical advancement" must be encouraged and that "the rights of private property and free choice of action under a system of private competitive capitalism must continue to be the foundation of our nation's peaceful and prosperous expanding economy." More important is this significant paragraph: "The inherent right and responsibility of management to direct the operations of an enterprise shall be recognized and preserved." [3]

Curiously enough, the National Association of Manufacturers, representing many thousands of manufacturers throughout the United States, refused to join in this declaration, fearful that its other provisions conceding the rights of labor might prove embarrassing to the N.A.M. program of securing labor legislation. [4]

Later in the year this promise of an understanding in respect to this issue vanished into thin air and suggested that the gulf between the parties might be as broad and as deep as differences in ideology. It at least appeared that, although in the first part of 1945 the National Association of Manufacturers was unwilling to write a broad definition of the respective functions of management and unions, in the latter part of the same year the unions were unwilling to be parties to any definite statement on this prickly and controversial subject.

It happened in this way. In November, 1945, President Truman issued invitations to the National Labor-Management Conference, composed of delegates from the American Federation of Labor, the Congress of Industrial Organizations, the United Mine Workers of America, the railway brotherhoods, the National Association of Manufacturers, and the Chamber of Commerce of the United States, in an endeavor to iron out the problems of postwar adjustments between labor and management. Among the committees established to deal with various aspects of the problems before the conference was Committee II on Management's Right to Manage. This committee found itself unable to reach any agreement, largely because management sought to stabilize the *status quo* while labor was totally unwilling to peg its future objectives. Except for this fundamental difference, it might not have been impossible to reach an understanding based on familiar boundaries.

The management members, reporting to the executive committee of the entire conference, stated that labor had been "unwilling to agree on any listing of specific management functions," which to the management members indicated that labor intended to expand the field of collective bargaining "into the field of management." Such philosophy, said the management representatives, means "joint management of enterprise," to which management members could not agree.[5]

These management representatives in presenting their contentions divided management functions into two classes. In the first class, management claimed exclusive jurisdiction. In the second class, management conceded the reviewability of its initial decision.

The first group of functions, which management claimed to be its exclusive responsibility, included the determination of products to be manufactured; services to be rendered customers; location of the business; methods, means, or materials to be used; determination of financial policies; and "the determination of the management organization of each producing or distributing unit and the selection of employees for promotion to supervisory and other managerial positions."[6] The second group of functions, as to which management conceded that its decisions might be subject to review, included discharges, seniority provisions, and disciplinary penalties.

The report of the labor members of this same committee was less detailed and factual. It reads in part:

Because of the complexities of these relationships, the labor members of the committee think it unwise to specify and classify functions and responsibilities of management. Because of the insistence by management for such specification, the committee was unable to agree upon a joint report. To do so might well restrict the flexibility so necessary to efficient operation.

It would be extremely unwise to build a fence around the rights and responsibilities of management on the one hand and the unions on the other.

The experience of many years shows that with the growth of mutual understanding the responsibilities of one of the parties today may well become
the joint responsibility of both parties tomorrow. . . .

Management and labor are both vitally concerned with full, regular and
efficient production. Each has functions to perform in the attainment of
that common objective.[7]

Labor was unwilling to define its ultimate goal. As Matthew
Arnold wrote: "Still bent to make some port he knows not where,
still standing for some false impossible shore." [8]

The labor members refused to make any recommendation relative to unionization of foremen "while cases involving this issue
are pending before the National Labor Relations Board." [9] The
employer members, however, detailed their arguments against the
recognition of foremen's associations for the purpose of collective
bargaining.

So there is the milk of the cocoanut. The unions convincingly
assert that "experience of many years shows that . . . the responsibilities of one of the parties today may well become the
joint responsibility of both parties tomorrow." The Federation
of Labor was asserting in September, 1949, that labor must "move
forward on the economic front" and "on the political front." [10]
But where? Our great experiment to ascertain whether under
modern industrial conditions, private management and private
capital can continue to function efficiently for the common good,
or whether envy of wealth and property on the one hand and the
fear of labor power on the other will deprive us of these values,
is still in the making. The issues cannot be frozen, particularly
in the present state of unrest and distrust. Union leaders are
empiricists—not idealists.

What then is the present state of the art? How far has collective bargaining encroached on private management? At the turn
of the century collective bargaining in the few industries in which
it truly prevailed, dealt almost entirely with wages and hours.
The Anthracite Award of 1903, with its provisions for a conciliation board and an umpire to settle grievances, was a beacon light
not thought of in most industries. Today if we glance at the
furthest frontiers of collective bargaining, we behold a startling
expansion of union demands and tremendous inroads on what
earlier would have been regarded as exclusive managerial functions. Although the outposts of the frontier may be extremes

and may be subject to the comment that one swallow does not make a summer, it must also be remembered that straws may show which way the wind blows.

The employer's choice of personnel is in many ways restricted. He may not discriminate against members of a union, regardless of its leadership, objectives, or practices. A few decades ago it was held to be the Constitutional right of the employer to choose his employees on almost any test of eligibility he might choose to apply. Union security as now demanded goes further and constitutes a direct restriction on the employer's choice of personnel, whether it takes the form of the closed shop, the union shop, maintenance of membership, or a union hiring hall. In either case the employer's right to select his employees is conditioned on the employees' relation to a particular union. In the case of jurisdictional disputes the employer is even told that in particular jobs he must restrict his choice to a member of the union that claims that work. It was only in 1947 that the Taft-Hartley Act placed some limitations on these practices.

Through seniority rules the employer is obliged to give precedence to length of service rather than ability in making layoffs, rehiring, and, in some cases, in making promotions. Apparently the union justifies this restriction, not on the ground that years of service should rank first, but on the ground that some rigid rule is necessary to avoid favoritism and arbitrary discrimination by management. Messrs. Golden and Ruttenberg assert it to be "the only equitable method proved practical of administration to eliminate favoritism and discrimination among a group of workers," [11] which seems to suggest that the rule is devised primarily to take discretionary power from the employer on the ground that he has abused it. So an uneconomic rule is adopted because, it is argued, the employer cannot be trusted impartially to choose employees according to their ability.

When negotiating for certain telephone companies, including the long lines of the American Telephone and Telegraph Company, we had a hard battle to wrest a concession from the union that there should be a small margin of tolerance where the company could prefer men of exceptional ability regardless of seniority, in order to develop a corps of leaders for supervisory positions. Even after this concession was written into one agreement the union later fought—in one case successfully—to have it eliminated. The provisions of some labor agreements that require seniority in making promotions are more troublesome. The requirement of superseniority for shop stewards and other union officials is less serious in large establishments.

Rigid rules that subordinate superior ability to length of service at least theoretically, and in many cases actually, tend to retard maximum productivity and to that extent injure both groups. In the long run they weaken the productive organization, although they tend to reduce turnover, promote stability, and remove worry from the mind of the worker.

Disciplinary action by the employer is in some aspects part of the same picture. The discharge, suspension, or discipline of employees for one reason or another is now pretty generally subject to grievance procedure, with arbitration as a last step, and only a few arbitrators have ventured to assert that the employer's action should necessarily be upheld unless it appears that he acted in bad faith, for an ulterior reason, in violation of contract, or arbitrarily and without reason. Too often the arbitrators proceed to substitute their judgment for that of the employer and frequently modify the penalty as too severe. I have tried in many instances, and have succeeded in some, to write clauses into agreements that in discharge cases the arbitrator should not undertake to substitute his judgment for that of the employer, and sometimes arbitrators have practically rejected the agreed limitation because of his sympathies—so strong is the feeling that the employee has a vested interest in his job.

Coupled with these arrangements affecting choice of personnel is the union insistence upon a voice in work assignments, content of job, and transfers. Strikes have been threatened because a man was transferred from a factory on one side of a river to a factory on the other side or from an office in one borough to an office in another borough. What work shall be done by women, what by apprentices and helpers, and what by skilled mechanics is a familiar subject of collective bargaining, in which the union men seek to protect their jobs and their wage scales.

The protection or expansion of job opportunities by the slowdown is a direct assertion of the right of the employee to protect his job. Those who believe that such practices are new or that we are going backward in such matters should read an article by John Stuart Mill in the *Fortnightly Review* of May, 1869, in which it is written that some union regulations go further than opposing improvements:

They are contrived for the express purpose of making work inefficient; they positively prohibit the workman from working hard and well, in order that it may be necessary to employ a greater number. Regulations that no one shall move bricks in a wheelbarrow, but only carry them in a hod, and then no more than eight at a time; that stones shall not be worked in a quarry while they are soft, but must be worked by the masons of the place where they are to be used; that plasterers shall not do the work of plasterers' laborers, nor laborers that of plasterers, but a plasterer and a laborer must both be employed when one would suffice; that bricks made on one side of a particular canal must lie there unused, while fresh bricks are made for work going on upon the other; that men shall not do so good a day's work as to "best their mates"; that they shall not walk at more than a given pace to their work when the walk is counted "in the master's time"—these and scores of similar examples, which will be found in Mr. Thornton's book, equally vexatious, and some of them more ridiculous, are all grave violations of the moral rule, that disputes between classes should not be so conducted as to make the world a worse place for both together, and ultimately for the whole of the community.[12]

Such accounts show not only the motivation of union leaders in erecting protection of this kind but also the infinite possibilities of sabotaging productivity by slowdowns and other passive efforts.

In many negotiations the question arises as to the right of the employer to sublet or subcontract any part of his work. This I encountered as a subject of intense bargaining in the communications industry. Then there is the converse. In the electrical industry and other construction industries, the union undertakes to require that certain work be done by the contractor on the job and not by the producer in the factory. During the war prefabricated houses were tabooed. In other cases the introduction of improved machinery or modern technology has been opposed because it eliminated jobs, and a familiar substitute is to require the employer to find other jobs for displaced persons. Duplication of work and other make-work provisions are well known. Full-crew provisions requiring the employer not to reduce his working forces and to increase the number attached to a particular task have been sought. The boycott of musical transcriptions and the employment of stand-by musicians are other examples. Material efficiency in the interest of all is again overridden by the uneconomic selfishness of a few.

Work-sharing and the allocation of work are another phase of industrial relations that has been introduced into union negotiations, and the complicated problem of merit increases, which depend so much on individual performance difficult to measure by definite data, has been thrown into the hopper.

The demand for a guaranteed wage, which is becoming more and more familiar, also reflects the growing desire for job security, which is closely related to the feeling that the worker owns the job. From the point of view of some social students the claim is not only to the job but to a full-time job, with the obligation of the employer permanently to take care of the worker's livelihood in this respect. "Call-in" pay, which requires the employer to pay a penalty for denying a worker a full day's work on arrival, and severance pay, for denying him continuity of employment for his lifetime, are part of the same trend. All these many-sided provisions point to the underlying philosophy that the employee has an inchoate title to his job and a full-time employment, as well as security on retirement.

These cumulative provisions, passing so many regulatory powers on to the union, reflect a growing philosophy, not only in the minds of unionists but in the minds of many thoughtful persons, that ownership and operation of private business should be subject to other controls than normal business management. Our attitude toward strikes that are an incident to collective bargaining reflects a similar trend.

No one wishes to go back to the old days when strikes merely brought strike-breaking tactics with vengeful reactions by employers. Public officials, as well as private citizens, are loath to look to strike breaking as the primary remedy, even for an unwarranted strike, to the point of protecting the employer and the replacements in their rights to do business together. Speaking the moral philosophy of the day, one might almost say that, although the business belongs to the owners for the purpose of management and returns on investment, the workers have an equitable lien on it for the purpose of their livelihood. The growing prevalence of that feeling in this country in the twentieth century is one of the most potent and significant factors to be weighed. Under the labor relations acts the employees who are out on strike for higher wages are by legal fiat still employees, although in fact they no longer have any connection with the business because of their inability to agree with their former employer on the terms of their employment. Thus the employee is protected not only in his right to quit but in his right to return. The extent to which we recognize the contention that the employee has a vested interest in the business is one of the anomalies of the free enterprise system. Even runaway shops, through which the employer has sought to avoid his former employees or their union by changing the location of his business, have been forbidden.

The subjects of insurance, social security, welfare provisions, and pensions have now entered the bargaining field. After determined opposition by the employers, the National Labor Relations Board and the courts have held that these subjects come under the statutory definition of "other terms and conditions of employment," concerning which the employer is legally required to bargain.

The contention now is that the rank and file workers have the same right to enjoy pensions at the expense of the company as its president, and that these payments must needs be continued, even after the contract that imposes them has expired. So the employer is to be held responsible for recognizing the worker's right to his job, as long as there is a job and the employee performs his work, and also to provide for his welfare and his old age. That is certainly socialization of business through collective bargaining, supplemented by national laws.

When it is recalled that these matters are not static, but dynamic, that the unions have recently refused to peg their objectives, and that the union membership is being taught to regard the employer as an oppressor who must be brought to terms, it would be a rash man indeed who would predict stability in present relationships. In the end stability must be a matter of compromise between industrial democracy and industrial efficiency, and the employers who value their social function to furnish goods at the lowest possible price can hardly be blamed when they resist any breakdown of management authority. A point of compromise consistent with the general welfare can be reached only through forbearance, restraint, and greater emphasis on practicality than ideology. Despite discouraging clashes from time to time, I still feel that an amazing amount of wisdom is often disclosed by both sides in respect to this important aspect of the class struggle. It is not

the attitude of present leaders but the opportunities for demagoguery that are being developed by hostile campaigns against
the employer that are to be feared.

The legal status of collective bargaining under the federal law,
before the passage of the Taft-Hartley Act, also indicates the extent to which unions and their members were to have a continuing
claim on business through the bargaining process. The employer
was obliged to bargain and, if an agreement could be reached, to
put it in writing. He was forced to bargain with the union over
changes in the agreement that were contrary to the terms of the
existing contract and even to bargain over changes when the union
was maintaining a strike in violation of an existing agreement.
The provisions of the anti-injunction laws denied the employer any
relief against such indefensible practices, and actions for damages
for such wrongs were not ordinarily maintainable in the federal
courts. The workers, through the unions, had a continuing legal
interest in their jobs, and the employer had no corresponding
rights that gave him any remedy for the wrongs so inflicted on
him by the union or those whom the law declared were still his
employees. The employer is still forced to contract with a union
that refuses to recognize its contract obligations. Now that this un-
balance of obligations has been changed by the Taft-Hartley Act,
the union is seeking to restore it.

Finally, let us turn to more startling examples of the progress
of workmen's rights through collective bargaining. Some unions,
not satisfied with the overtime provisions of the fair labor standards acts, have dictated the schedules that an employer shall maintain, and others have forbidden night work. Strikes have also
taken place, and others have been threatened, because of opposition to the managerial personnel. I have had occasion to deal
with a number of such situations. Unions have insisted—some
of them for many years—that they should bargain over the wages,
hours, and other terms and conditions of employment of first-line
supervision. Although the Taft-Hartley Act has ruled this form
of bargaining out as a matter of statutory obligation, it is nevertheless enforceable by industrial warfare. No one would expect
to prevent this in the printing or building trades. These trades,
like coal mining, need no Taft-Hartley Act to strengthen their
right to collective bargaining on any point they may choose to assert. Some unions have undertaken to dictate the products that

shall be manufactured and even the class of customers that shall be served, and some have sought to regulate prices. Other unions have limited the right of the employer in choosing the source or nature of the materials or equipment he shall use. Usually these regulations are negative and obstructive in character, but there have been regulations of a more constructive character.

To make the possibilities of this picture doubly clear, let us take the demands of one of the most brilliant leaders of one of the three largest unions in the country—Walter Reuther, president of the United Automobile Workers. Just before the end of 1945, I was acting as spokesman for the General Motors Corporation before the fact-finding committee established by President Truman to settle the pending strike against that company. The union had demanded that wage increases be measured by the individual ability of that company to pay and that it should be permitted to examine the company's books in order to establish its point. The company rejected the union contention on the ground that wages in that industry should not vary with the varying efficiency of each company, and that the price of labor, like the price of any commodity, should not depend on the ability of the purchaser to pay. A variation in wages among competing manufacturers of automobiles that depended on the efficiency of each manufacturer, it was urged, would destroy all incentive to keep costs and prices at the lowest possible level.

But President Reuther argued otherwise and thus developed his own theme song that the issue was not one of wages but of ideology. The issue, said Mr. Reuther, "is bigger than just an ordinary wage argument; it is bigger than the corporation or bigger than the union." The union sought to bargain on wages, profits, and prices; this demand included matters theretofore regarded as exclusively management functions. The union conceded that such demands would eventually lead to bargaining on the calculation of profits and the rewards and selection of the managerial staff. It declared publicly, through Mr. Reuther, that occasion might arise where it would be necessary for it to consider whether the company was "paying the president too much money," whether the directors "who aren't doing anything might be getting too much money," whether "the engineer ought to be sweeping the shop up instead of designing their products," and generally "whether the managerial personnel has gone to seed." In this over-all demand to settle wages, profits and prices by collective bargaining, the union declared, "We will make no compromise." I told the fact-finding board that the company was unwilling to accept a super-wage above that applicable to its competitors or other employers of like types of labor and that it would constitute a violation of the antitrust laws to bargain over profits and prices with a union that controlled all competing units in the industry. As to this there could be no doubt. For that reason I announced at a later session that, since the board insisted upon considering the issue of ability to pay, "the General Motors Corporation feels that it has no choice but to withdraw from this proceeding," which was accordingly done. That afternoon our seats were vacant.

If this position had been taken by some unimportant union, some Marxist union, or an unseasoned labor leader in the left wing, it would not deserve the importance I have attached to it. As the deliberate public position of an outstanding labor leader of one of the three largest unions in the United States, a leader who has fought the left wing within his union, it must be weighed as a rather complete flowering of the possibilities I have discussed and as an attempt to advance towards some new kind of syndicalism. It shows the thinness of the wall between some unions and radicalism.

Moreover, it is not unprecedented for unions to join with their employers in an effort to increase the revenues of the employer by increased service charges, and this is certainly sharing a management function. The transport workers' union joined with the city and the private bus lines in New York to obtain higher transit fares with which to pay higher wages, and utility workers have likewise plugged for higher gas and electric rates. The Brotherhood of Teamsters, on the other hand, joined with the produce merchants before the Interstate Commerce Commission to oppose additional charges, imposed on the merchants, covering produce unloaded in New York. The building service unions quietly backed demands for higher rent ceilings. In the garment trades, unions and employers join in supporting a program to promote the sale of dresses. The C.I.O. through Mr. Murray has advocated an ambitious program for industry councils of unions, employers, and government to prescribe industrial planning for basic industries, such planning to include production levels, amount of capital investment, prices, foreign trade, and the size and location of plants. The program sounds like an ambitious cartel, so typical in Germany before the war. It is forgetful of our antitrust policies, under which the exemptions of labor no longer control when the union collaborates with employers.

Mr. Murray says "Boards of Directors sitting in the financial centers of the nation pass economic legislation, based exclusively on their profit and loss statements. In one decision they wipe out a complete mill and ruin an entire town, and they do it apparently without any thought of responsibility for the social consequences of their decision." [13] Here is a challenge to management for failing to recognize the social consequences of its economic moves. Nor would it be surprising, with the growth of nationwide unions and nationwide bargaining, if the union demanded some voice as to plant location where it involves broad social consequences.

Union demands penetrate management and financial functions. Claims for wage increases are supported by referring to the dividends paid the investors or by charges of overcapitalization or excessive mortgage interest. Some contend that wage increases should be paid out of surpluses. The amounts paid company officials for salaries are frequently brought into the picture when the company pleads inability to pay.

But even if the claims of Mr. Reuther and Mr. Murray have been fairly well put at rest, for the moment, it cannot be denied that labor has an interest in productivity when it is constantly reminded that its wages depend on productivity. Having an interest in productivity, labor may wish to discuss many phases of management affecting productivity. A number of union contracts provide for union co-operation in promoting productivity.

The practical solution, it would seem, lies not so much in the field of ideology as in the field of economic efficiency, and existing union philosophy seems theoretically to accept this test when it looks with favor on private enterprise with all it implies. Those who think that the boundary line between union and management functions can be fixed where it now is are forgetful of the dynamic nature of our society.

One thoughtful and studious writer has recommended "that the protection of managerial rights in industrial enterprise is a matter of government concern." [14] This statement would seem to mean that the field of managerial rights should be fenced in by legislation. It is a proposition to give us pause. It seems to throw the whole subject of managerial rights into politics. The argument would be that the question of what "ism" should be pursued is a matter of governmental policy, and since the free-enterprise system is national policy, Congress should legislate against trends that conflict with it. If as a result of such an appeal by management to the political tribunal the scope of bargaining were broadened, it would place the employer in a more difficult position to resist demands within the bargaining area sanctioned by government. To the extent that the area of bargaining was restricted, the government should logically make unlawful any kind of industrial warfare to attain objects beyond the permitted area if the policy were to be enforced. Organized industrial warfare to force bargaining contrary to national policy, whatever it is, would not be sanctioned.

I can conceive of very few proposals that would offer a greater threat to our free economy than one that undertook by federal act to define the permissible limits of management sharing between management and unions, and I predict that in the long run the result of such an attempt would not be to protect, but to narrow, management rights. It is difficult to believe that the welfare of the nation would be more secure if the area of permissive bargaining were to be settled by statute rather than by the swaying forces of collective bargaining, tempered by the recognized exigencies of the contestants. After all, it seems almost inevitable that our only salvation lies in practical adjustments mutually acceptable to the parties. So far as management is concerned, I am quite sure it would settle for the elementary undertaking by government to enforce law and order and to protect existing elementary rights in times of industrial disturbance.

To look upon the area of bargaining as a static line seems to me the greatest of errors. It is a changing frontier, pricked out by experience. How far unions will encroach upon the domain of management is not predictable. In some industries it will be less and in others it will be more.

The needle trades offer outstanding examples where joint responsibility for matters ordinarily treated as exclusive functions of management has traveled far. It would take many pages to do justice to this particular detail of the subject. In that industry collective bargaining has included covenants that the employer install the most modern and efficient machines and has provided for joint committees to deal with safety, sanitation, elimination of waste, efficiency, public relations, fair trade practices, sales promotions, the study of nonunion production, and the suppression of nonunion competition. There seems to be no limit to joint responsibility for over-all results when the agreement provides that "the union further agrees to use its national influence wherever possible to increase the general business and profit of the firm." [15] The anthracite industry, notwithstanding its stormy experience with collective bargaining, presents a unique plan whereby the Commonwealth of Pennsylvania, the miners' union, and the coal operators are represented on a tripartite board that weekly fixes the amount of anthracite needed to meet market requirements. The aggregate being thus fixed, the actual allocation among the several operators is automatically controlled by predetermined percentages.

One of the best rationalizations of the union assertion of its undefined and almost unrestricted goal is found in a book published by two labor leaders, in which they say, "Workers join unions to get a voice in making the decisions that vitally affect them, and such a voice in economic matters is a path to industrial peace that cannot be by-passed, either by management or by unions." [16] And when the employers in collective bargaining talk of costs, profits, sales resistance and productivity, they certainly go far to invite joint discussions of these aspects of management.

Actual experience with labor-management committees, dealing with problems not customarily regarded as within the recognized scope of labor unions, offers both hope and discouragement.[17] The clothing industry and, to some extent, the glass-making industry are shining examples of union assistance to management in the solution of production problems. The plan started by the Baltimore & Ohio Railroad following the shopmen's strike of 1922 has survived these many years with benefits to both groups and has been applied by several other railroad systems. At the outset it was founded on the platform that "when the groups responsible for better service and greater efficiency share fairly in the benefits which follow their joint efforts, improvements in the conduct of the railroad are greatly encouraged." Through this plan it is claimed that "on all of the railroads where the cooperative program is in effect the shop employees through their unions have become very active indeed in securing new business as well as pro-

moting public good will." [18]   During the conferences between the
groups, it was further affirmed "the whole subject of the gains
due to cooperation and financial participation in these gains was
thoroughly reviewed" and agreed upon through direct negotiation.[19]

During World War II labor-management committees, advisory
in character and excluded from participation in collective bargaining, in some cases, achieved results although in others they
failed.   Perhaps these variations in results were due to the varying attitudes of the parties and a failure to search out the practical
limits of such co-operation.   Certainly any program so alluring
in theory should not be heedlessly discarded without practical experimentation so long as the final results are not proved incon-
trovertibly to be detrimental.   If both groups learn to apply the
standard of industrial efficiency, and not democratic idealism, as
the test of desirability, the desire for material progress should
lead to various adventures and the discovery of sound practice
through trial and error.

As unions advance in the field of economic research and engi-
neering and are forced to consider the impact of their decisions
not only on the economy of the employers but on the economy of
the nation, they should become better qualified to consider problems that formerly have been regarded as beyond their ken.   It
is when the starry-eyed talk idealistically of industrial democracy
and management-sharing for its own sake, without regard to the
desirability of greater productivity for the people as a whole, that
it is necessary to beware.   Less emphasis on ideology and continued increase in productivity should be our aim.

A workable program must be debated and determined on the
basis of an adjustment between productive efficiency and the health,
dignity, and security of the worker, as well as an adequate return
to the investor.

If unions will place as much emphasis upon the need of productivity as they do upon the dangers of a speed-up and will
reduce the virus they are injecting into the veins of their members,
there will be much less resistance to their efforts to assume an
enlarged responsibility.   So long as union men are taught to
view the employer as a plunderer, and employers in turn look upon
unions as agencies to deprive them of their rights, there can be no

stabilized policy and the battle line will prove as destructive of community interests as most battle lines.

There is real competition, between labor, management, and investor, that in a free economy automatically regulates many of these matters, and it is this competition that should in the long run restrain each group from overreaching. As a social ideal the greatest degree of industrial democracy consistent with efficiency is desirable, but equally desirable are the benefits that flow from unhampered disciplinary authority in the administration of industry. Where the line is to be drawn should be determined by experience rather than theory, and it must be drawn as a matter of mutual co-operation and accommodation if we are to avoid the possibilities of sabotaging any program of maximum productivity. Future safety lies in the elasticity of this issue and a frank acknowledgment of the mutual dependence of all groups upon a practical solution.

The report of the Twentieth Century Fund on *Trends in Collective Bargaining* clearly recognizes the possibilities of expanding the field of collective bargaining. It says:

> The ruling idea in today's economic thought is that prosperity is based on full employment, full production, internal price-cost equilibrium, and high levels of purchasing power. The stake of both labor and management in all four is beyond doubt. What a company decides in the way of work schedules, production quotas, and wages and prices is a concern of labor as of management. If employer and labor leader act on this assumption of mutuality of interests, collective bargaining may be applied to a whole range of industrial problems hitherto untouched by bilateral action.[20]

Taking an inventory of well-known items within the expanding area of collective bargaining has the advantage of exposing how completely step by step "the old order changeth yielding place to new." We are living in a reconstructing society, and since the present is fleeting and underlying forces are pushing us in one direction, it is well to understand that the reconstruction will become more radical. If all the implications growing out of the workers' inchoate right to a full-time job and compensation on retirement—controlled in important particulars by the union—are ever given full effect either by established custom or by governmental action, this will indeed become a society with changed

incentives and motivations and ultimately with changes in the reactions and conduct of individuals. The area of private management, meaning management by owners or their agents, is being
contracted not only by the extension of government but by the
extension of the rights of workers in the business. Another bad
depression might write these trends into a new social pattern. To
fear these trends is not to impugn motives. Mistaken idealism
can work havoc. In my family runs the story of the child who,
in trying to help her mother sweep the room with a broom, knocked
a priceless vase from the mantelpiece. Sobbing she cried out,
"I was so busy watching one end that I did not see what the other
end was doing"—the tragedy of the reformer.

The situation is bewildering because no one, not even those who
insist upon going, knows where we are going. In fact it would
be a thrilling symposium if the labor leaders of the country were
to give us an unguarded exposure of what they regarded as the
ultimate goal of unionism in its relation to private management.

I quote Mr. Gompers: "What does labor want? It wants the
earth and the fullness thereof." [21]

XXV

The Call to Battle

IMPORTANT ABOVE MOST MATTERS, but difficult to measure, is what goes on in the hearts and minds of multitudes of men and women. Dictators backed by a censorship can control this to an amazing extent. They know only too well that constant reiteration, without the corrective process of free speech, usually brings acceptance of an idea, whether it be true or false. In the field of labor relations, where a long history of antagonism so often leads the workers to give ready credulity to statements of labor leaders and incredulity to statements of employers, the situation is somewhat comparable to a censorship, and the opportunity and responsibility of union leaders to shape the attitude of their members toward employers and the results of the free enterprise system is indeed great. With this segment of society the employer to an important extent has lost his audience. The whole process, moreover, has been enormously accelerated by the political ascendancy of the New Deal and its crusade against property interests. To President Roosevelt, businessmen were money-changers profaning the temple of society, and that idea he helped to plant in the minds of the workers. Nor has President Truman sought to displace it.

In trying to appraise psychological trends in labor groups with a view to determining where they are heading, one is confronted with many contradictory facts. All currents are not running in the same direction.

The five-year agreement of 1950 between the U.A.W. and the General Motors Company recognized by mutual agreement the very thought I have been endeavoring to express. It implies that

353

the real basis for improvement in wages must depend to a large extent upon factors contributed by others than the employees. The president of the company refers to "substituting machines and mechanical power for human backs." Thousands of dollars stand as an investment behind each employee to give maximum effectiveness to his efforts. The agreement itself provides "the annual improvement factor herein recognizes that a continuing improvement in the standard of living of employees depends upon technological progress, better tools, methods, processes, and equipment, and a cooperative attitude on the part of all parties in such progress."[1] This is significant language. It means, as I read it, that industrial leaders, scientists, and bankers are the ones who hold out to the worker the real hope of advancement. If the vast membership of unions learns to recognize this fact and comes to look upon such important groups as its main benefactors instead of plunderers, the hopes for an improved era would be greatly enhanced.

The American Federation of Labor has taken an exceptional position on at least two occasions. Here is one of its statements:

"We do not seek to restrict profits to fixed ranges or to eliminate them. Profits are the incentive of employers, not because they are avaricious but because money is the key to other opportunities. If wage rates and profits compensate fairly, the experience, the resourcefulness, the know-how, and the dependability of workers and management will be potent for continued economic progress."[2]

Again the Federation affirms its faith:

We in the American Federation of Labor are determined that free enterprise shall survive in America, because it has brought to the people of our country a higher standard of living than is enjoyed by any other nation on earth.[3]

Mr. Buckmaster, president of the United Rubber Workers, C.I.O., speaking before an employers' group, is not so certain. He says:

The labor organizations of this country as democratic institutions are not wedded to any particular kind of economic system . . . we recognize and appreciate the great success which American industry has had under capitalism and we are ready and willing to try and make it work.[4]

Today nearly three-quarters of our industrial employees are working under collective-bargaining agreements, and many of these agreements reflect improved attitudes and methods in their negotiation and administration. Today with the workers enjoying higher standards of material welfare than have ever before been known anywhere and with unions almost invariably bringing back something from each bargaining table, the present basic order is acceptable. Today the dominant note of officialdom in the labor movement is opposed to Marxism, syndicalism, and the like. Labor asserts in general terms that it does not seek to overthrow private management or even the right of investors to a fair return on capital, but at the same time it is teaching that the employer is the enemy of the workingman.

Some support for this contradictory attitude may be read in the findings of the Labor Committee of the Twentieth Century Fund:

A close observation of the labor scene today reveals two strong forces working in opposite directions. One of these forces can tear our social fabric apart. Its source is power and its philosophy is conflict. The other, less dramatic, is slowly binding up the wounds of group dissension. It is gradually fashioning a code of mutual responsibility and plodding toward the goal of cooperation.[5]

To analyze these contradictory attitudes, which make us oscillate between hope and fear, is important. Labor agreements are often merely armed truces during which union members are warned by their leaders that they must not disarm.

There is often a sharp contrast between the co-operation that is going on between management and unions in the workaday world, coupled with the private expressions of top leaders during the negotiation and administration of collective-bargaining agreements, and the inflammatory messages that union leaders so often carry to the rank and file. That is the reason why agreements negotiated by union committees are sometimes voted down at union meetings; the leaders in their campaigns with their membership have encouraged and developed attitudes that are inconsistent with the talk across the bargaining table. Again and again have union leaders engaged in a tirade against me and my clients, in the presence of their followers, although later they have apologized and explained that it had to be done because of internal politics. To Mr. Bambrick of the building service union I was publicly a buzzard but privately was a brother to whom he wished peace and goodwill. Even though the employer is sympathetic and generous at the bargaining table, the report of the union officers to their membership does not reflect such an attitude.　Like Falstaff, they tell a story of a terrific battle with an imaginary foe and their valiant defense.　The union potency must be played up.　The employer must receive no credit.　Union leaders have long been boring from within by systematic propaganda, which some writers have called the "hate-the-employer campaign." They have nurtured emotional attitudes toward business and management, often with Wall Street as the symbol of wickedness, that are not different in their dynamic character from the feelings of the masses in Europe who hopefully look to Socialism and communism as the only effective means of securing justice in the economic world.　The unformulated utterance of such emotions requires that something be done to change the existing order and to prevent business from plundering society.　Anyone who is brave enough to speak in favor of an employer at a union meeting is usually regarded as a stooge and may become the victim of witch hunting.

Let me illustrate.　It was some time ago, when I was speaking one Sunday night in Lawrence, Massachusetts, before a public forum run by George Coleman, that this thought was concretely thrust upon me.　Mrs. Merritt had entered the meeting without me, and when I had finished my talk she turned to a fine-looking Scotch labor leader sitting next to her and said, "What do you think of Merritt?"　He looked at her and laughed, "He is just another capitalist dub."　She hesitated a moment and then replied, "Now that you have been so frank I must tell you that I am the dub's wife and I would like to know what you mean by a capitalist dub."　His answer, laughingly given, was, "A capitalist dub is anyone who believes that any good can come out of the present social order."

Perhaps this labor leader has been disillusioned and has now joined the ranks of those who believe in the capitalist system, but as the facts of the last half-century are studied, it becomes easy to understand why several important unions have been communistic. It is also clear why more unions contain strong left-wing groups and why an important percentage of union members, who have been warned against a left-wing movement, nevertheless entertain feelings of hostility and suspicion toward management and financiers. These feelings are dynamic. They seek an outlet—results.

At the C.I.O. convention held in November, 1946, various resolutions were passed and later circulated in pamphlet form for the guidance of union members as well as others. One of these resolutions included these resounding appeals:

The organizational gains of labor of the past ten years are threatened as never before by open-shop employers. . . . The expanded strength and the increased membership of CIO unions is our best defense against the anti-labor plotters of this country. . . . We must intensify our campaign to organize in areas where employers have sought to erect barriers of anti-union violence, intimidation and collusion with public authorities against the right of self-organization.[6]

Here is an inflammatory call to fight the employer, and it certainly contains no caution against the adoption of familiar methods of warfare. As a matter of fact Mr. Murray has everything in reverse. The changed public attitude was not due to any wave of antiunionism. On the contrary it was due to union excesses, a fact that Mr. Murray ignores. The railroad, coal, and maritime strikes, which with others in 1946 resulted in over three times as many days lost as in any previous year, and the organized violence, actual or threatened, that had accompanied the major strikes had conditioned the public mind for some kind of union regulation. But that did not make the public antilabor plotters.

An official pamphlet issued by the C.I.O. in January, 1947, in connection with the Taft-Hartley debates, includes attacks on the good faith of employers who criticized the one-sidedness of the Wagner Act. Mr. Murray in his introduction declares that this union pamphlet cuts through "the tissue of fabrications, false issues and deliberate distortion of labor's thoughts and action."[7] The employers, it is said, "hate and resist the challenge of the workers' union"[8] and are engaged in "propaganda of wilful distortion of oft-repeated calumnies and falsehoods. . . ." The pamphlet says: "Propaganda flows in a steady stream from the press and from most radio commentators and newspaper columnists for legislation to shackle labor. It is a campaign based upon misrepresentation and deceit."[9] Apparently all the world was out of step except labor, and according to Mr. Murray and the C.I.O. pamphlet, all who disagree with labor are actuated by dishonest motives.

That is how the poison is injected. It is not honest disagreement but charges of bad faith that become the issue.

"There are many areas in the United States," says the same pamphlet, "in which labor organizers are beaten and maimed by mobs instigated and paid by employers. . . . Today's anti-labor campaign is a smoke screen to conceal the most outrageous monopolistic plundering in our history." [10]

Mr. Murray in a speech called for "militancy around the bargaining table and militancy on the picket line." [11]

Another spokesman, Daniel J. Tobin, president of the teamsters union, the largest trade union in the United States with over a million members, is not to be outdone in attacking business and finance. He is becoming bitter toward the employers. He speaks of "the rich manufacturing mongrels of America." [12] He says they are suffering from almost "total blindness to the dangers ahead for the safety of capital, free enterprise and our present form of government." [13] He tells how he has lost his "respect for employers associations" and adds, "I am weakening somewhat in the opinion which I have held for fifty years as to big business and free enterprise. Free enterprise ruined England. Consequently England had no alternative but to take over business." [14]

Then comes this warning: "If the persecutions of capitalists carry on," and there is proper liberal leadership, labor will sweep to victory in 1952, "and when next labor has a majority of its friends in the Congress, it may have recourse to taking over greater control of big business which lives only for enormous profits." [15]

When Walter Reuther suggests that management may possibly have been responsible for the attempts to murder him and his brother Victor, he appeals to the basest instincts of the million members of his union and plants a seed that may reap a crop of thistles.

At the convention of the United Automobile Workers held in July, 1949, Walter Reuther railed against the manufacturers and financiers of the country saying:

The real allies of Joe Stalin are the people whom Franklin Roosevelt characterized as the economic royalists, the boys in Wall Street, the people who control the National Association of Manufacturers. They are sitting there in Wall Street on their fat money bags and instead of cutting prices and profits to keep our economy going in high gear they are cutting production and laying workers off.[16]

How dangerous has this become? Will the common sense of the workers immunize them from the extremes of such propaganda or will good sense be dethroned by passion? It is one thing to whip up emotions but it is quite another thing to calm them. "A word, once sent abroad, flies irrevocably."

In the *United Mine Workers Journal* for January 1, 1947, the following appears: "The moral concepts of the present-day business man as regards fair dealing are even far below those which prevailed in the Nation during the railroad buying and selling, stockjobbing days of Vanderbilt, Gould and Harriman."

Again this from the same *Journal:* "The National Association of Manufacturers and the U. S. Chamber of Commerce could well merge and call the amalgamation 'The Freebooters' Society for the Preservation and Promotion of Loot!' "

In the same *Journal* for April 1, 1948, we find this: "Hell belching its disgust is a mild appraisal of the operators' attempt to set themselves up as a segment of our population devoted to law observance. . . ."

The CIO News of August 1, 1949, with its large circulation, in referring to Philip Murray's remarks before the Steel Panel, published in large headlines across the page: "Murray calls steel industry: sanctimonious racketeers, . . . provocateurs, prevaricators."

The truculent John L. Lewis from time to time throws a faggot on the fire. In March, 1949, as already pointed out, he referred to employers and the banking interests of the nation as seeking to hold the workers "in irons while the jackboots of American finance kick out your economic teeth." Then he added, "We will not retreat, we will advance." [17] This has all the fire of *"Aux armes, citoyens."* How far has such truculent propaganda fertilized a revolutionary fervor?

Mr. A. J. Hayes, president of the International Association of Machinists, forgetful of trends to the contrary, tells his followers: "On every front organized labor meets with new and growing resistance." [18] Leaders like Lewis, Murray, and Reuther are now beginning to talk in terms of united capital against united labor. With them every major strike is represented as a struggle with embattled Wall Street. A single industry or a single employer is not depicted as the enemy. Here is the voice of class conflict, ever growing louder. The idea of mutual aid between A. F. of L.,

C.I.O. and the U.M.W. to fight the financial class is becoming more persistent. Early in 1950 Lewis called for a "mutual aid pact for common defense," giving as his reason that "the idea seems increasingly prevalent in industrial and financial circles that our great industrial unions should be attacked and crippled." [19] Although his proposal was rejected by his rival unionists on the ground that a formal pact was not necessary, there was no repudiation of the idea that the three groups should aid each other in future crises.

In April, 1950, the C.I.O. appealed to the American Federation of Labor, the United Mine Workers, the International Association of Machinists, and the railway unions to establish a joint committee "empowered to coordinate our efforts in the economic, legislative and political spheres." [20] In support of this proposal, it is stated "our economy suffers from the unrestrained greed of the trusts and monopolists," and that unless united action is taken without delay "the economic policies being pursued by the small financial group that dominates American industry will inevitably result in a disastrous depression. . . . A united committee of all American labor would strike fear in the hearts of those who block our road to progress. All that is needed, on our part, is the wisdom and courage to join together." [21] The United Mine Workers have accepted this appeal and others are considering it. A united front of one class against all others is in the making.

The nomenclature of warfare reflects these hostile teachings:

What this terminology reveals is an underlying concept of conflict, sometimes covert, sometimes open, and often violent and bloody. Unless this whole psychology of coercion is replaced with that of mutuality of interests, not as lip service, or a pep-talk platitude, but as down-to-earth reality, our postwar labor relations can become a "darkling plain where ignorant armies clash by night.[22]

This same book, referring to the struggle of unions for recognition, says:

The more prolonged and bitter the struggle the deeper are the concealed estrangements and antagonisms. Although the rational is by now supposed to supplant the emotional, this happens mainly in textbooks.[23]

The attack of union leaders on the employer sometimes extends even to his attorney. Anything to fire the hearers will serve the purpose. In the midst of conflict and excitement this is more understandable, but when it takes the form of a long-term program to increase the gulf between management and labor, it is less excusable and more dangerous. Thus one might smile indulgently when Mr. Bambrick, during the building service strike, compared me with the buzzards that swoop down to pluck eyes out of dying men, but unfortunately in some circles there is a deliberate building up of antiemployer and antiproperty feeling in times of industrial peace.

I cite one extreme example that fairly recently came within my personal experience. In February, 1947, a year after the General Motors Corporation had settled its strike, a speaker for labor broadcast in Pasadena, California, concerning the 1945 strike, and declared that its counsel, Mr. Merritt, had in the past purchased the most deadly type of gas and had "actually employed the gas against workers in the coal field." The speaker continued: "Under Mr. Merritt's able direction the lethal gas was actually used in coal mines during the last depression. A company report which appeared in the Congressional Record said . . . 'It was positively fascinating to watch the way the men squirmed and squealed as their life-blood was snuffed out of them.' " [24]

This charge, which contained no element of truth, was later retracted over the same broadcasting station. It was aimed not at me but at the General Motors Corporation for employing such a murderer and is a sample of the worst of the irresponsible statements designed to make the workers hate the employer.

Back of all the union demands to control hiring, layoffs, transfers, merit increases, and the many other assertions of an inchoate title to the job, as well as the demand for employer-paid pensions on retirement, is the conscious or unconscious grasp for the exclusive loyalty of the worker. That is the source of power. Does the employee owe his livelihood to the union or the employer? Whose is the hand that feeds him? Obviously, with the onward march of collective bargaining into the area of job control and the inculcation of hostility and suspicion toward the employer, loyalty and power swing more and more strongly to the union, and the rift that creates class cleavage becomes more and more definite.

Some union rules and practices openly emphasize job control. Local 3, International Brotherhood of Electrical Workers, forbids members to accept employment directly from an electrical contractor. The union, in supplying employees, rotates the men among different employers lest they develop a sense of loyalty to an employer. A violation of this rule in one instance led to a penalty of three years suspension. With the maritime workers job control became a major issue, and for the same reason no employer was allowed to maintain a regular crew. Hiring halls serve the union purpose in this respect. There must be no doubt as to who furnishes the employee with his work opportunities. That in one phase of the demand for the closed shop.

A conspicuous illustration of this attitude and the absurdities to which it leads is revealed by the union reaction when the American Telephone and Telegraph Company voluntarily improved its pensions throughout the Bell System. The company had instituted its benefit and pension system unilaterally about 35 years ago when unions among telephone workers were practically unknown. Today the various subsidiary corporations that the benefit plan covers recognize and deal with C.I.O., A. F. of L., or independent unions that have the right to bargain for the subsidiary employees but not for the employees of the system as a whole. To liberalize the existing pension benefits on a system-wide scale, through collective bargaining with these many unions, was impracticable. The company accordingly acted unilaterally in improving its unilateral plan. The unions' reaction was not one of applause. Of course not. The employer must not get the credit of doing something decent. So the unions, or some of them, shouted that the purpose was to destroy the union. Perhaps this clamor is understandable, but it is only understandable on the theory of class conflict. Hostility toward the employer, it is thought, must be sustained undiminished if unionism is to remain strong.

It is more than a coincidence that one of the clearest statements of this view was made before the impartial chairman by Harry Bridges, the communist labor leader on the Pacific water front:

Do we develop, agitate, educate or propagandize our men to be more loyal to the union than to the employer? You bet we do. No matter what happens in these proceedings we will never do otherwise. It is our union policy and an official policy—that we can't trust an employer; that if they depend upon an employer for any type of security or fair treatment, they'll get stung. And that is what we tell them—that their security comes through the union, and that their living comes through the union.[25]

In shaping the attitudes of union members toward our industrial society, union propaganda gives scant encouragement to any recognition of the proper functions of employers or the services they have rendered to society in supplying public needs and raising living standards. Labor does not like to admit that the employers of this country have done better by the workers than any other employers. That would weaken the call to battle. This attitude may have been excusable in the early days when labor lacked recognition and organizational campaigns were more dependent on the argument that the employer must be beaten to his knees, but today the unwillingness of union leaders to give the employer credit for a generous and humane impulse, where it may be conspicuously deserved, is most alarming. It certainly does not tend to stabilize the capitalistic system.

The invaluable contributions that the employer has made to our material welfare and his improved attitude toward unionism are not portrayed in the union hall. The cover of the September, 1949, issue of *The American Federationist* carried a picture of a parade with a banner that proclaims, "Labor Creates all Wealth." So why bother with employers? They are parasites and plunderers. Every advantage the worker secures must be portrayed as something wrested from the employer after the union has vanquished him. In fact there are few irritants that are more prevalent in labor-management relations than this question of whether the union or the employer, or both of them, are entitled to credit for some improvement in employment conditions. The question deeply affects the allegiance of the union member.

This attitude of labor is also strengthened by the fear of some unions that if they graciously accept anything from the well-intentioned employer they may be accused of being dominated by him contrary to the provisions of the labor relations acts. Co-operation became legally dangerous in some cases. I know, because I have faced such situations. The entire atmosphere of labor-management relations, encouraged by the legislation of the 1930's and fed by appeals that savor so much of the spirit of the class struggle, has been one of combat.

Only by appreciating these motivations can we explain many developments not otherwise explainable. They explain why class loyalty is sometimes put ahead of ordinary ethics. They explain why workers have been expelled from the union and discharged by the employer under the mandate of a closed-shop agreement because they reported thefts by a fellow employee, or because they

refused to violate the union agreement. They explain why Cecil
DeMille was expelled for refusing politically to conform to his
class, and why anyone making truthful statements favorable to the
employer from the floor of a union meeting runs the risk of un-
pleasantness.

Today, under changed conditions, labor suffers from the education of the last half-century to the effect that the government is
against it. "Labor distrusts the Congress of the United States," [26]
says one powerful labor leader. Mr. Lewis, in writing to the
President of the United States in 1950, said, "It is a travesty upon
justice that they [the coal miners] should now be slugged by a
legal blackjack to satisfy the overweening avarice of their reactionary employers." [27]

On April 20, 1948, Mr. Henry Mayer, representing many telephone unions, in writing to the *Herald Tribune,* declared:

Labor sincerely believes that our courts jump with alacrity on unions
and labor leaders who violate laws while they deal tenderly and consider-
ately with those who, for instance, make a sham and a mockery of our
anti-trust laws, Federal Trade Commission decrees and other regulatory
acts.

That is exactly what I mean and exactly what I fear about the
psychology created by labor's propaganda.

If labor distrusts employers, the Congress, and the courts under
present-day conditions, and nothing is done to correct that condition, there will be trouble ahead.

Labor leaders have a greater opportunity in this matter than
have employers. Theirs is the audience. The workers listen
to what they say. Do they realize that they may be unleashing
forces that may work immeasurable harm?

This barrier between individual employees and their employer,
which hinders employees in obtaining a balanced viewpoint, is
apparently regarded by union leaders as essential to the functioning of unions. The militant unionist is jealous of a direct contact
between the employer and the employees as individuals for fear
that the employee may look to the employer for fair treatment.
There must be no competition in doing good. That is the essence
of modern industrial relations [28] and as I have pointed out top
leaders have taken advantage of it to preach distrust and hostility
toward the employer.

The utterances of labor leaders selected to illustrate my point are not casual. They are not even spontaneous. They are typical, not freakish. They are not the ill-advised mistakes of local union officers. They are calculated utterances by the top level of officialdom of organizations that speak for a large part of the unionized industrial workers. Breathing hostility and distrust as these utterances do, what is their intended impact on the emotions of union members? Some workers may be wise enough to smile, but will the great majority quietly resolve to await *der Tag* in order to inflict retribution on the plunderers? If this propaganda continues from leaders to whom the workers extend the greatest credulity, there is always the possibility that some day the emotional hostility and suspicion so generated will be translated into action that the leaders themselves will regret. If we are to avoid such misfortune, all people, and particularly labor leaders, must have the courage to reject the tools of demagoguery and frankly recognize the value of industrial leadership. Labor leaders, not the employers, have the attentive ear of the workers.

Much of this colorful attack is in the nature of an abusive counteroffensive in respect to labor legislation rather than a discussion of the merits of any possible form of union regulation. Public officials and private citizens have constantly asked union leaders what kind of legislation they would tolerate or approve to correct admitted evils. This devastating question the C.I.O. pamphlet attempts to parry by replying that it means in effect, "What is your proposal for antilabor legislation?" [29] So long as this remains the official platform of unions and every challenge of it is met by tirade, rather than reason, the clouds of conflict grow blacker. Such intolerance of sincere criticism is lamentable. No less a figure than the late Frank P. Walsh made the statement in court that with one exception I had done more than anyone in the United States to wrong the workingman, but my belief in the necessity for unions was no less than his. In this field of industrial relations, honest differences of opinion seem to provoke outbursts instead of reasoned response.

Even with an aroused sense of grievance stirring resentment, it seems possible to maintain a working basis so long as union leaders are able to bring new advantages back to the union hall, just as compulsory arbitration in other countries has been reasonably successful in an upward swing in an economy. But the real test will arise when, under the economic limits of free economy, there is nothing more to give. As one successful leader said to me, "Walter, I do not ask for more now because I need to reserve something for next year. When the time comes—if it does come— that I have no further gains to offer my people, I am finished." The rapid improvement of the condition of industrial employees in the last ten years is enough to satisfy them without exploring the uncertainties of radical experiments. That resource will some-time be exhausted. Every communist recognizes this and is merely waiting for the time when it is believed that this basis of satisfaction with capitalism will cease to exist. Have labor leaders forgotten the famous declaration, "They have sown the wind and shall reap the whirlwind?" [30]

A real test may come when the economic forces inherent in the free enterprise system compel the union leader to return with an empty game bag, either because of a depression or because the system cannot increase labor costs. Will labor then be satis-fied to continue to accept the benefits that free enterprise has left to offer, or will new leaders, understanding the art of demagoguery and mindful of the emotions that have been nourished in the hearts of union members, possess the field with dreams of a promised land?

XXVI

Collective Bargaining or Class Conflict

In SEARCHING FOR INDUSTRIAL PEACE, we in the United States, notwithstanding flamboyant calls to battle, have chosen to follow the trail called free enterprise, or rather let us call it the trail of semifree enterprise. Fundamentally, the issue is one of adjustment between men and money or persons and property, and the approach to the problem is either free enterprise or totalitarianism or a combination of each. What we take of the one we lose of the other.

Under an absolutely free economy, the creative class, which is roughly the creditor class, accumulates too much power. Long ago society suffered from the oppression of usury and accordingly regulated the hiring of money. Nearly 4000 years ago the Code of Hammurabi provided that in case of crop failure the debtor need not pay his debt or any interest for that year. Our bankruptcy laws go even further. Transfers of property in perpetuity became a social vice that had to be forbidden. This was only a beginning. The United States, which still professes faith in a free economy, has added many restraints on property rights, surtaxes on large incomes, and death taxes on large inheritances, sometimes almost to the point of confiscation. From the opposite direction, but pointing to the same objective, are factory laws, wage and hour laws, social security laws, and union prerogatives to bolster the incomes and protect the lives of those who are economically too weak to protect themselves. These and general laws dealing with monopolies, unfair methods of competition, money control, and subsidies reflect the same effort to attain a democratic pattern of life without entirely abandoning the fundamental concept of a free economy.

The labor union movement in the United States, the Socialist program of the Labor Party in Great Britain, and the dictatorship of the proletariat in other countries are all born of the same emotional force: a desire to attain a greater degree of equalitarianism than is attainable under an uncontrolled individualistic economy, which some describe as the law of the jungle. The longed-for destination is human welfare and human happiness, not merely economic but spiritual; but dangers lurk in the pursuit of these ideals. Although it is true as Christian doctrine that strength can never shake off its debt to weakness, it may be equally true as economic doctrine that it cannot be forced by law to pay that debt. Moreover, one would like to give some scope to the spirit of voluntary altruism as well as self-help. Just at what point between free enterprise and governmental direction both toilers and leaders will be induced to render their best service and assume a maximum of social responsibility can only be settled by the trial and error process. It is quite certain, however, that a society that does not provide individual incentives or that protects failures and penalizes success will travel to its doom.

Our great experiment, like that of Great Britain before she abandoned it, is along the trail of free enterprise, with collective bargaining backed by union power as one of the stepping stones. Our journey will encounter many perils: There will be obstacles to cause us to falter, stumble, and fall; steep inclines along dizzy heights; and many ambushes. A safe arrival might be assured if one were to practice the Christian virtues of patience, tolerance, accommodation, and co-operation, as well as restraint and moderation in the demands that management, investors, and workers make upon society for their respective contributions. Competing with these Christian virtues, however, are elemental nonpeaceful forces, perhaps biological in nature, that throughout the course of known history mankind has never yet been able to control and that under given circumstances have heretofore always led to disaster. It is difficult to say whether industrial war or industrial peace await us. When once I addressed a church audience in Bridgeport on the subject of industrial peace, I was ironically marched in behind a surpliced choir singing "The Son of God goes forth to war."

Today there is a galvanized hope in this country that through the flexible process of collective bargaining some accommodation may be reached without plunging headlong into conflict or totalitarianism. Studies of the trends in collective bargaining, human relationships, labor-management co-operation, and the refinement of methods of working together and meeting problems that so often involve antagonisms are evidence of this hope and desire to work things out for the greater good of all. The broader acceptance of labor contracts, with arbitration clauses as the final step in grievance procedures, is convincing proof that in many important matters each group is ready to forego its assertion of power in respect to many exasperating controversies. Such compromises follow the path of management sharing, or partial management abdication to an arbitrator.

Unfortunate as it may be, much of the progress that has been made is born of a common fear. An uncle of mine always preached that a horrible warning was as useful as a saintly example, and this statement is certainly a factor in industrial relations. Both groups fear outside intervention and intermeddling. Both groups fear strike losses. Both groups desire to keep alive the spirit of free enterprise and have tentatively accepted the thought that only through collective bargaining is there any hope of mutual survival. Whether a settlement of conflicting claims is possible without destroying free enterprise is the underlying question that only time can answer. The facts of the call to battle that I have marshalled naturally tend to weaken hopes.

Paradoxical as it may seem, the two groups whose interests are most dependent on mutual co-operation, and upon whose co-operation the survival of our civilization depends, are operating in a state of acute conflict, and there is no convincing proof that the conflict is waning. Notwithstanding the homely truth, "United we stand, divided we fall," union leaders, whose followers have the most to lose by the downfall of the present system, are employing the language and tactics of battle to attack the inherent mechanics and results of the system to which they give lip endorsement. There seems to prevail a kind of war psychosis in our industrial relations.

Perhaps Macaulay's prediction, made nearly a century ago about this country, is too well known to be repeated in full, but we should not forget his fears. He declared that our free institutions would be lost through the appeals of the demagogue to class selfishness, greed and hate, and added "that the Huns and Vandals who ravaged the Roman Empire came from without, and that your Huns and Vandals have been engendered within your own country by your own institutions." [1] For this prophecy he had the authority of Greek history.

The continued preaching of enmity toward any one of our essential institutions, whether it is the industrial corporations, the banks, or the courts, is a disturbing aspect of present-day life to which Macaulay, were he living, would point as evidence that his prophecy is coming true. Preaching the gospel of hostility between classes inevitably leads toward a conflict destructive of human freedom. What can prevent all of those who are antagonistic to property rights from sometime uniting their forces, regardless of their particular ideology?

Can we clear the atmosphere of these dynamic forces that threaten to bring us nearer and nearer to some destructive climax? Admittedly there is fault on both sides, and admittedly the employer was once the greater offender, but when a comparison is made between the utterances of labor and management 25 and 50 years ago and their utterances today, it is clear that the employer, although obviously acting under pressure, has shown far greater progress toward moderate and modern thinking. With the growth of unionism and its increasing power and demands, as well as its encroachment on management prerogatives, there have developed among industrial managers a broader understanding and acceptance of union philosophy and union conduct. Discussions before such representative groups as the American Management Association and the National Industrial Conference Board, in which labor leaders and leaders of advanced intellectual thought often participate, are outstanding evidence of the ever-widening vision of management. Management has been more successful than labor in becoming more objective and less emotional.

Members of employers associations in their conventions listen to addresses such as that given by Professor Stefan Osusky before the American Management Association in Chicago in the winter of 1949:

In the light of present world trends, it is simply impossible to save a capitalistic system in which productive property is concentrated in the hands of several hundred or several thousand corporations if they are managed on the traditional principles of private property exclusively devoted to profit making.

. . . It is safe to say that the people of the United States, possessing a constitutional mechanism by which they can put their will into force, will not allow a few hundred corporations the control of America's life unless the management of those corporations can demonstrate to the satisfaction of America's citizens that it is successfully carrying out a great social and national trust and that it is a bulwark of human freedom.[2]

The researches of The Twentieth Century Fund discovered progress in this direction:

Then too the belligerent type of anti-union employer is disappearing from the top. He is being slowly elbowed aside by the executive who has proved his ability to get along with labor. At the annual convention of the National Association of Manufacturers in December 1947, all of the principal speakers stressed ways in which management could improve industrial relations.[3]

In the case of the union movement, as has been pointed out in Chapter XXV, "Call to Battle," most union leaders are afraid to bring home to their membership the outstanding contributions that employers have made to national welfare, as well as the necessity that management not be obstructed in the exercise of essential powers. Every labor leader of importance knows very well that in an economic sense a capable executive of a large corporation is seldom overpaid. Personally I disapprove of enormous salaries because men should be willing to serve society for moderate compensation, whatever their worth, and because conspicuous salaries cause misunderstanding and social irritation, but if the executive be of the type of which I speak, he is usually worth what he is paid.

If labor leaders were freely to acknowledge to their membership the indispensability, virtues, and social accomplishments of management, the cloud on the industrial horizon would seem less ominous. If we wish to preserve the free enterprise system and believe it can satisfactorily serve society through collective bargaining, the first essential toward its preservation is for all groups freely and publicly to pay homage to the growing need and importance of both management and unions. To talk of management as racketeers and plunderers is to sow the dragon's teeth. After all, in this country men more nearly start at scratch than ever before, and handicaps due to social conditions are fewer. That is why so many of our economic leaders have come from the bottom of the ladder. In the United States an outstanding fact is that the employers have more completely performed their service with resulting benefits to society than have the employers of any other country. To what extent government and unions will be satisfied with this record of high performance is one of the questions most difficult to answer, but the award, even by the unions, of the just credit due management for its splendid contribution to national welfare, whether in time of war or peace, should not be withheld. The scarcity of such praise in union literature and union utterances and the constant reference to the employers as a common enemy and as plunderers and deceivers are above almost any other factors the greatest danger to our system of free enterprise. Although industrial leaders have done a superb job, the leaders of labor to whom workers listen are woefully silent on this fact. So when the time comes—if ever it does come—when, through some kind of inexorability, "the strange desire to seek power and to lose liberty" possesses the field, this will be one of the contributing causes.

There is also another aspect that shows how easy it would be to throw the union movement on the side of radicalism if we do not mend our ways. Generally speaking, on all issues except the formal continuance of private management, which permits unions to deal with private employers rather than government, the unions support trends toward Statism and measures that tend to establish economic equality among all classes. That in itself is a cause for disquietude. With equality as a goal, a free enterprise system will find it more difficult to survive and Socialism will find it easier to enter. Liberty and equality are not associates. They travel in opposite directions. So we find this propaganda upholding the name of free enterprise against totalitarianism but challenging the essentials of free enterprise. It is here that many who think they eschew radicalism align themselves against liberty or a free economy.

Perhaps these propagandists, like many other people, feel that capitalism is the worst form of economic society—excepting all other forms known to man—and are vainly hoping that some new economic serum will come upon the market. The question is whether a free economy can be made acceptable to the noncreative group imbued with the propaganda of hostility toward success and a desire for greater economic equality. With unions unwilling to define their ultimate goals, it is difficult to know whether the dissatisfaction with present results is too fundamental to permit reconciliation.

The very exigencies that confront business leaders in a democracy make it improbable that business interests will stubbornly ignore the handwriting of history. Business cannot do otherwise than respond to the combined political and economic pressures of the times. Through taxes, antitrust laws and many other pressures, and through laws fostering unions and regulating conditions of employment, business is brought under the political controls of democracy. For its obedience to law, its property is a hostage to society. From the economic field, as distinguished from the political, comes another squeeze. Business cannot operate successfully without the co-operation of its employees and their unions. Here the alternatives to appeasement may be as extreme as sabotage, slowdowns, fake sick leaves, and other insidious devices difficult to handle. Caught between these two forces, capital and management can and will be compelled to acquit themselves of their responsibilities to society and to keep within the traces. They will continue to make adjustments, as they have been doing, unless forced to the wall. But can we say the same of the labor movement?

The future menace to our industrial democracy is more likely to come from uncontrollable resistance on the part of labor and from the inherent weaknesses of the democratic idea. Concerning the difficulty of imposing law enforcement on labor movements, I need not expatiate. It is too obvious. On other weaknesses of democracy, volumes have been written. Its tendency to seek economic equality, its drift toward the Marxian ideal, "from each according to his ability and to each according to his needs," and its jealousy of talent and leadership, all run counter to the free enterprise system and the human incentives upon which it relies. Every form of government carries the possible seeds of its own dissolution, and democracy is no exception. Its fundamental weakness is too much democracy and its drive against economic leadership. It is another paradox, noted by Mr. Macaulay, that democracy, which began by liberating the common man, may end by enslaving him.

So I reach the conclusion that while the labor movement, with its physical, economic, and political power, has been one of the great forces to promote democracy, at the same time it constitutes the greatest threat to the continuance of democracy and free enterprise. If we fail to make our free economy work, it will be because of too great curtailment of the rights and opportunities of capital and not because employers increase in power and arbitrariness. Unless unions will play their part in quieting the buncombe of equalitarianism and will promote a just appreciation of the services of industrial captains and financiers in increasing productivity, in promoting new industries, and in raising material standards, the fateful end, predicted by many pessimists, is sure to come. It is not too much to say that totalitarianism cannot be avoided without forebearance on the part of the labor movement. Although most labor leaders share the wish that unions will not become a roundabout route to more radical isms, apparently very few sense the danger of such an outcome. Those who sow the seeds of discord may harvest an unwished-for crop.

When Mr. Murray declares that "revolutionary changes with respect to the economic well-being of the American people have taken place during the last sixteen years," [4] it would be well for him to couple this with some slight assuagement of his assaults on those who crusaded for greater productivity and some slight recognition of the part they have played. An hour of labor today brings five times as much to the worker as it did 50 years ago, with less strenuous work. That is made possible only by the investor who puts thousands of dollars behind each employee. That is the contribution of the creative class under a free enterprise system.

Purchasing power of an hour's work almost doubled from 1914 to 1948, because the average factory worker's wages rose twice as much as prices. The 1948 worker had to work only 34 hours to supply his family with the higher living standards that were considered average in 1948.[5] Under Russian communism a worker has to labor over four times as long to earn a loaf of bread, 17 times as long to get butter, and 15 times as long to earn a woolen suit as in the United States. To state it otherwise, in Russia a worker must labor 81 hours, in Great Britain 19 hours, and in the United States eight hours for the same living needs.[6] For this advantage, I repeat, venture capital, improved technology, and the profit motive are entitled to a large measure of the credit. Dangerous it is for the workers to be kept in ignorance of this fact. One more item: Ten years ago, less than 70 per cent of all earned income went to the employed, but today they receive 84 per cent.

How short-sighted is the labor movement if it continues to misrepresent the attitudes and functions of the employing class! If democracy is to be regarded as a step forward in the cycle of civilization, as some people believe, and not as a final step toward the destruction of civilization, as others believe, broad education must be carried on to offset the evil tendency to be distrustful of leadership or overjealous of superiority and inequality.

Alfred Zimmern in his book on *Nationality and Government* declared, "it is one of the ironies of the modern age that democracy has become the dominant political creed at a time when the problems of society and government are more difficult and complex, less easy of understanding by the plain man, than ever before in history." [7]   The necessity of recognizing leadership, superiority, and executive ability is greater than ever before.

No institution, I repeat, is in as strategic a position to guard democracy against its besetting sin of devaluing leadership and special talents as the union movement.   To put it in a negative way, no institution in society is in a better position to lower our material standards and to bring about the downfall of free enterprise and democracy through wrong practices and wrong teachings.

This is the first and foremost lesson that labor unions should learn: In their desire for a free economy and material gains, they must preserve employers; in their present propaganda against private employers they are paving the way for radical labor leaders who will seek to bring about the extinction of private management and, correspondingly, the extinction of the rights of labor. Where do we read of A. F. of L., C.I.O., U.M.W., or railroad unions warning their membership, as did the officers of the United States Chamber of Commerce at a recent convention, that freedom will be lost if they are not more mindful of the rights of others? A continuance of the present policy will cultivate the soil for Marxism.   When employees in public transportation engage in a concerted slowdown on the nod and wink of the union president, when unprovoked men attack a factory, as was done in the Apex Hosiery Company Case, when workers engage in protest strikes against law enforcement, and so on, the Marxist spirit seems more predominant than the desire to preserve the free enterprise system with its dependence on co-operation and mutual recognition of rights and duties.   In ultimate results the distinction between the emotional attitude of a union member who hates his employer and defies the law and ideologists who would eliminate the employer may not be so great.   It would be no miracle if some of them joined forces.

Top officials of the C.I.O. unwittingly supported this conclusion when the communist locals of the C.I.O. were expelled in the late fall of 1949 and rival locals were chartered.   Emil Rieve, vice president of the C.I.O., declared that the C.I.O. did not throw out "its left wing" or "the radicals."   It merely threw out the east wing "that always looks to Moscow for guidance." [8]   James Carey, secretary of the C.I.O., in referring to injunctions secured to protect the rights of the members of the expelled locals, declared "Your chairman is not going to pay the least little bit of attention to any of these injunctions . . . and it is high time that the officers and locals of this organization take steps to defy these irresponsible actions by irresponsible, confused and ignorant judges." [8]

This rebellious dissatisfaction with industrial leadership and the results of our free enterprise system comes from the leaders of organized millions who, with their families, probably comprise over 40,000,000 of our citizens.   Whether or not greater social security, reducing the economic hazards of old age and unemployment, will prove more effective in tempering the heat of this dissatisfaction than the considerable elimination of excessive hours and low wages is hard to foretell.   Will the apostles of discontent merely raise their sights and ask for more than can be borne by a free economy?   "Wide is the gate and broad is the way which leadeth to destruction."   Certainly with the emotions that are being aroused, it is going to become more and more difficult to develop tolerance for the inescapable rigors of free economy and collective bargaining.

Alarming it was to some of us when, in April, 1950, a majority of the Joint Congressional Committee on the Economic Report advocated that steel companies should be required to give 30 days' notice of price increases so that hearings could be held to develop public opinion and that a study should be made to determine whether the industry had the characteristics of a public utility.   From important labor sources this report was highly praised, as well it might be in view of their heated criticism of the industry, but the startling observation is to note how little reliance can be placed on lip endorsement of a free economy.

The business leader is satisfied with a free economy and its results and is willing to exert every possible effort to perpetuate it. The leaders of organized labor, regardless of their opposition to foreign ideologies, are dissatisfied with the free enterprise system and are seeking fundamental changes.

The real import of the union appeal is class against class. If all the principal controversies involved in the Taft-Hartley debates were settled in favor of the labor movement, this trend, this dissatisfaction with the operation of existing institutions, would still be with us. It is fundamental and militant and moves forward without an ideology.

Statements of outstanding labor leaders such as I have quoted have a revolutionary flavor. Although no one will deny great credit to the labor movement for its contribution in defending this country against foreign ideology, it is nevertheless possible that, under the excitement of class exhortation, objectives that in the end will hamper the economic machine and lead to an ideology these leaders abhor may be pursued.

One is constrained to inquire whether collective bargaining or class conflict will be the pattern of tomorrow. Although the boundary between these two is not clear cut, in many respects they are opposites, the one representing economic bargaining within the structure of law and involving the elements of a commercial transaction and the other involving outbursts against society and existing institutions. The recognized right of workers to try to corner the labor market through the organization of labor unions is, after all, merely a means of promoting strong economic bargaining within the structure of our laws. The extent of our departures from that idea measure the extent to which we are promoting class conflict to displace or distort collective bargaining. Violence, political efforts to escape legal responsibility for wrong-doing or contract violations, political strikes, strikes for illegal objectives, and sympathetic strikes to coerce the public by stoppages designed to augment the privations of the public, rather than to pressure the employer, are all activities beyond the legitimate limits of collective bargaining. To the extent that we follow these departures we are following the course of class conflict as distinguished from collective bargaining.

Political action for high surtaxes, tax exemption for moderate incomes, social security, socialized housing and medicine, and wage-and-hour laws, although they are qualifications of our system of free enterprise and largely reflect a demand for class protection, is of a different nature, because such measures are obtained through the democratic political process. The question I am asking is whether militant labor groups having free access to the political process will be willing to confine their economic activities to the legitimate area of collective bargaining or whether they will insist on employing their economic and physical power against society itself.

The survival of our free economy, or the remains of it, depends on the conduct of the union movement. Will unions be willing to abandon the growing concept of class conflict and rely upon the process of collective bargaining to promote the welfare of the workers? Will they be willing to reject the lures of equality for the material advantages that flow from disciplinary management in the factory? Or will envy, provoked by inequalities of wealth and capacity, force us down the road of some form of socialization, wholly incompatible with freedom and with free enterprise?

Having posed these questions, I find it helpful specifically to enumerate familiar practices in the field of unionism that should be abandoned if we are seeking sincerely to evolve a workable pattern through collective bargaining rather than through the process of class conflict.

To begin with, unions must preach tolerance of management. As I have already indicated, our free economy cannot survive if the unions continue to inculcate the idea that the captains of industry, the bankers, and those who are styled "Wall Street" are parasites on society and inhuman enemies of the working classes. Such preachments are hostile to the essential structure of a free society. Unless labor leaders carry to their followers a more intelligent appraisal of the attitudes and social contributions of industrial and financial leaders, our system of free enterprise is doomed. You cannot be a friend of a free economy and an enemy of private management. You cannot preserve free enterprise and destroy the entrepeneur. "You take my house when you do take the prop that doth sustain my house."

The next need for change grows out of the union attitude toward industrial lawlessness in time of strike. Violence in labor disputes is no part of economic bargaining. It is tied up with class warfare against not only the employer, but society and government. In view of the lamentable failure of local authorities to maintain law and order in time of industrial strife, violence or disorderly conduct for the purpose of interfering with the production of goods for interstate commerce should be made a violation of the antitrust laws.

But more important, unions should frown on violence in industrial disputes and assume affirmative responsibility for the maintenance of law and order on the picket line. Such action should be the first expression of labor's faith in democratic government, and that above all other testimonials would win it greater support in the court of public opinion. If labor unions desire to fortify their position as great civic institutions like the church, the university, or the press, devoted to the furtherance of the democratic ideal and ever-acquiescent to the valid and Constitutional exercise of governmental powers, they must stand positively for law and order even in labor disputes. Today many of them not only tolerate but encourage organized violence and, instead of punishing the perpetrators and leaders of disorder, defend them. Has any C.I.O. or A. F. of L. convention ever condemned the organized violence of 1937 or 1946? Perhaps a characteristic viewpoint, not always frankly expressed, is given by the president of the National Federation of Telephone Workers when testifying before the Committee on Education and Labor of the House of Representatives in 1947:

Question: Then you are advancing a philosophy here, as I understand it, to the effect that the strikers and the pickets have a right to block passageways and to prevent people from going to their work or to their place of business?

Answer: I say I am sympathetically disposed towards those who do that.[8a]

The sworn testimony of John White, president of the United Mine Workers from April, 1911, to September, 1914, is significant if not startling:

Question: Has your organization ever announced that it would fine, suspend, expel or in any way discipline any member or officer of the union for lawlessness committed in connection with its strikes?

Answer: No.

Question: Has your organization ever disciplined any officer or member for crimes committed by him in connection with strikes that it was carrying on?

Answer: No.[9]

President White, in reporting to the Executive Board of the International Union in May, 1914, concerning the union destruction of the Arkansas mines, showed no shame or regret.   He said:

The boys simply marched in on him in a day down there and kicked his Colorado guards out of there and broke their jaws and put the flag of the United Mine Workers on the top of the tipple and pulled the fires out of the boilers, and that was all there was to it, and the mines have been idle in there ever since.[10]

If that is the dominant attitude of unions toward law and order and the rights of others, it explains why they are willing to raise millions for defense of lawbreakers and are so often unwilling to play a part in reducing lawlessness.   Violence in the Bell Aircraft strike in Buffalo in 1949 was a scandal and, according to reports, the union put up about $400,000 in bail.   So we have come to this tragic result: organized defense of organized violation of law.   That is exactly what communists would do.   If the labor movement in America wishes to be classed as an agency to promote democracy and resist isms that conflict with democracy, it can further such wishes by effectively stopping organized lawlessness on the picket line.   Union opinion on this subject should be revised.

When we consider the size and power of labor organizations, the extent to which they have been fostered by legislation and freed from familiar restraints, as well as the union pleas that society trust them to curb their own excesses and correct their own mischief, it can hardly be contended that inaction or a *laissez-faire* attitude in connection with industrial lawlessness should constitute full satisfaction of their obligation to society.   Professor Roscoe Pound speaks of liability arising through failure to restrain or prevent.   Employers have had experience with this rule; it is nothing new.

There is a rule of international law that when an army invades a country it is responsible for all the unlawful damage that could have been avoided by reasonable efforts on the part of the invaders to prevent it.   I think a union in charge of a strike should not escape the responsibility for lawlessness by just saying that it did nothing.   It should take active steps to maintain law and order.

Of course there are isolated and surprise acts for which the union should not be responsible, but in a case of systematic disorder going on day after day, the union should not escape responsibility by mere words. "It has," said the Anthracite Coal Commission in 1903, "by the concerted action of many aroused passions, which uncontrolled, threaten the public peace: it therefore owes Society the duty of exerting its power to check and confine these passions within the bounds of reason and of law." [11] It should not be permitted like Mark Anthony to say: "Now let it work. Mischief thou art afoot."

I repeat that unions should assume responsibility for keeping their corporate activities within legal limits. Anything short of this should be treated as negligence in the performance of their duties, just as corporate business is subject to responsibility for negligence. Once that responsibility is assumed, a labor dispute will become an economic battle and not a physical one, and industrial strife will become more civilized.

There can be no possible straddling of this issue if collective bargaining rather than class warfare is to dominate. Unions are either law-abiding civic institutions, ready to live within the framework of the laws of society, or they are revolutionary bodies reserving to themselves at all times the right to defy and, for practical purposes, to veto the laws of the land whenever in their opinion the emergency calls for such extremes. Why blink the facts?

There are an alarming number of people in this country, both in the North and South, who are faithful to the democratic process when it serves their interests, but who are all too ready to forsake it when they dislike the immediate result. The true democratic gospel is only half sold. As a matter of internal domestic policy, if we are to shudder at any ghost, let it be this deficiency in our education. If we need religious fervor to save our free institutions, it should be aimed not at isms, but at obstructions or perversions of the democratic process. So when we weigh the virtues and dangers of a powerful labor movement and the need for some degree of regulation, we must take into account labor's facilities for distorting the democratic process by disorder, violence, or economic prostration. That is the greatest internal threat of our day.

Closely related to this question of law and order in industrial disputes is another fundamental concept that labor unions would do well gracefully to embrace. Recognizing that industrial war is costly to labor, employers, and the community, they should at least concede that it should not be conducted to atttain illegal ends. Combinations to compel an employer to place union law above state law should be frankly repudiated.[12]   Years ago, as I have previously pointed out, Justice Brandeis, writing the unanimous opinion of the Supreme Court of the United States, held that "a strike may be illegal because of its purpose, however orderly the manner in which it is conducted." [13]   But we needed no Supreme Court to tell us that a strike to compel an employer to do an illegal act or something that he is not legally free to do is politically and morally indefensible.   It belittles the social functions of a strike, if its use is prostituted to attain forbidden ends.   In the pre-Taft-Hartley days, when a disgruntled union struck an employer to compel him to defy the rulings of the Labor Board or struck a common carrier to compel him to disregard his public duties to carry merchandise and passengers without discrimination, organized labor, as defenders of a democratic order, should at least have raised a voice of protest.   Again it was the very simple issue of whether they were prepared to side with democratic order and rely on lawful bargaining, or whether they were reserving the right to revolt.   If labor unions seek public approbation and the avoidance of discredit for the strike as an incident to collective bargaining, they should accept the idea that industrial strife should never be employed to frustrate or defy the laws of the land.   If a person who aids or abets an unlawful act becomes liable as a *particeps criminis*, it surely should follow that a union that seeks to promote a lawless purpose through the coercion of industrial strife is likewise liable.   Such conduct aggravates the usual offense by also injuring the community.   But even as conservative a leader as William Green testified, as late as February 27, 1947, before a Congressional committee, that the right to strike is an "unlimited right." [14]   Justice Jackson has pointed out in a Supreme Court opinion that the strike is particularly "vulnerable" to regulation because of its "impact upon the public interest." [15] Until labor stops prating about the absolute right to strike and stands four-square for submission to law, it cannot be regarded as an unqualified friend of democracy or an unqualified enemy of dictatorship. The provisions in the Taft-Hartley Act, which, in part, meet this argument, should never have been opposed.

Political strikes and strikes of governmental employees, in which no possible question can arise as to the balance of bargaining power, are a part of this same parcel. Some unions apparently wish to reserve the right to tell the government when they will, and when they will not, play ball. That attitude reflects itself in the reluctance of labor unions unequivocally to disclaim any right to employ the strike as a political weapon. Strikes have taken place for the purpose of preventing the shipment of goods to Yugoslavia and to disrupt aid to Britain. Protest strikes took place against both procedure and decisions of the War Labor Board. Not so long ago the transport workers' union in New York City, under the guidance of Michael Quill, their union president, threatened to paralyze the subways unless the city would agree not to sell certain power facilities to a private company, and seamen engaged in strikes to force the government to divert more ships for the homecoming of American soldiers. Petrillo threatened strikes against broadcasting companies if Congress enacted certain laws and again if the courts were to uphold the constitutionality of the Lea Act passed by Congress. Here was threatened economic action seeking to control the decisions of both the legislature and the judiciary. As pointed out in Chapter XVIII, general community strikes have been called as a protest against law enforcement, and usually government has yielded to the threat. President Green strengthened this feeling when he stood for the unlimited right to strike and when in 1946 he declared that if the President signed the Case Bill "the 7,500,000 members of the A. F. of L. would be rebels as long as that bill is on the statute books of the nation." [16] John Lewis told Congress that it had no authority to stop strikes or to legislate to stop strikes [17] and has taunted the government by his statement that you cannot dig coal with bayonets. President Whitney of the Brotherhood of Railway Trainmen, when asked by a Senatorial committee whether he thought "the maintenance of the right to strike would be superior to the right of government in operating its own railroads," replied, "I take the position that the right of freedom and the preservation of democracy for the worker and everyone is supreme to a dictatorial power on the part of anyone, including the government." [18]   All this is dangerous doctrine.   If we have faith in democracy we must not substitute economic coercion for the ballot.

One reads in the daily news from time to time of strikes against government in France, Italy, and even labor-governed Great Britain, and now this country can match them by a nationwide coal strike in the United States against government orders issued through the courts.   Even if the union and its leaders are acquitted on the contempt charges the union membership overwhelmingly united to defeat the ends of government.   Of course, there is a difference between these mass movements in Europe and this mass movement in the United States.   But what is it?   In both cases, as I have repeatedly stated, there is a common emotional resentment leading to mass resistance in conflict with the political ideals of law and order, however democratically controlled or administered.   The principle of control through the ballot box is one that cannot be compromised without compromising democracy. It is as fundamental as the choice between ballots and bullets. Every thoughtful person is asking whether or not this trend can be arrested.

The importance of this question is pointed up by the events of the summer of 1950.   Longshoremen engaged in strikes to prevent unloading of cargoes believed to have originated in Russia. This was obviously an attempt to usurp the functions of the State Department, but notwithstanding this fact various groups of considerable importance, and a newspaper as prominent as the New York *Journal-American,* applauded this action.   These groups seemed to be quite unmindful of what I regard to be the greatest menace to our democratic form of government.

Will unions accept unresistingly the democratic ideal and forswear all efforts to pressure government except through established political procedures?   Are American political philosophy and American civilization so different from European that the wedge between unionism and communism, or some form of proletarian dictatorship, can be broadened by confining strikes—meaning organized obstructions and not peaceful withdrawals—and other kinds of industrial strife to their proper frontiers?   In considering these questions, one should remember that the unions have sought and obtained the intervention of government through the Wagner Act to buttress their position.   The state helped to create them as they are. To the state they owe much. To deal with the state as an antagonist in industrial warfare is entirely inconsistent with the acceptance of the privileges granted and also with the idea of collective bargaining within the limits of law.

And now I go a step further. Recalling again the distressing concomitants and consequences of industrial strife and the losses it entails upon the parties, as well as the community, I think most reasonable people would agree that we should never be plunged into it except as a last resort and then only when necessary for a legitimate end. When, therefore, laws have been passed defining and forcing union recognition and collective bargaining and protecting the right to organize, resort to industrial warfare for the purpose of attaining these ends or ensuring these rights should be forsworn. Where governmental agencies, created at the instance of labor, exist to dispose of such disputes, their decisions should reflect a kind of compulsory arbitration binding on all concerned. Where a tribunal of reason is available, there is no excuse for resort to the tribunal of force. "Force is not a remedy."

In 1919 Senator Robinson of Arkansas, in discussing a labor disputes act for railroads said:

Once we recognize the right and power of the government representing the public to determine these questions, we of necessity, unless we wish to belittle the government and its agencies, must deny the right to strike for the purpose of enforcing the demands.[19]

To this proposal it will be objected that it takes too long for a union to secure relief from the National Labor Relations Board, and for that reason the union should also be permitted to resort to direct action. The answer to this misgiving, it seems to me, is to provide speedier and more summary remedies appropriate to each particular type of unfair labor practice. It may be that the present duty of the Board to secure a preliminary injunction pending the completion of its proceedings should be liberalized and expanded. That is the customary procedure in other types of suits for protecting the rights of parties pending a decision on the merits of a controversy. As the law now stands, strikes for actual or trumped-up charges that the Board is empowered to settle and strikes against certain types of decisions by the Board are permissible. Logic and reason support the argument that if we are to operate under a National Labor Relations Board, empowered to decide certain classes of disputes, both sides should be compelled to rely upon that Board for relief and to abide by its rulings. If two businessmen have a falling-out, they can terminate relations subject to contract obligations, but they are otherwise confined to their legal remedies and may not set out to obstruct each other.

So I repeat that where any detail of industrial relations is prescribed by government as a matter of public policy, the field of industrial conflict should to that extent be deemed narrowed, and disputes growing out of that subject matter should not become the football of private combat with community losses.

I should feel the same about union security if Congress, in addition to laying down the limits of lawful union security, had also provided that the employer must accept the Taft-Hartley type of union shop where a majority of employees so vote. When Congress decides on a policy and provides the parties with an enforcement tribunal, the remedy for private citizens should be limited to the legal procedure provided and should not include the alternative of ordeal by battle.

Again, if labor unions are to rank with civic and commercial organizations as defenders of democracy and collective bargaining, they should accept full responsibility as far as they control the situation for the observance of contracts they sign and should not oppose legislation for legal enforcement. This responsibility includes compliance with arbitration awards where the parties have agreed to arbitrate. Adequate legal and equitable remedies should be available to either party to secure adherence to the terms of such an important document as a collective-bargaining agreement. Nor can I discover any good reason why those remedies should not be of the same character and subject to the same tests as are applied in securing the rights of parties to less important contracts. Here again special immunities should have no place if collective-bargaining contracts are to be relied upon to stabilize labor relations and perpetuate our free institutions.

Already we have recourse to legal enforcement of matters relating to employment where provisions of the Wage and Hour Law, the labor relations acts, or the rights of veterans to re-employment are involved. It does not seem startling, therefore, to provide the usual enforcement remedies for other phases of the employment relationship that are covered by contract obligation. Special enforcement remedies are often embodied in the bargaining agreement.

In the bituminous coal industry for over 30 years district agreements, and for part of that period national agreements, provided penalties for unlawful stoppages by either operators or miners. These fines usually ran from 50 cents to $2.00 per man per day. Some agreements imposed fines for loading impurities and others for absenteeism beyond the second day of unexcused absence or for improper discharge. In order to avoid compromising these penalties, it was sometimes provided that no fine should be refunded except by mutual agreement of the accredited representatives of the parties and that double fines should be paid for non-collection. In most cases the fines were paid to agencies like the Red Cross or the Medical and Hospital Fund. On the whole these enforcement provisions were helpful, but now with the drift toward union irresponsibility all clauses have been formally set aside by the agreement of 1950.

Some collective-bargaining agreements require the parties to file a bond or to deposit cash as security for performance. Some specify a schedule of fines and penalties to be applied by a joint committee or an arbitrator, and some require that an arbitrator should decide all issues as to alleged contract breaches, including the imposition of penalties. Such provisions to promote compliance are not dissimilar to provisions in contracts in other fields of activity and tend to support the contention that, concerning enforcement, these contracts should be treated like contracts between other persons or groups of persons. Only recently in the case of a trucking company an arbitration award against a union, granting an employer $4,161.88 damages on account of an outlaw strike, was sustained by the courts.[20]

In October, 1950, the Michigan Supreme Court, reversing the decision of the lower court, which had held a strike to be a "spontaneous decision" of the employees, held the union liable for damages in the amount of $33,000, on the ground that a strike constituted a breach of contract and that "none of the stewards made an effort to prevent the walkout or tried to comply with contract grievance procedure." [21]

Curiously enough the greatest variety of compliance provisions in labor contracts are those imposed by unions on employers.

Here is an interesting sample: "It is hereby agreed that the union shall be entitled as a matter of right to equity relief restraining the employer from any breach or threatened breach of the agreement." [22] So what is the shouting about?

I believe that all the appropriate remedies in law or equity should be available to the parties in securing compliance with labor agreements, except in so far as the contract itself provides its own remedies for noncompliance, and that these latter remedies should be subject to judicial enforcement if flouted.

Furthermore, I would declare to be unenforceable and against public policy any contract clause exempting the parties from responsibility for stoppages in violation of the contract, where it appeared that such stoppages were due to any act of commission or omission of the contracting party. All agreements, wherever practicable, should cover a period of at least one year. Collective-bargaining contracts must become peace pacts for a substantial term. The law requires them to be put in writing if either party desires it and the law should put substance behind them.

This policy of contract enforcement through the courts, it will be recalled, was followed by the government in dealing with a coal strike in 1946. The injunction in that case was sought to prevent a strike, pending a determination by the court as to certain obligations arising under a contract between the union and the government. When the strike nevertheless took place, the government, as pointed out elsewhere in this volume, was successful in persuading the court to impose fines in contempt proceedings, which, when reduced by the Supreme Court, were finally enforced to the amount of $700,000 against the union and $10,000 against Mr. Lewis. Nor is the suggestion different in substance from that urged by President Truman and that found in the Canadian Act and our Railway Labor Act, that disputes as to the obligations of an existing contract be submitted to impartial adjudication. Of a related nature are the provisions of the Taft-Hartley Act requiring the parties to a collective-bargaining agreement to give 60 days' notice of a proposed modification or termination, together with a notification 30 days thereafter to the conciliation service if the parties are unable by that time to negotiate a new agreement.

As for jurisdictional strikes, they should be handled peacefully by interunion agreement, but where such arrangements are not forthcoming, and capacity for self-government is not demonstrated, the provisions of the Taft-Hartley Act, or equivalent provisions for peaceful adjudication, are necessary. The neutral employer and the neutral community should no longer continue to be the victims of such disturbances. Whatever may be the arguments for special privileges to unions to increase their bargaining strength with employers, they have little or no application to interunion battles. The Taft-Hartley Act, which gives the Labor Relations Board the power to determine the bargaining unit, was properly vested with power to decide jurisdictional questions that the parties cannot settle.

These enumerated situations, which afford no justification for the dislocations of industrial war, whether they be exceptional or frequent, are important for their moral content. Legal restraints are usually called for by the misconduct of a small group of wrong-doers and are applied to a few lest wrongdoing become a habit. Their efficacy as deterrents is to be measured not by the number of cases that come into court but by the unnumbered and unnoted cases where observance follows as a matter of course.

At least the prevailing attitude of unions, in respect to these various matters, is significant in interpreting the underlying philosophy of the labor movement. Generally speaking they could be wrapped into a single package. Lawlessness in industrial strife, strikes to promote violations of law, strikes of governmental employees, political strikes of employees in private industry, general strikes called to injure the community, strikes dealing with issues that are settled by law as a matter of governmental policy, and lastly strikes in violation of contract—all these situations should be regarded as forbidden areas for industrial strife. In asking for the unlimited right to strike, labor seeks to make legal rights of all these social wrongs.

To stimulate discussion I make one further suggestion. A strike is an exercise of power that the courts, without the aid of legislation, came to recognize as a social expedient. It is the lesser of two evils. It may be deliberately provoked by an offensive act of an employer or it may be an aggressive act of the union, but whoever causes it, the *raison d' être* of its recognition as a lawful movement is the need of giving the workers substantial power in dealing with employers. If we followed this historical philosophy, the employer who renounced his power by offering to arbitrate would not be faced by an aggressive attack to strangle

his business. Although legislation to support such a broad proposal would not be politically palatable, can we not meet the proposal half-way? The right to attack such an employer should not
be as broad as the right to attack an antiunion employer who, by
oppression, arbitrary conduct, or unfair labor practices, provokes
a strike. The right to secure replacements or discriminate against
strikers should not be restricted under such circumstances. I
suggest, therefore, that wherever an employer offers to arbitrate
in accordance with established statutory procedure and the union,
rejecting such offer, organizes a strike, there should be no right
to picket and that certain immunities afforded strikers under the
Norris-LaGuardia Act and the Labor Relations Act should not be
available. In the Norris-LaGuardia Act an employer is denied
the right to an injunction, even against fraud and violence, if he
has not exhausted the possibilities of peaceful settlement. An
employer who fails to embrace the opportunity to arbitrate forfeits
his right to such court relief.[23] Why not round out this idea by
denying the union the remedy of picketing if it rejects the available
processes of peaceful settlement?

The reaction of labor unions to such a suggestion might not be
uniform. John L. Lewis, speaking for the United Mine Workers,
as I have already pointed out, is opposed to arbitration in any form
and so have been most of the leaders of the railway brotherhoods.
On the other hand, the American Federation of Labor has in the
past at least professed its devotion to arbitration, while the C.I.O.
in an issue of the *Economic Outlook*, published in May, 1950,
makes this unqualified declaration:

It has always been the policy of C.I.O. to further the public interest by
utilizing all the resources of negotiation, mediation, fact-finding and voluntary arbitration. In almost all instances, it is only when these procedures
have been exhausted that strike action has been sanctioned.[24]

Notwithstanding this utterance, however, I do not recall any frank
condemnation by the C.I.O. of the railway brotherhoods or the
United Mine Workers when they have rejected arbitration. Today it has been the employing interest that has been more leery of
arbitration in industry.

Under my suggestion both sides would feel the pressure seriously to consider voluntary arbitration. A union which refused
arbitration would be hampered by its inability to picket and a loss

of some of the statutory privileges now extended to strikers. An employer who did not offer arbitration would be subject to the severities of picketing and the existing limitations on his right to hire replacements. Behind this idea would be sound social morality in giving preferred protection to employers and unions that yielded to arbitration. The Taft-Hartley Act embodies a comparable sanction when it requires 60 days' notice of termination and modification of an existing agreement and 30 days' notice to the conciliation service, with the right vested in the employer to discriminate against employees who engage in a strike during the 60-day period.

Down to the present time the labor movement as a whole has been unwilling to concede any distinction between its right to carry on damaging activities for antisocial purposes and its right to carry them on for proper purposes. Many others, not in the labor movement, apparently agree. There seems to be a defeatist attitude toward orderly, responsible collective bargaining regulated by law, an attitude that is in marked conflict with the philosophy that leans heavily on collective bargaining as a cornerstone of the social-industrial arch.

In an address before the Northwestern States Trade and Commercial Association Executives at Yale University in 1949, Herman W. Steinkraus, president of the United States Chamber of Commerce, said:

> Strikes are a device of a past era. They are incredibly costly to labor, management, and the community and are not necessary. No small group, for power reasons, should keep a whole community out of employment.
> Strikes are a bitter luxury for everyone, and, as workers come to assume more a greater part in controlling their own destinies, they will increasingly see that although strife is easy, yet in the long run the harder way—moderation—is most beneficial of all. We have often heard the idea that labor must preserve its right to strike. What is more important, however, is that it reserve its right to work.[25]

Mr. Steinkraus' remarks are eloquent arguments for keeping the strike in its rightful place. On the other hand, economic strikes, hurtful as they are,[26] should not be outlawed where there is no alternative form of protection for the workers. Why not start by limiting the area of industrial strife, by barring it where its use is unwarranted? The laws prescribe limitations on the unfair exercise of economic power by the employer, and there is no reason why they should not follow a like course in dealing with union power.

Without going further, it is clear—at least to my satisfaction —that a responsible, grown-up union movement, desiring to preserve a democratic government and a system of free enterprise, might well accept the limitations I have discussed with the assurance that such an acceptance would promote the standing and strength of unionism as a part of the framework of society. It would be an effective answer to those who now blacken the union movement with their denunciations and would make much clearer the demarcation between the labor union movement in the United States and the revolutionary movements in Europe. If the occasions multiply when it is necessary in this country for our government to make treaties with labor unions as though they were sovereign powers instead of domestic institutions, the walls of the temple of democracy will be cracked. Probably symptoms of internal rebellion are always with us when sections and groups feel frustrated, but it certainly behooves us to prevent the development of any large-scale habits of industrial warfare for purposes wholly inconsistent with collective bargaining and the democratic process. Why should the Norris-LaGuardia immunities extend to activities that are inherently wrong?

Violence in strikes and avoidable and unjustifiable strikes are recognized as breeders of communist sentiment.

Lozovsky in his book, *Marx and the Trade Unions,* quotes from a distinguished Marxian:

> Every strike is all the more valuable since it extends and deepens the gulf between the bourgeois class and the masses, for it proves to the workmen in the plainest way the absolute incompatibility of their interests with the interests of the capitalists and owners. . . . As a matter of fact, there is no better means of wresting the workmen away from the political influence of the bourgeoisie than a strike. . . .[27]

The same author in his book, *The World Economic Crisis,* says strikes "are only skirmishes that forge the class solidarity of the proletariat, that oppose class against class, and train the masses for the final struggle. . . . [28] Thus the strike movement trains the masses . . . for the dictatorship of the proletariat." [29]

Lenin said: "The final end of the strike struggle in the capitalist state is the destruction of the state apparatus." [30]

That we may not blind ourselves to the real danger and the door by which it may enter, if it does enter, I refer to one more distinguished proponent of radical philosophy. William Z. Foster looks upon our labor movement as undeveloped ideologically, but he adds, "Few countries have had a more violent class struggle than the United States. The trouble is that American workers have not yet drawn the full ideological meaning out of the class war which they themselves are waging." Then he adds, "The American workers are by no means wedded irrevocably to the capitalistic illusions. They are definitely on the march ideologically. . . ." [31]

"It is particularly important," said the program of the Communist International, "for the purpose of winning over the majority of the proletariat, to capture the trades unions, which are genuine mass working-class organizations closely bound up with the everyday struggles of the working class." [32]

A mathematical measure of the spread of Marxian thought in this country is of little significance, because it is the emotional attitude toward property rights, without a tag, that in the end will be of importance. Nevertheless it may be well to take a snapshot of the fluctuating strength of the Socialist vote since early in the century.

In 1905 the Industrial Workers of the World was organized, in response to what some people thought were reactionary policies of the A. F. of L. It aimed to set up a new type of labor organization to reach the low-paid unskilled workers, such as those who were later reached by the C.I.O. Mr. Debs was present at an initial conference in Chicago in January, 1905, "to discuss ways and means of uniting the working people of America in correct revolutionary principles." [33] The "class collaboration" of the A. F. of L. unions was condemned. A constitutional convention, composed of some 200 delegates representing nearly 150,000 workers, was called later in the year. Debs, speaking at this convention, declared that the sole purpose of the National Civic Federation was "to chloroform the working classes while the capitalistic class goes through their pockets." [34] The convention adopted a constitution declaring that the "working class and the employing class have nothing in common." [35]

During this era Mr. Debs and the Socialist party sought to woo the labor movement to the Socialist or Marxian ideology that there was no remedy for the workers except to abolish the wage system by taking over all means of production. Mr. Gompers, heading the A. F. of L., turned his back on any such plea, but in the meanwhile a Socialist party grew and commanded a considerable number of votes.

Debs received a Socialist vote of over 400,000 in 1904 and 1908; this vote he doubled in 1912, and by 1920 his Socialist vote of 919,299, added to the Farmer-Labor vote, established a record of nearly 1,180,000 votes. The radical vote was only a minor percentage of this record until 1932, when the combined vote of Norman Thomas, Socialist; William Z. Foster, Communist; and Verne L. Reynolds, Socialist-Labor, rose again to over 1,000,-000. Since then, whatever the reason, it has ebbed to about a quarter of a million, and in 1948 to about 100,000, unless we include the Wallace vote, which exceeded 1,000,000.

Whether these figures on the Socialist vote should allay our fears, or add to them, depends on the individual viewpoint. The radical writers pretend not to be discouraged. They feel that the American worker, being educated by the bitterness of class conflict, is ripe for ideological treatment, and it is difficult for the rest of us to appraise the trends. To date, the dominating voice of our labor movement has turned a deaf ear to Socialism, syndicalism, and communism as a remedy for the grievances of the working class, but nevertheless it is educating the membership to feel that the existing conditions are wrong, that employers are selfish exploiters of labor, and that radical changes must take place. They are still waiting to give capitalism a further trial.

Socialist writers, who are avowed enemies of the existing order, look upon our labor movement as a flaming movement that will produce conflagration. If the responsible labor leaders of today are to play their most effective role in preserving a capitalistic system and proving these radical writers to be false prophets, they must resort less to the teaching of hatred of capitalists and must frown on the use of their various sources of power in undemocratic ways to control political developments or defeat or resist our laws.

The tidal wave of fear and hatred of Russian ideology has greatly retarded the progress of radicals in this country and has given us needed breathing time to build our protection against that ideology, which most people wish to avoid. If only we will take full advantage of this!

Nor is there any reason why labor unions today should continue, as they did 25 years ago, to engender distrust of employers, bankers, courts, and public officials, and certainly there is no reason for believing that our democracy will hereafter short-change them, particularly as the percentage of wage workers is greatly expanding and therefore putting increasing political power in their hands.   By democracy I mean the rule of the people.   When through their government the people have spoken, acquiescence is the test of loyalty and patriotism.   It is the test of faith in democracy.   As votes, not dollars, are recorded in the final count, industrial workers and farmers hold the greatest political power, and large property owners, being a small minority, just have to take it.   So democracy becomes a form of government that gives preferred treatment to pressure groups.

Government in this country has drifted further and further from the checks and controls that were adopted by our founding fathers and has crept nearer and nearer to direct democracy.   The electoral college has been reduced to a mere form; direct election of Senators has taken the place of the original plan of selection by state legislatures.   Direct primaries, in many instances, have taken over the functions of party caucuses.   More judges are elected. The whittling away of certain individual rights under our Constitution has pointed toward greater collectivism, lobbies for the common people are more powerful, and above all, modern transportation and modern methods of communication, including the radio, have increased the facilities of the noncreative majorities to make their wishes effective.   Starting as a republic, fearful of tyranny arising from government by majorities, we have turned toward direct democracy.   The effect of this change has made itself felt with startling swiftness, and there is more to come.

Thus it may be said that the justification for such ultimate defenses as revolt or irregular resistance of any kind has faded. Hesitation as to law enforcement in industrial disputes should pass away.   However slothful society once may have been in giving labor full recognition of its just status, no such condition exists today.   With the changed conditions we have a right to seek changed attitudes, more in tune with the facts of the day.

But here again is a paradox.   Notwithstanding the advantages enjoyed by pressure groups, the greatest threat to orderly government in the Western world is the tendency of labor groups by direct action to challenge or resist democratic processes.   In France and Italy we behold them frequently defying authority and, like sovereign powers, embarking on treaty-making negotiations with their own government.   Can we prevent such an attitude from developing in this country?   Is organized labor satisfied with its position as one more social institution willingly operating within the framework of law or does it insist upon a reserve power of revolt, flying the historic flag, "Don't Tread on Me"?

In facing these issues I find myself convinced of the necessity of compromise between conflicting philosophies: between political concepts of individual self-reliance, such as our forefathers adopted, and collectivism and social security, of which these founders knew nothing.   Few, if any, political principles, or any principles, can be carried to a logical conclusion.   Those who believe in liberty, a free economy, and individual responsibility if not restrained may arrive at results just as destructive to human progress as their opposites, Socialism, authoritarianism, and social security.   Pursuing either ideal too far will throw civilization on the rocks.   Too much individualism means too much accumulation of property power in the hands of a few and too much inequality.   Too much control and too much social security hinder the development of the individual, upon which human progress depends.

So we are forced to this conclusion.   Nonsocialized individualism with its cumulative consequences breaks down civilization because of the disparity of human talents, but over-socialized individualism, with its jealousy of leadership and power, strikes at the very fountainhead of human growth.   Somewhere between these two extremes we must find the workable truth.   When we talk about equality of rights and equality of bargaining power, therefore, we should face the ultimate political problem: What curtailment of liberty and property rights and what qualifications of a free economy are necessary to maintain the essentials of free enterprise without impairing too profoundly the moral forces that make for individual effort?   Today the United States is earnestly and hopefully exploring this problem in the alluring fields of both theory and practice, but if any proposed solution is to succeed, it must reject all resort to violence and antisocial strife and give ungrudging support to leaders of real talent.   A democracy such as Plato describes as dispensing "a sort of equality to equals and unequals" will not promote the development of a nation.

The fundamental attitude of the labor unions, first toward the Case Bill of 1946, which was never enacted, and finally toward the Taft-Hartley Act, is a discouraging side of the picture. Any suggestion of any regulation of unionism was described as antilabor by top spokesmen. Union friends in the House of Representatives, as well as the Senate, pleaded with union leaders for constructive suggestions, but with no success. Labor would have none of it. The issue became the simple one of regulation or non-regulation—social control or no control—; the duty of government was to remedy outstanding social evils and to subordinate special interests to the general welfare. It was as elementary as that. Primarily the difference is between the philosophy of true collective bargaining as a commercial function and the philosophy of class conflict. The union attitude is all the more indefensible because it sought and accepted government aid to promote organization.

Mr. Gompers had a passion for freedom of the workers to act collectively and thus to shape the destiny of labor without statutory aid. He was as much opposed to laws to strengthen labor as he was to laws to restrict labor. His successors think otherwise. They would have their cake and eat it. In demanding government protection under the National Labor Relations Act and the Fair Labor Standards Act, they doff the mantle of Gompers. In demanding that government keep hands off the militant activities of unions, they again put on the mantle of Gompers. They ask government to bolster union power and oppose government regulation of the bolstered power! They have forgotten, what Gompers never forgot, that "The Lord giveth and the Lord taketh away." The public for its part insists upon controlling the institutions it has endowed.

The problems of union monopoly, closed-shop tyranny, organized violence, defiance of N.L.R.B. decisions, national emergency strikes in vital industries, attempts to force carriers not to serve the unorganized, boycotts and jurisdictional strikes, diversion of union funds for improper purposes, union dictatorships without union elections—these and other evils, crying aloud for some correction or restraint, were treated by union leaders as practices they themselves would correct in their own good time. They forget that human power does not naturally put on its own bridle and that they were only asked to take the same medicine capital had been taking for several decades. Although there was no other human activity in this country where so much mischief existed without some legal controls, Congressmen and Senators were threatened with political extinction if they dared break the line of nonregulation. There was no analysis of the varied problems presented with compromise suggestions that might help the legislators who sought to help labor. The demand was for no regulation, and as far as legal restraint was concerned, for the unqualified legal right to continue the wrongs that nearly everyone knew to exist. So when the Taft-Hartley Act was written and passed over the Presidential veto in 1947, it did not reflect any substantial collaboration from the labor movement.

The Act has its defects, defects of omission as well as defects in details, but on the whole it reflects careful study and restraint in dealing with a difficult problem and a sincere effort to comply with an insistent public demand. In general it is hospitable to unionism. If it had been passed in 1935 instead of the Wagner Act, it would have been hailed as a great advance for labor.

Such legislation, enacted in the face of stout opposition, revealed a courageous and surprising determination to make democracy work at a time when Europe had moved to the left, and organized industrial workers had tried to dictate to their governments, and at a time when Great Britain had repealed the labor legislation of 1926.

Some protest strikes took place pending legislative consideration of the Act; some of its legislative proponents were picketed at places where they spoke. When the act was passed over the Presidential veto, there were more protest strikes of many thousands of employees; and criticisms, instead of being discriminating, were rebellious and sweeping, as if government were profaning sacred precincts. Union leaders refused to accept it as an over-all legislative endeavor to bring them and their activities within the reach of law and, as in the case of other segments of society, to apply controls where public interests required it. They felt outraged at the very thought of regulation. All Congressmen and Senators who voted for this law were marked for political defeat. The demand was not for amendments but for a return in this field to an industrial system of no law. With the unions, this issue of social control versus no control transcended all other national problems. Men rendering invaluable services to this country in matters like foreign affairs were to be defeated because they differed with unions on this one point.

The failure of such unreasoned opposition to yield results later led the American Federation of Labor to summarize its grievances against the Act and its administration. At its sixty-eighth convention, held in the autumn of 1949, its specification of grievances ran thus:

The resurgence of the injunction as an anti-union weapon, the broadening application of "national emergency," the prohibition of inter-union assistance by the ban on secondary boycotts, the disappearance of union contract provisions requiring the union card as a condition of employment, the employers' use of free speech as a weapon against unions, prohibition of mass picketing without defining which acts are and are not illegal.[36]

Except for the desire to define more accurately the lawful bounds of mass picketing, this summary is but a reiteration of an unchanged, adamant position without any constructive suggestion for meeting the evils that grow out of these problems. Here are unanswered questions. As to the closed shop, what is to be done about the Cecil DeMilles when driven from their profession? What is to be done about the miner thrown out of a union because he called Mr. Lewis a dictator? As to secondary boycotts, how is it proposed to protect the right of the public to enjoy the free distribution of goods they wish to buy? Is the employer's song to be unsung by denying him the right of free speech? As to injunctions, why pick on them when their use is enjoyed by labor under the Labor Relations Act and the Fair Labor Standards Act, and is certainly to be preferred over criminal prosecutions and damage suits? How should government cope with organized violence? What should be the remedy against antisocial or unlawful strikes?

In evaluating the apparent reluctance of unions to consider reasonable regulation, the public is entitled to some real answers to many questions of the kind I have propounded and ought to be warned that complete nonregulation in matters of such grave importance would spell an inevitable drift toward something other than a balanced democratic government. On this issue, the title to the case is *Public* v. *Unions*. Someone is out of step. Either the unions or the public will have to revise their thinking. To one like the writer, who has a profound conviction as to the importance and necessity of unions in an industrial democracy, an undiscriminating attack on the general social purpose of the Taft-Hartley Act does not appear to be sound public relations. Far more effective in sloughing off charges of communism, and in winning public confidence, would be an affirmative program accepting reasonable regulation and opposing political strikes, strikes for unlawful purposes, and lawlessness in all strikes.

The explanation for labor's blind opposition is not far to seek. After giving a horse a free rein, one finds a sudden curb causes bucking, or to change the metaphor, a spoiled child reacts badly to attempts at discipline.

Industrial workers in many instances have suffered decades of mistreatment, which the unions have done much to remedy, and that historic fact inevitably led a democratic country to bolster the unions in many ways. When the propaganda of prounionism was sweeping the country in the 1930's, discriminatory laws contributed to a feeling that unions were under no obligation to adhere to social standards imposed on the rest of us. Regulatory laws, proceeding on the theory that only employers do wrong, forbade unfair labor practices on the part of employers and left the unions free from such restraint. Moreover the education of the workers was one-sided, since it was generally believed that employers were forbidden to present their viewpoint to their employees. When in addition to all this, violence was tolerated and strikes for unlawful ends were in effect sanctioned by statute and court decisions, union leaders cannot be blamed for feeling that a superior law existed to aid their highly idealized ends. No wonder they reacted unfavorably to any suggestion of accountability. The impact on the union mind of these double standards must have been impressive. So in this country there inevitably developed among the workers a new sense of divine right and power that made them prone to seize what they could reach, even though it was an unmannerly reach. To be asked suddenly to surrender the privilege of being a governmental pet inevitably provoked opposition. Is it strange that in this atmosphere the provisions of the Taft-Hartley Act, intended to harmonize union practices with established social standards and seeking equality of rights between management and unions, should meet with opposition from unions?

The inherent weakness of the unions' argument in pointing to their virtues and in asking the country to rely on self-correction is found throughout all history. "I am more and more convinced," wrote Abigail Adams, "that man is a dangerous creature and that power whether vested in many or a few is ever grasping and like the grave cries, Give, Give." [37] Human power does not easily contain itself. Wise labor leaders should begin to learn that legal remedies for evils inherent in any human organization like a labor union will in the long run be helpful to the movement itself. The forces of good in unionism need help to overcome the forces of evil. Unions should look upon the over-all purpose of the Taft-Hartley Act as a sincere effort to lessen unnecessary industrial warfare and to assert the supremacy of government for the protection of the public. As a social code this statute seems reconcilable with the legitimate interests of unions. It is not only the provisions requiring anticommunist affidavits, but all the other provisions giving legal standing to labor unions as social and economic agencies subject to normal responsibilities, that aim to drive a wedge between unions and revolutionary isms.

The intelligent labor leader must already have learned, just as capital had to learn, that excesses on the part of special interests inevitably lead to public discredit and legal restraints and that all the excesses in the 15 years preceding 1947, particularly those in 1937 and 1946, created the public sentiment that demanded a Taft-Hartley Act or its equivalent. If that lesson has been truly learned by both management and labor unions, it will constitute the most powerful inducement for them to compose their differences rather than to risk further curtailments of their rights. "The highest power may be lost by misrule."

Notwithstanding petulant protests against the Taft-Hartley Act, there are those who hope that it will lead to a more moderate course of union conduct and a tacit revision of labor's self-appraisal. Such a revision, according to these observers, might result in a greater reconciliation of interests between the labor movement and the public, as labor comes to realize that it is now confronted with something far more powerful and impartial than an employer attitude.

As for the voters, they may never understand all the complexities of labor legislation, but they will not endorse any campaign that offers nothing more constructive than the legislative erasure of the Taft-Hartley Act. They see no good reason why a country that pioneered in compelling union recognition and by positive law built up the unions should not also pioneer in requiring them to conduct themselves with due regard for the public good and traditional liberties. Consciously or unconsciously the public senses that the issue between collective bargaining and class conflict is well integrated with the issue of regulation or nonregulation.

The adjustment of individualism to collectivism is a question of public policy. Just how far must the rights of an individual worker be surrendered to the union in order to accomplish the greatest social good? Just how far must the rights and liberties of a single productive unit of employers and employees be submerged in industry-wide bargaining? Just how far should government delegate to unions and trade associations broad opportunities for self-government, and just what reservations should be made for government review in order to protect the public? The public will scarcely concede that issues so fundamental are beyond public concern and control.

When the Taft-Hartley Act was passed, I queried whether this remarkable response to an aroused public opinion could survive a well-organized political attack, and whether the Act, if politically upheld, could be and would be enforced. To date the answer to these questions must be in the affirmative. The law is being enforced. Notwithstanding the election of a President who vetoed the Act and labor's distorted claim that the popular vote in 1948 was a mandate to repeal the Act, it still stands. And why? Because the American people realize that the only hope of a free economy with collective bargaining lies in a labor movement that is under social controls. The temptations and vices inherent in labor monopolies, although they differ in their manifestations from the temptations and vices of a corporate monopoly, are nevertheless as heedless of social welfare. The American people, accustomed to legislative protection from economic overreaching, instinctively feel the need of protection against the evils from the labor segment.

The failure to repeal this measure of union regulation was also due in part to the stupid tactics of those who sought the repeal. Starting with the arrogant demand that there be no regulation and that we return to the state of legal vacuum that had proved so disastrous, the apostles of repeal never retreated to any significant extent.   Then in 1949, after repeal had been made a political issue, the unions, backed by the Administration, committed political hara-kiri by blunder number two.   They appeared to consent to some regulation to fill the vacuum left by the New Deal policy of the 1930's but insisted that this be done in two steps: (1) by the immediate repeal of the Taft-Hartley Act and a return to the vacuum now admitted to be politically unacceptable, and (2) by a prolonged investigation and debate as to what changes should be made for the future.   Thus Congress was to be stampeded into immediate action, creating a condition of nonregulation, and then during this labor millennium a real study of labor law—as if it had not already been made—would be undertaken.   If this had been done, the country would have started 1949 with the Taft-Hartley Act, followed by a second period of no regulation, and this in turn would be followed by a third period when a new law of unknown terms would take effect in the indefinite future.   Such a maneuver, creating uncertainty and a state of unsettlement in our factories, could only be explained as an indefensible attempt to force a political stampede.   When Congressmen and Senators began to feel the sense of the people back in their home towns, they knew better than to accede to such a program.   Once more the American people saw the need of protection from class dictation.   For the time being they have ruled that the Taft-Hartley Act shall stand until the groups most directly affected bring to the council chambers reasonable amendments designed to promote the public welfare.   As I write, prevailing winds are not from the east.

Why not hammer out the issues of industrial control by frank recognition of the merits of the claims on both sides, never forgetful of the claims of efficiency and productivity?   If such an approach, with its educational possibilities, is substituted for the language of emotional antagonism, which goes beyond the conflicting issues of the immediate dispute, there will be some hope of avoiding a dangerous clash.   If not, the rights of all will be lost in totalitarianism.   Am I too guileless in feeling that union membership can be held to solidarity by intelligent economic appeals, without resorting to extreme demagoguery?

More and more people incline to the philosophy that management should regard itself as a trustee for the investors, the employees, and the consumer.   By reason of unusual talent in-

dustrial managers are summoned to high command in the service
of society. Government can make or break them. Consumers
can make or break them. Unions can make or break them by
nonco-operation, just as Gandhi brought Great Britain to its knees
by nonco-operation. But it is in the interest of everybody that
management leadership should be stimulated by giving it the
fullest possible scope, consistent with economic and social progress.
Such service cannot be conscripted. To carry out this conception
and to guard against the menace of a contrary course, there must
be developed particularly among the working classes, an adequate
but balanced appreciation of the virtues of management and the
dependence of society upon the management.

Probably no system for the selection of leaders is more dependable and reliable than that which operates in big business.
The search for talent is always spurred by the necessities of competition and is ever on the alert. The old adage that there is
always room on top still holds. In a democratic world, where the
levelling process is ever a threat to the common welfare, emphasis
on the economic laws that select industrial captains, and the contribution that these captains make to the good of everybody, is not
misplaced. Well may we rue the day if, like the late Harold
Laski, we decide there is no need for leaders, or like Stalin we
are brought to the conclusion that any literate person can manage
a business. Those who vote for the free enterprise system—and
this classification includes most American labor leaders—must
remember that in its essence it is a system of free competition
between the investor and the worker and that it cannot thrive
unless unions will frankly recognize the normal claims of private
management and private capital and educate their followers to
such a recognition.

Perhaps the answer will be found in discovering definite standards for the division of the products of industry, but I think not.
It seems to me that the problem is deeper than that and calls for
a more positive campaign by union leaders to determine the proper
place of management and capital.

In theory profit sharing would seem to be an economic answer
to these trends toward the class struggle or the struggle of the
free enterprise system to survive. But neither labor nor management accepts this answer and its record of performance in
the limited number of cases in which it is applied is largely

against it. "Profit-sharing," preaches the powerful U.A.W., "is a step backward." [38]

Peter Henle, assistant economist of the American Federation of Labor, writing in *The American Federationist* for August, 1950, under the title of "What About Profit Sharing?" says this:

However, in our modern industrial society, the individual worker's effort can have only a very insignificant effect on the size of the firm's profits. Consequently, his portion of an annual or even a semi-annual profit sharing bonus cannot serve as an incentive for greater output, less waste or increased efficiency.

He also adds:

Under these circumstances, it is easy to see what has happened to many profit sharing plans. They proved successful when business was thriving and profits were plentiful, but once business declined and profits contracted, employee dissatisfaction mounted and in many cases the plan had to be abandoned.[39]

The unions may well look upon profit sharing as disruptive to national unionism, as it would to some extent substitute factory solidarity for class solidarity and in effect create competition between different groups of workers.

The conflict is something more than agreeing upon the division of the industrial income. Some submission to industrial leadership, some recognition of the limitations of industrial democracy, is essential. If conservative labor leaders seek to assure the preservation of private enterprise and private management, they must —before it is too late—give support not only to free enterprise in name but to all the essentials of private enterprise. Failure to do so makes their membership an easy recruiting ground for revolutionary groups. If the great body of union members believe that employers are enemies both of the workers and society and that our miraculous war production was merely the result of the patriotism of the workers, there would seem to be no basis for an appeal to treat them fairly, or even to tolerate their existence.

Not so many years ago the English labor movement operated more like our own, with Socialism gradually penetrating its thinking. At last English labor despaired of the trail we in this country are traveling and pushed the rudder in the wrong direction. But this is more significant. The British unions have so well educated their membership in uneconomic hostility toward property rights that they are slow to listen to the pleas of their own labor government.[40]   The London Dock Strike of 1950, carried on in opposition to the orders of the union leaders, was finally beaten by sending thousands of soldiers to protect willing workers and to perform the duties of strike breakers.   Other strikes have followed.   The emotions aroused by militant unionism throughout the decades are now difficult to direct.   The workers are not satisfied with the results of the democratic process which has substituted their government for the private employer.

To summarize, at the risk of slight repetition: The labor movement in this country thrives on the assertion that employers are oppressing labor and is pushing forward to undefined goals that will give it a greater participation in management and a larger share in the product.   It is characteristic of labor oragnizers, in talking to their constituencies, to depict employers as a common enemy and the labor movement as the most desirable means of meeting a common peril and to deny employers credit for good impulses or the outstanding services they have rendered society. To state it exactly, the labor union movement in the United States is an attack on capitalists but not on capitalism, because it believes that it has more to gain through its many-sided concentrated power by pitting its strength against capitalism than by overthrowing it.   The question, however, is how long you can attack capitalists without attacking the institution of capitalism.

Postscript

Fifty years is too short a time to distinguish between underlying currents and surface ripples.   That which seems of foremost importance in our time may be of little significance in the more distant future, and some trend that is actually shaping our future for years to come may pass unnoticed.   My purpose in this book has been to search for controlling forces that may exercise a tremendous influence on the future of the labor movement and private management, so that both groups will become conscious of the dangers ahead and endeavor to avoid them. From my viewpoint, management and labor have the most important of all objectives in common—the preservation of private management— and each can make its contribution to prosper that institution or to destroy it.   To me, the greater opportunity lies with restraint upon the part of the labor movement, because in a democratic government the trend is toward equalitarianism, which, if carried too far, means the death knell of private management.   Labor unions can, if they will, fend off that trend.   Ownership and private management should, of course, so conduct themselves as to win the co-operation of labor in this common objective, but ownership and management, as I view them, cannot again revert to outmoded extremes in their treatment of labor, since they are controlled by the overwhelming necessity of co-operating with both labor and government.   Any prediction as to whether the future holds the promise of co-operation or the disaster of class conflict depends in too large a degree upon the optimism or pessimism of those who dare to make a prediction.

For those who feel this book to be a jeremiad and for those who do not visualize the fragility and delicacy of adjustments between the creative and noncreative group, between those who earn the right to be acclaimed leaders and those who must accept the role of followers, I turn to ancient history.   Of Athens some 2300 years ago, it is written, "The poor schemed to despoil the rich by legislation or revolution, the rich organized themselves for protection against the poor. . . .   In this conflict more and more of the intellectual classes took the side of the poor.   They disdained the merchants and bankers whose wealth seemed to be in inverse proportion to their culture and taste; even rich men, among them men like Plato, began to flirt with communistic ideas.   Isocrates wrote, 'When I was a boy, wealth was regarded as a thing so secure, as well as admirable, that almost every one affected to own more property than he actually possessed.   Now a man has to be ready to defend himself against being rich as if it were the worst of crimes.' " [41]   And so Greece, torn by class conflict, became the weakened prey of an invading conqueror.

Toynbee looks upon class conflict and war as the causes of the downfall of any civilization.   So we all naturally wonder whether we are in the fell clutch of circumstance.   We hope not.   We hope there is nothing inexorable in the forces we face.

What happened 20 centuries ago is a far cry from what is likely to happen in the United States under conditions different, if we will but take advantage of the warnings of history and the accumulated knowledge and experience that are ours.   There is a way out of the discord and confusion, if mankind has developed sufficiently to control elemental human factors that so often have overridden reason. Idealists condemn eloquently those who would return to the law of the jungle, but equally to be shunned are unrealizable dreams of security and equality in a biological world where competition is the law of life and where strength and greatness should be allowed to play their part. It would be a great help to all of us if someone qualified to do so would attempt to discern the inevitable trends, which we will call the realities, and out of those materials would endeavor to paint the picture of a reconstructed society toward which we might reasonably struggle, changing our sights as we progress. Today the directors of our commercial life are too unmindful of what is happening, and too many of those who have vision are chasing a will-o'-the-wisp. Modern business, privately managed, and the modern labor movement cannot work out a solution unless a mutually acceptable pattern of industrial and social life is conceived.

Despite some tyranny and crime committed in the name of labor, despite antisocial interference with efficiency and production, despite some defiance of government and some revolutionary tendencies, despite privations inflicted upon an innocent society, and despite aims and philosophy that conflict with individual liberty, I still place my faith in labor organizations, in one form or another, as essential to the functioning of democracy in a commercial nation. I see no other solution between the extremes of private capitalism and totalitarianism.

I disagree with those who believe that the salvation of America lies in the destruction of the principles or practice of collective action among workers. I have not such confidence in the self-restraint of employers that I would leave the workers unorganized and unprotected. Nor have I such confidence in the organizations of the workers that I would leave employers and society unprotected from their excesses. Since when has absolute power been an infallible administrator of justice?

APPENDICES

A. State Legislation, 1937-1941 411
B. Summary of Provisions
   of Delaware Act of 1947 416
C. State Labor Legislation, 1947-1949 . . . 421

A

State Legislation, 1937-1946

BETWEEN 1937 AND 1946 13 states [1] enacted laws that forbade sitdown strikes.

At least 13 states [2] passed special acts in this period forbidding force, violence, intimidation and obstruction, and disorderly picketing. In 1939 Wisconsin condemned mass picketing by name. Some states [3] forbade picketing of a residence. Minnesota in 1939 forbade picketing by nonemployees unless a majority of the pickets were employees and permitted only one picket at all entrances if there was no dispute. Various states [4] forbade picketing in furtherance of unlawful or unauthorized strikes or for unlawful objectives. Idaho and South Dakota, acting in 1943, forbade all picketing of farms and ranches, but these laws came to grief in the courts. Some states specifically recognized the right of free speech for both employers and employees.

Between the disturbances of 1937 and 1946, eight states [5] passed laws requiring authorization by majority vote as a con-

---

[1] Tennessee (1937), Vermont (1937), Massachusetts (1938), Pennsylvania (1939), Minnesota (1939), Maryland (1941), Florida (1943), Kansas (1943), Louisiana (1946), Colorado (1943), Washington (1919), Michigan (1940), Wisconsin (1939).

[2] Alabama (1943), Arkansas (1943), Colorado (1943), Florida (1943), Kansas (1943), Louisiana (1946), Michigan (1943), Minnesota (1939), Mississippi (1942), Nebraska (1947), Pennsylvania (1939), Texas (1941), Virginia (1946), Wisconsin (1939).

[3] Colorado (1943), Kansas (1943), Wisconsin (1939).

[4] Pennsylvania (1939), Minnesota (1945), Colorado (1943).

[5] Alabama (1943), Colorado (1943), Florida (1943), Kansas (1943), Michigan (1939 et seq.), Minnesota (1939), Utah (1937), Wisconsin (1943). Delaware, Michigan, Missouri and North Dakota passed similar laws in 1947.

411

dition precedent to a lawful strike.   Included in these are Colorado and Wisconsin, which prohibit picketing and boycotting in connection with such strikes.   Some of these restrictions may not pass muster in the courts when subjected to constitutional tests, but it does not seem impracticable to draft valid regulations of this character.

Five states [6] required notices or certain procedural steps as a condition precedent to a lawful strike.

Six states [7] placed restrictions on jurisdictional strikes either by declaring them unlawful or banning picketing or boycotting in connection therewith.

Ten states [8] forbade or restricted boycotting in one form or another.

Seven states [9] outlawed or provided legal remedies against strikes in violation of agreements.

Subsequent to 1937 but prior to 1947, ten states [10] in the South and Middle West, four of them by constitutional amendment, placed restrictions on the closed shop by forbidding discrimination on account of membership or nonmembership in a union or by regulating the conditions under which union security would be permissible.   Michigan required a majority vote.   Wisconsin required a two-thirds vote.   Colorado required a three-fourths vote and further specified that there should be no check-off except on individual authorization revocable on 30 days' notice.   Texas in 1943 required all agreements providing for the check-off to be filed with the secretary of state.   Utah pointed the other way. As early as 1937 it required the employer to comply with a check-off authorization, but limited the amount.   In 1943 Alabama, Texas, and Massachusetts forbade a union from requiring the payment of a fee as a condition of employment.

---

[6] Minnesota (1939), Michigan (1939), Wisconsin (1939), Georgia (1941), Colorado (1943).

[7] Minnesota (1939), Oregon (1939), Pennsylvania (1939), Wisconsin (1939), Florida (1943), Kansas (1943). The Oregon Act was declared unconstitutional by the State Court, *A. F. of L. & C.I.O.* v. *Bain*, 106 Pac. 2d 544 (1940).

[8] Massachusetts (1938), Minnesota (1939 and 1945), Wisconsin (1939), California (1941), Alabama (1943), Colorado (1943), Idaho (1943), Kansas (1943), South Dakota (1945), Texas.

[9] California (1941), Colorado (1943), Louisiana (1946), Minnesota (1939), New York (1940), Pennsylvania (1939), Wisconsin (1939).

[10] Alabama (1943), Arizona (constitutional amendment, 1946), Arkansas (constitutional amendment, 1944), Colorado (1943), Florida (constitutional amendment, 1944), Kansas (1943), Nebraska (constitutional amendment, 1946), South Dakota (1945), Texas (a mild restriction, 1943), Wisconsin (1939).

In 1943 Colorado followed the Wisconsin Act of 1939 by making it an unfair labor practice not to accept the decision of any tribunal on an issue that it had authority to decide or where the parties had agreed to accept the decision. Puerto Rico did the same in 1945. In 1939 Pennsylvania forbade combinations to bring about a violation of state or federal labor relations laws [11] and Minnesota in 1945 forbade economic combinations to upset a labor board's decree in certifying a bargaining agency.[12]

Alabama in 1945 and Minnesota, Colorado, and Wisconsin in their labor relations acts excluded supervisory employees from the bargaining unit.

Florida and Kansas in 1943 enacted laws requiring the licensing of union agents, and Texas the same year required them to carry identification cards that must be issued as a matter of course to all but aliens and felons. Both of these laws have been invalidated by decisions of the Supreme Court on the ground that they conflicted with the federal law but not on the ground that government has no power to enact regulations of this character.[13]

Colorado in 1943 provided for compulsory incorporation of unions.

Many of these statutes, like the Minnesota legislation in 1945, wisely distinguish in some way between legitimate and illegitimate objectives by restricting or forbidding strikes, picketing, and boycotting for improper objectives—just the distinction Congress has been so slow to learn. Moreover, a considerable number of the states [14] recognized the right of anyone injured by violations of the labor relations acts to secure injunctive relief, but some of them deny relief to a violator of the act. Others [15] adopted special provisions making unions liable for their unlawful acts.

In this period 12 states and two territories [16] passed some regulation requiring union registration, filing of reports, or keeping of financial records available to the membership, and some otherwise regulated the internal administration of union affairs.

---

[11] Penn. No. 163 (1939) Sec. 4 (c).

[12] Minnesota Chap. 414 (1945).

[13] *Hill* v. *Watson*, 325 U.S. 538 (1945); *Thomas* v. *Collins*, 323 U.S. 56 (1945).

[14] California (1941), Colorado (1943), Minnesota (1939), Pennsylvania (1939), Wisconsin (1939).

[15] Minnesota (1939), Kansas (1920 et seq.), Michigan (1939), North Dakota (1941).

[16] Oregon (1939), Alabama (1943), Colorado (1943), Florida (1943), Idaho (1943), Kansas (1943), Minnesota (1943), South Dakota (1943), Texas (1943), Massachusetts (1946), Wisconsin (1939), Utah (1937), Puerto Rico (1945), Hawaii (1945).

Some states regulated the methods for fixing dues or the amount of dues, and some of them fixed the amount of the entrance fee.[17] In 1939, Oregon forbade any union from charging fees, dues, or fines "which will create a fund in excess of legitimate requirements in carrying out lawful purposes or activities,"[18] and in 1943 Texas substantially duplicated this law. In 1943 Florida excused ex-service men from the payment of dues, and Texas permitted the union to excuse such men from the payment of back dues and assessments as a condition of reinstatement.

Efforts were also made to promote regularity of union elections by the enactment of state laws.[19] In 1943, Florida, Minnesota, and Texas passed measures regulating the election of officers. Texas made aliens and felons ineligible.

In 1943 Minnesota supplemented its labor relations laws by the Minnesota Labor Union Democracy Act, providing that officials be elected for limited terms by secret ballot and that statements of receipts and expenditures be furnished members. To deal with charges of violations a labor referee is appointed by the governor. If the referee sustains the charges, the union is disqualified from representing the employees until such time as the disqualification is removed as provided in the Act.

In 1943, four states[20] enacted laws making it unlawful for unions to contribute funds for the support of political parties or their candidates. None of them seems to make any distinction between a union that operates under some form of union security and a union that does not discriminate against nonmembers, although the most convincing argument against political contributions by unions arises where a man is forced to join the union in order to pursue his trade and the money so conscripted is then diverted to the political support of candidates he may disapprove.

In the same period various states[21] forbade membership discrimination on the grounds of race, color, creed, and so on. Wisconsin in 1945 decided to investigate the problem. Kansas in

---

[17] Florida (1943), Idaho (1943), Oregon (1939), South Dakota (1943), Texas (1943).

[18] Oregon Chap. 2 (1939), Sec. 4.

[19] Florida (1943), Minnesota (1943), Texas (1943).

[20] Alabama, Colorado, Pennsylvania, Texas.

[21] Colorado (1943), Kansas (1941), Massachusetts (1946), Nebraska (1941), New Jersey (1945), New York (1940).

1941 provided that any union that discriminates may not be the bargaining agent. That same year Nebraska declared that discrimination in collective bargaining is against the policy of the state.

B

Summary of Provisions of Delaware Act of 1947

The term *labor dispute* excludes the following:

1. A dispute between parties who do not stand in the proximate relation of employer and employee.

2. The refusal of an employer to enter into an all-union agreement.

3. A jurisdictional dispute.

4. The refusal to employ or the discharge of a person on account of incompetence, dishonesty, and so on, unless such refusal or discharge is in violation of contract.

It is an *unfair labor practice* for an employee individually or in concert to do any of the following acts:

1. To coerce another employee, intimidate his family, or picket his domicile, or to injure the person or property of such employee or any member of his family.

2. To induce an employer to interfere with the labor rights of an employee.

3. To violate a collective-bargaining agreement or an agreement to accept an arbitration award.

4. To refuse to accept as conclusive the final determination of any competent tribunal having jurisdiction or whose jurisdiction the employees have accepted.

5. To engage in picketing or any other act in connection with a strike, unless a majority of the employees involved have voted by secret ballot at a special meeting to call a strike, and to induce others to do so.

6. To hinder the pursuit of lawful work by mass picketing, threats, or coercion or by obstructing approaches, highways, ways of travel, and also approaches to a home.

7. To engage in a secondary boycott, which means a combination to compel neutrals to join in a combination to injure others, and to hinder or prevent anyone by intimidation, sabotage, and so on, from obtaining, using, or disposing of materials, and all picketing, loitering, or patrolling in furtherance thereof.

8. To remain in unauthorized possession of property, real or personal, and "to interfere with production except by leaving the premises in an orderly manner for the purpose of going on strike."

9. To engage in a slowdown or sitdown.

10. To fail to give notice of intention to strike as required by the statute.

11. To commit any crime or misdemeanor in connection with any controversy as to employment relations.

12. To require or demand "stand-by" employees.

It is a *fair labor practice* for an employer to refuse to grant a closed shop or an all-union agreement.

Both employer and employees have the right freely to express their views concerning labor relations.

Unlawful labor practices include the use of violence, coercion, intimidation, threats, or insulting, annoying, abusive, or threatening language to a worker or a member of his family; following or photographing a worker for the purpose of inducing him to join or refrain from joining a union or to refrain from going to work; interfering with the exercise of the lawful right to work; and loitering or patrolling for such purposes.

The *checkoff*, except when directed by a court, is unlawful, and no provision for a checkoff shall be embodied in a contract.

A *strike vote* is necessary. No strike shall be lawful except when authorized by a majority vote of those in the bargaining unit, taken by secret ballot at a special meeting duly noticed for that purpose.

Arbitration agreements and *awards* made pursuant to them shall be enforceable in court.

In the case of *collective-bargaining agreements*, the courts are given jurisdiction over suits for their violation or enforcement and may enjoin the union and its officers from inducing, influencing, or advising any member to participate in stoppages that are in violation of contract.

Unions are responsible for the acts of their authorized agents acting within the scope of their authority. Unions can sue and be sued, and judgments shall be enforceable against the union and members who have been made parties, except that money judgments against the union shall be enforceable only against organization funds. Any employee who strikes in violation of the collective-bargaining agreement or otherwise interferes with its performance may be held in damages.

Injunctions may issue to prevent any unfair or unlawful labor practice, unlawful strike, or secondary boycott, or to enforce labor agreements.

Injunctions against picketing may limit the number of pickets, prescribe distance from plant where pickets may be permitted, or the manner of picketing, and may prohibit the use of weapons or threats or intimidation.

Any person in interest, or any organization or person or persons representing any public interest, may seek an injunction.

Reports must be filed with the Secretary of State; these must give name; constitution and bylaws; principal office of union; names and titles of officers and members of governing bodies and their salaries; the companies and industries with which it deals; initiation fees, dues, and assessments; limitations of membership and number of members; date and results of last election and method of election; and the date of last financial statement and the method of publication. Working agreements must be filed with the Secretary of State within 20 days after execution.

It is unlawful for any officer, organizer or agent of any union to fail to file reports, as required, and all persons holding any such position at time of failure forfeit their office and shall be ineligible for re-election for a period of one year. In addition thereto the Attorney General shall apply to court to enforce compliance.

Filing a false report is a criminal offense subject to fine and imprisonment, and anyone filing such a false report is barred from holding any union office for a period of five years after conviction.

Unions' constitution and bylaws shall provide a representative form of government and the term of office of any officer or agent shall not exceed one year. Any provision in the constitution or bylaws seeking to impose conditions of employment, limitations on the quality of work to be performed, or the use of labor-saving devices shall be null and void.

Initiation fees and dues shall not be increased or special assessments levied without a majority vote and no initiation fee shall exceed $25.00.

Elections of officers and voting on strikes are subject to elaborate statutory regulations. The tabulation and count of votes is to be supervised by an impartial person who must certify the results under oath. A court may review the election under certain circumstances. Any employer who may be affected by the vote may attend the special meeting and state orally the proposals he has made.

Payments of fees, dues, or assessments to secure a work permit from a union are forbidden.

The right to vote shall be accorded to every person paying dues.

No communist, alien, or felon shall hold any union office, except a felon whose citizenship rights have been restored.

Hiring halls and placement bureaus are forbidden when operated to direct the employer to employ persons recommended by the union.

Political contributions shall not be made by a union.

Accounts must be kept by local unions and shall be open to inspection of members, public officials, and grand juries and for legal proceedings.

Suspension or expulsion of a union member shall be unlawful except for good cause and after a fair public hearing on specific written charges. A court may order reinstatement where a member is suspended or expelled without good cause.

Members of armed forces shall not be required to pay back dues as a condition of reinstatement.

Penalties for violation of any provision of the act where no specific penalty is prescribed shall be a maximum of $500 fine and 60 days' imprisonment or both except for third conviction when the prison sentence may be as heavy as six months.

Damage suits may be maintained by any person injured by

violation of the major provisions of the Act. A person injured because the union induces a person against his will to violate a contract may recover treble damages.

Union security agreements and yellow dog antiunion agreements in general are against public policy and unenforceable.

The extraordinary part of this statute is the elaboration of unfair and unlawful practices, with some of them calling for administrative judgment and flexibility of application, without any provision for action by an administrative board before the parties may resort to court.

C

State Labor Legislation, 1947-1949

1947 Legislation

Seventeen states [1] enacted laws forbidding discrimination on account of nonmembership in a union, forbidding discrimination on account of nonmembership or membership, or forbidding or regulating closed- or union-shop agreements.

In 1947 five states [2] regulated or forbade the check-off; these with Utah in 1937 and Texas in 1943 made a total of seven dealing with this subject. Texas required an agreement containing provisions for the check-off to be filed with the secretary of state, but this statute was declared unconstitutional. [3] Delaware made it unlawful to check off dues, except when the employer is directed to do so by a court of competent jurisdiction, and forbade the incorporation of check-off provisions into the collective-bargaining agreement. Three states make the check-off unlawful unless authorized by the individual employee. Iowa requires that there be a written authorization, signed by the employee and spouse and terminable at pleasure on 30 days' notice.

Closely allied to this question of collection of dues are the provisions of the statutes of seven states, [4] all passed in 1947, dealing with the collection of dues or fees of any kind for work permits or otherwise as a condition of securing employment.

---

[1] Arizona, Arkansas, Delaware, Georgia, Iowa, Maine, Massachusetts, Nebraska, New Hampshire, New Mexico, North Carolina, North Dakota, Pennsylvania, South Dakota, Tennessee, Texas, and Virginia. Five states had previously enacted some statute of this character: Florida (1944), Louisiana (1934), Maryland (1939), Nevada (1929), Colorado (1943).

[2] Delaware, Georgia, New Hampshire, Texas, and Virginia.

[3] *A. F. of L.* v. *Main*, XVI, L.R.R. 307 (1945).

[4] Arkansas, Delaware, Georgia, Iowa, North Carolina, Tennessee, and Virginia.

The same year eight states [5] took direct cognizance of industrial disorders by passing special laws against violence, intimidation, threats, and injury to persons or property in connection with industrial disputes, as Virginia and Louisiana had done in 1946.

Two more states, following the lead of eight others, outlawed sitdowns, including slowdowns, and a few others dealt with this subject in connection with public utilities.

Delaware made it a special offense, as Wisconsin had done in 1939, to commit misdemeanors in connection with industrial disputes.

Picketing received special attention by way of restrictive regulations from eight different states.[6]

Several states [7] forbade picketing of residences. Pennsylvania outlawed picketing by nonemployees, and South Dakota forbade picketing where no dispute existed. Texas forbade picketing of public utilities. Others forbade picketing for illegitimate ends.

Mass picketing was forbidden by name by seven states,[8] South Dakota defining mass picketing as any number in excess of 1 per cent of the strikers. Texas had a different definition. It declared that picketing by more than two pickets within 50 feet of an entrance and within 50 feet of other pickets constituted mass picketing. An injunction issued in Wisconsin against mass picketing and picketing of homes remained undisturbed by the Supreme Court of the United States.[9]

Twelve states outlawed or severely restricted secondary boycotts.[10]

Jurisdictional strikes were outlawed or severely restricted by seven states.[11] Four states [12] outlawed sympathetic strikes.

Thirteen states [13] either forbade or drastically regulated strikes

---

[5] Arizona, Delaware, Georgia, Iowa, Michigan, South Dakota, Texas, and Utah.

[6] Connecticut, Delaware, Georgia, Michigan, Pennsylvania, South Dakota, Texas, and Utah.

[7] Connecticut, Michigan, and Utah.

[8] Delaware, Georgia, Massachusetts, Michigan, South Dakota, Texas, Utah.

[9] *Allen Bradley* v. *Board*, 315 U.S. 740 (1942).

[10] California, Delaware, Georgia, Idaho, Iowa, Minnesota, Missouri, North Dakota, Oregon, Pennsylvania, Texas, Utah.

[11] California, Iowa, Massachusetts, Michigan, Missouri, Pennsylvania, and Wisconsin.

[12] Iowa, Missouri, North Dakota, Texas.

[13] New Jersey, Florida, Indiana, Massachusetts, Minnesota, Michigan, Missouri, Nebraska, North Dakota, Pennsylvania, Texas, Virginia, Wisconsin.

on public utilities, and eight[14] forbade strikes by public employees.

Strikes were otherwise regulated in seven states[15] by requiring strike notices and an opportunity for negotiation and conciliation, by requiring approval by a majority vote taken through secret ballot, or by both such restrictions. In Oregon a vote against a strike remains effective for one year; in Missouri the industrial commission supervises the strike vote.

Four states[16] forbade strikes in violation of contracts or provided legal remedies for the enforcement in court of contracts and arbitration awards.

A number of states[17] restricted strikes by minority groups or bargaining by employers with minority groups, and some of them forbade picketing and boycotting in connection with strikes of minority groups or where there is no dispute as defined in the act. Missouri outlawed strikes for recognition where the representatives have not been legally selected and designated. Inconsistent though it was with the fundamental philosophy of labor relations acts, Texas preserved for the individual employee the right to bargain individually.

Outstanding is the fact that 14 states[18] provided for the issuance of injunctions against unions for activities of the kind I have enumerated. In 1946 Louisiana had authorized injunctions with the proviso that they should not run against strikes, free assembly, or peaceful picketing.

Four states[19] dealt with the suability of unions or their liability for the acts of their agents. Here again Louisiana had already dealt with the same subject in 1946.

Delaware followed the provisions of Wisconsin and Puerto Rico, making it unlawful or an unfair labor practice to refuse to recognize or accept as conclusive the final determination of any tribunal having competent jurisdiction or whose jurisdiction the employees had accepted.

---

[14] Massachusetts, Missouri, Nebraska, New York, Ohio, Pennsylvania, Texas, and Wisconsin.

[15] Delaware, Michigan, Massachusetts, Missouri, North Dakota, Oregon, and Utah.

[16] Delaware, Iowa, Michigan, Missouri, North Dakota, South Dakota, Texas.

[17] Delaware, North Dakota, and Texas, thus following the action of Oregon, Pennsylvania, and Wisconsin in 1939.

[18] Arizona, California, Delaware, Georgia, Iowa, Massachusetts, Minnesota, New Hampshire, North Dakota, Oregon, Pennsylvania, South Dakota, Texas, and Wisconsin.

[19] Arizona, Delaware, Minnesota, South Dakota.

The record of 1947 does not show a well-rounded legislative program dealing with the purely internal affairs of unions. Various states [20] did require registration or the filing of information or reports or the rendering of financial statements, and the Delaware Act regulated elections. Some [21] regulated dues or assessments and the manner of levying them. Delaware limited the maximum amount of initiation fees, and New Hampshire empowered the labor commissioner to pass on the reasonableness of dues. Delaware joined the ranks of the states that forbade political contributions. Three states,[22] one in 1946, passed laws prohibiting union discrimination on account of race, color, and creed.

Delaware in its 1947 Act required that in union elections the ballots be counted and tabulated under supervision of an impartial judge who shall not be a member of the union and the results must be made known to the president and the secretary in the presence of the members. Elections influenced by inducements, threats, or intimidation are invalid. Finally, any member may petition a court to review the election within 15 days after the result is announced.

Under the 1947 enactments of North Dakota the union seeking recognition with the alternative of the strike is required to join in the appointment of a board to hold an election, and no strike is permitted until 30 days after the result of the election is certified. No bargaining agent may act, and no strike may be called, unless 51 per cent of the employees vote in favor of it. Picketing is unlawful except when 51 per cent of the employees favor the strike and even then only one picket is allowed for each establishment. For the violation of these provisions suits for injunctions or damages are authorized. Boycotting and sympathy strikes are subject to injunction and damage suits. This Act became effective when approved by referendum in 1948.

Legislation 1948–1949

As an even year when few state legislatures convened, 1948 saw very little labor legislation by the states. Louisiana repealed its 1946 law that regulated union activities and passed a law against the importation of strike breakers.

---

20 Delaware, New Hampshire, North Dakota.
21 Delaware, New Hampshire.
22 Connecticut, Massachusetts, New Hampshire.

A legislative year for so many states, 1949 saw a larger crop of labor legislation than 1948, but the crop was so moderate as to indicate that the results of the tillage of 1946 had been spent. Delaware, Missouri, and New Hampshire repealed their regulatory laws, and Michigan liberalized its restrictions. Michigan abandoned its requirement for compulsory arbitration of labor disputes on public utilities and substituted voluntary arbitration, or if that was not acceptable, fact finding by a commission appointed by the governor. New Jersey remedied the defects of its public utility law, which had been declared unconstitutional because it had not provided standards for arbitration.

Massachusetts provided that arbitration awards, when made pursuant to agreement, shall be enforceable in court, and also required the filing of financial statements. Nebraska forbade mass picketing, which it defined as more than two pickets within 50 feet of an entrance or within 50 feet of other pickets.

Four more states [23] passed laws forbidding race discrimination by unions, and three others took notice of the problem.

---

[23] New Mexico, Oregon, Rhode Island and Washington. California, Kansas, and Nebraska took notice of the problem.

Bibliographical References

Chapter II

[1] *Convention Proceedings of A.F. of L. for 1897*, pp. 200–206.
[2] *The American Federationist*, February, 1902, p. 232.
[3] *Ibid.*, November, 1902, p. 808.
[4] Report of the President to 1900 Convention of the United Hatters of North America.
[5] Minutes of Danbury Hat Finishers, February 7, 1900.
[6] Report to 1903 Convention of United Hatters of North America.
[7] Transcript of Record, Lawlor v. Loewe, 235 U. S. 522, p. 1021.
[8] Transcript of Record, First Trial, Loewe v. Lawlor, 187 Fed. 522, pp. 4071 *et seq.*
[9] Transcript of Record, Lawlor v. Loewe, 235 U. S. 522, p. 1018.
[10] *Ibid.*, p. 1019.
[11] *Ibid.*, p. 541.
[12] *Ibid.*, p. 553.
[13] *Journal of the United Hatters*, September, 1902, p. 22.
[14] *Ibid.*, October, 1902, p. 7.
[15] *Ibid.*, April, 1903, p. 7.
[16] Transcript of Record, Lawlor v. Loewe, 235 U. S. 522, p. 584.
[17] *Ibid.*, p. 642.
[18] Loewe v. Lawlor, 208 U. S. 274.
[19] *The American Federationist*, March, 1908, p. 181.
[20] *Ibid.*, March, 1910, p. 197.
[21] *Convention Proceedings of A.F. of L. for 1908*, p. 259.
[22] *The American Federationist*, April, 1908, p. 269.
[23] *Ibid.*, June, 1908, p. 454.
[24] *Ibid.*, p. 457.
[25] Job 29.
[26] Loewe v. Lawlor, 187 Fed. 522.
[27] Lawlor v. Loewe, 209 Fed. 721.
[28] Lawlor v. Loewe, 235 U. S. 522.
[29] Savings Bank v. Loewe, 242 U. S. 357.

Chapter III

[1] *The American Federationist*, January, 1908, p. 27.
[2] *Ibid.*, January, 1908, p. 27.
[3] *Ibid.*, September, 1908, p. 688.
[4] *Ibid.*, June, 1908, pp. 467–468.
[5] *Ibid.*, October, 1907, p. 791.
[6] *Ibid.*, p. 792.
[7] *Garment Workers Journal*, January 31, 1908.
[8] *Proceedings of the Nineteenth Convention of the United Mine Workers of America*, p. 204.
[9] Gompers v. Buck Stove & Range Co., 221 U. S. 418.
[10] Gompers v. U. S., 233 U. S. 604.
[11] *Ibid.*
[12] *The American Federationist*, March, 1908, p. 92.

Chapter IV

[1] *The American Federationist,* October, 1915, p. 853.
[2] *New York Sun,* April 6, 1904.
[3] *The American Federationist,* April, 1906, p. 228.
[4] *Ibid.,* October, 1903, p. 1042.
[5] *Ibid.,* May, 1904, p. 399.
[6] *Ibid.,* May, 1906, pp. 295–296.
[7] *Ibid.,* November, 1906, p. 881.
[8] *Ibid.,* September, 1906, pp. 646–681.
[9] *Ibid.,* May, 1906, p. 319.
[10] *Albany Evening Journal,* July 27, 1906.
[11] *The American Federationist,* October, 1906, p. 801.
[12] *Ibid.,* p. 811.
[13] *Ibid.,* December, 1906, p. 970.
[14] *Ibid.,* December, 1906, p. 972.
[15] *Ibid.,* June, 1912, p. 459.
[16] *Ibid.,* p. 460.
[17] *American Industries,* October, 1909, p. 16.
[18] *Ibid.,* February, 1910, pp. 17–18 and September, 1911, p. 44.
[19] *Ibid.,* February, 1910, p. 18.
[20] *Ibid.,* June, 1911, p. 14.
[21] *Ibid.,* June, 1911, p. 24.
[22] *Ibid.,* August, 1911, p. 10.
[23] *The American Federationist,* June, 1912, p. 462.
[24] *Ibid.,* June, 1912, p. 464.
[25] *Ibid.,* November, 1912, p. 909.
[26] *Ibid.,* November, 1914, p. 967.
[27] *Ibid.,* p. 971.
[28] *Ibid.,* p. 951.
[29] *Ibid.,* p. 958.
[30] *Ibid.,* pp. 971–972.
[31] *New York World,* October 12, 1912.
[32] *The American Federationist,* February, 1915, p. 116.
[33] *Ibid.,* November, 1914, pp. 973–974.
[34] Milo Blish Pinkerton, *The Right to Work versus Slavery,* page 77. Madison, Wis.: The author, 1941; Robert Perry Shepherd, "Turgot and the Six Edicts," *Studies in History, Economics and Public Law,* Vol. XVIII, F. 2, page 186. New York: Columbia University Press, 1903.
[35] Bogni v. Perotti, 112 N.E. (Mass.) 833.
[36] *The American Federationist,* August, 1916, p. 653.
[37] *Ibid.,* August, 1916, p. 664.
[38] *Ibid.,* August, 1916, p. 685.
[39] *Ibid.,* August, 1916, p. 687.
[40] *Ibid.,* January, 1917, p. 31.
[41] *Ibid.,* January, 1918, p. 37.
[42] *Ibid.,* March, 1918, p. 225.

Chapter V

[1] Irving v. Joint District Council, 180 Fed. 896.
[2] Irving v. Neal, 209 Fed. 471.
[3] Secretary's Report to the 1906 Convention of the United Brotherhood of Carpenters and Joiners of America.
[4] President's Report to the 1906 Convention of the United Brotherhood of Carpenters and Joiners of America.
[5] Paine Lumber Co. v. Neal, 212 Fed. 259.

6 Paine Lumber Co. v. Neal, 214 Fed. 82.
7 Paine Lumber Co. v. Neal, 244 U. S. 459.

Chapter VI

1 *New York Times*, October 27, 1912, p. 15.
2 *Ibid.*
3 *1912 Biennial Convention of United Brotherhood of Carpenters*, p. 447.
4 *Ibid.*, p. 194.
5 *Ibid.*, p. 450.
6 *Ibid.*, p. 735.

Chapter VII

1 Transcript of Record, Duplex v. Deering, 254 U. S. 443, p. 96.
2 *Ibid.*, p. 97.
3 *Ibid.*, p. 66.
4 *Ibid.*, p. 115.
5 *Machinist Monthly Journal*, September, 1914; Transcript of Record, Duplex v. Deering, 254 U. S. 443, p. 45.
6 *Machinist Monthly Journal*, February, 1914; Transcript of Record, Duplex v. Deering, 254 U. S. 443, p. 41.
7 Transcript of Record, Duplex v. Deering, 254 U. S. 443, p. 111.
8 Duplex v. Deering, 247 Fed. 192.
9 Duplex v. Deering, 252 Fed. 722.
10 Duplex v. Deering, 254 U. S. 443.
11 Kemp v. Division, 241 99 N.E. Rep. 289 (Ill.).
12 *The American Federationist*, February, 1921, p. 135.
13 *Ibid.*
14 *The American Federationist*, March, 1921, p. 222.
15 *Ibid.*, April, 1921, p. 296.

Chapter VIII

1 Boyle v. U. S., 259 Fed. 803.
2 Harold Seidman, *Labor Czars*, p. 60. New York: Liveright Publishing Corp., 1938.

Chapter IX

1 Bedford Co. v. Stone Cutters, 9 F. 2d 40.
2 Bedford Co. v. Stone Cutters, 274 U. S. 37.
3 Decorative Stone Co. v. Building Trades, 18 F. 2d 333.
4 Decorative Stone Co. v. Building Trades, 23 F. 2d 423.
5 Aeolian Co. v. Fischer, 27 F. 2d 560.
6 Aeolian Co. v. Fischer, 29 F. 2d 679.
7 Aeolian Co. v. Fischer, 40 F. 2d 189.
8 *Cong. Record*, Vol. 93, No. 167, p. A5190.

Chapter X

1 In re Debs, 158 U. S. 564.
2 In re Lennon, 166 U. S. 548.
3 Toledo A.A. & N.M.R.R. Co. v. Penn Co., 54 Fed. 730.
4 Chicago & A.R. Co. v. Pillsbury, 8 N.E. 803.
5 *The American Federationist*, January, 1895, p. 68.
6 *New York Times*, May 6, 1920,

[7] Burgess v. Stewart, 112 Misc. (N. Y.) 354; 114 Misc. (N. Y.) 673.
[8] Buyer v. Guillan, 271 Fed. 65.

Chapter XI

[1] New York Lumber Trade Assn. v. Lacey, 245 App. Div. 262.
[2] New York Lumber Trade Assn. v. Lacey, 269 N. Y. 595, 677.

Chapter XII

[1] *The American Federationist*, November, 1917, p. 989.
[2] Pamphlets privately published by the League for Industrial Rights, New York City.
[3] Average output per man hour in manufacturing from a report of Solomon Fabricant, National Bureau of Economic Research.

Years	Basic Increase	% Increase
1899 to 1909	100 to 118	18+
1909 to 1919	118 to 135	14+
1919 to 1929	135 to 238	77+
1929 to 1939	238 to 305	28+

Chapter XIII

[1] Felix Frankfurter and Nathan Greene, *The Labor Injunction*, p. 215. New York: Macmillan Company, 1930.
[2] U. S. v. Hutcheson, 312 U. S. 219.
[3] Aikens v. Wisconsin, 195 U. S. 194.
[4] Dorchy v. Kansas, 272 U. S. 306.
[5] I.B.E.W. v. N.L.R.B., 181 F. 2d 34.
[6] U. S. v. United Brotherhood of Carpenters, 330 U. S. 395.
[7] Phila. & Reading, etc. v. Derby, 55 U. S. 468.
[8] Taff-Vale, etc., 17 Times L. R. 698.
[9] Bussy v. The Amalgamated Society, 24 Times L. R. 437.
[10] Conway v. Wade, 24 Times L. R. 874.
[11] Coronado Coal Co. v. United Mine Workers of America, 259 U. S. 344.
[12] Brotherhood of Railroad Trainmen, etc. v. Toledo, Peoria, etc. R.R. 321 U. S. 50.
[13] U. S. v. Local 807, 315 U. S. 521.

Chapter XIV

[1] U. S. v. Hutcheson, 312 U. S. 219.
[2] U. S. v. Building & Construction Trades Council, 313 U. S. 539.
[3] U. S. v. International Hod Carriers, 313 U. S. 539.
[4] U. S. v. American Federation of Musicians, 318 U. S. 741.
[5] Report of Department of Justice, 1946.
[6] Transcript of Record, Allen Bradley & Co. v. Local Union 3, 325 U. S. 797, pp. 1211–1212.
[7] "Soliloquy of the Spanish Cloister" by Robert Browning.
[8] 21 Congressional Record 2461.
[9] Allen Bradley Co. v. Local Union 3, 41 F. Supp. 727.
[10] Allen Bradley Co. v. Local Union 3, 51 F. Supp. 36.
[11] Allen Bradley Co. v. Local Union 3, 145 F. 2d 215.
[12] Allen Bradley Co. v. Local Union 3, 325 U. S. 797.
[13] *Ibid.*
[14] *Ibid.*
[15] *Ibid.*
[16] *Ibid.*

Chapter XV

[1] *The American Federationist*, April, 1907, p. 258.

[2] Adair v. U. S., 208 U. S. 161.

[3] Hitchman Coal & Coke Co. v. Mitchell, 245 U. S. 229.

[4] Atchison v. Gee, 139 Fed. 582.

[5] Truax v. Corrigan, 257 U. S. 312; Bogni v. Perotti, 224 Mass. 152; Am. Steel Foundries v. Tri-City Central Trades Council, 257 U. S. 184.

[6] Thornhill v. Alabama, 310 U. S. 88; A.F. of L. v. Swing, 312 U. S. 321.

[7] Carpenters & Joiners Union v. Ritter, 315 U. S. 322; Giboney v. Empire Storage & Ice Co., 336 U. S. 490; Note in *Chicago Law Rev.*, Vol. XVI, No. 4, p. 701.

[8] *The American Federationist*, March, 1908, p. 163.

[9] Lawlor v. Loewe, 208 U. S. 274.

[10] American Steel Foundries v. Tri-City Central Trades Council, 257 U. S. 184; Duplex v. Deering, 254 U. S. 443.

[11] U. S. v. Hutcheson, 312 U. S. 219.

[12] Connolly v. Union Sewer Pipe Co., 184 U. S. 540.

[13] State v. Coyle, 80 Okla. Crim. Cas. 686.

[14] Aikens v. Wisconsin, 195 U. S. 194.

[15] U. S. v. Hutcheson, 312 U. S. 219.

[16] Dorchy v. Kansas, 272 U. S. 306.

[17] Hammer v. Dagenhart, 247 U. S. 251; U. S. v. Darby, 312 U. S. 100.

[18] Kirschbaum v. Walling, 316 U. S. 517, 697.

[19] Brooklyn Savings Bank v. O'Neil, 324 U. S. 697.

[20] Lochner v. New York, 198 U. S. 45; Wilson v. New, 243 U. S. 332; Adkins v. Children's Hospital, 261 U. S. 525.

[21] Fair Labor Standards Act of 1938.

[22] Ribnik v. McBride, 277 U. S. 350.

[23] Olsen v. Nebraska, 313 U. S. 236.

[24] Swift v. Tyson, 16 Peters 1.

[25] Erie R. R. v. Tompkins, 304 U. S. 64.

[26] *Ibid.*

[27] West. Va. State Board of Education v. Barnette, 319 U. S. 624.

[28] Mercoid Corp. v. Mid-Continent Investment Co., 320 U. S. 661.

[29] Mahnich v. Southern S. S. Co., 321 U. S. 96.

[30] Smith v. Allwright, 321 U. S. 649.

[31] H. A. Washington, *Writings of Thomas Jefferson*, Vol. VII, page 216. Washington: Printed by Order of Congress, 1853.

Chapter XVI

[1] Butchers Union v. Crescent City, 111 U. S. 757.

[2] Callan v. Wilson, 127 U. S. 540.

[3] Truax v. Corrigan, 257 U. S. 312, 338.

[4] Martell v. White, 185 Mass. 255.

[5] *Open Shop Encyclopedia for Debaters*, p. 215. National Association of Manufacturers, 1921.

[6] Harold Cox, editor of the *Edinborough Review*, in the *London Times*, April 10, 1922; 4 Law and Labor (1922) 250.

[7] *Report to the President on the Anthracite Coal Strike of May–October 1902*, p. 83. Washington: Government Printing Office.

[8] *The American Federationist*, December, 1903, p. 1304; *North American Review*, August, 1905, p. 223.

[9] Constitution of Typographical Union.

[10] 4 Law & Labor 112, April, 1922.

[11] *The American Federationist*, December, 1903, p. 1282.

[12] Hitchman Coal & Coke Co., 245 U. S. 229.

[13] 2 Law and Labor 7, July, 1920, p. 166.
[14] *Ibid.*
[15] *Quarterly Journal of Economics*, February, 1949, p. 7.
[16] Connors v. Connolly, 86 Conn. 641.
[17] Court Files of Connors v. Connolly.
[18] *New York Times*, April 5, 1915.
[19] J. I. Case Co. v. N.L.R.B., 321 U. S. 332.
[20] Lincoln Federal Union v. Northwestern Iron & Metal Co., 335 U. S. 525.
[21] *The Open Shop and Industrial Liberty*, p. 26. Privately published by the League for Industrial Rights, New York City (1922).

Chapter XVII

[1] Sir Henry Maine, Ancient Law (No. 734, Everyman's Library), p. 100. New York: E. P. Dutton.
[2] Graham v. Brotherhood, 338 U. S. 232.
[3] J. I. Case Co. v. Labor Board, 321 U. S. 332.
[4] Stuart Chase, *Democracy Under Pressure*, p. 81. New York: Twentieth Century Fund, 1945.
[5] Rudyard Kipling, "The Gods of the Copy Book Headings."

Chapter XVIII

[1] Ryan v. Union, 216 Fed. 13.
[2] *Ibid.*
[3] *Ibid.*
[5] Transcript of Record, United Mine Workers v. Coronado Coal Co., 259 U. S. 344, p. 2355.
[6] *Ibid.*, p. 1118.
[7] United Mine Workers v. Coronado Co., 259 U. S. 344; Coronado Co. v. United Mine Workers, 268 U. S. 295.
[8] Penn Mining Co. v. United Mine Workers, 300 Fed. 965; 28 F. 2d 851.
[9] Grand Jury Report.
[10] *Ibid.*
[11] 5 Law & Labor 211; 6 Law & Labor 295; Russell v. Central Labor Council.
[12] Ex parte Bernat, 255 Fed. 429; *The Industrial Worker*, published by the I.W.W.; I.W.W. statements in Paterson, New Jersey, in 1913; U. S. v. Swelgin, 254 Fed. 884.
[13] *The I.W.W., Its History, Structure and Methods*, pp. 17–18.
[14] *The Industrial Worker*, June 12, 1913, published in Spokane, Washington.
[15] "The Survey" (New York City, June 28, 1919), 1 Law and Labor (August, 1919) 16.
[17] *Detroit Saturday Night*, January 24, 1914.
[18] *Labor Review*, April 11, 1916.
[19] *Ibid.*, April 28, 1916.
[20] James H. Maurer in the *New York Times*, April 10, 1916, p. 2, col. 4.
[21] *The American Federationist*, July, 1916, p. 577–578.
[22] *Ibid.*
[23] Statement of W. G. Lee, president, in Brotherhood of Railroad Trainmen Hearings before House Committee on Interstate and Foreign Commerce, H.R. 19730, p. 71, January 17 to 23, 1917.
[24] 1 Law and Labor (December, 1919) 23.
[25] Ray Stannard Baker and William E. Dodd (Editors), *Public Papers of Woodrow Wilson*, Vol. 2 (*The New Democracy*), p. 307. New York: Harper & Bros., 1926.
[26] 46 Monthly Labor Review 1063–1064 (May, 1938).
[27] *Congressional Digest*, Vol. 16, No. 2, pp. 135–138 (May, 1937).
[28] *New York Times*, January 27, 1937, p. 1, col. 1.
[29] 1 Monthly Labor Review, March, 1937, pp. 666–670.

[30] Frederick H. Harbison and Robert Dubin, Patterns of Union Management Relations, p. 20. Chicago: Science Research Associates, 1947.

[31] Apex Hosiery Co. v. Leader, 90 F. 2d 155.

[32] Ibid.

[33] Apex Hosiery Co. v. Leader, 310 U. S. 469.

[34] Frances Perkins, The Roosevelt I Knew, p. 321. New York: Viking Press, 1946.

[35] Ibid., pp. 321–322.

[36] "The Truth about C.I.O.," 1935–1945 The First Ten Years, p. 3. Publication No. 132 of the Department of Research and Education, C.I.O.; For C.I.O. Stewards, p. 9. C.I.O. Department of Research and Education, 1949.

[37] Labor Board v. Fansteel, 306 U. S. 240.

[38] Ibid.

[39] Carnegie Steel Co. v. United Steel Workers, 45 Atl. 2d 856.

[40] Ibid.

[41] Printed circular issued by Timken Roller Bearing Company.

[42] New York Times, October 28, 1945.

[43] General Elec. Co. v. U.E.R. & M., Court of Common Pleas, Cuyahoga County, Ohio, No. 559,712, January 29, 1946.

[44] General Electric Co. v. U.E.R. & M., 17 Labor Reference Manual 866; No. 3615 Court of Common Pleas No. 4, Philadelphia, February 21, 1946.

[45] Ibid.

[46] Westinghouse v. United etc. Electrical Workers, 46 Atl. 2d 16.

[47] New York Times, November 15, 1945, p. 13.

[48] Ibid., December 29, 1945.

[49] Ibid., December 30, 1945, and January 1, 1946.

[50] Ibid., January 4, 1946.

[51] Hearings before Senate Committee on Labor on S.55 and SJ.Res.22, February, 1947, Part 1, p. 445.

[52] New York Evening Post, March 23, 1903.

[53] John Mitchell, Organized Labor, p. 317. Philadelphia: American Book and Bible House.

[54] Osgood Nichols and T. R. Carskadon, Can Labor and Management Work Together? p. 5. New York: The Twentieth Century Fund, 1949.

Chapter XIX

[1] Report by the Anthracite Coal Strike Commission, p. 35. Washington: Government Printing Office, 1903.

[2] McAlister Coleman, Men & Coal, p. 70. Toronto: Farrar-Rinehart Company, 1943.

[3] Ibid.

[4] Report by the Anthracite Coal Strike Commission, p. 14. Washington: Government Printing Office, 1903.

[5] Ibid., p. 38.

[6] Ibid., p. 65.

[7] Ibid., p. 64.

[8] Ibid., p. 65.

[9] Ibid., p. 67.

[10] Ibid., p. 67.

[11] Ibid., p. 68.

[12] Ibid., p. 73.

[13] Ibid., p. 75.

[14] Ibid., p. 76.

[15] Ibid., p. 78.

[16] New York Times, March 22, 1903.

[17] The American Federationist, May, 1903, pp. 370 and 373.

[18] New York Times, March 22, 1903.

[19] *Report of the Anthracite Coal Strike Commission and Subsequent Reports*, p. 281. Washington: Government Printing Office, 1903.

[20] *Ibid.*, p. 283.

[21] Ray Stannard Baker and William E. Dodd (Editors), *Public Papers of Woodrow Wilson*, Vol. II *(War and Peace)*, pp. 498–499. New York: Harper & Bros., 1926.

[22] *Convention Proceedings of United Mine Workers of America, 1921*, p. 148.

[23] *The Anthracite Coal Strike of 1922*. Submitted on behalf of the General Policies Committee of the Anthracite Operators to the United States Coal Commission, April 13, 1923.

[24] *The Anthracite Strike of 1922*. Issued by The Anthracite Bureau of Information.

[25] *Issues in the Anthracite Strike of 1925*. Published by The Anthracite Operators Conference, Philadelphia.

[26] *New York Times*, August 19, 1922.

[27] *The Issues in the Anthracite Strike of 1925*. Issued by the Anthracite Operators Conference, Philadelphia.

[28] *The Anthracite Coal Strike of 1922*. Submitted on behalf of the General Policies Committee of Anthracite Operators to United States Coal Commission, April 13, 1923.

[29] *The Anthracite Strike of 1922*. Issued by the Anthracite Bureau of Information, Philadelphia.

[30] Cecil Carnes, *John L. Lewis*, p. 122. New York: Robert Speller Publishing Corp., 1936.

[31] *Ibid.*, p. 142.

[32] *The Anthracite Strike of 1923*. Issued by the Anthracite Bureau of Information, Philadelphia.

[33] Paragraph VI of the Award of the Anthracite Commission of 1903.

[34] *Outlaw Strikes in the Anthracite Fields*. Submitted by the General Policies Committee of the Anthracite Operators to the United States Coal Commission, May 1, 1923.

[35] Report of U. S. Coal Commission.

[36] *Ibid.*

[37] *Ibid.*

[38] *The Issues in the Anthracite Strike of 1925*. Issued by Anthracite Operators Conference.

[93] *The Anthracite Strike of 1925–26*. Issued by The Anthracite Bureau of Information.

[40] Agreement of February 17, 1926 between Districts 1, 7, 9 U.M.W., and Anthracite Operators, Section 2.

[41] *Ibid.*, Section 3.

[42] *Ibid.*

[43] *Ibid.*

[44] Agreement of May 7, 1936 between U.M.W. and Anthracite Operators, Section 7.

[45] Agreement of May 26, 1939 between U.M.W. and Anthracite Operators, Section 9.

[46] Minutes of Hearings before National War Labor Board in re Five Anthracite Coal Companies, pp. 123–124.

[47] *New York Times*, January 20, 1943.

[48] Agreement of June 7, 1946 between Mine Workers and Anthracite Operators.

[49] *Ibid.*, Section 8.

[50] *Ibid.*, Section 7.

[51] *Supra*, p. 197.

[52] See note 48.

[53] 48 D.L.R. (March 11, 1949) A2.

[54] Bituminous Agreement, July, 1948.

[55] 57 Daily Labor Report A 3–4, March 24, 1949.

[58] *The American Federationist*, September, 1902, p. 506.

[59] *Ibid.*

Chapter XX

[1] *New York American,* October 27, 1934.
[2] *New York Sun,* October 31, 1934.
[3] *New York American,* October 27, 1934.
[4] *New York Times,* January 31, 1941.
[5] *New York Sun,* November 1, 1934.
[6] *New York Herald-Tribune,* November 3, 1934.
[7] *New York Sun,* November 3, 1934.
[8] *Building Service Review,* November 7, 1934.
[9] *New York Herald-Tribune,* October 28, 1934.
[10] *New York Times,* October 27, 1934; *New York Journal,* November 20, 1934.
[11] *New York Herald-Tribune,* November 8, 1934.
[12] *New York Times,* November 20, 1934.
[13] Committee Letter to Mayor LaGuardia dated November 21, 1934, in files of Realty Advisory Board on Labor Relations and known as Mayor's Agreement of November 21, 1934.
[14] *Ibid.*
[15] *Ibid.*
[16] *Ibid.*
[17] *New York World Telegram,* February 18, 1935.
[18] *New York Sun,* January 24, 1936.
[19] *New York Times,* February 3, 1936; Edward D. Sullivan, *The Labor Union Racket.* New York: Hillman-Curl, Inc., 1936.
[20] Broadcast over WEVD on February 27, 1936.
[21] *Building Service,* June, 1938, p. 10.
[22] *New York Herald-Tribune,* February 2, 1939.
[23] *New York Journal American,* April 18, 1939.
[24] Panel Report, July 17, 1942, in N.W.L.B. #141.
[25] *New York Herald-Tribune,* September 22, 1945; *New York Times,* September 22, 1945.
[26] *New York Herald-Tribune,* September 29, 1945.
[27] *New York Times,* October 1, 1945.
[28] Agreement between Realty Advisory Board on Labor Relations, Inc. and Local 32-B, B.S.E.I.U., A.F. of L., dated June 3, 1948 and effective April 21, 1948, Article VI, Section 3.
[29] In re Bethlehem Steel Co., 63 NLRB 1230, 1236.
[30] State Labor Relations Board vs. Metropolitan Life Insurance Co., 295 N. Y. 839.

Chapter XXI

[1] See page 35, *supra.*
[2] *The American Federationist,* May, 1949, p. 6.
[3] *Works of Theodore Roosevelt,* Vol. 17, p. 507. New York: Charles Scribner's Sons, 1925.
[4] McComb v. Jacksonville Paper Co., 336 U. S. 187, p. 196.
[5] *The American Federationist,* February, 1922, p. 118; *ibid.,* January, 1913.
[6] LaCrosse Tel. Co. v. Wisconsin Labor Relations Board, 336 U. S. 18; Auto Workers v. Wisconsin Board, 336 U. S. 245.
[7] Contract dated June 23, 1950 between Hat Corporation of America and United Hatters Cap, etc. International Union. See also C. F. Mugridge, "Better Management and Better Union Leadership." *Labor Relations and the Public, The Annals,* November, 1946, published by the American Academy of Political and Social Science, Philadelphia.

[8] In re Debs, 158 U. S. 564.

[9] *Ibid.*

[10] See page 192, *supra.*

[11] Graham v. Brotherhood, 338 U. S. 232.

[12] Louis D. Brandeis, *Business a Profession*, p. 26. Boston: Hale, Cushman and Flint, 1933.

[13] *Resolutions of the Eighth C.I.O. Convention*, p. 30. Washington: C.I.O., 1946.

Chapter XXII

[1] Sidney and Beatrice Webb, *Industrial Democracy*, p. 305. New York: Longmans Green and Co. Ltd., 1926.

[2] It may be that the antitrust laws now apply because the collective-bargaining agreement with a nonlabor group is not exempt from the antitrust laws, but so far the Department of Justice has refrained from pursuing that theory.

[3] *The Settlement of Labor Disputes*, p. 179. Philadelphia: American Academy of Political and Social Science, 1910.

[4] The Industrial Relations and Disputes Investigation Act of Canada, enacted June 30, 1948.

[5] *Railway Age*, May 25, 1946, pp. 1049–1050. New York: Simmons-Boardman Publishing Corp.

[6] *Railway Wages and Labor Relations 1900–1946*, p. 134. Bureau of Information of Eastern Railways, 1947.

[7] Bryce M. Stewart and Walter J. Couper, *Fact-Finding in Industrial Disputes*, p. 21. New York: Industrial Relations Counsellors, Inc., 1945.

[8] *The Daily Worker*, New York, August 29, 1950.

[9] *The Albany Times-Union*, August 28, 1950.

[10] *Railway Age*, July 22, 1950, p. 13. New York: Simmons-Boardman Publishing Corp.

[11] *Ibid.*, July 1, 1950, p. 12.

[12] Senate Report 986, Part 5, 80th Congress, 2nd Session (Labor-Management Relations, West Coast Maritime Industry), December 31, 1948, p. 14.

[13] *Personnel Series #133*, p. 27. New York: American Management Association.

[14] Section 8 of the War Labor Disputes Act.

[15] *Ibid.*

[16] Section 3 of the War Labor Disputes Act.

[17] Section 6 of the War Labor Disputes Act.

[18] Sections 206–207 of Labor Management Relations Act, 1947.

[19] 52 Daily Labor Report G1, March 16, 1948.

[20] 56 Daily Labor Report A14, March 22, 1948.

[21] 119 Daily Labor Report A16, June 18, 1948.

[22] Report of the President's Commission on Labor Relations in the Atomic Energy Installations, U. S. Atomic Energy Commission, April, 1949.

[23] 66 Monthly Labor Rev. No. 5, May, 1948, p. 531; 66 Monthly Labor Rev. No. 6, June, 1948, p. 644.

[24] International Union United Mine Workers v. U. S., 177 F. 2d 29.

[25] *Ibid.*

[26] 66 Monthly Labor Rev. No. 4, April, 1948, p. 112; International Union U.M.W. v. U. S., 177 F. 2d 29.

[27] 66 Monthly Labor Rev. No. 6, June, 1948, p. 645; International Union U.M.W. v. U. S., 177 F. 2d 29.

[28] *Ibid.*

[29] International Union U.M.W. v. U. S., 177 F. 2d 29.

[30] *Ibid.*

[31] *Ibid.*

[32] *Ibid.*

[33] 66 Monthly Labor Rev. No. 6, June, 1948, p. 645.

[34] 67 Monthly Labor Rev. No. 1, July, 1948, p. 49.

[35] 108 Daily Labor Report A 18 (1948).

[36] 67 Monthly Labor Rev. No. 1, July, 1948, p. 49; 67 Monthly Labor Rev. No. 3, September, 1948, p. 289; 67 Monthly Labor Rev. No. 4, October, 1948, p. 411.

[37] 67 Monthly Labor Rev. No. 4, October, 1948, p. 395.

[38] 67 Monthly Labor Rev. No. 5, November, 1948, p. 517.

[39] 67 Monthly Labor Rev. No. 6, December, 1948, p. 629.

[40] 67 Monthly Labor Rev. No. 3, September, 1948, p. 289; Bay Ridge Operating Co. v. Aaron, 334 U. S. 446.

[41] 110 D.L.R. (June 8, 1949) A7.

[42] U.M.W. Resumption Order November 30, 1949, 218 D.L.R. (November 9, 1949) 83.

[43] Saul Alinski, *John L. Lewis, an Unauthorized Biography*. New York: G. P. Putnam's Sons, 1949.

[44] Report of Board of Inquiry, 30 Daily Labor Report (February 13, 1950), pp. D5–6.

[45] Injunction issued by Judge Keech on file in District Court, 30 Daily Labor Report (February 13, 1950) D10.

[46] *Ibid.*

[47] 34 Daily Labor Report (February 17, 1950), A11.

[48] 76 Daily Labor Report (April 19, 1948), p. E4.

[49] 42 Daily Labor Report (March 2, 1950), p. E2.

[50] *Ibid.*

[51] *Supra*, p. 202.

[52] *Ibid.*

[53] 43 D.L.R. (March 31, 1950), p. F1–2.

[54] *Ibid.*

[55] Chapter XXIII, p. 302.

[56] Agreement of March 5, 1950 between Coal Operators and U.M.W., 44 D.L.R. (March 6, 1950) p. D8–9.

[57] *Ibid.*

[58] *Ibid.*

[59] *Ibid.*

[60] *Ibid.*

[61] Julia E. Johnson, "Compulsory Arbitration of Labor Disputes." *The Reference Shelf*, Vol. XVII, No. 6, pp. 134–135 (1945).

[62] Wolf Packing Co. v. Court of Industrial Relations, 262 U. S. 522; 267 U. S. 522.

Chapter XXIII

[1] In commenting on state legislation, I have checked the work of Charles and Beverly Killingsworth in their book entitled *State Labor Relations Acts* (1946, University of Chicago Press) against the report of the United States Department of Labor.

[2] Eldridge Foster Dowell, *History of Criminal Syndicalism Legislation in the United States*. Baltimore: Johns Hopkins Press, 1939.

[3] *Ibid.*, p. 39.

[4] N.L.R.B. v. Jones & Laughlin Corp., 301 U. S. 1.

[5] Utah in 1937 required labor unions to register, and Wisconsin had a pious utterance about unfair practices and a violation of union agreements by either group but without any sanctions.

[6] William G. Rice, "Wisconsin Labor Relations Act in 1937." *Wisconsin Law Review*, March, 1938, p. 229.

[7] Laws of Wisconsin 1939, Chap. 57, Sec. 1.

[8] The percentage vote was changed from the original requirement.

[9] Auto Workers v. Wisconsin Board, 336 U. S. 245.

[10] *Ibid.*

[11] U. S. v. Petrillo, 332 U. S. 1.

[12] New Title 18 Chap. 95, Section 1951 U.S.C. Hobbs Act; U. S. v. Local 807, 315 U. S. 521.

[13] Section 8(2), Labor Management Relations Act, 1947.

[14] Section 14(b), Labor Management Relations Act, 1947.

[15] Section 305, Labor Management Relations Act, 1947.

[16] Lincoln Federal Labor Union v. Northwestern Iron and Metal Company, 335 U. S. 525; American Federation of Labor v. American Sash & Door Co., 335 U. S. 538.

[17] *Ibid.*

[18] *Ibid.*

[19] *Speakers Book of Facts,* p. 162. Washington: C.I.O.-P.A.C., 1950.

[20] *Ibid.*

[21] Lincoln Federal Labor Union v. Northwestern Iron & Metal Co., 335 U. S. 525, p. 546.

[22] Justice Frankfurter's concurring opinion in Lincoln Federal Labor Union v. Northwestern Iron & Metal Co., 335 U. S. 542.

[23] *Cleveland Plain Dealer,* December 27, 1949.

[24] Cleveland v. Division 268, No. 609,819 Journal Entry, December 26, 1949.

[25] *Ibid.*

[26] Wolff Packing Co. v. Court of Industrial Relations, 262 U. S. 522; 267 U. S. 552.

[27] *Ibid.*, page 33.

[28] Florida, Indiana, Massachusetts, Michigan (Minnesota as to Hospitals), Missouri, Nebraska, New Jersey (1946 and 1947), North Dakota, Pennsylvania, Texas, Virginia, Wisconsin. Mississippi declared obstructions of utilities by force or violence to be felonies.

[29] Florida, Indiana, Michigan, Minnesota, Missouri, Nebraska, New Jersey, Pennsylvania, Wisconsin.

[30] Massachusetts, Missouri, New Jersey, Virginia.

[31] State v. Traffic Telephone Workers, 66 Atl. 2d 616.

[32] Laws of Wisconsin 1947, Chap. 414, Sec. 111.52.

[33] *Ibid.*

[34] *Ibid.*

[35] Mass. Chap. 596, approved June 27, 1947.

[36] Local 170 v. Gadola, 34 N.W. 2d 71.

[37] Laws of Pennsylvania 1947, Vol. II, No. 485, Secs. 7, 12, 14, 15.

[38] Virginia Code, Vol. 6, Chap. 4, Art. 4, Sec. 4, par. 4, Secs. 40–88.

[39] Laws of Nebraska 1947, Chap. 178, Legislative Bill 537, Secs. 3, 18, 19, 21.

[40] Texas General and Special Laws 1947, Chap. 84, Secs. 4, 5, 6.

[41] See end of Appendix C.

[42] Massachusetts, New York, Pennsylvania, Utah, Wisconsin, Minnesota, Michigan, Rhode Island, Colorado, Kansas, Connecticut, Delaware, Puerto Rico, Hawaii, Wilcox County, Alabama.

[43] New York, Connecticut, Rhode Island.

Chapter XXIV

[1] Neil W. Chamberlain, *The Union Challenge to Management Control,* p. 105. New York: Harper & Bros., 1948.

[2] *Ibid.,* p. 101.

[3] Frank P. Huddle, "Labor Policy after the War." *Editorial Research Reports,* Vol. 1, No. 19 (May 18, 1945), p. 377. 64 D.L.R. (March 28, 1945) AA1.

[4] 109 D.L.R. (May 31, 1945) p. A1.

[5] *The President's National Labor-Management Conference* (November 5–30, 1945). Published by U. S. Department of Labor.

[6] *Ibid.*

[7] *Ibid.*

[8] Matthew Arnold, "A Summer Night."

[9] See Note 5.

[10] *The American Federationist,* September, 1949, p. 5.

[11] Clinton S. Golden and Harold J. Ruttenberg, *The Dynamics of Industrial Democracy,* p. 129. New York: Harper & Bros., 1942.

[12] *Fortnightly Review*, Vol. V N.S., May 1, 1869. London: Chapman & Hall.

[13] Phillip Murray, "Technological Unemployment." *Steelworkers Handbook*, p. 13. Published by C.I.O.

[14] Ludwig Teller, *Labor Policy for America*. New York: Baker, Voorhis & Co., 1945.

[15] *Collective Bargaining Provisions, Union-Management Cooperation*. U. S. Dept. of Labor, Bul. 908–910; see also *Collective Bargaining Contracts*, Bureau of National Affairs, Inc., Washington, D.C.

[16] Clinton S. Golden and Harold J. Ruttenberg, *The Dynamics of Industrial Democracy*, p. 163. New York: Harper & Bros., 1942.

[17] 52 Monthly Labor Review (June, 1941) 1351; 67 Monthly Labor Review No. 2 (August, 1948), p. 123.

[18] Otto Beyer, "Management and Labor Cooperation on the Railroads." *Industrial Management*, May, 1927, p. 269.

[19] *Ibid.*

[20] S. T. Williamson and Herbert Harris, *Trends in Collective Bargaining*, p. 187. New York: The Twentieth Century Fund, 1945.

[21] *The American Federationist*, April, 1950, p. 8.

Chapter XXV

[1] 111 Daily Labor Report, June 8, 1950, p. D1.

[2] William Green, "The American Federation of Labor's Wage Policy." *The Annals*, November, 1946, p. 5. Published by the American Academy of Political and Social Science.

[3] *The American Federation of Labor Weekly News Service*, May 11, 1948.

[4] L. S. Buckmaster, "Union Philosophy on Pensions." *N.I.C.B. Pension Conference*, November 22, 1949. Published by National Industrial Conference Board, New York City.

[5] *Partners in Production*, pp. 6–7. New York: Report of the Labor Committee of the Twentieth Century Fund, 1949.

[6] *The Drive against Labor*, p. 4. Washington: C.I.O.

[7] *The Drive against Labor*.

[8] *Ibid.*

[9] *Ibid.*

[10] *Ibid.*

[11] *New York Times*, November 30, 1949.

[12] *International Teamsters*, May, 1949.

[13] *Ibid.*, November, 1949.

[14] *Ibid.*

[15] *Ibid.*

[16] *New York Times*, July 11, 1949.

[17] *Supra*, page 204.

[18] *The Machinist.* Published by International Association of Machinists.

[19] 45 D.L.R. (March 7, 1950) A3.

[20] 65 D.L.R. (April 4, 1950) A5–6.

[21] *Ibid.*

[22] S. T. Williamson and Herbert Harris, *Trends in Collective Bargaining*, p. 198. New York: The Twentieth Century Fund, 1945.

[23] *Ibid.*, p. 200.

[24] Station KXLA, Pasadena, California, February 5, 1947.

[25] *Labor-Management Relations, West Coast Maritime Industry*, p. 59. Senate Report 986, Part 5, 80th Congress.

[26] *Investigation of the Causes of Labor Disputes.* Hearings before the Committee on Education and Labor, House of Representatives, 79th Congress, July, 1946, Part 2, p. 120.

[27] 25 D.L.R. (February 6, 1950) AA3–4.

[28] Solomon Barkin, "A Trade Unionist Appraises Management Personnel Philos-

ophy." XXVIII Harvard Business Review, No. 5, September, 1950, p. 59.

29 *The Drive against Labor*, p. 34. Washington: C.I.O.

30 Hosea VIII: 7.

Chapter XXVI

1 George Trevelyan, *Life and Letters of Lord Macaulay*, Vol. II, Appendix, p. 410. New York: Harper & Bros., 1875.

2 *The Practical Meaning of Management Statesmanship.* American Management Association Personnel Series No. 124 (1949).

3 *Partners in Production*, p. 14. New York: The Twentieth Century Fund, 1949.

4 *Youngstown Vindicator*, October 12, 1949.

5 *What an Hour's Work Would Buy 1914–48*, Studies in Labor Statistics No. 3. New York: N.I.C.B., March, 1950.

6 *U. S. News*, March 11, 1949 and October 29, 1948.

7 Alfred Eckhard Zimmern, *Nationality and Government*. London: Chatto & Windus, 1918.

8 *New York Times*, November 30, 1949.

8a Hearings, Committee on Education and Labor, 80th Congress, 1st Session, p. 2244 (1947).

9 An abbreviated statement of the testimony of John White, president of the United Mine Workers, pp. 480–482 of the printed record in the case of U.M.W. v. Coronado, 259 U. S. 344.

10 *Ibid.*, p. 2390. See also statement of William Morgan, commissioner of markets, in Edward Dean Sullivan, *This Labor Union Market*. New York: Hillman-Curl, Inc., 1936.

11 *Report of Anthracite Coal Commission*, p. 75. Washington: Government Printing Office, 1903.

12 Gibboney v. Empire Storage Co., 336 U. S. 490.

13 *Ibid.*, p. 86.

14 *House Committee on Education and Labor*, Vol. III, p. 1701, February 26, 1947.

15 Auto Workers v. Wisconsin Board, 336 U. S. 245, p. 259.

16 *New York Times*, June 4, 1946.

17 *Appointment of Fact-Finding Boards.* Hearings before House Committee on Education and Labor, House of Representatives on H.R. 4908, December 10, 1945, p. 19.

18 Hearings before Senate Committee on Labor on S.55 and S.J.Res., 22 March 1947, Part IV, p. 2093.

19 Buel W. Patch, "Restrictions on the Right to Strike." *Editorial Research Reports*, Vol. XI, No. 2, July 10, 1937, Washington.

20 Matter of Motor Haulage Co., 298 N. Y. 208.

21 Michigan Supreme Court Decision, October 3, 1950, in General Magnetic Corp. v. U.E.R., 44 N.W. 2d 140.

22 *Special Report of Bureau of Labor Collective Bargaining Provisions, Enforcement of Union Agreements*, p. 24. U. S. Dept. of Labor, Bureau of Labor Statistics, March, 1949.

23 Brotherhood of Trainmen v. Toledo, etc. R.R. Co., 321 U. S. 50.

24 *Economic Outlook*, May, 1950. Published by C.I.O.

25 154 D.L.R. (August 10, 1949) A9.

26 The National Industrial Conference Board estimates that from 1937 to 1948 the workers lost directly three billion dollars in wages because of strikes.

27 A. Losovsky, *Marx and the Trade Unions*, p. 132. New York: International Publishers, 1942.

28 A. Losovsky, *The World Economic Crisis*, p. 57. Moscow: State Publishers, 1931.

29 *Ibid.*, p. 60.

30 *Ibid.*

[31] William Z. Foster, *The Twilight of World Capitalism,* p. 63. New York: International Publishers, 1949.

[32] William H. Chartener, *Reds in Trade Unions,* p. 475. Washington: Editorial Research Reports, Vol. XI, July 22, 1949.

[33] Herbert M. Morais and William Cahn, *Gene Debs,* p. 72. New York: International Publishers, 1948.

[34] *Ibid.,* p. 74.

[35] *Ibid.*

[36] *Proceedings of the 68th Convention of the A. F. of L.,* p. 462 (1949).

[37] Abigail Adams' letter to her husband, John Adams, November 27, 1775.

[38] *Ammunition,* April, 1949. Published by United Automobile Workers.

[39] *The American Federationist,* August, 1950.

[40] Norman Angell, "The Workers under British Socialism." *Reader's Digest,* November 1, 1949.

[41] Will Durant, *The Life of Greece,* pp. 465–466. New York: Simon & Schuster, 1939.

Index

A

Abbott, Lawrence F., 123
Ability to pay theory, 273–274
"Able and willing" clause, 295
Absolutism for property, 303
Adams, Abigail, 401
Advisory coal labor commission, 261
Aeolian Company, 67
AFL, 8–26, 27–28, 30, 31, 33–36, 59
  anthracite award reaction, 190
  at National Labor-Management Conference, 336–338
  Atlantic City Convention of 1911, 39
  Baltimore convention of, 43–44, 162
  "Bill of Grievances" of, 35
  boycott of CIO goods, 95
  building service strike, 216
  defeat by CIO unions, 102
  grievance list against Taft-Hartley Act, 399
  Iowa state-wide political strike, 174
  political campaign activities, 33–44
  stand on free enterprise, 354
  stand on profits, 354
Alabama "little Taft-Hartley Act," 318
Albany Times Union, 269
Alinsky, Saul, 289, 298
Allis-Chalmers Company, 103
Allocation of work, 341–342
Amalgamated Association of Street, Electric Railway and Motor Coach Employees of America, 320
Amalgamated Clothing Workers of America, 179, 332
American Anti-Boycott Association, 10, 18, 28, 34, 50–53
American Federation of Full Fashioned Hosiery Workers, 167
American Federation of Labor (see AFL)
American Federationist, The (see Federationist, The)
American Management Association, 370
American Newspaper Publishers' Association, 57
American Railway Union, 69

American Telephone and Telegraph Company, 286, 339, 362
"Americans, Wake Up!," 43
Anderson, Judge, 65
Anheuser-Busch Brewing Company, 102
Ann Arbor Railroad, 70
Anthony, Mark, 381
Anthracite and bituminous merger, 192–193
Anthracite Coal Strike Commission, 11–12, 122–123
Anthracite Commission Award of 1903, 90
Anthracite Commission Board of Conciliation, 188
Anthracite Health and Welfare Fund, 203, 204
Anthracite sales, 185
Anthracite strike:
  of 1902, 185–190
  of 1942, 201–202
Anti-injunction laws, 239, 303, 344
Antimonopoly statutes, 253
Antipicketing ordinance of San Francisco, 161
Antiracketeering law, federal, 94, 311
Anti-Russia strike, 384
Antiunion employment contracts, 303
Apex Hosiery Company strike, 167–170, 375
Apostles of discontent, 376
Appalachian Joint Wage Agreement, 295
Appropriations Act of 1913, 303
Arbitration Reports of the Bureau of National Affairs, 4
Arizona Anti-Injunction Law, 41
Arkansas mines destruction, 380
Armour & Company, 282
Arnold, Matthew, 338
Arnold, Thurman, 110
Associated Press, 57
Athens, 407
Atom bomb, 281
Atomic Trades and Labor Council, 281–282
Attachment of homes, 17–18, 22–24
Australia, compulsory arbitration in, 256

442

B

Baer, George F., 186, 206
Baldwin, Governor, 179
Ball, Senator Joseph H., 177
Ballots vs. bullets, 384
Baltimore & Ohio Railroad, 349
Baltimore Convention of AFL, 43–44, 162
Balzac, 24
Bambrick, James J., 211–212, 214, 215–216, 219–221, 223, 225–226, 355, 361
Bankruptcy laws, 367
Bar Association of the City of New York, 224
Bargaining:
  government, 6
  political, 6
Beach, John K., 20, 21
Beattie, Charles Maitland, 50, 52
Beck, James M., 34
Bedford-Bloomington district, 65
Bell Aircraft Company strike, 180–181, 380
Bell System, 286, 362
Belmont, August, 38, 186
Berg & Company, 12–13, 16
Bijur, Judge, 51
Billings, Josh, 131
Bituminous and anthracite merger, 192–193
Bituminous coal contract dispute, 286
Bituminous coal emergency of 1948, 282–286
Black, Judge Edward D., 165
Black, Justice, 117
Blackball, 46
Black Hand Society, 38
Blacklist, 124, 189–190, 304
Blue Cross Hospitalization Plan, 232
Board of Conciliation, use of, 188
Board of Survey for building service strike, 221–222
Boston police strike, 319
Boycott, 9–26, 28, 31
  Anthracite commission's statement on, 189
  distinction between secondary and primary, 95
  legalization of, 94–95
  of electrical goods shipped to New York, 106–107
  of musical transcriptions, 341
  primary, 58, 95
  secondary, 44, 45–49, 58, 78, 95, 308
Boyle, Mike, 62–64
Brandeis, Justice, 58, 66, 86, 115, 123, 248, 382

Bridgeport strike threat, 163–164
Bridgeport trial, 130
Bridges, H. Styles, 284–285
Bridges, Harry, 272, 287, 362
Briggs & Stratton Corporation, 309
British Labor Party, 80
British Socialism, 251
Broad-scale bargaining (see Industry-wide bargaining)
Bronx Board of Trade, 74
Brooklyn Chamber of Commerce, 73–74
Brotherhood of Locomotive Engineers, 70, 122, 248, 266
Brotherhood of Locomotive Firemen and Enginemen, 267–268
Brotherhood of Railroad Trainmen, 266, 268, 383
Brotherhood of Teamsters, 346
Browning, 106
Buckmaster, Mr., 354
Buck Stove and Range Company, 19, 27–29, 31, 59
Building Service Employees' International Union:
  factional fight in, 225
  Local 32B, 209, 211, 216–217, 223, 236
  Local 32J, 209
  Local 219, 233
Building service industry:
  Administrative Board for, 216
  arbitration hearings, 215–216
  closed shop in, 218
  Committee on Arbitration for, 213–215
  compared to anthracite industry, 234–236
  composition of, 209
  history of, 209–236
  "Peace Plan" for, 230
  problem of decentralization, 210
  protest strike, 216
  "replacement clause" in, 214
  special apartment building plan, 231–232
  strike of 1934, 211–215
  strike of 1936, 220–221
  strike of 1939, 224–225
  strike of 1942, 227
  strike of 1945, 229
  unionization of building superintendent, 233–234
  War Labor Board hearings on, 227–228, 229
Building Trades Council of Minneapolis, 161
Building Trades Council of Westchester County, 66, 104
Building Trades Employers' Association, 106

Bullets vs. ballots, 384
Bureau of Information of the Eastern Railways, 267
Bureau of Labor Statistics, 173
Burgess Brothers Company, 74
"Button strikes," 196
Buyer & Company, 75

C

Cadillac strike, 166
California State Federation of Labor, 16
"Call-in" pay, 342
Calumet & Hecla mines strike, 159
Camden *Courier-Post* strike, 174
Canada, 3
Canadian Compulsory Investigations Act, 256
Can Labor and Management Work Together?, 184
Cannon, Joe, 37
Capitalist dub, 356
Carbide and Chemical Corporation dispute, 280–282
Carey, James, 376
Carnegie-Illinois Steel Corporation strike, 175–176
Carnes, Mr., 194
Carpenters' union, 45–54
Cartels, German, 347
Case Bill, 311, 397
Cathedral of St. John the Divine, 46
Cease and desist orders, 241, 249
Censorship, 353
Central Cooperative Field, 151
Chamber of Commerce:
  of San Francisco, 160–161
  of the Borough of Queens, 74
  of the State of New York, 73
  of the United States, 336, 391
Chase, Stuart, 144
Checkoff, the, 191, 193, 201
Chevrolet strike, 166
Chicago Building Trades Council, 61, 62
Chicago Switchboard Manufacturers Association, 61
Ching, Cyrus, 286
Christian doctrine, 368
Christian virtues, 368
Churchill, Winston, 245
CIO:
  appeal to labor unity, 360
  at National Labor-Management Conference, 336–338
  communist locals expelled from, 376
  convention of 1946, 357
  Labor Board election victories of, 102

CIO (*Cont.*):
  pamphlet on Taft-Hartley Act, 357–358
  strikes, 171, 173–174, 179
CIO News, The, 359
Citizens' Alliance, 159
Citizens' Committee, 74, 75
Citizens' Trucking Company, 74, 75
City Trades Council, 9
Civil service strike laws, 318–319
Clark, Dr. Victor R., 256
Clark, Justice, 48, 58
Clayton Act, 40, 41, 44, 55, 57–58, 65, 114, 302, 303
Cleveland, President, 8, 93, 160
Cleveland rapid transit strike, 320–321
Closed shop:
  Anthracite commission condemnation of, 188
  Connecticut Supreme Court decision against, 129
  court attitude towards, 124
  expulsions and fines under, 126
  in building service industry, 211–214, 218
  loss of political rights under, 141
  New Hampshire treatment of, 329
  opinions on, 122–123
  problems created by, 126
  restrictive practices of, 127
  suggested regulation for, 132
  suggested safeguards for, 134
Coal crisis of 1949–50, 288–299
Coal strike:
  of 1922–1923, 193–196
  of 1925–1926, 198–199
  of 1949, 204–205
Coast Line Steamship Companies, 72
Code for labor unions, 99
Code of Hammurabi, 367
Coleman, George, 356
Collective bargaining:
  adherance to arbitration awards, 386
  encroachment of private management, 338–339
  expanded field of, 334–335, 337
  for pensions, 343
  hopes of, 368–369
  in needles trade, 348–349
  on prices, 345–346
  on profits, 346
  on sublet or subcontract of work, 341
  onward march of, 332–352
  under Taft-Hartley Act, 334
Collectivism, 5, 31, 84, 136
Colorado Fuel & Iron Company, 80, 151
Colorado Industrial Commission, 33, 322
Commerce Clearing House, Inc., 4
Commercial suffrage, right of, 96

Committee of twelve, 201
Committee on Education and Labor, 379
Committee II on Management's Right to Manage, 337
Communication Workers of America, 324
Communism, 332, 356
Communist International, 393
Communists, expulsion of, 304–305
Comparative need doctrine, 93
Compulsory arbitration:
  discussion of, 299–300
  in Australia, 256
  in Canada, 256
  in New Zealand, 256
  in railway industry, 262
  under Railway Labor Act, 256
Compulsory old age insurance, 33, 142
Conciliation Service, 280
Conestoga Transportation Company strike, 173
Confiscation taxes, 367
Congressional Record, 361
Connors, Dominick, 128–131
Conroy, Robert, 226
Constant reiteration, power of, 353
Constitutional Convention of 1789, 96
Contraband goods, 27, 96
Contract enforcement, 387–388
Coolidge, President, 198
Cooling-off periods, 273
Cooper Union, 53
Cost of living index, 259
County Lawyers' Association, 223
Court-packing bill, 84
Courts, duties of the, 242
"Covenant running with the land," 227
Cox, Harold, 137
Cram, Ralph, 46
Creative class contribution, 374
"Creeping Socialism," 332
Criminal Court of Appeals of Oklahoma decision, 114–115
Criminal syndicalism, 303
Croly, Herbert, 122
"Crop of 1937, the," 306
"Crop of 1946, the," 306
Cudahy Packing Company, 282
Cummings, Homer S., 130
Cummings, Lawrence B., 212, 213–214
Curran award, 216–217
Curran, Henry H., 215–216, 217

D

Dailey, Clarke, 215
Daily Labor Reports, 4
Daily Worker, The, 269
Damage suit, 17–18, 22–24, 27

Danbury, Connecticut, 7
Danbury Hatters Case, 8–9, 17–26, 34, 58, 113
Darling, Justice, 91
Darrow, Clarence, 186
Daugherty, Dr. Carroll R., 274
Davenport, Daniel, 17, 20, 34
Death taxes, 367
Debs Case, 58, 246
Debs, Eugene V., 69–70, 246, 393–394
Decorative Stone Company, 66
Delaware labor relations act, 318
Demagoguery, 344, 366
DeMille, Cecil B., 126, 364, 399
Democratic process within unions, 142–144
Depression of 1929, effects of, 147
Dewey, Governor, 229
Dewey investigation, 226
Dictators, 353
Direct election of Senators, 395
Direct primaries, 395
Disciplinary action, 340
Discrimination against negroes, 248
"Divine Right" Baer, 186
"Don't Tread on Me" slogan, 396
Douglas, Justice, 117
Dred Scott decision, 18, 41
Dub, capitalist, 356
Duplex Printing Press Company, 55–57
Duplication of work, 341
Duquesne Power & Light Company strike, 173
Dynamiting conspiracy of 1910, 148–150

E

East Coast dockworkers dispute, 288
Economic Outlook (see Outlook)
Economic Stabilization Director, 264–265
Edinborough Review, The, 137
Edward the First, 88
Egypt, 5
Eightieth Congress, 240
Election of judges, 395
Electoral college, 395
Electrical Case, 108–110
Electrical switchboards, purchase of, 61
Eliot, Charles W., 122
Embargo of docks and piers, 76
Eminent domain, power of, 69
Employee representation plans, 79–80, 82
Employment contracts, antiunion, 303
Employment exchanges, 116–117
England, 3
English unions, 334
Enormous salaries for executives, 371
Equalitarianism, 368, 407

Era of unbalanced liberalization, 302
Erle, Chief Justice, 18
Espionage, 15
Evening Bulletin, 178
Evening Post, New York, 181, 190
Everett, Washington violence, 157–158
Excessive mortgage interest charges by union, 347
Explusion of communists, 304–305

F

Fact finding procedures, 273, 345
Factory manager in Russia, 333
Factory Solidarity or Class Solidarity, 80
Fair Employment Practices Committee, 277
Fair Labor Standards Act, 96, 147
Fake sick leaves, 373
Falstaff, 356
Fansteel Metallurgical Corporation strike, 171
Farmer-Labor vote, 394
Farwell, Justice, 90–91
Federal antiracketeering law, 94
Federal Mediation Service, 312
Federal Shipping Act, 74, 77
Federal Trade Commission, 122, 364
Federationist, The, 9, 10, 28–29, 34, 39–41, 43, 59, 70, 155, 190, 206, 240, 299, 366, 405
Fire insurance decision, 118
Fisher 2 plant riot, 165, 166
Five-year agreement between UAW and General Motors, 353–354
Flint Alliance, 166
Ford, Justice, 51
Forshey, O. B., 33
Fortnightly Review, 340–341
Foster, William Z., 393, 394
Four C's—Contact, Conference, Confidence, Cooperation, The, 80–81
France, strikes in, 384
Frankenthaler, George, 230
Frankfurter, Justice, 85, 117, 317
Free contract, system of, 139, 142
"Freebooters' Society, The," 359
French, Mr., 46
French helmets, 81
Full-crew provisions, 341
Furuseth, Andrew, 22, 59, 135

G

Gadola, Judge Paul V., 167
Gandhi, 404
Gandhi policy of noncooperation, 5
Gardner, Congressman, 37

Garment area building strike, 211–212
Garment-center agreement, 219
General Electric Company, 61, 103, 107, 177–178
General Motors Corporation, 164–166, 180, 255, 345–346, 361
General Motors Corporation sitdown strike, 164–166, 180
German cartels, 347
Gibbons, Cardinal, 122
Gillett, Congressman, 37
Gold, Frank, 226
Golden, Mr., 339
Goldsborough, Judge, 292–293
Gompers, Samuel, 9–12, 19, 22, 27–32, 33, 35–37, 40, 41, 43, 53, 59, 80, 111, 114, 123, 157, 163, 186, 239, 242, 352, 394, 397
Gould, Jay, 359
Gould, Justice, 28, 29
Governmental seizure, practice of, 275–279
Government bargaining, 6
"Government by Injunction," 94
Government intervention, 33, 34
Grand Central Palace, 57
Grape Nuts, 30
Gray, Judge George, 187
Great Britain, 4
Greater New York Council, 212
Greek history, 370, 407
Green, William, 256, 336, 382, 383
Greene, Professor, 85
Grievance procedure, 82
Group bonus for labor, 79
Guaranteed wage demand, 342
Guffey Act of 1935, 260
Gwynne Committee of Congress, 68

H

Hammond, John Hays, 195
Hammond Commission, 195–197, 203
Hand, Judge Learned, 86
Hanna, Mark, 10, 38, 186
Harding, Warren, 136, 193–194
Harriman, 359
Hartford, Connecticut general strike, 174
Hastings' department store strike, 174
"Hate-the-employer" campaigns, 356
Hatters, Danbury, 7–26
Hayes, A. J., 359
Hayward, Allen S., 287
Health and Welfare Fund, 203, 204, 298
Heney, Francis J., 54
Henle, Peter, 405
Herald Tribune, New York, 364
Hiring halls, purpose of, 362
Hitchman Coal & Coke Company, 124

Hitler, Adolph, 195
Holmes, Oliver Wendell, 21, 58, 92, 115
Hoover, Herbert, 80, 122
"Hot cargoes," 78, 88, 272
Hotel Astor, 72
House that Jack Built, The, 16
Houston, Texas, general strike, 173
Houston Central Trades Council, 173
Hughes, Charles Evans, 19, 48
Humphrey, Judge, 77
Huns, 370
Hunter, Colonel, 153, 154
Hygrade Food Products Corporation, 282

I

"Illegal Suspension of Work" clause, 295
Increased service charges agitation, 346
Individual incentives, 368
Individualism, 5, 31, 84, 124, 136
Individual rights under Constitution, 121–122, 124
Industrial Magna Carta, 40, 44
  downfall of, 55–60
Industrial planning for basic industries, 346–347
Industrial Union Marine & Shipbuilding Workers of America, 179
Industrial Workers of the World, 42, 393
Industry councils of unions, employers and government, 346–347
Industry-wide bargaining:
  adverse effects of, 250
  alternatives of, 251–252
  clothing, 250
  economic consequences of, 251
  English, 250
  glass, 250
  reasons for need of, 252–253
  Scandinavian, 250
  UMW of A, 254
Industry-wide stoppages, protection against, 259
Ingersoll, Raymond V., 213–214, 217
Injunction:
  against unlawful picketing, 247–248
  as aid to conservative union leader, 247
  CIO condemnation of, 249
  phobia, 239–249
  propaganda against, 239–240
  suggested uses for, 243–245
  suits, 27, 28–29, 35, 46–47, 57–58
  use of, 240–241
  where used, 241
"Injunction judge, the," 65
"Injunction Mania, The," 35
Inquirer, Philadelphia, 178
Insull, Samuel, 63

Insurance, old age (*see* Compulsory old age insurance)
Interlocking directorates, 258
Internal price-cost equilibrium, 351
International Association of Bridge and Structural Iron Workers, 148
International Association of Machinists, 55–56, 179, 180, 359
International Brotherhood of Electrical Workers, 103, 361
International Brotherhood of Teamsters, 77
International Harvester Company, 80
International law concerning invasion, 380
International Longshoremen's and Warehousemen's Union, 287
International Longshoremen's Association, 77, 288
Intershareholding controls, 258
Interstate Commerce Commission, 71, 122, 254, 262, 270, 346
Iowa state-wide political strike, 174
Ireland, Archbishop, 186
Irving & Casson, 46
"Isms," 332
Isocrates, 407
Italy, strikes in, 384
IWW, 155, 157–159

J

Jackson, Justice, 382
Jefferson, Thomas, 119
Job, 20
"Job action," 271
John Morrell & Company, 282
Johnson, Eric, 336
Johnson, Walter, 195
Johnston, Mr., 57
Joint Congressional Committee on the Economic Report, 376
Joint District Council of Carpenters, 51
Journal-American, New York, 384
Journeyman Stone Cutters' Association, 66
"Judicial legislation," 111, 114
"Judicial nullification," 116
Jurisdictional strike, 308, 314

K

Kahn's department store strike, 174
Kansas Court of Industrial Relations, 321–322
Kansas Industrial Court Act of 1920, 300, 321
Kearns, Daniel, 25–26
Keating, Michael J., 8
Keech, Judge, 290–291, 292–293, 296–298

Kennedy, Thomas, 202
King, Mackenzie, 80
Kipling, 144–145
Kirby, John, 27, 49
Knights of Labor, 121
Knudsen, William S., 165
Koster, Frederick J., 72
Krug, Mr., 279
Krug-Lewis Agreement, 279
Ku Klux Klan, 38, 155

L

Labor Committee of Twentieth Century
    Fund, 355
"Labor Creates All Wealth" banner, 363
Labor Czars, 64
Labor dictatorship, defense against, 301
Labor Injunction, The, 85
Labor-management charter, 336
Labor-management committees, 350
Labor Management Relations Act (see
    Taft-Hartley Act)
Labor pressure groups, 183
Labor Relations Reporter, 4
Labor Review, 161–162
Labor's Magna Carta (see Industrial
    Magna Carta)
LaGuardia, Mayor, 213, 217, 230
Lancaster, Pennsylvania general strike,
    173
Lancaster Central Labor Union, 173
Lang, Harry C., 320–321
Lansing agreement, 166
Large-scale bargaining (see Industry-
    wide bargaining)
Laski, Harold, 404
Lawlor, 12–13
Law of the jungle, 408
Lea Act, 311, 383
Leader, Bill, 168–169
League for Industrial Rights, 18, 125
Legal theory of contract stability, abon-
    donment of, 203–204
Leitch, John, 79
Lenin, 139, 392
Lennon, Engineer, 70
Lennon, John B., 28
Lethal gas, use of, 361
Lewis, John L., 10–11, 25, 140, 151, 153,
    165, 166, 191, 192, 194, 198, 202,
    204–206, 222, 248, 258–260, 279,
    282–286, 288–299, 359, 383, 388,
    390, 399
Lexington Avenue Theatre debate, 135
Liberty of contract, right of, 112
Liberty of the trader, 27, 122
Lincoln, Abraham, 123, 188

Literary Digest, 11
Littlefield, Charles E., 36, 51, 68
Little steel strikes, 172
"Little Wagner Acts," 305
Local 134 of electricians' union, 61–62
Local 376 of electrical workers' union,
    61–62
Loewe, D. E., 12–16, 18, 20, 22–24, 31–32
Loewe & Company, 12, 15–17
London Dock Strike, 406
Longshoremen's Union of New York, 127
Loss of liberty by workingman, 138–145
Loyalty to employer, 361–362
Lozovsky, 392
Ludlow Massacre, 151

M

McCall, Congressman, 37
Macauley's paradox, 373
Macauley's prediction, 369–370
McDowell, 154
McGrady, Edward F., 217
McManigal, 149
McNamara, James B., 149
McNamara, John J., 149
Mafia, the, 38, 155
Magna Carta, Industrial (see Industrial
    Magna Carta)
Maher, James P., 12–13
Mahoney, Judge Jeremiah T., 219
Mahoney agreement, 219
Maine, Sir Henry, 139
Maintenance of membership clause:
    bad features of, 131–132
    good features of, 131
Make-work provisions, 341
Mallory hats, 8
Management contribution to national wel-
    fare, 371–372
Management functions, classes of, 337
Management-sharing, 333–334, 337
Management's Right to Manage, Com-
    mittee II on, 337
Mann Act, 211
Marat, 10
Marine Cooks and Stewards, 287
Marine Firemen, 287
Maritime workers' dispute, 286–288
Martin, Governor, 177
Martin, Homer, 165
Martin, Joseph, 284
Martin, Judge, 21
Marx and the Trade Unions, 392
Marxism, 355, 375
Massachusetts Anti-Injunction Law, 41
Massachusetts Labor Relations Act, 315–
    316, 325–326

Massacre at Herrin, Illinois, 153
Mass picketing, 399
Maurer, James H., 162
Mayer, Henry, 364
Mayor's Board of Survey agreement, 222
Meaney, Thomas P., 320–321
Meany, George, 240
Medical and Hospital Fund, 387
"Memorial stoppage," 204, 260
Merchants' Association of New York, 73
Mergenthaler Linotype Corporation strike, 176
Merit increases, 342
Merritt, Mrs., 356
Merritt's bodyguard, 8
Meyer, Arthur S., 3, 225, 226
Meyer, Mr., 168–169
Michigan civil service strike law, 319
Michigan Sheriffs' Association, 167
Michigan Supreme Court decision, 387
Midtown Realty Owners' Association, 218
Mill, John Stewart, 340–341
Million Against One, 9
Minimum wage laws, 33, 142
Minnesota Act, the, 322, 326
Misbranded goods, 96
Missouri civil service strike law, 319
Missouri Pacific Railroad System, 267
Mitchell, John, 19, 28, 30, 38, 123, 124, 181, 185, 186–187, 206, 235
Model Anti-Injunction Bill, 39–40, 43
Moffitt, John, 12, 14, 16, 20, 22
Molly Maguires, the, 155
"Mona Scalisa," 211
Monopolies, regulation of, 253
Monopoly bargaining, 261
Morgan, J. Pierport, 155, 187
Morrison, Frank, 28, 30, 199–200
Moscow, 376
Moyer, 159
Mulholland, Frank L., 20, 21
Multi-employer bargaining, 261
Murphy, Justice, 109, 165–166, 172, 317
Murray, Philip, 25, 207, 287, 336, 346–347, 357, 358, 359, 374
Musical transitions boycott, 341
Mussolini, Benito, 120

N

NAM, 27, 31, 38, 50, 336
National Association of Manufacturers (see NAM)
National Bituminous Coal Strike Agreements, 291, 295
National Civic Federation, 10, 38, 186, 393
National Coal Act, 257–258, 259–262

National Exposition Company, 56–57
National Federation of Shipping, Inc., 271
National Federation of Telephone Workers, 379
National Grange, 36
National Industrial Conference, 300, 370
National Industrial Recovery Act (see National Recovery Act)
Nationality and Government, 375
Nationalization of industry, 261
National Laboratory at Oak Ridge, 281
National Labor-Management Conference, 336–338
National Labor Relations Act of 1935:
    affirmation of validity of, 305
    author's remarks on, 99
    cause of passage of, 147
    discrimination against union man under, 112
    effect of passage of, 164
    purpose of, 98
    terms of, 97–98
National Labor Relations Board, 82, 280
    duties under suggested national coal act, 260
    improvements suggested for, 385–386
    powers of, 304
National maritime strike, 174–175
National Maritime Union, 287, 288
National Mediation Board, 263–264
National Railroad Adjustment Board, 263
National Recovery Act of 1933, 147, 251, 304
National Wage Stabilization Board, 175
National War Labor Board:
    adoption of maintenance of membership clause, 131
    anthracite strike of 1942, 202
    government seizure under, 276
    protest strikes against decisions of, 383
Neal, Eldridge H., 53
Nebraska civil service strike law, 319, 327
Needle trades industry, 348–349
Neglected Side of Trade Unionism, The, 11
Negro discrimination, 248
New Deal:
    appointments to Supreme Court, 111
    as result of depression, 147
    crusade against property interests of, 353
    errors of, 97
    legislation (see Norris-LaGuardia Act; see also National Labor Relations Act)
New Hampshire statute of 1947, 316
New Jersey acts against public utility strikes, 322–324

New Jersey Telephone Company strike, 323–324
New Republic, 122
News, Danbury, 25
New York Board of Trade and Transportation, 74
New York Civil Service Law amendment, 319
New York Law Journal, The, 56
New York Shipping Association, 76
New York State Board of Mediation, 224–225
New York World's Fair, 225
New Zealand, compulsory arbitration in, 256
Night work provisions, 344
Niles-Bemont-Pond Company strike, 174
NIRA (*see* National Recovery Act)
NLRA (*see* National Labor Relations Act)
"Nod-and-wink" strike, 297, 375
Noncooperation, policy of, 5
Norris-LaGuardia Anti-Injunction Act, 78, 83
  author's indictment of, 85
  objections to, 86–90, 92–93
  passage of, 147
  primary aim of, 97
  purpose of, 85, 304
  rule of *respondent superior* under, 88–89
  Supreme Court's interpretation of, 114
North Dakota military law, 322
Northern Michigan Railroad, 70
Northwestern States Trade and Commercial Association Executives, 391

O

Oakland, California general strike, 174
Ohio Act of 1947, The, 320
Old age insurance, compulsory (*see* Compulsory old age insurance)
Old Dominion Transportation Company, 75
Omar Khayyám, 117
Open shop:
  Anthracite commission indorsement of, 183
  court attitude towards, 124
  opinions on, 122–123
Orange, New Jersey, 12
Order of Railway Conductors, 268
Oregon State Federation of Labor, 16
Osusky, Professor Stefan, 370
Outcries against public authority, 150–164
Outlaw strikes, 195–197

Outlook, 11, 123, 390
Overcapitalization charges by union, 347
Overtime pay, 142

P

P.A.C. (*see* Political Action Committee of the CIO)
Pacific American Ship Owners Association, 287
Packinghouse Emergency, the, 282
Palmer, Congressman, 37
Parker, Alton B., 20, 21, 22
Parks, Sam, 149
Particeps criminis, 382
Party caucuses, 395
Patent laws, 253
Patronage boycott (*see* Boycott: secondary)
"Peace Plan" for building service industry, 230
Penal Law of New York State:
  Section 280, 50–51
  Section 600, 101
Pennsylvania Act of 1947, 326
Pennsylvania arbitration law, 101
Pennsylvania civil service strike law, 319
Pennsylvania Mining Company, 152–153
Pennsylvania Railroad Company, 70, 80
Pennsylvania State Federation of Labor, 162
Penn Zone Association, 218
Pensions, 343
Pepper, Senator, 194
Perkins, Frances, 166, 170, 172
Petrillo, James Caesar, 311, 383
Phyfe furniture, 46
Picketing rights, 113
Pitney, Justice, 58
Pittsburgh general strike threat, 173
Plato, 396
Platt, Judge, 21
Political Action Committee of the CIO, 317
Political bargaining, 6
Portal to Portal Act, 116
Portland Trades Council, 16
Post, Mr., 30
Postscript, author's, 406–408
Postum, 30
Potter, Bishop, 186
Pound, Professor Roscoe, 380
Power of eminent domain, 69
Prairie Creek Mine, 152
Prefabricated houses, 341
Preferential shop, 131
Prentice-Hall, Inc., 4
"Preparedness Parade," 161

President's Second Industrial Conference of 1920, 82
Pressure groups, 395
Primary boycott (*see* Boycott: primary)
Production quotas, 351
Professional strike breakers, 156
Profit motive, 374
Profit sharing, 404–405
Propaganda, importance of, 239
Property in perpetuity, 367
Protest strike, 383
Public v. Unions, 399
Pullman Company, 69
Pullman disturbances, 4, 8
Purchasing power levels, 351
Purchasing power of hour's work, 374

Q

Quarterly Journal of Economics, 126
Quasi-public agencies, types of, 69
Quill, Michael, 383

R

Radicalism, restraints on, 333
Railroad emergency board, 263, 264
Railroad strike threats, 162–163, 264–266
Railroad Yardmasters, 268
Railway Age, The, 266, 269
Railway Labor Act, 256, 262–268, 269
Rape:
of Ethiopia, 184
of Manchuria, 184
Rate-fixing laws, 253
Rawlins, William D., 235
Razor-sharpening machine, 33
Real Estate Board of New York, 212
Realty Advisory Board on Labor Relations, Inc., 209, 210, 215, 217, 218–219, 223–224
Record, Philadelphia, 178
Red Cross, 387
Reed, Senator, 194
Referenda on union shop, 317–318
"Replacement clause," 214
Report of committee of Massachusetts to the Senate and House, 134
Representation plans, employee (*see* Employee representation plans)
Republican party, 10
Republic Steel Battle, 172
Reserve power of revolt, 396
Resolution of New York City merchants, 1920, 73–74
Respondeat superior doctrine, 88–89
Restraints on radicalism, 333
Reuther, Victor, 358

Reuther, Walter, 273–274, 345, 347, 358
Reynolds, Verne L., 394
Rieve, Emil, 376
"Rights Judicially Purloined," 59
Right to labor, 41–42
Roberts, Justice, 85, 110, 114, 117–118
Robertson, Hugh, 222
Robinson, Senator, 385
Rochester, New York general strike, 173–174
Rockefeller Center strike, 106–107
Rockefeller, John D., 155
Rock Island Railroad, 268
Roelofs & Company, 13, 14, 16
Roman Empire, 370
Romer, Lord Justice, 91
Roosevelt, Eleanor, 86
Roosevelt, Franklin D., 111, 170, 172, 202, 210, 265, 353, 358
Roosevelt, Theodore, 11, 116, 122, 187, 240
Roosevelt Award of 1903, 191
Roosevelt I Knew, The, 170
Root, Elihu, 130
Roth, Almon E., 271, 287
Rublee, George, 199–200
Rule of irresponsibility, 296
Rule of responsibility, 296
Runaway shops, 343
Russia, 5, 333
Russian communism, 374
Ruttenberg, Mr., 339
Ryan, Frank M., 148–150

S

Sabotage, 373
Salaries for executives, 371
San Diego disturbances, 159
San Francisco Employers Council, 287
San Francisco Labor Council, 16
San Francisco violance, 160
Scab labor, 56, 122
Scalise, George, 211–212, 220, 225–226
Seafarers International Union, 287
Seattle Central Labor Union, 16
Secondary boycott (*see* Boycott: secondary)
Second Industrial Conference, 1920, 82.
Secretary of Labor, 4
Secret ballot of Labor Relations Board, 280
Section 280, Penal Law of New York State, 50–51
Section 600, Penal Law of New York State, 101
Securities & Exchange Commission Act, 241
Semi-annual profit sharing, 405

Semi-free enterprise system, 333, 367
Senate Labor Committee, 271
Seniority rules, 339–340
Settlement of coal strike of 1949, 295–296
Severance pay, 342
Shamokin convention, 186
Sharfman Emergency Board, 265
Sheraton furniture, 46
Sherman, Congressman, 37, 108
Sherman Anti-Trust Law, 4, 17, 18, 39, 113, 122
Shopmen's strike of 1922, 349
Shop stewards, 340
Silcox, Ferdinand A., 222
Sit-down strikes, 147, 164–172
　Apex Hosiery Company, 168–170
　General Motors, 164–167
　government attitude toward, 172
　in building service industry, 222
　number of, 164
　Supreme Court ruling on, 171–172
S.K.F. Industries strike, 176
Slichter, Sumner H., 126–127, 134
Sloan, Alfred P., 166
Slowdown, the, 340–341, 373, 375
Smith-Connolly Act, 228, 277
Snead, W. A., 153
Socialism, 322, 356, 372
Socialist commonwealth in England, 334
Socialist party in United States, 393–394
Socialized housing, 378
Socialized medicine, 378
Southern Coal Producers Association, 205, 290, 298
Southern Illinois Coal Company, 153
Speakers Book of Facts, The, 317
Speed-up dangers, 350
Squeezes on Business, 373
Stack, Robert, 320
Stacy, Judge, 265
Stalin, Joe, 358, 404
Stamford, Connecticut general strike, 173, 180
Stand-by musicians, 341
State Department, usurpation of functions of, 384
States Electric Company, 62
"State Wagner Acts," 305
Station WEVD, 221
Statism, 332, 372
Status, definition of, 139
Statutory compulsion to bargain, 334–335
Steelman, John R., 268
Steel Panel, 359
Steffens, Lincoln, 123
Steinkraus, Herman W., 391
Stern, Harold, 109
Stone, Chief Justice, 106, 118

Stone, Warren S., 122
Stone Cutters Case, 65–68
Story, Justice, 117
Street & Electrical Railway Employees, 173
Strike, definition of, 243
Strike breakers, professional, 156
Subcontracting work, 341
Sublet of work, 341
Sullivan, David, 226, 229, 231, 235
Sun, New York, 34
Super grammaticam, 91
Super legem, 91
Superseniority, 340
Supreme Court of New York State, 51, 74, 77
Supreme Court of the United States, 18, 21, 29–30, 41, 48, 58, 65–68, 77, 85–86, 109, 111
　affirmation of validity of NLR Act, 305
　change in personnel in, 112
　decision concerning yellow-dog contract, 125
　decisions on state labor laws, 316–317
　fire insurance decision of, 118–119
　Kansas Act decision by, 321
　legislation by, 112
　picketing rights according to, 113
　reversals by, 111–120
　ruling on employment exchanges, 116–117
　ruling on Wisconsin Act, 309–310
　sit-down strike ruling, 171–172
Surtaxes, 367, 378
Swift & Company, 282
Switchmen's Union of America, 268
Swope Plan, 251
Syndicalism, criminal, 303, 332

T

Tacoma Trades Council, 16
Taff-Vale Case, 90–91
Taft-Hartley Act:
　Attorney General's duties under, 280
　bituminous coal emergency under, 282–286
　carbide and carbon chemical emergency under, 280–282
　checkoffs under, 314
　CIO pamphlet on, 357–358
　Civil Service strikes under, 314
　coal crisis of 1949–50 under, 288–299
　collective bargaining under, 334–335
　communist affidavit under, 313
　compared to state acts, 315, 327
　discrimination clauses in, 312

Taft-Hartley Act (*Cont.*):
East Coast dockworkers dispute under, 288
hospitality toward labor, 398
information unions must file, 313
injunctions under, 248
jurisdictional strikes under, 314
lack of disciplinary authority under, 133–134
maritime dispute under, 286–288
mass picketing provision, 399
national emergency strikes under, 314–315
noncommunist affidavits under, 287
omissions in, 315
outlawing of union hiring halls by, 287
packinghouse emergency under, 282
power of patronage under, 95
presidential fact finding board under, 274
presidential veto of, 312
protest strike over, 174
provision omitted from, 251
refusal to bargain clauses in, 312–313
regulation of dues by nonunion men, 132
regulations for initiation fees, 313
secondary boycott under, 95, 314
60 and 30 day notice requirement, 388, 391
strike review under, 279–280
success of, 402
telephone emergency under, 286
treatment of supervisor's union under, 313
union political contributions under, 314
union-shop requirements under, 137
unlawful strikes and boycott clauses in, 313
Taft, William Howard, 36, 39, 70, 122
Technological progress, 354
Telephone emergency dispute, 286
Temple of Apollo, 145
Ten Eyck Low-Cost Housing Project, 106
Terminal strikes, 200
Texas public policy strike law, 319–320, 327
Textile Workers Union of America, 179
Thomas, Norman, 394
Thornton, Mr., 341
Three days' operation of coal mines, 205, 260
Times, London, 137
Times, New York, 53, 131, 177, 180, 190
Timken Roller Bearing Company strike, 176
Tobin, Daniel J., 358
"Token" strikes, 269

Toynbee, 407
Trade Commission Act, 96
Trades and Labor Assembly of Minneapolis, 161
Trades Dispute Act, 91
Trade Union Act, 3
Transportation Trades Council, 71, 76
Trends in Collective Bargaining, 351
Triborough Bridge, 107
Tribune, Chicago, 64
Triest & Company, 16
Trucking company award, 387
Truckman's Union, 73
Truman, Harry S., 138, 140, 263, 268, 280–281, 293–295, 311, 336, 353
Tugboat workers stoppage, 311
Tumulty, Mr., 41
Turgot, 41
Tweedy, Edmund, 7
Twentieth Century Fund, 351, 355, 371
Typographical union pledge requirement, 123

U

UAWA, 167, 180, 345
"Umbrella Mike," 62–64
UMW of A, 29, 38, 140
abuses of power by, 258–259
acceptance of CIO appeal to labor unity, 360
Arkansas mine strike, 380
at National Labor-Management Conference, 336–338
coercion of society by, 260–261
conference with anthracite operators, 185–186
District 10 of, 153
District 21 of, 152
industry-wide bargaining of, 254
Ludlow Massacre, 151
national suspension order of 1922, 193
President Wilson's condemnation of, 192
strike of 1946, 279
strike of 1948, 282–286
strike of 1949–50, 288–299
unpopularity of, 257–259
violation of antitrust laws by, 253–254
war against open shops, 150–155
Unbalanced liberalization, era of, 302
Underwriters Laboratories, Incorporated, 107
Union liability, 89–90
Union of Telephone Workers, CIO, 286
Union rights, definition of, 304
Unionism, 332, 370
avoidance of violence in, 378–379
illegal purpose of strikes by, 382

Unionism (*Cont.*):
  observance of contracts, 386
  organized picket-line violence, 379–380
  tolerance of management, 378
United Aircraft Corporation strike, 174
United and True Assistant Society of
  Hatters in Danbury, 7
United Auto Workers of America, 167,
  180
United Brotherhood of Carpenters and
  Joiners of America, 45–54
  Biennial Convention of, 53–54
United Electrical Workers, 173
United Electrical and Radio Workers, 180
United Furniture Workers of America,
  179
United Hatters, Cap and Millinery
  Workers, 25
United Hatters of North America, 12, 13
United Mine Workers Journal, The, 126,
  151, 155, 206, 359
United Mine Workers of America (*see*
  UMW of A)
United Packinghouse Workers dispute,
  282
United Rubber Workers, 354
United States Coal Commission, 195
United States Fuel Administration, 191
United States Steel Company, 274
United Steel Workers, 180
  nationwide strike, 175–176
Usury, oppression of, 367

V

"Vacation strike," 192
Van Cleave, James W., 27–30
Vandals, 370
Vanderbilt, 359
Venture capital, 374
Veterans rights, 386
Vicarious liability of employer, 88
Vinson, Judge, 265
Virginia law against government em-
  ployee strikes, 319, 326–327
Virginia telephone strike, 327

W

Wage and Hour Law, 386
Wagner Act of 1935, 82, 304–305, 330
Wallace, Henry, 394
Wall Street as a symbol, 356, 378
Walsh, Frank P., 109, 365
Ward's Island sewage plant, 107
War Labor Board (*see* National War
  Labor Board)
War Labor Disputes Act of 1943, 261,
  275–279
War psychosis in industrial relations, 369

Washington State Federation of Labor, 16
Waterfront Employers Association, 287
Water-front workers, 71–75
Webb, 251
Webster, Daniel, 108
Weeks, Congressman, 37
Welfare Fund (*see* Health and Welfare
  Fund)
West Coast maritime industry, 271–272
Western Central Labor Union, 16
Western Electric Company, 277
Western Federation of Miners, 159
Westinghouse Electric & Mfg. Company,
  61, 103, 178
"What About Profit Sharing?," 405
"What Shall Be Done with Judges Who
  Violate the Constitutional Rights
  of Labor?," 43
Wheeler, Burton K., 77
Wheeling Steel Company, 93
White, John, 379–380
Whitney, President, 383
Wilcox County, Alabama, 318
Wilson & Company, 282
Wilson Commission, 196
Wilson, William B., 160, 187, 191
Wilson, Woodrow, 40, 44, 64, 122, 162,
  163, 191
"Wings Over Africa," 221
Wisconsin Employment Peace Act:
  dealing with public utility strikes, 324–
  325
  employee unfair labor practices, 308
  passage of, 306
  policy of, 307
  unfair labor practices by employer,
  307–308
  union financial reports under, 309
Wisconsin Employment Relations Board,
  309
Wolcott, Sheriff Thomas, 165, 167
Work assignments, 340
Works councils, 80–82, 84
Work-sharing, 341
World, New York, 20, 40
World Economic Crisis, The, 392
World's Work, 10

Y

Yale & Towne Company strike, 173, 179–
  180
Yale University, 391
Yates, Governor Ralph F., 177
Yellow-dog contracts, 97, 124, 304

Z

Zaritsky, Max, 25
Zimmern, Alfred, 375